TEST PREP SERIES

2021 Edition

VIBRANT
PUBLISHERS

GRE®

QUANTITATIVE REASONING:
520 PRACTICE QUESTIONS
Fourth Edition

520 Quantitative Reasoning
Practice Questions

Answer Key and Detailed explanation
included for all questions

10 Timed Practice Exercises with
questions in-line with the real GRE

GRE® Quantitative Reasoning: 520 Practice Questions
Fourth Edition

Paperback ISBN-10: 1-63651-019-1

Paperback ISBN-13: 978-1-63651-019-4

Library of Congress Control Number: 2017918248

This publication is designed to provide accurate and authoritative information in regard to the subject matter covered. The Author has made every effort in the preparation of this book to ensure the accuracy of the information. However, information in this book is sold without warranty either expressed or implied. The Author or the Publisher will not be liable for any damages caused or alleged to be caused either directly or indirectly by this book.

Vibrant Publishers books are available at special quantity discount for sales promotions, or for use in corporate training programs. For more information please write to **bulkorders@vibrantpublishers.com**

Please email feedback / corrections (technical, grammatical or spelling) to **spellerrors@vibrantpublishers.com**

For general inquires please write to **reachus@vibrantpublishers.com**

To access the complete catalogue of Vibrant Publishers, visit **www.vibrantpublishers.com**

Table of Contents

Dear Student,

Thank you for purchasing **GRE Quantitative Reasoning: 520 Practice Questions.** We are committed to publishing books that are content-rich, concise and approachable enabling more students to read and make the fullest use of them. We hope this book provides the most enriching learning experience as you prepare for your **GRE** exam.

Should you have any questions or suggestions, feel free to email us at **reachus@vibrantpublishers.com**

Thanks again for your purchase. Good luck for your GRE!

- Vibrant Publishers Team

facebook.com/vibrantpublishers

///////////// GRE Books in Test Prep Series /////////////

6 Practice Tests for the GRE

GRE Analytical Writing: Solutions to the Real Essay Topics - Book 1

GRE Analytical Writing: Solutions to the Real Essay Topics - Book 2

GRE Analytical Writing: Solutions to the Real Essay Topics - Book 3

GRE Analytical Writing Supreme: Solutions to the Real Essay Topics

GRE Master Wordlist: 1535 Words for Verbal Mastery

GRE Quantitative Reasoning: 520 Practice Questions

GRE Reading Comprehension: Detailed Solutions to 325 Questions

GRE Words in Context: The Complete List

GRE Verbal Reasoning Supreme: Study Guide with Practice Questions

GRE Text Completion and Sentence Equivalence Practice Questions

Verbal Insights on the GRE General Test

GRE Words in Context: List 1

GRE Words in Context: List 2

GRE Words in Context: Challenging List

GRE Wordlist: 491 Essential Words

For the most updated list of books visit
www.vibrantpublishers.com

Chapter **1**

Overview of the GRE General Test

The Graduate Record Examinations (GRE) General Test is required for admission to most graduate programs. The most competitive programs tend to require comparatively higher scores. This book is designed to prepare students for the GRE General Test. The GRE revised General Test was renamed in 2016 and is now known as the GRE General Test, but content and scoring of the test remain the same. Note that some graduate programs require applicants to take specialized GRE Subject Tests which will not be covered in this book. Before preparing to take the GRE, please review the admissions criteria for the programs that you are interested in applying to so that you know whether you need to take subject tests in addition to the GRE General Test. To learn more about subject tests, visit the Subject Tests section at ets.org.

The GRE General Test is not designed to measure your knowledge of specific fields. It does not measure your ability to be successful in your career or even in school. It does, however, give a reasonably accurate indication of your capabilities in certain key areas for graduate level work, such as your ability to understand complex written material, your understanding of basic mathematics, your ability to interpret data, and your capacity for reasoning and critical thinking. By using this book to prepare for the GRE General Test, you will not only improve your chances of scoring well on the test, you will also help to prepare yourself for graduate level study.

General Information of the Format of the GRE General Test

Whether you are taking the paper or computer version of the GRE General Test, the format of the test will be essentially the same. The test consists of three main components: Analytical Writing, Verbal Reasoning and Quantitative Reasoning. The total time for the test will be between 3 ½ and 3 ¾ hours, depending on the version you are taking.

The first section of the test is always the Analytical Writing component which is broken into two sections. In the first, you will be asked to write an argumentative essay that takes a position on an issue of general interest. In the second, you will be asked to analyze an argument for logical validity and soundness. You will be given 30 minutes for each section.

The remainder of the test will be split between sections devoted to Verbal Reasoning and sections devoted to Quantitative Reasoning. There will be two sections devoted to Verbal Reasoning, and another two devoted to Quantitative Reasoning. You will be given between 30-40 minutes to complete each section, and each section will contain approximately 20 questions. At any point during the test, you may be given an unscored section on either Verbal or Quantitative Reasoning; since this section will not be identified, it is important that you try your best at all times. Also, it is possible that you will be asked to complete a research section that will allow ETS to test the efficacy of new questions. If you are given a research section, it will appear at the end of your General Test. Unscored and research sections may vary in number of questions and time allotted.

Outline of the GRE General Test

The following will briefly introduce the three main components of the GRE General Test.

Analytical Writing Assessment

The first section of the GRE General Test is the Analytical Writing assessment. This component of the GRE is designed to test your ability to use basic logic and critical reasoning to make and assess arguments. The Analytical Writing assessment is broken into two assignments, each of which must be completed within 30 minutes. In the first assignment, you will be asked to develop a position on an issue of general interest. You will be given an issue and a prompt with some specific instructions on how to approach the assigned issue. You will be expected to take a position on the issue and then write a clear, persuasive and logically sound essay defending your position in correct English. You will be assessed based on your ability to effectively defend your positions with supporting evidence and valid reasoning, your skill in organizing your thoughts, and your command of English. In the second assignment, you will be presented with a passage in which the author sketches an argument for their position on an issue. Here, you will be expected to write an essay that critically evaluates their argument in terms of the evidence they use and the logical validity of their reasoning. You will be assessed based on your ability to parse the author's argument and effectively point out the strengths and weaknesses of their reasoning using good organization and correct English.

Task	Time Allowed	Answer Format
Analyze an Issue	30 minutes	Short essay on an issue of general interest that clearly and carefully addresses the prompt
Analyze an Argument	30 minutes	Short essay that analyzes another person's argument for validity, soundness and supporting evidence

The Analytical Writing assessment tests your ability to:

- Coherently develop complex ideas

- Write in a focused, organized manner

- Identify relevant evidence and use it to support your claims

- Critically evaluate another person's argument for clarity and effectiveness

- Command the elements of standard written English

Verbal Reasoning

The Verbal Reasoning portion of the GRE assesses your reading comprehension, your ability to draw inferences to fill in missing information, and your vocabulary. You will be given two sections on Verbal Reasoning, each consisting of approximately 20-25 questions and lasting 30-35 minutes. Verbal Reasoning questions on the GRE General Test are mostly multiple choice and will be drawn from the following three types: Reading Comprehension, Text Completion, and Sentence Equivalence. Reading Comprehension questions will ask you to read a short passage several paragraphs long, and then answer questions about the passage. Text Completion questions will have a short passage with 1-3 blanks which you will need to fill in by choosing the best of several multiple-choice options. The Sentence Equivalence section will ask you to fill in the blank in a passage using the two words that will complete the sentence in such a way that the meaning will be as similar as possible.

Time	Question Type	Answer Format
You will have 30-35 minutes to complete the entire section, which will include a mixture of different question types	Reading Comprehension	• Multiple choice: select one answer choice • Multiple choice: select one or more answer choices • Highlight a section of text
	Text Completion	Multiple choice: fill in one or more blanks to complete the text
	Sentence Equivalence	Multiple choice: select the two options that produce two sentences with the most similar meanings

The Verbal Reasoning section tests your ability to:

- Comprehend, interpret and analyze complex passages in standard written English

- Apply sophisticated vocabulary in context

- Draw inferences about meaning and authorial intent based on written material

Quantitative Reasoning

The Quantitative Reasoning section of the GRE evaluates your ability to use basic mathematics, read and interpret graphs and figures and engage in basic reasoning involving math and numbers. You will be given two sections on Quantitative Reasoning, each with about 20-25 questions. You will have 35-40 minutes to complete each section. There are two basic question types, multiple choice and numerical entry. For multiple choice questions, you will be asked to choose the best answer or answers from several possibilities; for numerical entry questions, you will be asked to enter a numerical answer from your own calculations. Some questions will be designed to test your knowledge of basic algebra and geometry; others will be designed to test your ability to read and interpret different presentations of data.

Time	Question Type	Answer Format
You will have 35-40 minutes to complete the entire section, which will include a mixture of different question types	Multiple Choice	• Select one answer choice • Select one or more answer choices
	Numeric Entry	Solve the problem through calculation and enter a numeric value
	Quantitative Comparison	Evaluate two quantities to decide whether one is greater than the other, whether they are equal, or whether a relationship cannot be determined
	Data Interpretation	• Multiple choice: choose the best answer or answers • Numeric entry: enter a value

The Quantitative Reasoning section tests your ability to:

- Use mathematical tools such as basic arithmetic, geometry, algebra and statistics

- Understand, interpret and analyze quantitative information

- Apply basic mathematical and data interpretation skills to real-world information and problems

Paper Based and Computer Based GRE General Test

The Paper Based GRE General Test

If you are taking the paper-based version of the test, the format will be slightly different than the computer-based version. The typical format for the paper version of the test will be as follows:

Component	Number of Questions	Time Allowed
Analytical Writing	1 Analyze an Issue 1 Analyze an Argument	30 minutes 30 minutes
Verbal Reasoning (2 sections)	25 questions per section	35 minutes per section
Quantitative Reasoning (2 sections)	25 questions per section	40 minutes per section

Note that if you are taking the paper-based test, you will not be given an unscored section or a research section. You will enter all answers in your test booklet, and you will be provided with an ETS calculator for doing computations. You will not be allowed to use your own calculator.

The Computer Based GRE General Test

If you are taking the computer-based version of the test, the format will be slightly different than the paper-based version. Also, unlike the paper-based test, the Verbal Reasoning and Quantitative Reasoning sections of the computer-based version is partially adaptive. This means that the computer will adapt the test to your performance. Since there are two sections each of Verbal Reasoning and Quantitative Reasoning, the difficulty of the second section will depend on how well you did on the first section. The format for the computer-based version of the test will be as follows:

Component	Number of Questions	Time Allowed
Analytical Writing	1 Analyze an Issue	30 minutes
	1 Analyze an Argument	30 minutes
Verbal Reasoning (2 sections)	Approximately 20 questions per section	30 minutes per section
Quantitative Reasoning (2 sections)	Approximately 20 questions per section	35 minutes per section
Unscored	Variable	Variable
Research	Variable	Variable

While taking the computer-based GRE General Test:

- You can review and preview questions within a section, allowing you to budget your time to deal with the questions that you find most difficult.

- You will be able to mark questions within a section and return to them later. This means that if you find a question especially difficult, you will be able to move on to other questions and return to the one that you had trouble with, provided that you stay within the time limit for the section.

- You will be able to change or edit your answers within a section. This means that if you realize that you made a mistake, you can go back and correct yourself provided you stay within the time limit for the section.

- You will have an onscreen calculator during the Quantitative Reasoning portions of the test, allowing you to quickly complete any necessary computations.

Registering for the GRE

Before you register to take the GRE, be sure to consider your schedule and any special accommodations that you may need. Be aware that the availability of testing dates may vary according to your location, and that paper-based testing only takes place on certain set dates. Be sure to give yourself plenty of time to prepare for the GRE and be sure that you know the deadlines for score reporting and application deadlines for all the schools you are applying to. For general information about deadlines and the GRE, visit GRE section at ets.org. For more information on how to register for the GRE, visit the Register for GRE section at ets.org. For information on special accommodations for disabled students, visit Disabilities section at ets.org.

How the GRE General Test is Scored

Scoring for the Analytical Writing Section

In the Analytical Writing section, you will be scored on a scale of 0-6 in increments of .5. The Analytical Writing measure emphasizes your ability to engage in reasoning and critical thinking over your facility with the finer points of grammar. The highest scores of 5.5-6.0 are given to work that is generally superior in every respect - sustained analysis of complex issues, coherent argumentation and excellent command of English language. The lowest scores of 0.0-0.5 are given to work that is completely off topic or so poorly composed as to be incoherent.

Scoring for the Verbal and Quantitative Reasoning Sections

The Verbal and Quantitative Reasoning sections are now scored on a scale of 130-170 in 1-point increments.

General Strategies for Taking the GRE

There are strategies you can apply that will greatly increase your odds of performing well on the GRE. The following is a list of strategies that will help to improve your chances of performing well on the GRE:

- Review basic concepts in math, logic and writing.

- Work through the test-taking strategies offered in this book.

- Work through mock GRE tests until you feel thoroughly comfortable with the types of questions you will see.

- As you are studying for the GRE, focus your energy on the types of questions that give you the most difficulty.

- Learn to guess wisely. For many of the questions on the Verbal and Quantitative Reasoning Sections, the correct answer is in front of you - you only need to correctly identify it. Especially for questions that you find difficult, you should hone your ability to dismiss the options that are clearly wrong and make an educated guess about which one is right.

- Answer every question. You won't lose any points for choosing the wrong answer, so even a wild guess that might or might not be right is better than no answer at all.

Preparing for Test Day and Taking the GRE

How you prepare for the test is completely up to you and will depend on your own test-taking preferences and the amount of time you can devote to studying for the test. At the very least, before you take the test, you should know the basics of what is covered on the test along with the general guidelines for taking the GRE. This book is designed to provide you with the basic information you need, and give you the opportunity to prepare thoroughly for the GRE General Test.

Although there is no set way to prepare for the GRE, as a general rule you will want to

- Learn the basics about the test - what is being tested, the format, and how the test is administered.

- Familiarize yourself with the specific types of questions that you will see on the GRE General Test.

- Review skills such as basic math, reading comprehension, and writing.

- Learn about test-taking strategies.

- Take a mock GRE test to practice applying your test-taking skills to an actual test.

Remember, you don't need to spend an equal amount of time on each of these areas to do well on the GRE - allot your study time to your own needs and preferences. The following are some suggestions to help you make the final preparations for your test, and help you through the test itself:

Preparing for Test Day

- In the time leading up to your test, practice, then practice some more. Practice until you are confident with the material.

- Know when your test is, and when you need to be at the testing center.

- Make a "practice run" to your testing center, so that you can anticipate how much time you will need to allow to get there.

- Understand the timing and guidelines for the test and plan accordingly. Remember that you are not allowed to eat or drink while taking the GRE, although you will be allowed to snack or drink during some of the short breaks during testing. Plan accordingly.

- Know exactly what documentation you will need to bring with you to the testing center.

- Relax, especially in the day or night before your test. If you have studied and practiced wisely, you will be well prepared for the test. You may want to briefly glance over some test preparation materials but cramming the night before will not be productive.

- Eat well and get a good night's sleep. You will want to be well rested for the test.

The Test Day

- Wake up early to give yourself plenty of time to eat a healthy breakfast, gather the necessary documentation, pack a snack and a water bottle, and make it to the testing center well before your test is scheduled to start.

- Have confidence: You've prepared well for the test, and there won't be any big surprises. You may not know the answers to some questions, but the format will be exactly like what you've been practicing.

- While you are taking the test, don't panic. The test is timed, and students often worry that they will run out of time and miss too many questions. The sections of the test are designed so that many students will not finish them, so don't worry if you don't think you can finish a section on time. Just try to answer as many questions as you can, as accurately as possible.

- Remember the strategies and techniques that you learn from this book and apply them wherever possible.

Frequently Asked Questions

General Questions

What changes have been made to the GRE revised General Test?

The GRE revised General Test (introduced on August 1, 2011) is now known as the GRE General Test. Only the name of the test has changed. Content and scoring have remained the same. Study materials that reference the GRE revised General Test are still valid and may be used for test preparation.

Why did the name of the test change from GRE revised General Test to GRE General Test?

The name of the test was changed from GRE revised General Test to GRE General Test in 2016 because the word "revised" was no longer needed to distinguish the version of the GRE prior to August 1, 2011. The scores from that version of the test are no longer reported.

How do I get ready to take GRE General Test?

To take the GRE General Test, there are several steps you'll need to take:

- Find out what prospective graduate/professional programs require: Does the program you're interested in require additional testing beyond the GRE General Test? What is the deadline for receipt of scores?

- Sign up for a test date. You need to sign up for any GRE testing. For computer-based testing, there will generally be numerous dates to choose from, although acting in a timely manner is essential so that you have plenty of time to prepare and are guaranteed that your scores will be sent and received on time. For paper-based testing, testing dates are much more restricted, so if you know that you will need to take the paper-based GRE General Test, make arrangements well in advance of the application deadline for your program.

- Use this book and the resources provided by ETS to familiarize yourself with both the format of the GRE and the types of questions you will face. Even if you are confident about taking the test, it is essential to prepare for the test.

Does the GRE General Test Measure my proficiency in specific subject areas?

No. The GRE General Test is designed to measure general proficiency in reading, critical reasoning, and working with data, all abilities that are critical to graduate work. However, you won't be tested on your knowledge of any specific field.

Where can I get additional information on the GRE General Test?

Educational Testing Service (ETS), the organization that administers the GRE, has an informative website entirely devoted to information about the test at the GRE section at ets.org. There, you can find links that further explain how to sign up for testing, fees, score reporting and much more.

Preparing for the Test

How should I start to prepare for the test?

The first thing you should do is thoroughly familiarize yourself with the format of the GRE General Test. Once you've decided whether you're taking the paper-based test, or the computerized version, learn exactly what you can expect from the version of the test you're taking - how many sections there are, how many questions per section, etc. You can find general information about the structure of the test earlier in this chapter.

How do I prepare for the questions I will be asked on the GRE General Test?

There are plenty of resources by Vibrant Publishers, including this book to help you prepare for the questions you will face on the GRE General Test. A list of books is provided at the end of this book. For the most updated list, you may visit www.vibrantpublishers.com.

How much should I study/practice for the GRE?

Study and practice until you feel comfortable with the test. Practice, practice and practice some more until you feel confident about test day!

Are there additional materials I can use to get even more practice?

Yes. ETS offers a free full-length practice test that can be downloaded from the GRE section at ets.org. Also, after you have signed up for testing through ETS, you are eligible for some further test preparation materials free of additional charge.

Test Content

How long the GRE General Test is?

- The computer-based version of the test is around 3 hours and 45 minutes including short breaks.

- The paper-based version of the test will take around 3 hours and 30 minutes.

What skills does the GRE test?

In general, the GRE is designed to test your proficiency in certain key skills that you will need for graduate level study. More specifically:

- **The Analytical Writing section** tests your ability to write about complex ideas in a coherent, focused fashion as well as your ability to command the conventions of standard written English, provide and evaluate relevant evidence, and critique other points of view.

- **The Verbal Reasoning section** tests your ability to understand, interpret and analyze complex passages, use reasoning to draw inferences about written material, and use sophisticated vocabulary in context.

- **The Quantitative Reasoning section** tests your knowledge of basic, high school-level mathematics, as well as your ability to analyze and interpret data.

What level of math is required for the Quantitative Reasoning section?

You will be expected to know high school level math - arithmetic, and basic concepts in algebra and geometry. You will also be expected to be able to analyze and interpret data presented in tables and graphs.

Scoring and Score Reporting

How are the sections of the GRE General Test scored?

The GRE General Test is scored as follows:

- **The Verbal Reasoning section** is scored in 1-point increments on a scale of 130-170.

- **The Quantitative Reasoning section** is scored in 1-point increments on a scale of 130-170.

- **The Analytical Writing section** is scored on a scale of 0-6 in increments of .5.

When will my score be reported?

It depends on which version of the test you are taking, and also when you decide to take the GRE General Test. In general, scores for the computer-based version of the test are reported within two weeks; for the paper-based test, they are reported within six weeks. Check the GRE section at ets.org for updates on score reporting and deadlines.

How long will my scores be valid?

In general, your score for the GRE General Test will remain valid for five years.

Other Questions

Do business schools accept the GRE instead of the GMAT?

An increasing number of business schools accept the GRE as a substitute for the more standard test for admission to an MBA program, the GMAT. Before you decide to take the GRE instead of the GMAT, make sure that the programs you are interested in applying to will accept the GRE. You can find a list of business schools that currently accept the GRE in the GRE section at ets.org.

How is the GRE administered?

The GRE is administered at designated testing centers, where you can take the test free from distraction in a secure environment that discourages cheating. The computer-based version of the test is administered continuously year-round at designated testing centers. In areas where computer-based testing is unavailable, the paper-based version of the test is administered at most three times a year on designated dates. For information on testing centers in your area and important dates, visit the GRE section at ets.org.

I have a disability that requires me to ask for special accommodation while taking the test - what sort of accommodation is offered?

ETS does accommodate test-takers with disabilities. For information on procedures, visit the GRE section at ets.org.

Will there be breaks during testing?

Yes. You will have a 10-minute break during the test. On the computer-based version of the test, the 10-minute break will fall after you have completed the first three sections of the test. On the paper-based version, you will be given a 10-minute break following the Analytical Writing sections.

Will I be given scratch paper?

If you are taking the computer-based version of the test, you will be given as much scratch paper as you need. If you are taking the paper-based version of the test, you won't be allowed to use scratch paper, however, you will be allowed to write in your test booklet.

Should I bring a calculator to the test?

No. If you are taking the computer-based version of the test, there will be an onscreen calculator for you to use. If you are taking the paper-based version of the test, an ETS-approved calculator will be issued to you at the testing center.

Chapter 2

The Quantitative Reasoning Section of the GRE

Overview

The Quantitative Reasoning Section of the GRE® (Graduate Record Examinations) is designed to test and measure the ability to solve problems that require fundamental skills in arithmetic, algebra, geometry, and data analysis. The section consists of three modules:

- Quantitative Comparisons, which involves less computations or calculations than the other modules but requires reasoning ability and the skills to describe problems in a logical manner. The module is about 35% of the GRE Quantitative Section.

- Math Problem Solving, which tests basic mathematical skills. Problems in this module are usually multiple-choice questions that can be solved fairly quickly.

- The Numeric Entry module requires entering solutions of math problems into an answer box.

- Solving these problems requires basic mathematical skills.

Question Types

There are four types of questions in the Quantitative Reasoning Section.

Quantitative Comparison Questions

The Quantitative Comparison (QC) Questions are a subset of Quantitative Reasoning Section, which assesses

- Basic mathematical skills

- Understanding of fundamental mathematical concepts

- Ability to use quantitative methods to logically reason and model practical problems.

In Quantitative Comparison questions, you will be provided with information on two quantities, such as Quantity A and Quantity B. From the given information, you should compare Quantity A and Quantity B, and select an answer that is based on these choices:

- Quantity A is greater.

- Quantity B is greater.

- Quantities A and B are equal.

- The relationship cannot be determined from the information given.

Hints for answering questions:

- Carefully examine answers (a) through (c), before selecting choice (d).

- Avoid unnecessary and lengthy computations. Sometimes, you need to simplify the results of computation in order to find the answer in choices (a) through (c).

- Keep in mind that geometric figures may not be drawn to scale.

- If quantities A and B are mathematical expressions, plug your answer into the expressions in order to validate your choice of answer.

- You may need to simplify the mathematical expressions for quantities in order to use them effectively.

Multiple-Choice Select One Answer Questions

The Multiple-choice-Select One Answer Questions form a subset of the Quantitative Reasoning Section, which assesses

- Basic mathematical skills

- Understanding of fundamental mathematical concepts

- Ability to use quantitative methods to logically reason and to model practical problems.

In the MCSO (Multiple-choice-Select One) section, you will be asked to select only one answer to a question from a list of choices.

Hints for answering questions:

- Carefully compute to validate the selected answer.

- Avoid unnecessary and lengthy computations but check your calculations for careless errors.

- Keep in mind that geometric figures may not be drawn to scale.

- If you need to guess at the answer, you should perform validation tests (such as plugging the selected answer into the problem).

- You may need to simplify the mathematical expressions for quantities in order to use them effectively.

Multiple-Choice-Select Multiple Answers Questions

The Multiple-Choice-Select Multiple Answers Section of the GRE is a subset of the Quantitative Reasoning Section, which assesses

- Basic mathematical skills

- Understanding of fundamental mathematical concepts
- Ability to use quantitative methods to logically reason and to model practical problems.

In the MCSM (Multiple-choice-Select Multiple) Section, you will be asked to select one or more answers to a question from a list of choices.

Numeric Entry Questions

Numeric Entry (NE) questions are one of the four types of questions in the Quantitative Reasoning Section of the GRE. Questions of the NE type ask you to answer a question by typing your answer into a box. For paper-based tests, answers are submitted by filling incircles in a grid. Your answers may be integers, decimals, or fractions, and they could be negative quantities.

Because there are no answer choices for an NE question, it is necessary to read the question carefully, and to answer the question in the form that is expected. It is also important to pay attention to units (such as feet, yards, miles/hour, km/hour, and so on), and to give answers that are fractions or percentages, if requested. You may be asked to round an answer to a certain number of decimal places.

Because NE questions do not allow you to guess at an answer, it is necessary to check your answer carefully after you have expended some time to obtain it.

This page is intentionally left blank

Chapter **3**

Arithmetic Practice Questions

This chapter consists of *80 Arithmetic* practice questions. The questions cover all the question types as explained in Chapter 2 and are segregated into 3 levels of difficulty - Easy, Medium and Difficult. You may choose to start solving the Easy questions first and then move on to higher levels of difficulty or solve the questions in any random order. You will find answers and detailed explanations towards the end of this chapter.

Level: Easy

1. What is 21% of 19? Write your answer in the answer box up to two significant digits.

   [   ]

2. Which of the following decimals are greater than 5.04078 and less than 6.1035?

   Select all that apply.

   (A) 5.1703
   (B) 5.0405
   (C) 5.709
   (D) 5.00231
   (E) 6.123
   (F) 6.046

3. 30 liters of a certain drink is to be divided between the students of 5th and 10th class. A school teacher is appointed on that duty. He gave $\frac{3}{7}$ liter drink to each of 5th class student and then the remaining drink with $\frac{3}{2}$ liters to each of 10th class student. If there are 21 students of 5th class, then what will be the number of students of 10th class and what will be their percentage to the total number of students?

    Select all that apply.

    (A) 12 students

    (B) 14 students

    (C) 16 students

    (D) 40%

    (E) 50%

    (F) 60%

4.

    Integers m and n when individually divided by the number 5, their remainders are 2 and 1 respectively.

Quantity A	**Quantity B**
Remainder obtained when sum of m and n is divided by 5	Remainder obtained when product of m and n is divided by 5

    (A) Quantity A is greater.

    (B) Quantity B is greater.

    (C) The two quantities are equal.

    (D) The relationship cannot be determined from the information given.

5.

Quantity A	**Quantity B**
$1 + \frac{1}{2} + \frac{1}{4} + \frac{1}{16} + \frac{1}{32} + \frac{1}{64}$	2

    (A) Quantity A is greater.

    (B) Quantity B is greater.

    (C) The two quantities are equal.

    (D) The relationship cannot be determined from the information given.

6. If $(2^{2x+1})(3^{2y-1}) = 2^{3x}3^{3y}$, then $x + y =$

    (A) -2

    (B) -1

    (C) 0

    (D) 1

    (E) 2

7. How many inches are in m yards and n feet?

    (A) $m + n$

    (B) $36m + 12n$

    (C) $36(m + n)$

    (D) $3m + n$

    (E) $12(m + n)$

8. Which of the statements shown below is true for $x = \dfrac{\left(\frac{1}{3}+\frac{1}{4}-\frac{2}{5}\right)}{4-\left(\frac{1}{2}-\frac{3}{5}+\frac{1}{8}\right)}$?

    Select all that apply.

    (A) $x < 0.04$

    (B) $x < 0.02$

    (C) $x > 0.03$

    (D) $x > 0.04$

9.

$$\left\{\frac{m}{n}=\frac{2}{3}; n \neq 3\right\}$$

Quantity A	**Quantity B**
$\dfrac{m+3}{n+3}$	$\dfrac{5}{6}$

    (A) Quantity A is greater.

    (B) Quantity B is greater.

    (C) The two quantities are equal.

    (D) The relationship cannot be determined from the information given.

10. If the average (arithmetic mean) of four distinct positive integers is 11, what is the greatest possible value of any one of the integers?

    (A) 35

    (B) 38

    (C) 40

    (D) 41

    (E) 44

11. The ratio of the arithmetic mean of two numbers to one of the numbers is 3 : 5. What is the ratio of the smaller number to the larger?

   (A) $1:5$

   (B) $1:4$

   (C) $1:3$

   (D) $1:2$

   (E) $2:3$

12. Total income of a family of 5 members is $27,000. The average income of three of them is $4,500. Then what will be average income of remaining 2 persons?

   Write your answer in the answer box.

   $ [   ]

13. The average of $\frac{5}{6}, \frac{3}{4}, \frac{2}{7}, \frac{5}{3}$ and $\frac{7}{2}$ is?

   Write your answer in the answer box up to two significant digits.

   [   ]

14.

   x is the geometric mean of $(2a - b)$, $(2a + b)$, and $(4a^2 + b^2)$, and

   y is the geometric mean of $(2a - b)$, $(4a^2 - b^2)$, and $(2a + b)$.

   x and y are equal.

Quantity A	**Quantity B**
b	0

   (A) Quantity A is greater.

   (B) Quantity B is greater.

   (C) The two quantities are equal.

   (D) The relationship cannot be determined from the information given.

15. The mean value of ten numbers in a list is 7. The mean value of the seven lowest numbers in the list is 5. Determine the mean value of the highest three numbers in the list to 2 decimal place accuracy.

   [   ]

16.

The relationship between the cost and the pounds of laundry washed by two different laundry services is shown below:

Laundry A	
Laundry washed (lbs)	Cost ($)
1	16
2	18
3	20
4	22

Laundry B	
Laundry washed (lbs)	Cost ($)
1	6
2	10
3	14
4	18

Which laundry will charge more to wash 30 pounds of laundry?

Quantity A

Laundry A

Quantity B

Laundry B

(A) Quantity A is greater.

(B) Quantity B is greater.

(C) The two quantities are equal.

(D) The relationship cannot be determined from the information given.

17.

Quantity A

The number of prime numbers between 1 and 100

Quantity B

The number of odd numbers between 1 and 100

(A) Quantity A is greater.

(B) Quantity B is greater.

(C) The two quantities are equal.

(D) The relationship cannot be determined from the information given.

18. A pie divided into 3 equal parts. The first part is divided equally between 2 people, the second part is divided equally between 4 people, and the third part is divided equally between 5 people.

What percentage is the ratio between the smallest serving of the pie, to the largest serving of the pie (to the nearest integer)?

☐ %

19. A cricket player played 3 matches against team A with an average of 42 runs. Then he played 5 matches against team B with an average of 38 runs. What will be his average in all 8 matches?

Write your answer in the answer box.

☐

20. A salesman's income was divided between commission and regular salary. His salary, therefore, varied from week to week. His weekly salaries over a 5-week period were $406.20, $413.50, $420, $425 and $395.30. What was his average weekly salary over the 5-week period?

    (A) $400.40

    (B) $408.90

    (C) $410.40

    (D) $412

    (E) $2060

21. The AM(Arithmetic Mean) of 6 numbers is 24. Find the AM of 2 numbers, if the sum of the other 4-numbers is 96.

    (A) 12

    (B) 24

    (C) 48

    (D) 72

    (E) 96

22. The AM(Arithmetic Mean) of 3 successive numbers is M. State which of the following statements must be true to fulfill the previous statement.

    I   One of the three numbers must be M

    II   The AM of two numbers is M

    III M is an integer

    Select all that apply.

    (A) I

    (B) II

    (C) III

    (D) I & II only

    (E) I &III only

23. Stella has some coins with her. She can bundle the coins equally into 6 bags with no coins left over. She can also pack the coins equally into 4 bags with no coins left over. However, when she bundles them into 7 bags, she has one coin left over. What is the least number of coins Stella could have?

    (A) 36

    (B) 29

    (C) 25

    (D) 12

    (E) 48

24. Sequence S is defined as $S_n = 3S_{n-1} - 3$. If $S_1 = 3$, then $S_5 - S_4 =$

    (A) 79

    (B) 80

    (C) 81

    (D) 82

    (E) 83

25. If a and b are positive integers and $a^{-3}b^{-2} = \frac{1}{36}$, what is the value of $a^{-2}b^{-3}$?

    (A) $\frac{1}{6}$

    (B) $\frac{1}{36}$

    (C) $\frac{1}{216}$

    (D) 216

    (E) 36

26.

$$\text{Given: A} = \frac{3}{4} - \frac{5}{4} + \frac{9}{4}, \text{B} = \frac{3}{6} - \frac{5}{12} + \frac{7}{24}, \text{and C} = \frac{3}{8} + \frac{1}{8}.$$

Quantity A	**Quantity B**
C% of (A + B)	$\frac{17}{160}$

    (A) Quantity A is greater.

    (B) Quantity B is greater.

    (C) The two quantities are equal.

    (D) The relationship cannot be determined from the information given.

27. The average laptop price today is \$700. If the average laptop price 5 years ago was 75% of the average laptop price today, what was the percentage increase in the average laptop price over the past 5 years?

    (A) 15%

    (B) 20%

    (C) $33\frac{1}{3}$%

    (D) 50%

    (E) $66\frac{1}{6}$%

28. Which of the following is between 5 and 5000?

    (A) 0.5×10^{-3}

    (B) $50000(0.00005)$

    (C) $0.05 \div 10^{-6}$

    (D) 5×10^3

    (E) $10^{-5} \div 10^{-7}$

29. Simplify the following expression:

    $17 - 3[5 - 6 \div 3 \times 2 + 3^2 - (4 - 2)^3]$

    (A) -4

    (B) 2

    (C) 11

    (D) 14

    (E) 20

30. In a bag of candy, there are 19 red candies, 25 blue candies, 18 green candies, 21 brown candies, and 6 yellow candies. What percent of the candies are green, blue, or yellow?

    (A) 27%

    (B) 48%

    (C) 49%

    (D) 55%

    (E) 72%

31.

    It is given that n is a positive integer and $p = 4 \times 5 \times 6 \times 11 \times n$

Quantity A	**Quantity B**
Remainder when p is divided by 88	Remainder when p is divided by 40

    (A) Quantity A is greater.

    (B) Quantity B is greater.

    (C) The two quantities are equal.

    (D) The relationship cannot be determined from the information given.

32. 60% of the trees in a section of forest are maple and birch in a ratio of 3 :5. If there are a total of 440 trees in this section of forest, how many are birch?

    (A) 33

    (B) 99

    (C) 165

    (D) 264

    (E) 275

Level: Medium

33. If we divide 5000 into $(k^2 - 16)$ equal parts where $\left(\dfrac{k+4}{25}\right)$% of each part is equal to 1, what is k?

34. A motor draws 15 kilowatts (kW) of power while it is running. During the 12-hour day shift, the motor kicks on four times per hour and runs for 4 minutes every cycle. The motor runs at 85% efficiency (transmits 85% of the power into the equipment) during the workday, with the remaining power being lost to heat and friction. During the 12-hour night shift, the motor switches to an operating scheme that runs 3 times per hour for 6 minutes every time. The night time efficiency is 74%. The power company rates are $0.14 per kilowatt – hours (kWh) during the day and $0.11 per kWh during the night. What is the total amount of money (in dollars) spent per day on wasted power (power lost to heat and friction)?

$

35. A survey of 100 individuals revealed that 96% are actively using Instagram and 85% are active on their Pinterest accounts. If 83% of the surveyed individuals have both Instagram and Pinterest accounts, what percent of these individuals do not use Instagram or Pinterest?

 %

36. $(2 + 2 \times 2) + \left(\dfrac{3}{5} + \dfrac{9}{7}\right) \times \dfrac{5}{6} =?$

Write your answer in the answer box as a reduced improper fraction.

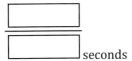

37. A train 200 m long is travelling at a speed of 60 km/h. How long will the train take to pass a person walking at 3 km/h in the opposite direction? Give your answer as a fraction in seconds.

 seconds

38. A woman drives 200 miles in a week. She drove 80 miles as "stop and go driving" and her mileage was 18 mile/gallon. She drove the remaining 120 miles on the highway and her mileage was 24 miles/gallon. Determine her average miles/gallon for the week to one decimal-place.

mi/gal

39. A man travels 200 miles on 8 gallons of gas if his average traveling speed is 55 miles/hour. If he travels at 65 miles/hour, his gas consumption rate is 18 miles/gallon, and if he travels at 45 miles/hour, his gas consumption rate is 28 miles/gallon.

He travels 300 miles in the following manner:

(i) 100 miles at 55 miles/hour,

(ii) 150 miles at 65 miles/hour, and

(iii) the remaining distance at 45 miles/hour.

Determine the gallons required (to 1 decimal place) for the trip.

 gal

40. $17^3 + 17^4 = ?$

Select all that apply.

(A) 17^7

(B) $17^3(18)$

(C) $17^6(18)$

(D) $2(17^3) + 17$

(E) $2(17^3) - 17$

(F) $2(17^3)(3^2)$

(G) $2(17^4) + 17$

(H) $2(17^4) - 17$

(I) $3(17^3)(6)$

41. What is the value of $\dfrac{\sqrt[3]{64} + 3^3}{(16)^{\frac{1}{4}}}$?

(A) $\dfrac{17}{4}$

(B) $\dfrac{31}{4}$

(C) $\dfrac{17}{2}$

(D) $\dfrac{35}{4}$

(E) $\dfrac{31}{2}$

42. What is the value of the expression $\dfrac{2\frac{2}{3} + 1\frac{5}{6}}{4\frac{4}{5}}$?

   (A) $\dfrac{85}{108}$

   (B) $\dfrac{125}{144}$

   (C) $\dfrac{15}{16}$

   (D) $1\dfrac{1}{16}$

   (E) $21\dfrac{3}{5}$

43. Which of the following are smaller than $\dfrac{2}{3}$?

   Select all that apply.

   (A) $\dfrac{33}{50}$

   (B) $\dfrac{8}{11}$

   (C) $\dfrac{3}{5}$

   (D) $\dfrac{13}{27}$

   (E) $\dfrac{5}{8}$

44. Jack started a business with an investment of $12,000. Two months later, his friend James joined him in the business by investing $16,000. After three months of James, Harry also joined them in the same business by investing $20,000. After a year from the start of the business, there was a profit of $78,000. What will be the share of each partner in the profit?

   Select all that apply.

   (A) $24,595

   (B) $25,297

   (C) $27,835

   (D) $28,108

   (E) $28,263

   (F) $25,570

45. Tony and John started a business. Tony invested $50,000 and John invested $36,000. After one month, they had a profit of $20,000. How much of the profit did John and Tony receive according to their investments?

    Select all that apply.

    (A) $8,372

    (B) $9,232

    (C) $10,000

    (D) $10,768

    (E) $11,628

46. If $8^x = 128^3$, what will the value of x be?

    Select all that apply.

    (A) $\dfrac{21}{3}$

    (B) $\dfrac{5}{3}$

    (C) 5

    (D) 7

    (E) 21

47.

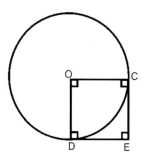

    Circumference of the circle O is 12π. What is the ratio of the area bounded by the circle, CE, and DE to the area of the square?

    (A) $4\pi - 1$

    (B) $1 - \dfrac{\pi}{4}$

    (C) $\dfrac{\pi}{4} - 1$

    (D) $\dfrac{1}{4} + 1$

    (E) $4\pi + 1$

48. A boat travels with a speed of 13 miles/hour in still water. If the ratio of the speed of the boat upstream to the speed of the boat downstream is 4:9, how much longer does it take the boat to travel 60 miles upstream than it takes to go 60 miles downstream?

    (A) 3 hours and 20 minutes
    (B) 5 hours
    (C) 4 hours and 30 minutes
    (D) 7 hours
    (E) 4 hours and 10 minutes

49.

a_2, a_3, a_5 and a_6 are the second, third, fifth and sixth terms respectively in a geometric progression.

$$a_6 - a_3 = 3024$$
$$a_5 - a_2 = 756$$

Quantity A	**Quantity B**
The first term a_1	The common ratio

   (A) Quantity A is greater.

   (B) Quantity B is greater.

   (C) The two quantities are equal.

   (D) The relationship cannot be determined from the information given.

50. One milk distributor visits Harry's local stores in every 3 days and another milk distributor visits his local stores in every 7 days. If both milk distributors visited today, when is the next time both milk distributor will visit on the same day?

    (A) 4th day from today
    (B) 5th day from today
    (C) 10th day from today
    (D) 21st day from today
    (E) Can't be determined

51. Clive saved $25 in the first month, $42 in the next month, $59 in third month and so on. If he followed the pattern for 10 months, which of the following statements are true?

    Select all that apply.

    (A) The mean of his savings for 10 months is $101.5

    (B) The mean for his savings for 5 months is $50.75

    (C) The median of his savings for 10 months is $101.5

    (D) The ratio of the median for the savings in the first 5 months to the median for the savings in the next 5 months is 59 : 144.

    (E) The amount saved in the 10th month is $178.

    (F) The amount saved in the 10th month exceeds the amount saved in the 5th month by $58.

52. a, b, and c form an arithmetic progression, and 20% of a, 40% of b, and 60% of c form a geometric progression. Which of the following is true?

    (A) $\dfrac{a}{c} + \dfrac{c}{a} = 1$

    (B) $\dfrac{a}{c} - \dfrac{c}{a} = 1$

    (C) $\dfrac{a}{c} + \dfrac{c}{a} = 0$

    (D) $\dfrac{a}{c} + \dfrac{c}{a} = -1$

    (E) $\dfrac{a}{c} - \dfrac{c}{a} = -1$

53.

In a geometric progression, the sum of its 1st and 4th term is 18. 12 is the sum of its 2nd and 3rd term. The common ratio is more than 1.

Quantity A	Quantity B
Common Ratio	2

    (A) Quantity A is greater.

    (B) Quantity B is greater.

    (C) The two quantities are equal.

    (D) The relationship cannot be determined from the information given.

54. The set of five terms of an arithmetic progression is 10, and their product is 320. What is the common difference of the progression?

    (A) 3 or 3

    (B) −2 or 3

    (C) −3 or 2

    (D) 3

    (E) −3

55.

The sum of the first five terms of an arithmetic progression is 175 less than the sum of the next five terms. The first term is a and the common difference is d.

__Quantity A__	__Quantity B__
$3d + 7$	$4d - 7$

(A) Quantity A is greater.

(B) Quantity B is greater.

(C) The two quantities are equal.

(D) The relationship cannot be determined from the information given.

56. A water tank has $6m^3$ of water. The tank has one outlet drawing water at different rates based on the user's need. If the tap is allowed to supply water at a constant rate of flow for two days, identify the rates that would reduce the water by more than a third of the initial capacity within that period of time.

Select all that apply.

(A) $16cm^3/s$

(B) $10cm^3/s$

(C) $12cm^3/s$

(D) $14cm^3/s$

(E) $9.5cm^3/s$

(F) $9cm^3/s$

57. $\dfrac{1}{a+b}, \dfrac{1}{b+5}$, and $\dfrac{1}{a+5}$ are three consecutive terms of an arithmetic progression. Which of the following represents three consecutive terms in an arithmetic progression?

(A) $25, 2a, 2b$

(B) $2a, 25, 2c$

(C) $a^2, 5^2, b^2$

(D) $a^2, b^2, 5^2$

(E) $5^2, a^2, b^2$

58.

John and Eva save the money over a period of 10 months as per the patterns shown below:

John's pattern: John saves $4 in the first month, $8 in the second month, $16 in the third month and so on.

Eva's pattern: Eva saves, $100 in the first month, $150 in the second month, $200 in the third month and so on.

Quantity A	**Quantity B**
Total money saved by John over a period of 10 months.	Total money saved by Eva over a period of 10 months.

(A) Quantity A is greater.

(B) Quantity B is greater.

(C) The two quantities are equal.

(D) The relationship cannot be determined from the information given.

59. A prize of $600 is to be distributed among 20 winners, each of whom must be awarded at least $20. If $\frac{2}{5}$ of the prize will be distributed to $\frac{3}{5}$ of the winners, what is the greatest possible individual award?

(A) $20

(B) $25

(C) $200

(D) $220

(E) $300

60. Mark the correct answers of the sum of first 3-terms and first 7-terms in a geometric progression (GP) if the 2nd term of the GP is $\frac{2}{9}$ and the 4th term is $\frac{8}{81}$.

Select all that apply.

(A) $\frac{2059}{2187}$

(B) $\frac{2}{27}$

(C) $\frac{2059}{6561}$

(D) $\frac{64}{2187}$

(E) $\frac{7}{27}$

(F) $\frac{19}{27}$

61. Select all the alternate equivalents of $\dfrac{\sqrt{x}}{x^2}$.

    Select all that apply.

    (A) $x^{\frac{-3}{2}}$

    (B) $\dfrac{1}{\sqrt{x^3}}$

    (C) $\dfrac{1}{x\sqrt{x}}$

    (D) $\sqrt[3]{x}$

    (E) $\dfrac{x^{-2}}{-\sqrt{x}}$

    (F) $\dfrac{x^{-2}}{\sqrt{x}}$

62.

$$\text{If } A = (22)^5 + (33)^5, B = (33)^5 + (44)^5, C = (44)^5 + (22)^5, \text{ and } M = (2.2)^5 + (3.3)^5 + (2.2)^5.$$

Quantity A	**Quantity B**
$(10^5)M$	$(A + B + C)$

   (A) Quantity A is greater.

   (B) Quantity B is greater.

   (C) The two quantities are equal.

   (D) The relationship cannot be determined from the information given.

63.

   If P dollars borrowed or invested for *t* years at the interest rate *r* compounded *n* times per year, then

$$\text{the future value (A) will be} A = P\left(1 + \frac{r}{n}\right)^{nt}$$

   Two individuals, M and N invested P dollars with the following conditions and both gained the same future value at the end of the investment period:

   M invested \$P at the interest rate $\dfrac{r-5}{100}$ for 6 years compounded 4 times per year

   N invested \$P at the interest rate $\dfrac{r+5}{100}$ for 4 years compounded 6 times per year.

Quantity A	**Quantity B**
r	25

   (A) Quantity A is greater.

   (B) Quantity B is greater.

   (C) The two quantities are equal.

   (D) The relationship cannot be determined from the information given.

64.

| **Quantity A** | **Quantity B** |

$$\sqrt{2014 + 2 \times (1 + 2 + 3 + \cdots + 2013)}$$

$$(\sqrt{\sqrt{2014} + 1} \times (\sqrt{\sqrt{2014} + \sqrt{2013}} - \sqrt{\sqrt{2014} - \sqrt{2013}}))^2$$

(A) Quantity A is greater.

(B) Quantity B is greater.

(C) The two quantities are equal.

(D) The relationship cannot be determined from the information given.

65. Richmond Publishing Company is planning to look for some simple interest loan between $120,000 and $150,000 at an annual interest rate of 6% for three years. What will be the range of the interest I of this loan?

(A) $21,800 $<I<$ $27,000

(B) $21,600 $<I<$ $27,000

(C) $21,600 $<I<$ $29,000

(D) $22,800 $<I<$ $29,200

(E) $23,600 $<I<$ $31,000

66. A car travels 140 miles in 4 hours, while the return trip takes $3\frac{1}{2}$ hours. What is the average speed in miles per hour for the entire trip?

(A) 35

(B) $\dfrac{371}{3}$

(C) $\dfrac{371}{2}$

(D) 40

(E) 75

Level: Difficult

67.

A and B form $\dfrac{1}{2}$ of the square, while C and D form the other $\dfrac{1}{2}$ of the square. The area of A is $\dfrac{1}{2}$ the area of B, while the area of C is $\dfrac{2}{5}$ the area of D.

What fraction of the square is the area of C? Give the ratio in the simplest form.

68. If n and m are even integers, which of the following are even integers?

    Select all that apply.

    (A) $3mn$

    (B) $(3m + 2)(3n - 2)$

    (C) $3(2m - 3)(3n - 1)$

    (D) $5(5m + 2)(5n - 6)$

    (E) $\dfrac{1}{64} m^3 n^3$

    (F) $m^2 n^3$

69. Sherry, Tom, Kim and Jolene invested $250, $100, $150 and $200 respectively to start a business. At the end of two months, they all shared half of the total profit in proportion with their contribution. If they earned a total amount of $1400 after two months, which partner(s) got less than a seventh of the total profit?

    Select all that apply.

    (A) Jolene

    (B) Tom

    (C) Kim and Jolene

    (D) Sherry and Jolene

    (E) Kim

    (F) None of them

70. When $\dfrac{y}{x} > y$, which of the following answers are true?

    Select all that apply.

    (A) y is infinite

    (B) x is infinite

    (C) $y < 0$ and $x < 0$

    (D) $y > 1$ and $x > 1$

    (E) $y > 0$ and $0 < x < 1$

71. A homeowner would like to fill up a pool and add chlorine to the water. Starting with an empty pool, the homeowner places a hose in the pool that discharges water at a constant rate of 10 gallons per minute. After letting the hose run for 2.5 hours, the homeowner pours 1 ounce of liquid chlorine solution into the pool. The hose runs for another 2 hours, and when the homeowner comes to check on the pool, he bumps a bucket next to the pool that contains a 1 :15 by volume mix of liquid chlorine to water, and 24 ounces of this solution spills into the pool. The homeowner opens a drain, still letting the hose run, and drains out water at a rate of 3 gallons per minute for 1.5 hours, then shuts both the drain and the hose. 5% of the chlorine was lost out of the drain. What is the final concentration of chlorine in the pool, in ounces/1,000 gallons of water?

    (A) 0.67

    (B) 0.93

    (C) 1.5

    (D) 2

    (E) 0.73

72. Boat A can travel in still water at a speed of 30 feet per second, known as its base speed. Boat A is currently traveling upstream (against the current) in a river that is flowing at a constant speed of 11 feet per second. Boat B is also traveling upstream at a base speed of 29 feet per second, and begins to catch up to Boat A.

    When the two boats are even with each other, the motor in the Boat A suddenly stops and the boat begins to drift downstream with the current. The operator starts to fix the engine and makes it run 30 seconds later, at which point Boat A instantly begins upstream again at half of its base speed.

    Another 30 seconds past that point, the operator is able to increase the speed to 40 feet per second. He continues for another two minutes and then drops a buoy in the water, which begins to float downstream. What is the distance, in feet, between Boat B and the buoy 45 seconds after the buoy is dropped in the water?

    (A) 465

    (B) 30

    (C) 75

    (D) 495

    (E) 164

73. A particular vehicle dealer sells only cars and trucks. The ratio of cars to trucks is 3 :4, the ratio of four-wheel-drive trucks to two-wheel-drive trucks is 7 :3, and the ratio of luxury cars to non-luxury cars is 3 : 2? If there are 108 luxury cars, what is the ratio of two-wheel-drive trucks to non-luxury cars?

    (A) 1:1

    (B) 1:2

    (C) 2:3

    (D) 3:2

    (E) 14:9

74. A food distributor must ship out 4,000 pounds per day of each one of their products. The products they carry, along with the product densities are:

- Asparagus   28 pounds per cubic foot
- Cherries   40 pounds per cubic foot
- Corn   20 pounds per cubic foot
- Grapes   30 pounds per cubic foot
- Lemons   40 pounds per cubic foot

The conveyors begin to run at 6 A.M. at the following rates:

- Asparagus   0.27 cubic feet per minute
- Cherries   0.22 cubic feet per minute
- Corn   0.45 cubic feet per minute
- Grapes   0.25 cubic feet per minute
- Lemons   0.19 cubic feet per minute

The conveyors stop running at 4 P.M. for the day.

During the loading process, portions of the produce were removed due to spoilage. Spoilage consists of fully-spoiled and half-spoiled portions of the produce.

The following are percentages of the produce that was fully spoiled and had to be removed from the conveyors:

- Asparagus   11% by weight
- Cherries   7% by weight
- Corn   10% by weight
- Grapes   6% by weight
- Lemons   9% by weight

The half-spoiled portion represents a portion of the product that required removal of half of its weight due to spoilage. The other half of the percentage was allowed to remain on the conveyor.

The following are percentages of the produce that was half spoiled:

- Asparagus   11% by weight
- Cherries   29% by weight
- Corn   24% by weight
- Grapes   14% by weight
- Lemons   4% by weight

Which products fulfilled the required daily quota of 4,000 pounds?

Select all that apply.

(A) Asparagus

(B) Cherries

(C) Corn

(D) Grapes

(E) Lemons

75. Two workers produce the same part. For the first worker it takes 5 minutes longer than second worker to complete the manufacturing of a part. Within 8 hours, the second worker produces 16 parts more than the number of parts the first worker makes. During this time period, how many parts two workers produce?

   (A) 28

   (B) 32

   (C) 33

   (D) 45

   (E) 48

76. A moving cargo train takes 5 minutes to pass a polar bear moving in opposite direction at a speed of 15 miles per hour. If the length of the train is 1.25 miles, what is the speed of the train?

   (A) 21.25 miles per hour

   (B) 30 miles per hour

   (C) 45 miles per hour

   (D) 20 miles per hour

   (E) 60 miles per hour

77. An investment in the amount of $245,000 was made at the beginning of Year 0 with an interest rate of 3.5%, compounded yearly. At the end of year 3, the investor places another $50,000 in the investment and the yearly interest rate has now increased to 5.5%. The investor pulls out all of the money at the end of Year 20. If the investor would have had $125,000 as an initial investment and could only start adding money at the end of year 5, the regular installment amount that would need to be added at the end of each year, given the interest rates provided above, to equal the same amount at year 20, is closest to:

   (A) $30,000

   (B) $19,000

   (C) $45,500

   (D) $21,000

   (E) $13,500

78.

   m is defined as the largest integer that is smaller than 12.022.

   n is defined as the smallest integer that is greater than 23.032.

   p is defined as the middle integer of the integers that lie between 34.43 and 43.34.

Quantity A	**Quantity B**
m^{n+p}	n^{m+p}

   (A) Quantity A is greater.

   (B) Quantity B is greater.

   (C) The two quantities are equal.

   (D) The relationship cannot be determined from the information given.

79. A couple was planning to make a purchase of a home with a price of $250,000. They knew that the down payment would be 18% of the home's price. Since they did not have the down payment money available, they invested $20,000 with an annual interest rate of 8% compounded annually. They invested the money at the beginning of Year 0. At the end of year 6, the couple realized that the home price had increased to $378,000, and the annual interest rate would change and would also be compounded quarterly. If the couple only has another 4 years to invest in order to reach the down payment amount, what should the minimum annual interest rate be, to the nearest whole number?

    (A) 19

    (B) 25

    (C) 18

    (D) 11

    (E) 8

80.

A positive integer n has a remainder of 5 when divided by 7.

$$\frac{m + 3}{5} \text{ is an integer greater than 1.}$$

Quantity A	**Quantity B**
The remainder when $(5n + 3)$ is divided by 7	The remainder when m is divided by 5

(A) Quantity A is greater.

(B) Quantity B is greater.

(C) The two quantities are equal.

(D) The relationship cannot be determined from the information given.

Answers and Explanations

Level: Easy

1. **Sub topic: Percent**

   The correct answer is 3.99.

   To solve, convert the percent to its decimal form.

   $21\% \div 100 = 0.21$

   Now multiply the 19 by the decimal form of the percent.

   $19 \times 0.21 = 3.99$

2. **Sub topic: Decimals**

   The correct answers are (A), (C) and (F).

   First, we compare the value in the ones place. The numbers are between 5 and 6. Of the choices we have, they are all between 5 and 6.

   Now we compare numbers in the tenths place, which are 5.0 and 6.1. The choices we are given are A. 5.1, B 5.0, C. 5.7, D. 5.0, E. 6.1, and F. 6.0.5.1 and 5.7 are between 5.0 and 6.1. A and C are between the two numbers.

   Now we compare numbers in the hundredths place. We want numbers between 5.04 and 6.10.

   Of the choices we have left, B 5.04, D 5.00, E.6.12 and F 6.04,D is less than 5.04 and E is greater than 6.10, but F is a solution because 6.04 is between 5.04 and 6.10.

3. **Sub topic: Percent/Fraction**

   The correct answers are (B) and (D).

   Total drink drunk by 5th class students $= \left(\frac{3}{7}\right) \times 21 = 9$ liters

   Remaining drink $= 30 - 9 = 21$ liters

   As each student of 10th class is given $\frac{3}{2}$ liter of drink then 21 liters will be given to $\frac{21}{\frac{3}{2}} = 14$ students.

   Percentage will be $\left(\frac{14}{35}\right) \times 100 = 40\%$

4. **Sub topic: Integers**

   The correct answer is (A).

   The variable m can be any integer that ends in either a 2 or a 7. n can be any integer that ends in either a 1 or a 6. Plugging in will show that in any case, $m + n$ will leave a remainder of 3 when divided by 5, and mn will leave a remainder of 2 when divided by 5, so Quantity A is greater.

5. **Sub topic: Fractions**

   The correct answer is (B).

   The easiest method is by inspection (and/or addition). Quantity A is approaching 2 but will not get there. Mathematically getting a common denominator and adding gives

   $1 + \frac{1}{2} + \frac{1}{4} + \frac{1}{16} + \frac{1}{32} + \frac{1}{64}$ or

$$1 + \frac{32}{64} + \frac{16}{64} + \frac{4}{64} + \frac{2}{64} + \frac{1}{64}$$

$$1 + \frac{55}{64}$$

$$1 + \frac{55}{64} < 2$$

6. **Sub topic: Exponents**

The correct answer is (C).

Since both bases on either side of the equation are different primes, we can set the exponents of each respective base equal to one another:

$2x + 1 = 3x$, so $x = 1$

$2y - 1 = 3y$, so $y = -1$

Therefore, $x + y = 1 + (-1) = 0$.

The correct answer is (C).

7. The correct answer is (B).

Since m yards $= 36m$ inches and n feet $= 12n$ inches, m yards and n feet $= (36m + 12n)$ inches.

8. **Sub topic: Fractions**

The correct answers are (C) and (D).

Add fraction in denominator and numerator separately.

$$x = \frac{\left(\frac{1}{3} + \frac{1}{4} - \frac{2}{5}\right)}{4 - \left(\frac{1}{2} - \frac{3}{5} + \frac{1}{8}\right)} = \frac{\left(\frac{20 + 15 - 24}{60}\right)}{4 - \left(\frac{20 - 24 + 5}{40}\right)} = \frac{\frac{11}{60}}{4 - \frac{1}{40}} = \left(\frac{11}{60}\right)\left(\frac{40}{159}\right) = \frac{440}{9540} = 0.046$$

9. **Sub topic: Fractions**

The correct answer is (D).

This question has variables in it, so we should plug in. We simply have to obey the rules that $\frac{m}{n} = \frac{2}{3}$ and $n \neq 3$.

Let's start with $m = 4$ and $n = 6$. In this case, Quantity A becomes $\frac{7}{9}$ which is less than $\frac{5}{6}$, so we can eliminate A and C. Now let's try some weird numbers. How about $m = -6$ and $n = -9$? These satisfy the condition that $\frac{m}{n} = \frac{2}{3}$. In this case Quantity A becomes $\frac{-3}{-6}$, which is equal to $\frac{1}{2}$. This is larger than Quantity B, so we can eliminate B and our answer must be D.

10. **Sub topic: Averages**

The correct answer is (B).

Use an Average Pie to solve this one. Write in the number of things, which is 4, and the average, which is 11.

Multiply to find the total, which is 44. Now you have to be careful with the vocabulary in the question. We know that the four distinct positive integers add up to 44. To find the greatest possible value of one of them, you need to figure out the smallest possible value of the other three. Since distinct means different, the other three numbers have to be the smallest positive integers: 1, 2, and 3. Those add up to 6, so the fourth number must be 44-6, or 38.

11. **Sub topic: Ratios**

The correct answer is (A).

Calling the number x and y, $\dfrac{x+y}{2} = x\dfrac{3}{5}$, that is $\dfrac{x+y}{2x} = \dfrac{3}{5}$

Cross multiplying: $5x + 5y = 6x$, $5y = x$

Hence, one number is five times as large as the other, so their ratio is $1:5$.

Alternatively, AM is 3 parts and One number is 5 parts. We know that 2 times AM = Sum of the two numbers. So, Sum = 6 parts, hence the smaller number is $(6-5)$ parts = 1 part. Hence the ratio is $1:5$

12. **Sub topic: Averages**

The correct answer is $6,750.

Total income of three $= 4500 \times 3 = \$13,500$

Remaining income $= 27000 - 13500 = \$13,500$

Average of the two $= \$6,750$

13. **Sub topic: Fractions**

The correct answer is 1.4.

$\dfrac{5}{6} + \dfrac{3}{4} + \dfrac{2}{7} + \dfrac{5}{3} + \dfrac{7}{2} = \dfrac{591}{84}$

Average $= \dfrac{591}{84 \times 5} = \dfrac{591}{420} = 1.41$

Up to 2 significant digits it will be 1.4

14. **Sub topic: Progressions**

The correct answer is (C).

$\sqrt[3]{(2a-b)(2a+b)(4a^2+b^2)} = \sqrt[3]{(2a-b)(4a^2-b^2)(2a+b)}$

$(2a-b)(2a+b)(4a^2+b^2) = (2a-b)(2a+b)(4a^2-b^2)$

$(4a^2+b^2) = (4a^2-b^2)$

$b^2 = -b^2$

Critical Argument: A number can be equal to its negative only when the number is zero.

15. **Sub topic: Average**

The correct answer is 11.67.

Let the numbers be $x_1, x_2, \ldots \ldots, x_{10}$

Without the loss of generality assume, $x_1 < x_2 < x_3 < \ldots < x_{10}$

Therefore, the mean of the 10 numbers is

$$m = \frac{1}{10}(x_1 + x_2 + \ldots + x_{10}) = 7 \rightarrow x_1 + x_2 + \ldots x_{10} = 70 \qquad (1)$$

The mean value of the seven lowest numbers in the list is 5. Therefore

$$\frac{1}{7}(x_1 + x_2 + \ldots + x_7) = 5 \rightarrow x_1 + x_2 + \ldots x_7 = 35 \qquad (2)$$

Subtract equation (2) from equation (1): $x_8 + x_9 + x_{10} = 70 - 35 = 35$

This is the sum of the highest three numbers.

The mean of the highest three numbers $= \frac{1}{3}(x_8 + x_9 + x_{10}) = \frac{35}{3} = 11.67$ (2 decimal place accuracy)

Answer: 11.67

16. **Sub topic: Progressions**

The correct answer is (B).

Analyzing the data given in the two tables, we can see that the costs charged by both the laundries are in arithmetic progression.

At Laundry A, the cost progresses with weight as:$16, $18, $20, $22...

First term $a = \$16$

Common difference $d = \$18 - \$16 = \$2$

The cost of washing 30 pounds of cloth at Laundry A $= 30^{\text{th}}$ term

$= a + (n - 1)\, d$

$= 16 + (30 - 1)\, 2$

$= 16 + 29 \times 2$

$= 16 + 58$

$= \$74$

At Laundry B, the cost progresses with weight as:$6, $10, $14, $18...

First term $a = \$6$

Common difference $d = 10 - 6 = \$4$

The cost of washing 30 pounds of cloth at Laundry B $= 30^{\text{th}}$ term

$= a + (n - 1)\, d$

$= 6 + (30 - 1)4$

$= 16 + 29 \times 4$

$= 16 + 116$

$= \$132$

Laundry A charges $74 for washing 30 pounds of clothes, while laundry B charges $132 for the same weight.

Hence, Laundry B charges more for washing 30 pounds of clothes.

17. **Sub topic: Integers**

The correct answer is (B).

All prime numbers- except for 2-are odd, but not vice-versa. Think of 9, 21, 35; all factors other than 1 and themselves. Consequently, there are more odd numbers than prime numbers.

18. **Sub topic: Fractions**

    The correct answer is 40%.

    1st group: Each person receives $\left(\frac{1}{2}\right)\left(\frac{1}{3}\right) = \frac{1}{6}$

    2nd group: Each person receives $\left(\frac{1}{4}\right)\left(\frac{1}{3}\right) = \frac{1}{12}$

    3rd group: Each person receives $\left(\frac{1}{5}\right)\left(\frac{1}{3}\right) = \frac{1}{15}$

    Ratio of smallest/largest serving $= \dfrac{\frac{1}{15}}{\frac{1}{6}} = \frac{2}{5} = 40\%$

    Answer: 40%

19. **Sub topic: Averages**

    The correct answer is 39.5.

    Total score in 3 matches against team A $= 3 \times 42 = 126$ runs

    Total score in 5 matches against team B $= 5 \times 38 = 190$ runs

    Total scores in 8 matches $= 316$ runs

    Average $= \dfrac{316}{8} = 39.5$

20. **Sub topic: Averages**

    The correct answer is (D).

    Add up all the weekly wages: $406.20 + 413.50 + 420.00 + 425.00 + 395.30 = \$2,060.00$.

    Divide \$2,060.00 by 5 to get the average weekly wage, \$412.00.

21. **Sub topic: Averages**

    The correct answer is (B).

    This is an average problem, so use the average formula. If the average of 6 numbers is 24, we can solve for their sum: $6 \times 24 = 144$. If four of these numbers total 96, then by subtracting 96 from 144, we get the sum of the other two numbers, 48. To find the average of these two numbers, we divide their sum by their number: $\dfrac{48}{2} = 24$.

22. **Sub topic: Averages**

    The correct answers are (A), (B) and (C).

    Let the integers be $(x - 1)$, x, $(x + 1)$. Then M $= \dfrac{x - 1 + x + x + 1}{3} = \dfrac{3x}{3} = x$

    So, all I, II and III are true.

23. **Sub topic: Integers**

The correct answer is (A).

Since no coins were left over when she packed them into 4 or 6 bags, the number of coins should be a multiple of their LCM.

LCM of 4 and 6 is 12.

When she packs them into 7 bags, one coin is left over.

Multiples of 12 are 12, 24, 36, 48,.......

One less than these multiples should be a multiple of 7.

The least number that fulfills this condition is 36 (as 36 – 1 = 35 is indeed a multiple of 7).

Hence, the least number of coins Stella has is 36.

24. **Sub topic: Integers – Sequences**

The correct answer is (C).

We can use the formula to calculate the first 10 values of S:

$S_1 = 3$ $S_2 = 3(3) - 3 = 6$ $S_3 = 3(6) - 3 = 15$

$S_4 = 3(15) - 3 = 42$ $S_5 = 3(42) - 3 = 123$ $S_5 - S_4 = 123 - 42 = 81.$

Alternatively, we could solve this problem by noticing the following pattern in the sequence:

$S_2 - S_1 = 3$ or (3^1)

$S_3 - S_2 = 9$ or (3^2)

$S_4 - S_3 = 27$ or (3^3)

We could extrapolate this pattern to see that $S_5 - S_4 = 3^4 = 81.$

The correct answer is (c).

25. **Sub topic: Exponents and Roots**

The correct answer is (C).

As per the question,

$$a^{-3}b^{-2} = \frac{1}{36}$$

$$\frac{1}{(a^3b^2)} = \frac{1}{36}$$

$$a^3b^2 = 36$$

The only positive integers that satisfy this expression are $a= 1$ and $b = 6$.

Therefore, the value of $a^{-3}b^{-2} = \frac{1}{a^2b^3} = \frac{1}{(1)^2(6)^3} = \frac{1}{216}$

The correct answer is (C).

26. **Sub topic: Fractions and Percent**

The correct answer is (B).

Simplify all the given numerical statements A, B, and C first.

Combine all the ratios in each expression.

$$A = \frac{3}{4} - \frac{5}{4} + \frac{9}{4}$$

$$A = \frac{3 - 5 + 9}{4}$$

$$A = \frac{7}{4}$$

In (B), multiply the denominator and numerator of the first fraction by 4 and of the second fraction by 2 to make all the denominators the same, and then simplify.

$$B = \frac{12}{24} - \frac{10}{24} + \frac{7}{24}$$

$$B = \frac{3}{8}$$

In (C), denominators are the same. Keep the same denominator and add the numerators.

$$C = \frac{4}{8} = \frac{1}{2}$$

Next, find A + B. Replace A and B with their values found above.

$$A + B = \frac{7}{4} + \frac{3}{8}$$

$$A + B = \frac{17}{8}$$

Replace the values of (A + B) and C found above in the expression below:

$$C\% \text{ of } (A + B) = \left(\frac{1}{2}\%\right)\left(\frac{17}{8}\right)$$

$$= \left(\frac{1}{200}\right)\left(\frac{17}{8}\right)$$

$$= \frac{17}{1600}$$

Since $\frac{17}{1600} < \frac{17}{160}$, thus the choice (B) is correct.

27. **Sub topic: Percent**

The correct answer is (C).

The formula for percentage change is change/original × 100.

In this case, the average laptop price five years ago represents the original amount. The original amount = 75% of $700 or 75% × $700 = $525.

The change is the difference between the original and new prices = $700 − $525 = $175.

Thus, the percentage increase = $175/$525 × 100 = $33\frac{1}{3}$%.

28. **Sub topic: Percent**

The correct answer is (E).

Rewrite each answer choice in simplest form.

(a) $0.5 \times 10^{-3} = 0.0005$

(b) $50000(0.00005) = 2.5$

(c) $0.05 \div 10^{-6} = 50000$

(d) $5 \times 10^3 = 5000$

(e) $10^{-5} \div 10^{-7} = 100$

Only 100 is between 5 and 5000.

The correct answer is (e).

29. **Sub topic: Order of Operations**

The correct answer is (C).

To evaluate using order of operations, we need to use PEMDAS.

P: Parenthesis

E: Exponents

M/D: Multiplication and Division done from Left to Right.

A/S: Addition and Subtraction

$17 - 3[5 - 6 \div 3 \times 2 + 3^2 - (4 - 2)^3]$

$= 17 - 3[5 - 6 \div 3 \times 2 + 9 - (2)^3]$

$= 17 - 3[5 - 6 \div 3 \times 2 + 9 - 8]$

$= 17 - 3[5 - 2 \times 2 + 9 - 8]$

$= 17 - 3[5 - 4 + 9 - 8]$

$= 17 - 3[2]$

$= 17 - 6$

$= 11$

Therefore, the correct answer is (C).

30. **Sub topic: Percent**

The correct answer is (D).

To begin this problem, we need to first find the total number of candies in the bag.

19 Red + 25 Blue + 18 Green + 21 Brown + 6 Yellow = 89 Total

Now we determine how many of the candies are green, blue or yellow.

18 Green + 25 Blue + 6 Yellow = 49 Green, Blue or Yellow

Now we can calculate the percentage of the candies that fit our description.

$\% = \dfrac{Number\ That\ Fit\ Description}{Total\ Number} \times 100$

$\% = \dfrac{49}{89} \times 100 = 0.55 \times 100 = 55\%$

55% of the candies are Green, Blue, or Yellow. The correct answer is D.

31. **Sub topic: Percent**

The correct answer is (C).

$p = 4 \times 5 \times 6 \times 11 \times n \rightarrow p = 2 \times 2 \times 5 \times 2 \times 3 \times 11 \times n.$

Therefore $p = 88 \times 15$ or $p = 40 \times 33$. So, p is divisible by both 88 and 40 and remainder will be zero in both the cases.

Hence, the correct answer is (C)

32. **Sub topic: Percent and Ratios**

The correct answer is (C).

First determine how many trees are maple and birch by calculating 60% of 440, $0.6 \times 440 = 264$. The ratio of maple to birch is 3 :5, which means $\frac{3}{8}$ are maple and $\frac{5}{8}$ are birch.$\frac{5}{8} \times 264 = 165$. There are 165 birch trees.

Level: Medium

33. The correct answer is 6.

Divide 5000 first into$(k^2 - 16)$equal parts: $\frac{5000}{k^2 - 16}$.

Then, $\frac{k+4}{25}$ % of$\frac{5000}{k^2 - 16} = 1$

Write percent notation $\frac{k+4}{25}$ % in a fraction form

$\frac{\frac{k+4}{25}}{100} \times \frac{5000}{k^2 - 16} = 1$

Simplify the first fraction and factor the denominator of the second fraction.

$\frac{k+4}{2500} \times \frac{5000}{(k-4)(k+4)} = 1$

Simplify

$\frac{2}{k-4} = 1$

$k - 4 = 2$

$k = 6$

34. The correct answer is 2.56.

To find the answer, the number of kilowatt-hours must be determined for each shift. During the day shift, the motor run four times per hour at four minutes each for a total of 16 minutes per hour, or $\frac{16}{60} = 0.27$ hour. The shift is 12 hours long, so the total run time is $12 \times 0.27 = 3.24$ hours. Since the motor draws 15 kW, the total power draw during the day shift is $15 \times 3.24 = 48.6$ kWh. The percentage of power lost to heat and friction during the day shift is $100\% - 85\% = 15\%$. The cost of the lost day shift power is 48.6 kWh $\times$ 15% $\times$ \$0.14/kWh = \$1.02.

During the night shift, the motor runs 3 times per hour at 6 minutes each for a total of 18 minutes per hour, or $\frac{18}{60} = 0.30$ hour.The shift is 12 hours long, so the total run time is $12 \times 0.30 = 3.6$ hours.Since the motor draws 15 kW, the total power draw during the night shift is $15 \times 3.6 = 54$ kWh.The percentage of power lost to heat and friction during the night shift is $100\% - 74\% = 26\%$.The cost of the lost night shift power is 54 kWh $\times$ 26% $\times$ \$0.11/kWh = \$1.54.

The total cost for power loss during the day is $1.02 + 1.54 = $2.56.

35. **Sub topic: Percent**

The correct answer is 2%.

Those who do not use Instagram nor Pinterest can be represented as $P(A \cup B)'$. First, let's solve for

$P(A \cup B) = P(A) + P(B) - P(A \cap B)$

Substituting the given values in decimal form,

$P(A \cup B) = 0.96 + 0.85 - 0.83 = 0.98$

$P(A \cup B)' = 1 - P(A \cup B)$

$P(A \cup B)' = 1 - 0.98 = 0.02$

The percentage form of the answer is 2%.

36. **Sub topic: Order of Operations**

The correct answer is $\dfrac{53}{7}$.

Use order of operations to solve.

$(2 + 2 \times 2) + \left(\dfrac{3}{5} + \dfrac{9}{7}\right) \times \dfrac{5}{6}$

$= (2 + 4) + \left(\dfrac{3}{5} + \dfrac{9}{7}\right) \times \dfrac{5}{6}$

$= 6 + \left(\dfrac{66}{35}\right) \times \dfrac{5}{6}$

$= 6 + \dfrac{11}{7}$

Find a common denominator.

$= \dfrac{42}{7} + \dfrac{11}{7}$

$= \dfrac{53}{7}$

37. **Sub topic: Time and Distance**

The correct answer is $\dfrac{80}{7}$.

Remember that the formula for distance is Distance = Speed $\times$ Time.

The train is moving in a direction opposite to the person, therefore the relative speed of the train with passer by stationary is $(60 + 3)$ km/h= 63 km/h.

The relative speed of train in $\dfrac{m}{s}$ is $\dfrac{63\,\text{km}}{h} \times \dfrac{1000\,\text{m}}{1\,\text{km}} \times \dfrac{1h}{3600\,\text{s}} = \dfrac{35}{2}$.

Therefore, time in which the train will pass the person is the length of the train divided by the relative speed of the train.

$\left(\dfrac{200}{\frac{35}{2}}\right) = \left(\dfrac{80}{7}\right)$ seconds

38. **Sub topic: Time and Distance**

The correct answer is 21.2mi/gal.

Math procedure	Strategy/Explanation
80 miles / (18 miles/gal) $$= (80\text{mi})\left(\frac{1}{18}\frac{\text{gal}}{\text{mi}}\right) = 4.444 \text{ gal}$$	Calculate gallons required for 80 miles of "stop and go" driving.
120 miles / (24 miles/gal) $$= (120\text{mi})\left(\frac{1}{24}\frac{\text{gal}}{\text{mi}}\right) = 5.0 \text{ gal}$$	Calculate gallons required for 120 miles of highway driving.
Total gallons used $$= 4.444 + 5.0$$ $$= 9.444 \text{ gal}$$ Average miles/gallon $$= \frac{200}{9.444}\frac{\text{mi}}{\text{gal}}$$ $$= 21.177 \text{ mi/gal.}$$	9.444 gallons were used to drive 200 miles. Compute average miles per gallon for 200 miles. When rounded to 1 decimal place, we have 21.2 mi/gal.

39. **Sub topic: Time and Distance**

The correct answer is 14.1gal.

Strategy: Determine fuel consumption rate at the different traveling speeds.

At 45 mi/hr, fuel consumption = 28 mi/gal

At 55 mi/hr, fuel consumption = (200mi)/(8gal) = 25 mi/gal

At 65 mi/hr, fuel consumption= 18 mi/gal

His trip:

100 miles at 55 mi/hr consumes $(100\text{mi})\dfrac{1}{25}\dfrac{\text{gal}}{\text{mi}} = 4\text{gal}$

150 miles at 65 mi/hr consumes $(150\text{mi})\dfrac{1}{18}\dfrac{\text{gal}}{\text{mi}} = 8.333\text{gal}$

50 miles at 45 mi/hr consumes $(50\text{mi})\dfrac{1}{28}\dfrac{\text{gal}}{\text{mi}} = 1.786\text{gal}$

Total gallons consumed on trip = 4.0 + 8.333 + 1.786 = 14.119 gal = 14.1
(to 1 decimal place).

40. **Sub topic: Exponents and Roots**

The correct answers are (B), (F) and (I).

Since $17^3 = 17^3 \times 1$ and $17^4 = 17^3 \times 17$, then 17^3 may be factored out of each term. It follows that $17^3 + 17^4 = 17^3(1 + 17) = 17^3(18)$.

(B) $17^3 (18)$

(F) $2(17^3)(3^2) = 2(17^3)(9) = (17^3)(18)$

(I) $3(17^3)(6) = 17^3 (18)$

Rest all other options are incorrect as they cannot be simplified to $17^3(18)$form.

41. **Sub topic: Exponents and Roots**

The correct answer is (E).

To determine the value of the expression, we need to simplify each part of the equation.

$$\frac{\sqrt[3]{64} + 3^3}{(16)^{\frac{1}{4}}}$$

- $\sqrt[3]{64}$ - This is the cube root of 64. In other words, what three numbers that are the same will multiply to 64. $4 \times 4 \times 4 = 64$, so $\sqrt[3]{64} = 4$.

- 3^3 - We are raising 3 to the third power meaning we have $3 \times 3 \times 3$ or 27.

- $(16)^{1/4}$ - To simplify a fractional power, use the following property $a^{m/n} = \sqrt[n]{a^m} = \left(\sqrt[n]{a}\right)^m$

$(16)^{\frac{1}{4}} = \sqrt[4]{16} = 2$

Now put the pieces together into one problem.

$$\frac{\sqrt[3]{64} + 3^3}{(16)^{\frac{1}{4}}} = \frac{4 + 27}{2} = \frac{31}{2}$$

42. **Sub topic: Fractions**

The correct answer is (C).

To simply the expression we need to follow these rules:

- Adding/Subtracting Fractions: Get a common denominator for both fractions, combine the numerators, and simplify the fraction.

- Multiplying Fractions: Multiply straight across the numerator and denominator to obtain your answer.

- Dividing Fractions: Keep the first fraction. Change the division to multiplication and take the reciprocal of the second fraction. Simplify.

First, we need to change each mixed number to an improper fraction.

$$2\frac{2}{3} = \frac{3 \times 2 + 2}{3} = \frac{8}{3}$$

$$1\frac{5}{6} = \frac{6 \times 1 + 5}{6} = \frac{11}{6}$$

$$4\frac{4}{5} = \frac{5 \times 4 + 4}{5} = \frac{24}{5}$$

Second, simplify the numerator.

$$\frac{8}{3} + \frac{11}{6} = \frac{8 \times 2}{3 \times 2} + \frac{11}{6} = \frac{16}{6} + \frac{11}{6} = \frac{27}{6}$$

And last, we divide the resulting fraction

$$\frac{\frac{27}{6}}{\frac{24}{5}} = \frac{\frac{27}{6}}{\frac{24}{5}} = \frac{27}{6} \times \frac{5}{24} = \frac{135}{144} = \frac{45}{48} = \frac{15}{16}$$

43. **Sub topic: Fractions**

The correct answers are (A), (C), (D) and (E).

Let $\frac{a}{b}$ be a fraction in which a and b are both positive. Then $\frac{a}{b} < \frac{2}{3}$ if and only if $3a < 2b$. Test each of the given fractions.

(A) For $\dfrac{33}{50}$, since $3(33) = 99, 2(50) = 100$, and $99 < 100$, then $\dfrac{33}{50} < \dfrac{2}{3}$

(B) For $\dfrac{8}{11}$, since $3(8) = 24, 2(11) = 22$, and $24 > 22$, then $\dfrac{8}{11} > \dfrac{2}{3}$

(C) For $\dfrac{3}{5}$, since $3(3) = 9, 2(5) = 10$, and $9 < 10$, then $\dfrac{3}{5} < \dfrac{2}{3}$

(D) For $\dfrac{13}{27}$, since $3(13) = 39, 2(27) = 54$, and $39 < 54$, then $\dfrac{13}{27} < \dfrac{2}{3}$

(E) For $\dfrac{5}{8}$, since $3(5) = 15, 2(8) = 16$, and $15 < 16$, then $\dfrac{5}{8} < \dfrac{2}{3}$

So, except $\dfrac{8}{11}$ all other fractions are smaller than $\dfrac{2}{3}$

44. **Sub topic: Ratios**

The correct answers are (A), (B) and (D).

The ratio of each in the business with respect to the duration of their involvement

Jack: James: Harry

$12,000 \times 12 : 16,000 \times 10 : 20,000 \times 7$

36:40:35

Sum of the Ratios $= 36 + 40 + 35 = 111$

Jack's share $= 36 \times \dfrac{78,000}{111} = \$25,297$

James's share $= 40 \times \dfrac{78,000}{111} = \$28,108$

Harry's share $= 35 \times \dfrac{78,000}{111} = \$24,595$

45. **Sub topic: Profit and Loss**

The correct answers are (A) and (E).

John's share according to his investment is

$(\text{profit}) \times \dfrac{\text{John's investment}}{\text{total investment}}$

$= (20000) \times \dfrac{36,000}{86,000}$

$= \$8,372$

Tony's share of the profit is $= 20,000 - 8,372 = \$11,628$

46. **Sub topic: Exponents and Roots**

The correct answers are (A) and (D).

To solve, first convert $8^x = 2^{3x}$. Next, convert $128^3 = 2^{7\times3} = 2^{21}$

Now relate the two exponents and solve for x.

$3x = 21$

$x = 7$

47. **Sub topic: Ratios**

The correct answer is (B).

The circumference of a circle is the product of a radius and 2π. So, dividing the circumference by 2π gives the measure of a radius. Denote the length of a radius by r. Then

$$r = \frac{12\pi}{2\pi}$$

Reduce the fraction by 2π.

$$r = 6$$

Denoting by Q, find the area of one-quarter of the circle.

$$Q = \frac{1}{4}\pi(6^2)$$

$$= 9\pi$$

A side of the square is same as a radius of the square. Denoting by S, find the area of the square.

$$S = 6^2$$

$$= 36$$

The difference between S and Q is the area of the region bounded by the circle, CE, and DE.

$$S - Q = 36 - 9\pi$$

$$= 9(4 - \pi)$$

We are asked to find the ratio of S – Q to S. To do so, replace the known values in $\frac{S-Q}{S}$

$$\frac{S - Q}{S} = \frac{9(4 - \pi)}{36}$$

Reduce the right fraction by 9.

$$\frac{S - Q}{S} = \frac{(4 - \pi)}{4}$$

Decompose the right fraction.

$$\frac{S - Q}{S} = \frac{4}{4} - \frac{\pi}{4}$$

$$\frac{S-Q}{S} = 1 - \frac{\pi}{4}$$

48. **Sub topic: Boat and Stream**

The correct answer is (E).

Boat speed upstream = Speed in still water − Speed of the water current

Boat speed downstream = Speed in still water + Speed of the water current

If we divide the above equations

$$\frac{\text{Boat speed upstream}}{\text{Boat speed downstream}} = \frac{\text{Speed in still water } - \text{ Speed of the water current}}{\text{Speed in still water } + \text{ Speed of the water current}}$$

$$\frac{4}{9} = \frac{13 \text{ miles/hour } - \text{ Speed of the water current}}{13 \text{ miles/hour } + \text{ Speed of the water current}}$$

52 miles/hour + 4 × Speed of the water current = 117 miles/hour − 9 × Speed of the water current

$$\text{Speed of the water current} = \frac{117 \text{ miles/hour} - 52 \text{ miles/hour}}{13} = 5 \text{ miles/hour}$$

If we now substitute the values, we know:

Boat speed upstream = 13 miles/hour − 5 miles/hour = 8 miles/hour

Boat speed downstream = 13 miles/hour + 5 miles/hour = 18 miles/hour

Time taken to travel 60 miles upstream = 60/8 hours = $7\frac{1}{2}$ hours = 7 hours and 30 minutes

Time taken to travel 60 miles downstream = 60/18 hours = $3\frac{1}{3}$ hours = 3 hours and 20 minutes

7 hours and 30 minutes − 3 hours and 20 minutes = 4 hours and 10 minutes

Therefore, (E) is the correct answer, it takes the boat 4 hours and 10 minutes longer to travel 60 miles upstream than it takes to travel 60 miles downstream

49. **Sub topic: Ratios**

The correct answer is (B).

The formula for calculating the *n-th* term in a geometric progression is:

$a_n = a_1 r^{n-1}$

Where a_1 is the first term and r is the common ratio

In this case we can re-write the system of equations:

$a_6 - a_3 = 3024 \rightarrow a_1 r^5 - a_1 r^2 = 3024$

$a_5 - a_2 = 756 \rightarrow a_1 r^4 - a_1 r^1 = 756$

If we divide the two equations $\rightarrow \dfrac{a_1 r^5 - a_1 r^2}{a_1 r^4 - a_1 r^1} = \dfrac{3024}{756}$

$\dfrac{a_1 r^2 (r^3 - 1)}{a_1 r (r^3 - 1)} = \dfrac{3024}{756}$

We can now simplify the left side by $a_1 r(r^3 - 1) \rightarrow r = \dfrac{3024}{756} = 4$

In order to find a_1 we substitute r in the second equation $a_1 r^4 - a_1 r^1 = 756$

$a_1 = \dfrac{756}{r(r^3 - 1)} = \dfrac{756}{4 \times 63} = \dfrac{756}{252} = 3$

The common ratio (4) is greater than the first term (3), hence the right column is greater than the left column and (B) is the correct answer.

50. **Sub topic: Real Numbers and Operations**

The correct answer is (D).

This problem simply asks you to find the LCM of the visits of the two milk distributors. Since both milk distributors visited today, the next time when they will visit together will be the LCM of their visiting frequency 3 and 7, which is 21. So, they will visit again on the 21st day from today.

51. **Sub topic: Progressions**

The correct answers are (A), (C), (D) and (E).

The monthly savings of Clive are $25, $42, $59

Note that Clive's savings are in Arithmetic Progression.

The first term of AP, $a = 25$

Common difference $d = 42 - 25 = 17$

Total savings in 10 months = Sum of 10 terms of AP

$= \dfrac{10}{2}[2 \times 25 + (10 - 1)17]\left[\text{Using } S_n = \dfrac{n}{2}(2a + (n - 1)d)\right]$

$= 5 \times [50 + 153]$

$= 5 \times 203$

$= 1015$

So, Clive's total savings in 10 months is $1,015

Mean of saving for 10 months $= \dfrac{\text{Total amount saved in 10 months}}{10}$

$= \dfrac{1,015}{10} = \$101.5$

So, the mean of Clive's savings for 10 months is $101.5

Total savings in 5 months = Sum of 5 terms of AP

$= \dfrac{5}{2}[2 \times 25 + (5 - 1)17] \left[\text{Using } S_n = \dfrac{n}{2}(2a + (n - 1)d)\right]$

$= 2.5 \times [50 + 68]$

$= 2.5 \times 118 = 295$

So, Clive's total savings in 5 months is $295

Mean of saving for 5 months $= \dfrac{\text{Total amount saved in 5 months}}{5}$

$= \dfrac{295}{5} = \$59$

So, the mean for Clive's savings for 5 months is $59.

Since, number of month $n = 10$ is an even number, median will be the average of 5th and 6th terms.

Median $= \dfrac{a_5 + a_6}{2}$

$= \dfrac{a + 4d + a + 5d}{2}$

$= \dfrac{2a + 9d}{2}$

$= \dfrac{2 \times 25 + 9 \times 17}{2}$

$= \dfrac{50 + 153}{2}$

$= \dfrac{203}{2}$

$= \$101.5$

So, the median of Clive's savings for 10 months is $101.5.

Since, for the first 5 months, $n = 5$ is an odd number, median will be the third term.

Median $= a_3$

$= a + 2d$

$= 25 + 34$

$= 59$

So, the median of Clive's savings for first 5 months is $59.

Since, for the next 5 months, $n = 5$ is an odd number, median will be the third term starting from the sixth term i.e. eighth term.

Median $= a_8$

$= a + 7d$

$= 25 + 119$

$=144$

So, the median of Clive's savings for next 5 months is \$144.

Hence, the ratio of the median for the savings in the first 5 months to the median for the savings in the next 5 months is $59 : 144$

Now, the amount saved in the 10th month = 10th term of the AP

$= a_{10}$

$= a + 9d$

$= 25 + 9 \times 17$

$= 25 + 153$

$= \$178.$

So, Clive saved \$178 in the 10th month.

The difference between the amount saved by Clive in the 10th and the 5th months $= a_{10} - a_{5.}$

$= (a + 9d) - (a + 4d)$

$= 5d$

$= 5 \times 17$

$= 85$

So, the difference between the amount saved by Clive in the 10th and the 5th months is \$85.

So, options A, C, D and E are correct.

52. **Sub topic: Progressions**

The correct answer is (A).

Write the relationships between the terms of both progressions.

(1) $a + c = 2b$

(2) $(0.2a)(0.6c) = (0.4b)^2$

Square (1), and simplify (2)

(3) $a^2 + c^2 + 2ac = 4b^2$

(4) $3ac = 4b^2$ [Multiply (2) by 100 and divide by 4 on both sides]

Replace (4) in (3).

$a^2 + c^2 = ac$

$\dfrac{a}{c} + \dfrac{c}{a} = 1$

53. **Sub topic: Progressions**

The correct answer is (C).

$a + aq^3 = 18$

$aq + aq^2 = 12$

Factor.

$a(1 + q)(1 - q + q^2) = 18$

$aq(1 + q) = 12$

Divide.

$$\frac{1 - q + q^2}{q} = \frac{3}{2}$$

$$2q^2 - 5q + 2 = 0$$

$$q = 2 \text{ or } \frac{1}{2}$$

54. **Sub topic: Progressions**

The correct answer is (A).

Denote the consecutive terms of the progression by $(a - 2d)$, $(a - d)$, a, $(a + d)$, and $(a + 2d)$. Then

$(a - 2d) + (a - d) + a + (a + d) + (a + 2d) = 10$

$5a = 10$

$a = 2$

Also,

$(2 - 2d)(2 - d)(2)(2 + d)(2 + 2d) = 320$

$2(4 - d^2)(4 - 4d^2) = 320$

$(4 - d^2)(1 - d^2) = 40$

$d^4 - 5d^2 + 4 = 40$

$(d^2 - 9)(d^2 + 4)$

$d = -3 \text{ or } d = 3$

55. **Sub topic: Progressions**

The correct answer is (A).

Denote the first term by a and the common difference by d. Then

Sum of the first five terms $= 5a + (d + 2d + 3d + 4d)$

$= 5a + 10d$

Sum of the second five terms $= 5a + (5d + 6d + 7d + 8d + 9d)$

$= 5a + 35d$

Apply the difference of two sums and set up the following equation.

$5a + 10d + 175 = 5a + 35d$

$d = 7$

$3d + 7 = 3(7) + 7 = 28$

$4d - 7 = 4(7) - 7 = 21$

56. **Sub topic: Pipe & Cistern**

The correct answers are (A), (C) and (D).

Converting the given volume of the water in the tank to cm^3, we have $6m^3 \times \frac{1000000cm^3}{1m^3} = 6,000,000$ cm^3.

2 days' time in seconds is 2 days $\times$ 24 hours/day $\times$ 3600 seconds/hour = 172,800 seconds

The rate of flow necessary to drain the tank by $\frac{1}{3}$ is $\frac{1}{3} \times \frac{6000000\,cm^3}{172800\,sec}$ = approximately 11.57.

The answer choices which are greater than 11.57 ($12cm^3$, $14cm^3$, $16\ cm^3$) are all acceptable solutions.

The correct options are A, C, and D.

57. **Sub topic: Progressions**

The correct answer is (E).

$$\frac{1}{a+b} + \frac{1}{a+5} = \frac{2}{b+5}$$

$$\frac{2a+b+5}{(a+b)(a+5)} = \frac{2}{b+5}$$

Cross multiply.

$2ab + b^2 + 5b + 10a + 5b + 25 = 2a^2 + 2ab + 10a + 10b$

Move all the terms from right side to the left except $2a^2$. Then cancel out the like terms.

$b^2 + 25 = 2a^2$ or $b^2 + 5^2 = 2a^2$

58. **Sub topic: Progressions**

The correct answer is (A).

Analyzing the data given in the two patterns, we can see that John's saving is in the geometric progression and Eva's saving is in the arithmetic progression.

To find the amount saved by each of them, we need to find the sum of 10 terms of each progression.

John's pattern is: $4, $8, $16, $32 .....

So, the first term of this geometric progression is $a = 4$.

And the common ratio is $r = \frac{8}{4} = 2$

Sum of the n terms of a geometric progression is given by the expression

$$S = a\left(\frac{r^n - 1}{r - 1}\right); r > 1$$

$$S = 4\left(\frac{2^{10} - 1}{2 - 1}\right)$$

$$S = 4(2^{10} - 1)$$

$$S = 4(1024 - 1)$$

$$S = 4 \times 1023$$

$$S = 4092$$

So, John saves $4092 in 10 months.

Eva's pattern is: $100, $150, $200, $250.....

So, the first term of this arithmetic progression is $a = 100$.

And the common difference is $d = 150 - 100 = 50$

Sum of the n terms of an arithmetic progression is given by the expression: $S = \frac{n}{2}\{2a + (n-1)d\}$

$$S = \frac{10}{2}\{2 \times 100 + (10 - 1)50\}$$

$$S = 5\{200 + 450\}$$

$$S = 5\{650\}$$

$$S = 3250$$

So, Eva saves $3250 in 10 months.

Hence, John saved more money in 10 months.

59. **Sub topic: Percentages**

The correct answer is (D).

If $\frac{2}{5}$ of the prize $\left(\frac{2}{5}$ of \$600 = \$240$\right)$ is distributed to $\frac{3}{5}$ of the winners $\left(\frac{3}{5}$ of 20 is 12 winners$\right)$, this indicates that each of those 12 winners will receive a minimum of \$20.

That leaves \$360 to be divided among 8 remaining winners. If 7 of those winners receive minimum \$20 (total \$140), then the eighth winner would receive all the remaining prize money, $360 − \$140 = \$220$.

60. **Sub topic: Progressions**

The correct answers are (A) and (F).

The *n-th* term of a geometric progression is given by $a_n = ar^{n-1}$ where the letters have there usual meaning.

The second term $ar = \frac{2}{9}$, the fourth term is $ar^3 = \frac{8}{81}$

Therefore $\dfrac{ar^3}{ar} = \dfrac{8}{81} \times \dfrac{9}{2}$

$r^2 = \frac{4}{9}; r = \frac{2}{3}$

The common ratio is $\frac{2}{3}$

The first term $a = \frac{2}{9} \times \frac{3}{2} = \frac{1}{3}$

The first, second and third term is $\frac{1}{3}$, $\frac{2}{9}$ and $\frac{2}{9} \times \frac{2}{3} = \frac{2}{27}$

The sum of the first three terms is $\frac{1}{3} + \frac{2}{9} + \frac{4}{27} = \frac{19}{27}$

Using the formula for the first *n* terms, $S_n = \dfrac{a(1-r^n)}{1-r}$, we have,

$S_7 = \dfrac{\frac{1}{3}\left(1 - \frac{2^7}{3^7}\right)}{1 - \frac{2}{3}} = \dfrac{2059}{2187}.$

61. **Sub topic: Rules of Exponents**

The correct answers are (A), (B) and (C).

Let us rewrite the expression given in the question.

$\dfrac{\sqrt{x}}{x^2} = \dfrac{x^{\frac{1}{2}}}{x^2}$

$= \dfrac{1}{x^{-\frac{1}{2}} \times x^2}$

$= \dfrac{1}{x^{-\frac{1}{2}+2}}$

$= \dfrac{1}{x^{\frac{-1+4}{2}}}$

$= \dfrac{1}{x^{\frac{3}{2}}} = x^{-\frac{3}{2}}$

Let us now rewrite each option and compare with $x^{-\frac{3}{2}}$.

Option A is $x^{-\frac{3}{2}}$. Hence, option A is correct.

Option B is $\frac{1}{\sqrt{x^3}}$.

$$\frac{1}{\sqrt{x^3}} = \frac{1}{(x^3)^{\frac{1}{2}}}$$

$$= \frac{1}{x^{\frac{3}{2}}} = x^{-\frac{3}{2}}$$

Hence, option B is correct.

Option C is $\frac{1}{x\sqrt{x}}$

$$\frac{1}{x\sqrt{x}} = \frac{1}{x \times x^{\frac{1}{2}}}$$

$$= \frac{1}{x^{1+\frac{1}{2}}}$$

$$= \frac{1}{x^{\frac{2+1}{2}}}$$

$$= \frac{1}{x^{\frac{3}{2}}} = x^{-\frac{3}{2}}$$

Hence, option C is correct.

Option D is $\sqrt[3]{x}$.

$$\sqrt[3]{x} = x^{\frac{1}{3}}$$

$$x^{\frac{1}{3}} \neq x^{-\frac{3}{2}}$$

Hence, option D is incorrect.

Option E is $\frac{x^{-2}}{-\sqrt{x}}$

$$\frac{x^{-2}}{-\sqrt{x}} = \frac{x^{-2}}{-1 \times \sqrt{x}}$$

$$= \frac{x^{-2}}{x^{\frac{1}{2}}}$$

$$= -x^{-2} \times x^{-\frac{1}{2}}$$

$$= -x^{-2+\left(-\frac{1}{2}\right)}$$

$$= -x^{\frac{-4-1}{2}} = -x^{-\frac{5}{2}}$$

Hence, option E is incorrect.

Option F is $\frac{x^{-2}}{\sqrt{x}}$

$$\frac{x^{-2}}{\sqrt{x}} = \frac{x^{-2}}{x^{\frac{1}{2}}}$$

$$= x^{-2} \times x^{-\frac{1}{2}}$$

$$= x^{-2+\left(-\frac{1}{2}\right)}$$

$$= x^{\frac{-4-1}{2}} = x^{-\frac{5}{2}}$$

Hence, option F is incorrect.

62. **Sub topic: Exponents**

The correct answer is (B).

Start from Quantity B

$A + B + C$

$= (22^5 + 33^5) + (33^5 + 44^5) + (44^5 + 22^5)$

$= 2 \times 22^5 + 2 \times 33^5 + 2 \times 44^5$

$= 2(22^5 + 33^5 + 44^5)$

$= 2[(2.2 \times 10)^5 + (3.3 \times 10)^5 + (4.4 \times 10)^5]$ (rewrite 22, 33, 44 as 2.2×10 etc. so that thenumbers 2.2, 3.3, 4.4 found in M, show up)

$= 2(2.2^5 \times 10^5 + 3.3^5 \times 10^5 + 4.4^5 \times 10^5)$

$= 2 \times 10^5(2.2^5 + 3.3^5 + 4.4^5)$

$= 2 \times A$

As Quantity B is 2 times Quantity A, Quantity B is greater.

Therefore, the choice (B) is correct.

63. **Sub topic: Compound Interest**

The correct answer is (C).

The future values for M and N are as follows:

$$A_M = P\left(1 + \frac{r - 5}{100 \times 4}\right)^{4 \times 6}$$

$$A_N = P\left(1 + \frac{r + 5}{100 \times 6}\right)^{4 \times 6}$$

Set both future values equal and simplify.

$$P\left(1 + \frac{r - 5}{400}\right)^{24} = P\left(1 + \frac{r + 5}{600}\right)^{24}$$

Divide both sides by P and take 24th root of each side.

$$\left(1 + \frac{r - 5}{400}\right) = \left(1 + \frac{r + 5}{600}\right)$$

$$\frac{r - 5}{400} = \frac{r + 5}{600}$$

$$\frac{r - 5}{2} = \frac{r + 5}{3}$$

$$3r - 15 = 2r + 10$$

$$r = 10 + 15 = 25$$

64. **Sub topic: Exponents and Roots**

The correct answer is (B).

We try to simplify the first expression $\sqrt{2014 + 2 \times (1 + 2 + 3 + \cdots + 2013)}$

The sum $1 + 2 + 3 + \ldots + 2013$ is the sum of a finite arithmetic progression. So, it can be calculated as the number of terms being added (here 2013) multiplied by the sum of the first and last number in the progression (here 1 and 2013) and divided by 2.

Thus, $1 + 2 + 3 + \dots + 2013 = \dfrac{2013 \times (1+2013)}{2} = 2013 \times 1007$

$\sqrt{2014 + 2 \times (1 + 2 + 3 + \dots + 2013)} = \sqrt{2014 + 2 \times 2013 \times 1007}$

$= \sqrt{2014 + 2013 \times 2014}$

$= \sqrt{2014(1 + 2013)}$

$= \sqrt{2014^2}$

$= 2014$

Next, we try to simplify the second expression

$\left(\sqrt{\sqrt{2014} + 1} \times \left(\sqrt{\sqrt{2014} + \sqrt{2013}} - \sqrt{\sqrt{2014} - \sqrt{2013}}\right)\right)^2$

$= (\sqrt{2014} + 1) \times \left(\sqrt{2014} + \sqrt{2013} - 2 \times \sqrt{(\sqrt{2014} + \sqrt{2013})(\sqrt{2014} - \sqrt{2013})} + \sqrt{2014} - \sqrt{2013}\right)$

$= (\sqrt{2014} + 1) \times (2 \times \sqrt{2014} - 2 \times \sqrt{2014 - 2013})$

$= (\sqrt{2014} + 1) \times 2 \times (\sqrt{2014} - 1)$

$= 2 \times (2014 - 1)$

$= 2 \times 2013$

2×2013 is greater than 2014. Hence the quantity on the right is greater, so the correct answer is B.

65. **Sub topic: Simple Interest**

The correct answer is (B).

We use the formula $I = P \times t \times r$, where I is the simple interest for principle P during t years at annual rate t.

We are given 120,000 $<P<$ 150,000

Multiplying all parts of this compound inequality by the product of rate $r = 6\%$ and the number of years $t = 3$ gives the following compound inequality:

(120,000) (6%)(3) $<P(3)(6\%) <$ (150,000)(6%)(3)

Simplify this inequality.

21,600 $<P(3)(6\%) <$ 27,000

The middle expression represents the varying amount of the interest I.

Then,

$21,600 <I< \$27,000$

66. **Sub topic: Simple Interest**

The correct answer is (B).

The car travels a total distance of 280 miles $7\dfrac{1}{2}$ hours for the road trip. Its average

$280 \div 7\dfrac{1}{2} = \dfrac{280}{1} \div \dfrac{15}{2}$

Speed in miles per hour is $\dfrac{280}{1} \times \dfrac{2}{15} = \dfrac{560}{15} = \dfrac{112}{3} = 37\dfrac{1}{3}$ here and simply divided 280 by 7.5, getting

37.333, or $37\dfrac{1}{3}$

Level: Difficult

67. **Sub topic: Ratios**

The correct answer is $\frac{1}{7}$.

Let the area of the square be s sq. units.

Let the area of C be represented as c square units and the area of D be represented as d square units.

It is given that area of C $= \frac{2}{5}$ area of D

Hence, Area of D $= \frac{5}{2}$ area of C

We also know that,

Area of C + Area of D $= \frac{1}{2}$ area of the square

Therefore,

$$c + \frac{5}{2}c = \frac{1}{2}s$$

$$\frac{2c + 5c}{2} = \frac{s}{2}$$

$$\frac{7c}{2} = \frac{s}{2}$$

$$\frac{c}{s} = \frac{1}{2} \times \frac{2}{7}$$

$$\frac{c}{s} = \frac{1}{7}$$

68. **Sub topic: Integers**

The correct answers are (A), (B), (D) and (F).

Define the even integers m and n as follows, where a and b are some integers.

(1) $m = 2a$

(2) $n = 2b$

Examine all the answer choices using the definitions (1) and (2).

Choice (A): $3mn = [3(2a)(2b)]$: Replace m and n with their equivalents.

$= 12ab$: Multiply the numbers on the right.

This is an even integer.

Choice (B): $(3m + 2)(3n - 2) = [3(2a) + 2][3(2b) - 2]$: Replace m and n with their equivalents.

$= [2(3a + 1)][2(3b - 1)]$: Factor 2 out within each bracket.

The result is divisible by 4. So, the choice (B) is an even integer, as well.

Choice (C): Using (1) and (2), we have $3(2m - 3)(3n - 1) = 3[2(2a) - 3][3(2b) - 1]$

$= 3(6a - 3)(6b - 1)$: Find the product inside each bracket.

$= 3[3(2a - 1)][3(2b - 1)]$: Factor 3 out within each parenthesis.

$= 27(2a - 1)(2b - 1)$: Multiply the factors 3.

Clearly, $(2a - 1)$ and $(2b - 1)$ are odd integers for all integers a and b. So, the product $27(2a - 1)(2b - 1)$ is an odd integer as a result. Therefore, this expression produces an odd integer for the integers m and n defined in the problem.

Choice (D): Using (1) and (2), we have

$5(5m + 2)(5n - 6) = 5[(5(2a) + 2][5(2b) - 6]$

$= 5(10a + 2)(10b - 6)$: Find the product inside each bracket.

$= 20(5a + 1)(5b - 3)$: Factor 2 out of each parenthesis.

Clearly, $(5a + 1)$ and $(5b - 3)$ are odd integers for all integers a and b.

However, the product$20(2a - 1)(2b - 1)$ is an even integer due to the coefficient 20.

Choice (E): Using (1) and (2), we have

$\dfrac{1}{64} m^3 n^3 = (2a)^3 (2b)^3$: Replace m and n with their equivalents.

$= \dfrac{1}{64}(8a^3)(8b^3)$: Raise inside each parenthesis to its power.

$= a^3 b^3$: Multiply the coefficients.

Since a and b can be odd numbers, then $a^3 b^3$ is not divisible by 2.

Choice (F): Using (1) and (2), we have

$m^2 n^3 = (2a)^2 (2b)^3$: Replace m and n with their equivalents.

$= (4a^2)(8b^3)$: Raise inside each parenthesis to its power.

$= 32a^2 b^3$: Multiply the coefficients.

Since $32a^2 b^3$ is divisible by 2, $m^2 n^3$ is divisible by 2, and it is an even integer.

69. **Sub topic: Profit and loss**

The correct answers are (B) and (E).

The total capital $= 250 + 100 + 150 + 200 = \$700$

Total amount earned $= \$1,400$

Total profit $= (400 - 700) = \$700$

Half of total profit $= \dfrac{1}{2} \times (1400 - 700) = \$350$

A seventh of the profit $= \dfrac{1}{7} \times 700 = \$100$

Ratio of their contributions: $250 : 100 : 150 : 200 = 5 : 2 : 3 : 4$

Each received the following in profit:

Sherry $= \dfrac{5}{14} \times 350 = \$125$

Tom $= \dfrac{2}{14} \times 350 = \$50$

Kim $= \dfrac{3}{14} \times 350 = \$75$

Jolene $= \dfrac{4}{14} \times 350 = \$100$

By observation, Tom and Kim got less than $\$100 \left(\dfrac{1}{7} \text{ of the profit}\right)$

70. **Sub topic: Fractions**

The correct answers are (C) and (E).

In order for $\dfrac{y}{x} > y$, either both x and y should be negative numbers (as in answer C) or y is not negative and x must be a decimal number between 0 and 1.

71. **Sub topic: Pipe & Cistern/Rates**

The correct answer is (E).

Start by determining how much water and chlorine are in the pool after 2.5 hours.

Volume of water = 10 gallons per minute × 150 minutes = 1,500 gallons. 1 ounce of chlorine is poured into the pool to create a concentration (at that instant) of 0.67 oz/1,000 gallons.

After 120 minutes, the homeowner bumps the mixed solution into the pool. To determine the amount of liquid chlorine that spilled into the pool:

$$\frac{24\ oz\ solution}{16\ parts} = 1.5\ oz\ per\ part$$

So, the amount of chlorine spilled into the pool is 1.5 ounces. The pool has been running for 120 minutes at 10 gallons per minute, so the total volume of water at this point is 1,500 + 120 × 10 = 2,700 gallons. The total amount of liquid chlorine is 1 + 1.5 = 2.5 oz. The concentration is:

$$\frac{2.5}{2,700} = \frac{x}{1,000} \rightarrow x = 0.93\ \frac{oz}{1,000\ gallons}$$

The homeowner opens a drain that empties water at 3 gallons per minute, so the total water flow rate is 10 gallons in minus 3 gallons out, or 7 gallons per minute. 7 gallons per minute for another 90 minutes = 630 gallons. The final volume of water is 2,700 + 630 = 3,330. The final amount of chlorine is 2.5 ounces −(2.5 × 0.05) = 2.4 oz. The final concentration is:

$$\frac{2.4}{3,300} = \frac{x}{1,000} \rightarrow x = 0.73\ \frac{oz}{1,000\ gallons}$$

72. **Sub topic: Boat and Stream**

The correct answer is (A).

To find the position of Boat B and the buoy, determine the distance that each has traveled since the point that the boats were even with each other. The engine on the Boat A quits at this point and it drifts downstream for 30 seconds, or −11 feet per second (fps) × 30 seconds = −330 feet.

Once the engine starts, Boat A begins to travel at half of its base speed, or 30 × 0.5 equals 15 fps minus the river speed of 11 feet per second for a total speed of 4 fps. This continues for 30 seconds for a distance of 30× 4 =120 feet. The speed then increases to 40 fps minus the river speed of 11 fps for 2 minutes (120 seconds) for a distance traveled of 29 fps × 120 = 3,480 feet.

At this point the buoy is dropped into the water and float downstream at 11 feet per second for 45 seconds, traveling 45 × 11 = 495 feet in the other direction.The total distance traveled by the buoy, both inside Boat A and in the river is −330 + 120 + 3,480 − 495 = 2,775.

Boat B travels for 3 minutes (180 seconds) after the engine failure in Boat A at a constant speed of 29 fps minus the river speed of 11 fps for a total distance of (29−11) × 180 = 3,240. The distance between Boat B and the buoy is 3,240 − 2,775 = 465 feet.

The correct answer is A.

73. **Sub topic: Ratios**

The correct answer is (A).

Begin with what you know.

Cars:

There are 108 luxury cars which is $\frac{3}{5}$ of all cars. The total number of cars is:

$$\frac{3}{5}x = 108$$

$x = 180 -$ total cars

This means there are $\frac{2}{5} \times 180$ or 72 non-luxury cars.

Trucks:

From above we know that there are a total of 180 cars which is $\frac{3}{7}$ of all vehicles. The total number of vehicles

is $\frac{3}{7}x = 180x = 420 -$ total vehicles

This means there are $\frac{4}{7} \times 420$ or $240 \times$ trucks. Of these trucks $\frac{3}{10}$ are two-wheel drive or $240 \times \frac{3}{10} = 72$.

The ratio of non-luxury cars to two-wheel drive trucks is 72:72 or 1:1.

74. **Sub topic: Percentages**

The correct answers are (B), (C) and (E).

Start by determining the mass of product moving down the conveyors.

First, the product density is multiplied by the conveyor rate to provide a rate in pounds of product per minute:

Product	Density (pounds per cubic foot)		Conveyor Rate (cubic feet per minute)		Pounds per Minute
Asparagus	28		0.27		7.6
Cherries	40		0.22		8.8
Corn	20	×	0.45	=	9.0
Grapes	30		0.25		7.5
Lemons	40		0.19		7.6

Next, determine the total spoilage percentage of the products:

Product	Full-Spoilage Percentage		Half-Spoilage Percentage × 0.5		Total Spoilage Percentage
Asparagus	11%		11% × 0.5 = 5.5%		16.5%
Cherries	7%		29% × 0.5 = 14.5%		21.5%
Corn	10%	+	24% × 0.5 = 12%	=	22%
Grapes	6%		14% × 0.5 = 7%		13%
Lemons	9%		4% × 0.5 = 2%		11%

Finally, determine the pounds of product loaded per day:

Product	Pounds per Minute		100% − Total Spoilage Percentage		Minutes per 10-hour shift		Pounds Loaded per Day
Asparagus	7.6		(100 − 16.5) %				3,807
Cherries	8.8		(100 − 21.5) %				4,145
Corn	9.0	×	(100 − 22) %	×	600	=	4,212
Grapes	7.5		(100 − 13) %				3,915
Lemons	7.6		(100 − 11) %				4,058

The answers are: B, C and E.

75. Sub topic: Time and Distance

The correct answer is (B).

Let x be the number of minutes it takes the first worker to produce one part. Then, it takes the second worker $(x − 5)$ minutes to produce one part.

Eight hours is equal to $8 \times 60 = 480$ minutes. Within this period of time the number of parts two workers can produce are as follows:

Number of parts the second worker can make within eight hours $= \dfrac{480}{x}$

Number of parts the second worker can make within eight hours $= \dfrac{480}{x − 5}$

Within eight hours also the first worker makes 16 parts less than the second workers. Therefore,

$\dfrac{480}{x} + 16 = \dfrac{480}{x − 5}$

Multiply each side of this equation by $x(x − 5)$ to eliminate fractions.

$480(x − 5) + 16x(x − 5) = 480x$

Divide each side by 16 and then solve.

$30(x − 5) + x(x − 5) = 30x$

$30x − 150 + x^2 − 5x − 30x = 0$

$x^2 − 5x − 150 = 0$

$(x − 15)(x + 10) = 0$

This equation gives $x = 15$ and $x = −1$, which only $x = 15$ is admissible since x represents the measure of time.

Thus, the first worker produces $\dfrac{480}{15} = 32$

76. Sub topic: Trains

The correct answer is (B).

Let x be the speed of the train.

The relative speed of the train in relation to the polar bear $= x − 15$ and by using this effective speed, the bear can be considered still

In this case, the distance travelled by the train to completely pass the polar bear = its length = 1.25 miles

The time taken $= \dfrac{5}{60} = \dfrac{1}{12}$ hours

Distance travelled $\dfrac{1}{12}(x - 15) = 1.25 = \dfrac{5}{4}$

$x - 15 = 15$

$x = 30$ miles per hour

77. **Sub topic: Compound Interest**

The correct answer is (B).

First, find the balance of the original investment at Year 20. To determine the value up until the end of Year 3, the compound interest formula is used:

$A = P\left(1 + \dfrac{r}{n}\right)^{nt}$

Where:

A = amount of money accumulated after "n" years

P = principal amount (amount invested)

r = annual interest rate (as a decimal)

n = number of times per year that interest is accumulated

t = number of years that the principal is invested

Therefore, for the first four years (Years 0, 1, 2, 3) the value is:

$A = \$245{,}000\left(1 + \dfrac{0.035}{1}\right)^{4} = \$281{,}143$

At this point $50,000 is added to the investment for a total of $281,143 + $50,000 = $331,143 at the end of Year 3.

The interest rate then changes to 5.5% for the remainder of the investment from Year 4 through Year 20 (17 years).

The final value is therefore:

$A = \$331{,}143\left(1 + \dfrac{0.055}{1}\right)^{17} = \$822{,}824$

In order to find the answer to the problem,

Determine the amount, A, at the end of year 5 without having made any additions to the investment:

At the end of Year 3:

$A = \$125{,}000\left(1 + \dfrac{0.035}{1}\right)^{4} = \$143{,}440$

At the end of year 5, the total is:

$A = \$143{,}440\left(1 + \dfrac{0.055}{1}\right)^{2} = \$159{,}652$

The future value of the original investment at the end of year 20 =

$A = \$159{,}652\left(1 + \dfrac{0.055}{1}\right)^{15} = \$356{,}419$

The future value of the installments using the Uniform Series Compound Amount Factor =

$F = \dfrac{A[(1 + i)^{n} - 1]}{i} \rightarrow \$822{,}825 - \$356{,}419 = A\dfrac{[1.055^{16} - 1]}{0.055}$

$\$466{,}406 = 24.6A \rightarrow A = \$18{,}960$

The correct answer is B, 19,000.

78. **Sub topic: Integers and Exponents and Roots**

The correct answer is (B).

The largest integer that is smaller than 12.022 is 12 thus $m = 12$

The smallest integer that is greater than 23.032 is 24 thus $n = 24$

The middle integer of the integers that lie between 34.43 and 43.34 is the middle integer among the following integers: 35, 36, 37, 38, 39, 40, 41, 42, and 43. The middle number is 39. Thus p = 39

Next, find the given expressions:

$m^{n+p} = 12^{24+39} = 12^{63}$

$m^{m+p} = 24^{12+39} = 24^{51}$

Let's compare these two expressions by placing a question mark between them.

$12^{63} \boxed{?} 24^{51}$

Simplify both sides using the rules of exponents.

$12^{63} \boxed{?} (2 \times 12)^{51}$

$12^{63} \boxed{?} 2^{51} \times 12^{51}$

$12^{12} \boxed{?} 2^{51}$

$(2^2 \times 3)^{12} \boxed{?} 2^{51}$

$2^{24} \times 3^{12} \boxed{?} 2^{51}$

$3^{12} \boxed{?} 2^{27}$

Take logarithm of both sides.

$12 \log 3 \boxed{?} 27 \log 2$

The difference between the log 3 and log 2 is a very small decimal. But the coefficient of log 2 is 15 more than the coefficient of log 3. Thus, the result of the right side will come out far more than the result of the left side.

79. **Sub topic: Compound Interest**

The correct answer is (C).

First, determine the value of the couple's investment at the end of year 6:

$V = P\left(1 + \frac{r}{100n}\right)^{nt}$, where V is the value of the investment, P is the principal amount invested, r is the percentage rate, n is the number of times per year that the interest is compounded, and t is the number of years that the principal amount is invested.

Initially, the rate is 8% compounded annually, and the investment is held for 7 years (Year 0 through Year 6):

$V = \$20,000\left(1 + \frac{8}{100}\right)^7 = \$34,277$

The home price has increased to \$378,000, so the down payment goal is \$378,000 × 18%, or \$68,040.

The couple invests for another 5 years; set the formula as greater than or equal to the goal:

$\$68,040 \le \$34,277\left(1 + \frac{r}{400}\right)^{4\times4} \rightarrow 1.99 \le \left(1 + \frac{r}{400}\right)^{16} \rightarrow \sqrt[16]{1.99} \le 1 + \frac{r}{400}$

$r \ge 400\left(\sqrt[16]{1.99} - 1\right) \rightarrow r \ge 400\left(\sqrt{\sqrt{\sqrt{\sqrt{1.99}}}} - 1\right) \rightarrow r \approx 18$

The correct answer is (C).

80. **Sub topic: Integers**

    The correct answer is (B).

    If the integer n has a remainder of 5 when divided by 7, then the integer can be written in the form of:

    $n = 7k + 5$, where k is also a positive integer

    $5n + 3 = 5 \times (7k + 5) + 3 = 35k + 28 = 7 \times (5k + 4)$

    The remainder of the division of $(5n + 3)$ by 7 is 0

    Let $\dfrac{m+3}{5} = j$ where j is an integer greater than 2

    $m + 3 = 5j \rightarrow m = 5j - 3$

    This can be written as $m = 5 \times (j - 1) + 5 - 3 \rightarrow = 5 \times (j - 1) + 2$

    As j is an integer greater than 1, the remainder of the division of m by 5 is 2

    2 is greater than 0

    The right column is greater than the left column, so (B) is the correct answer.

Chapter **4**

Algebra Practice Questions

This chapter consists of *80 Algebra* practice questions. The questions cover all the question types as explained in Chapter 2 and are segregated into 3 levels of difficulty - Easy, Medium and Difficult. You may choose to start solving the Easy questions first and then move on to higher levels of difficulty or solve the questions in any random order. You will find answers and detailed explanations towards the end of this chapter.

Level: Easy

1. If $\frac{(x^2 + 7x + 6)}{2} = 3$, then x could equal:

    (A) -6

    (B) 0

    (C) -1

    (D) 1

    (E) 3

2.

$$\text{Inequality 1: } 4(x + 2) \leq 2(x + 5) + 14$$

$$\text{Inequality 2: } \sqrt{16 - 8y + y^2} \leq 9$$

Quantity A	**Quantity B**
x, where x is a solution of Inequality 1	y, where y is a solution of Inequality 2

(A) Quantity A is greater.

(B) Quantity B is greater.

(C) The two quantities are equal.

(D) The relationship cannot be determined from the information given.

3. Find the value of y given that $\dfrac{4^{y^2}}{64} = 2^{-y}$ and $y < |y|$

    ☐

4.

    It is given that $(x - 5)(x + 6) = 0$

    Quantity A   **Quantity B**

    $x - 6$ 0

    (A) Quantity A is greater.

    (B) Quantity B is greater.

    (C) The two quantities are equal.

    (D) The relationship cannot be determined from the information given.

5. If z is not equal to zero, and $z = \sqrt{(8zs - 16s^2)}$, then z equals:

    (A) s

    (B) 4s

    (C) 4s²

    (D) $-\dfrac{4s^2}{3}$

    (E) −4s

6.

    It is given that $a \,@\, b = a^2 + ab - 10$

    Quantity A   **Quantity B**

    $2 \,@\, 3$ 0

    (A) Quantity A is greater.

    (B) Quantity B is greater.

    (C) The two quantities are equal.

    (D) The relationship cannot be determined from the information given.

7. If $|x - 2| \le 4$; then the solution set will be?

    Select all that apply.

    (A) $2 \le x \le 6$

    (B) $-2 \le x \le 6$

    (C) $2 \le x \le -6$

    (D) $-2 \le x \le -6$

    (E) $2 \ge x \ge -6$

8.

It is given that $@x = x^2 - 11$ and $\#x = x^2 - x + 11$

Quantity A	**Quantity B**
$(@2)(\#3)$	$(\#2)(@3)$

(A) Quantity A is greater.

(B) Quantity B is greater.

(C) The two quantities are equal.

(D) The relationship cannot be determined from the information given.

9. For what value of k will the quadratic equation $x^2 - kx + 9 = 0$ have real and equal roots?

Select all that apply.

(A) 6

(B) 4

(C) -4

(D) -6

(E) -3

10.

It is given that $4x - 10 \geq x + 8$

Quantity A	**Quantity B**
x	5

(A) Quantity A is greater.

(B) Quantity B is greater.

(C) The two quantities are equal.

(D) The relationship cannot be determined from the information given.

11.

It is given that $1.3 < w < 1.3101$ and $1.3033 < y$

Quantity A	**Quantity B**
w	y

(A) Quantity A is greater.

(B) Quantity B is greater.

(C) The two quantities are equal.

(D) The relationship cannot be determined from the information given.

12. What is the value of $a - b + c - d - e$ if $a = 5, b = 2, c = 3, d = -8$, and $e = 10$?

   (A) -8

   (B) -4

   (C) -2

   (D) 4

   (E) 8

13. If $x^2 - 2x - 15 = 0$ and $x > 0$, which of the following must be equal to 0?

   Select all that apply.

   (A) $x^2 - 6x + 9$

   (B) $x^2 - 7x + 10$

   (C) $x^2 - 10x + 25$

   (D) $x^2 + 6x + 9$

   (E) $x^2 + 7x + 10$

   (F) $x^2 + 10x + 25$

14.

It is given that $0 < p < 1$

Quantity A	**Quantity B**
$\dfrac{1}{p^2}$	$\dfrac{1}{(p+1)^2}$

   (A) Quantity A is greater.

   (B) Quantity B is greater.

   (C) The two quantities are equal.

   (D) The relationship cannot be determined from the information given.

15. A certain deck of cards contains r cards. After the cards are distributed evenly among s people, 8 cards are left over. In terms of r and s, how many cards did each person receive?

   (A) $\dfrac{s}{8-r}$

   (B) $\dfrac{r-s}{8}$

   (C) $\dfrac{r-8}{s}$

   (D) $s - 8r$

   (E) $rs - 8$

16.

It is given that F > 0

Quantity A	**Quantity B**
$\dfrac{2F - 5}{2}$	$\dfrac{4F - 1}{4}$

(A) Quantity A is greater.

(B) Quantity B is greater.

(C) The two quantities are equal.

(D) The relationship cannot be determined from the information given.

17.

15 more than $5x = 55$

Quantity A	**Quantity B**
11	x

(A) Quantity A is greater.

(B) Quantity B is greater.

(C) The two quantities are equal.

(D) The relationship cannot be determined from the information given.

18.

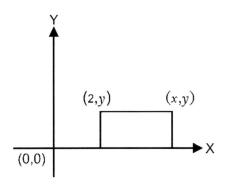

If the figure above is a rectangle, then what is the area of the figure, expressed in terms of x and y?

(A) xy

(B) $4x$

(C) $8x$

(D) $y(x - 2)$

(E) $x(y - 2)$

19. Which of the statements shown below is true for $y = \dfrac{1}{x} - \dfrac{1}{x+1}$?

    Select all that apply.

    (A) $y = \dfrac{1}{x(x+1)}$

    (B) $y = \dfrac{\frac{1}{x}}{x+1}$

    (C) $y = \dfrac{\frac{1}{x^2}}{\frac{1+1}{x}}$

    (D) $y = \dfrac{x}{x+1}$

    (E) $y = \dfrac{x}{x-2}$

20. Two vehicles, a car and a bus, are traveling directly towards each other at the speed of 68 mph and 30 mph, respectively. If the distance between them is 792 feet, determine how much time (in seconds) it will take for them to meet.

    ☐ seconds

21.

There are x employees in Company A. The number of employees in Company B is 85% of 20 less than thrice the employees in company A.

Quantity A	**Quantity B**
Employees in company B	$0.85(3x - 20)$

(A) Quantity A is greater.

(B) Quantity B is greater.

(C) The two quantities are equal.

(D) The relationship cannot be determined from the information given.

22.

$$a > 1$$
$$a - 1 = b$$

Quantity A	**Quantity B**
b^2	$a^2 - 1$

(A) Quantity A is greater.

(B) Quantity B is greater.

(C) The two quantities are equal.

(D) The relationship cannot be determined from the information given.

23. For all integers $n \neq 1$, let $< n > = \frac{n+1}{n-1}$. Which of the following has the greatest value?

    (A) $< 0 >$
    (B) $< 2 >$
    (C) $< 3 >$
    (D) $< 4 >$
    (E) $< 5 >$

24.

$$x = -y$$

Quantity A	**Quantity B**
x	y

    (A) Quantity A is greater.
    (B) Quantity B is greater.
    (C) The two quantities are equal.
    (D) The relationship cannot be determined from the information given.

25.

$$3 > p > 1$$

Quantity A	**Quantity B**
$\dfrac{p}{2}$	$\dfrac{p+2}{4}$

    (A) Quantity A is greater.
    (B) Quantity B is greater.
    (C) The two quantities are equal.
    (D) The relationship cannot be determined from the information given.

26. Determine the positive value of y, where the graphs of $y = x^2 - 2$ and $y = 2x + 1$ intersect.

    ☐

27.

There are x books in a bookstore. After $\frac{1}{4}$ of them were purchased by customers the bookstore received a shipment of 15 more books, bringing the total number of books on hand to 105.

Quantity A	**Quantity B**
x	105

(A) Quantity A is greater.

(B) Quantity B is greater.

(C) The two quantities are equal.

(D) The relationship cannot be determined from the information given.

28.

$$n > 0$$

Quantity A	**Quantity B**
$\dfrac{n^2 + 2}{n}$	$n + \dfrac{1}{n}$

(A) Quantity A is greater.

(B) Quantity B is greater.

(C) The two quantities are equal.

(D) The relationship cannot be determined from the information given.

29. The following numerical expressions are given:

$K = \left(\frac{2}{3}\right)$ of $\left(\frac{3}{2} + a\right)$

$L = \left(\frac{3}{4}\right)$ of $\left(\frac{4}{3} + b\right)$

$M = \left(\frac{a}{b}\right)$ of $\left(\frac{3}{5} + 3\right)$

Which of the following statements are true?

Select all that apply.

(A) $12(K + L) = 8a + 9b + 24$

(B) $20(K + L) = \dfrac{2a + 3b + 7}{2}$

(C) $20(L + M) = \left(\dfrac{15b^2 + 20b + 72a}{b}\right)$

(D) $(L + M) = \left(\dfrac{15b^2 + 20b + 48a}{5b}\right)$

(E) $(K + M) = \left(\dfrac{10ab + 15b + 54a}{15b}\right)$

(F) $(K + M) = \left(\dfrac{10ab + 5b + 48a}{5b}\right)$

(G) $(L - K) = \left(\dfrac{2a + 3b - 1}{3}\right)$

30.

A man buys 16 shirts. Some of them cost $13 each, while the remainder cost $10 each. The cost of all 16 shirts is $187.

Quantity A	**Quantity B**
The number of $13 shirts purchased	The number of $10 shirts purchased

(A) Quantity A is greater.

(B) Quantity B is greater.

(C) The two quantities are equal.

(D) The relationship cannot be determined from the information given.

31.

Quantity A	**Quantity B**
Slope of the straight line $2y + 3x - 5 = 0$	$\dfrac{3}{2}$

(A) Quantity A is greater.

(B) Quantity B is greater.

(C) The two quantities are equal.

(D) The relationship cannot be determined from the information given.

Level: Medium

32. If $f(x) = ax^4 - 5x^2 + ax - 5$, then $f(b) - f(-b)$ will equal:

(A) 0

(B) $2ab$

(C) $3ab^4 - 7b^2 - 8$

(D) $-3ab^4 + 7b^2 + 8$

(E) $3ab^4 - 4b^2 + 5ab - 6$

33. The following sets are given, where x is an integer greater than 1:

$A = \{(-1 + x + x^2), (1 - x + x^2), (1 + x + x^2)\}$

$B = \{(-1 + x^2 + x^3), (1 - x^2 + x^3), (1 + x^2 + x^3)\}$

Which statements are true?

Select all that apply.

(A) The greatest element of A is less than the least element of B.

(B) The greatest element of A is greater than the least element of B.

(C) The greatest element of A is less than the greatest element of B.

(D) The average of the elements of A is greater than the average of the elements of B.

(E) The average of the elements of A is smaller than the average of the elements of B.

(F) The average of the elements of A is equal to the average of the elements of B.

(G) The average of the elements of A is twice the average of the elements of B.

34.

$$f(x) = 3x - 15 \text{ for all numbers } x, \text{ and } g(x) = (x + 3)^2 + 3 \text{ for } x \geq -3.$$

$$f^{-1}(x) \text{ is the inverse of } f(x) \text{ and } g^{-1}(x) \text{ is the inverse of } g(x) \text{ respectively.}$$

Quantity A	**Quantity B**
$f^{-1}(-3)$	$g^{-1}(4)$

(A) Quantity A is greater.

(B) Quantity B is greater.

(C) The two quantities are equal.

(D) The relationship cannot be determined from the information given.

35. If $\dfrac{5x^2 + ax + b}{3x^2 + 7x + 5} = x$ and $3x^3 + 2x^2 - b = 0$, where $x \neq 0$, what is the value of a?

[　　　　]

36. What is $x + y - z$ if $x + y = 8$, $x + z = 11$, $y + z = 7$?

(A) 23

(B) 3

(C) 6

(D) 13

(E) 12

37. Which of the following functions can be obtained by transferring the function
$y = 4x^2 - 3x^2 - x + \frac{2}{3}$?

    Select all that apply.

    (A) $y = 4x^4 + 3x^3 + 2x^2 + x + \frac{2}{3}$

    (B) $y = 4x^4 + 3x^3 + 6x^2 - x + \frac{2}{3}$

    (C) $3y = 12x^4 - 6x^3 + 3x^2 - 15x + 2$

    (D) $y = 12x^4 - 3x^3 + 2x^2 - x + 3$

    (E) $y = 4x^4 - 3x^3 + 2x^2 - x + 1$

    (F) $y = 4x^4 - 3x^3 + 2x^2 - x + \frac{2}{3}$

    (G) $y = 4x^3 - 3x^2 + 2x + \frac{2}{3}$

38.

It is given that $h + k < 7$, $g + 2h = 12$ and $k = 3$.

Quantity A	**Quantity B**
g	6

(A) Quantity A is greater.

(B) Quantity B is greater.

(C) The two quantities are equal.

(D) The relationship cannot be determined from the information given.

39. If $x > y$, $x < 9$, and $y > -4$, what is the largest prime number that could be equal to $x + y$?

    (A) 17

    (B) 11

    (C) 13

    (D) 7

    (E) 5

40.

Quantity A	**Quantity B**
The number of real roots in the quadratic equation $f(x) = 2x^2 - 3x + 1$	The number of real roots in the quadratic equation $f(x) = x^2 - 7x - 8$

(A) Quantity A is greater.

(B) Quantity B is greater.

(C) The two quantities are equal.

(D) The relationship cannot be determined from the information given.

41. A company employs 150 persons who are 25 years or older. 30% of employees in the age group 25- 35, and 63% of employees in the 35+ age group contribute to the defined benefits plan. If 52% of all employees contribute to the plan, how many employees are over 35 years of age?

    ┌─────────────┐
    │   │
    └─────────────┘

42. If $x^2 - 6x - 27 = 0$ and $y^2 - 6y - 40 = 0$, what is the maximum value of $2(x - y)$?

    (A) 21

    (B) 19

    (C) 26

    (D) 18

    (E) 17

43. Identify the domain of the given rational function:

    $$f(x) = \frac{x^3 - 9x}{\sqrt{3x^2 - 6x - 9}}$$

    Select all that apply.

    (A) -1

    (B) 0

    (C) 1

    (D) 2

    (E) 3

    (F) 5

44.

$$y \geq 6$$

Quantity A	**Quantity B**
$\dfrac{10 + y}{8}$	y

    (A) Quantity A is greater.

    (B) Quantity B is greater.

    (C) The two quantities are equal.

    (D) The relationship cannot be determined from the information given.

45. If $x^2 - 6x - 27 = 0$ and $y^2 - 6y - 40 = 0$, what is the minimum value of $x + y$?

    (A) -4

    (B) -5

    (C) -7

    (D) -6

    (E) -3

46. If $b < 2$ and $2x - 3b = 0$, then which of the following can be values of x ?

    Select all that apply.

    (A) 4

    (B) 3

    (C) 2

    (D) 1

    (E) 0

    (F) −1

    (G) −2

    (H) −3

    (I) −4

47.

Quantity A	**Quantity B**
$8x - 5$	$x^2 + 16$

    (A) Quantity A is greater.

    (B) Quantity B is greater.

    (C) The two quantities are equal.

    (D) The relationship cannot be determined from the information given.

48. For any three-digit number, *abc*, *abc*= $(3^a)(5^b)(7^c)$. What is the value of *(g − f)* if *f* and *g* are three-digit numbers for which *f* = $(3^r)(5^s)(7^t)$ and *g* = *(25)(f)*?

    (A) 250

    (B) 220

    (C) 200

    (D) 20

    (E) 2

49. Two functions are defined as $f(x) = 1 + x^3$, and $g(x) = \frac{x}{1+x}$ for all real and positive values of x. Compute $f[g(2)]$ to 2 decimal place accuracy.

    [   ]

50. If x, y and z are three non-zero numbers and $xy > 0$ and $yz < 0$, which of the following must be negative?

    Select all that apply.

    (A) xyz

    (B) xyz^2

    (C) xy^2z

    (D) xy^2z^2

    (E) $x^2y^2z^2$

    (F) x^2yz

    (G) $-(x^2y^2z^2)$

    (H) x^2yz^2

    (I) $x(-y)z^2$

    (J) $-(xyz^2)$

51. If x is real, then $x - 1 + \dfrac{1}{x}$ CANNOT have these values:

    (A) 0.8

    (B) 1.2

    (C) 4.5

    (D) -2.5

    (E) $\sqrt{0.87}$

52.

$$y = 3x^2 + 8x - 10$$

Quantity A	**Quantity B**
x	$y - 10$

    (A) Quantity A is greater.

    (B) Quantity B is greater.

    (C) The two quantities are equal.

    (D) The relationship cannot be determined from the information given.

53. $620 is to be divided among three brothers A, B and C so that A gets $\dfrac{2}{3}$ of what B gets and B gets $\dfrac{2}{5}$ of what C gets. What is the approximate amount A, B and C will each get?

    Select all that apply.

    (A) $86

    (B) $168

    (C) $213

    (D) $283

    (E) $321

    (F) $366

54. If $-5x + 2y = 9$ and $3x - 4y = -4$, then what is the value of $7x + 10y$?

   (A) -19

   (B) -17

   (C) -9

   (D) 9

   (E) 19

55. The two curves $y = x^2$ and $y = |3x|$ intersect at several points. Which of the following statements are true?
   Select all that apply.

   (A) The two curves have identical values for x and y at one point.

   (B) The two curves intersect at $x = -3$.

   (C) The value of $y = x^2$ is greater than $y = |3x|$ for $x = 2$.

   (D) Both curves show symmetry about the y-axis.

56. Which of the following quadratic equations opens downward and has x-intercepts of 5 and $\frac{2}{3}$?

   (A) $f(x) = 3x^2 - 17x - 10$

   (B) $f(x) = -3x^2 + 17x + 10$

   (C) $f(x) = 3x^2 - 17x - 10$

   (D) $f(x) = -3x^2 + 17x - 10$

   (E) $f(x) = -3x^2 - 17x - 10$

57. Determine values of x that satisfy the equation $|x^2 - x + 1| = 2x - 1$
   Select all that apply.

   (A) $x = -1$

   (B) $x = 1$

   (C) $x = 3$

   (D) $x = 2$

   (E) $x = -3$

58.

$$x > y$$
$$xy \neq 0$$

Quantity A	**Quantity B**
$\dfrac{x}{y}$	$\dfrac{y}{x}$

   (A) Quantity A is greater.

   (B) Quantity B is greater.

   (C) The two quantities are equal.

   (D) The relationship cannot be determined from the information given.

59. The function $f(x) = 2x^2 - 5x$ and $g(x) = x^2 + x - 3$

What is the value of $(f.g)(-2) - [f(3) + g(2)]$

(A) -6

(B) -1

(C) 0

(D) 1

(E) 14

60.

$$x > 0$$
$$0 < x^2 < 1$$

Quantity A   **Quantity B**

$1 - x^2$ $1 - x$

(A) Quantity A is greater.

(B) Quantity B is greater.

(C) The two quantities are equal.

(D) The relationship cannot be determined from the information given.

61. If $x + y = z$ and $x = y$, then of the following all are true EXCEPT

(A) $2x + 2y = 2z$

(B) $x - y = 0$

(C) $x - z = y - z$

(D) $x = \frac{z}{2}$

(E) $z - y = 2x$

62. Jack purchases 8 apples, 5 pears, and 6 oranges for $8.70.

Cindy purchases 10 apples, 4 pears, and 3 oranges for $7.95.

Sarah purchases 5 apples, 7 pears, and 8 oranges for $8.90.

Select all that apply.

(A) An apple costs more than a pear.

(B) An orange costs more than a pear.

(C) An orange costs $0.45.

(D) An orange costs less than an apple.

(E) An orange costs less than a pear.

63.

$$x > 1$$
$$y > 0$$

Quantity A

y^x

Quantity B

$y^{(x+1)}$

(A) Quantity A is greater.

(B) Quantity B is greater.

(C) The two quantities are equal.

(D) The relationship cannot be determined from the information given.

(E) A mathematical operation is defined as:

64. $a\$b = \dfrac{\sqrt{a}}{\sqrt{a} + \sqrt{b}}$ for positive square root.

Compute 1\$(4\$9) with 3 decimal place accuracy.

```
┌──────────┐
│          │
└──────────┘
```

65. If $\dfrac{(3a + 2b)}{(3a + 4b)} = \dfrac{15}{32}$, then what is $\dfrac{(3a + b)}{7b}$?

(A) $\dfrac{1}{3}$

(B) $\dfrac{1}{2}$

(C) $\dfrac{2}{3}$

(D) $\dfrac{3}{4}$

(E) $\dfrac{4}{5}$

66.

$$c = d + 2$$

Quantity A

$c^2 - d^2$

Quantity B

$4d$

(A) Quantity A is greater.

(B) Quantity B is greater.

(C) The two quantities are equal.

(D) The relationship cannot be determined from the information given.

67. When the two curves $y = x^2 - x + 4$ and $y = 4x - 1$ intersect, the value of x satisfies which of the following conditions?

    Select all that apply.

    (A) $x < 1$

    (B) $x > 1$

    (C) $x < 4$

    (D) x is undefined

    (E) $x = 0$

68.

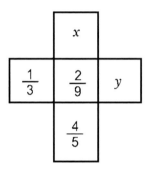

    The sum of the numbers in the horizontal row of boxes equals the sum of the numbers in the vertical row of boxes.

Quantity A	**Quantity B**
x	y

    (A) Quantity A is greater.

    (B) Quantity B is greater.

    (C) The two quantities are equal.

    (D) The relationship cannot be determined from the information given.

69. Jim has $50 in his piggy bank. His money consists of $31.50 bills and 350 pennies. The remaining amount consists of nickels, dimes, &quarters. There are thrice as many nickels as quarters and three more dimes than nickels in the piggy bank.

    Select all that apply.

    (A) He has 16 quarters.

    (B) He has 66 dimes.

    (C) He has 48 nickels.

    (D) The sum of the dimes and nickels has a value greater than $7.00.

    (E) He has 66 dimes.

    (F) He has 48 quarters.

70.

$$x \geq 1$$

Quantity A	**Quantity B**
$x^{(x+2)}$	$(x+2)^x$

(A) Quantity A is greater.

(B) Quantity B is greater.

(C) The two quantities are equal.

(D) The relationship cannot be determined from the information given.

71. If $m - n = 1$, where $m \neq -n$, which of the following statements is true?

(A) $m(m-1) = n(n+1)$

(B) $m(m+1) = n(n-1)$

(C) $n(m+1) = m(n-1)$

(D) $n(m-1) = m(n+1)$

(E) $m(m+n) = n(m-n)$

Level: Difficult

72. Find the shortest distance from the line of symmetry of $y = 2x^2 - 16x + 29$ to the line $x = -3$.

(A) 1 unit

(B) 6 units

(C) 11 units

(D) 15 units

(E) 7 units

73. If $m - n = 1$, where $m \neq -n \neq 0$, which of the following equations are valid?

Select all that apply.

(A) $m(m-1) = n(n+1)$

(B) $m(m+1) = n(n-1)$

(C) $n(m+1) = m(n-1)$

(D) $n(m-1) = m(n+1)$

(E) $m(m+n) = n(m-n)$

(F) $\dfrac{1}{mn^2} - \dfrac{1}{m^2n} + 1 = \dfrac{1 + m^2n^2}{m^2n^2}$

(G) $\dfrac{1}{mn^2} - \dfrac{1}{m^2n} + 1 = \dfrac{1 + mn}{mn}$

74.

$$-5x + 12y = 18$$

$$2x - 6y = -11$$

Quantity A	**Quantity B**
The value of the product of x and y	The value of the sum of x and y

(A) Quantity A is greater.

(B) Quantity B is greater.

(C) The two quantities are equal.

(D) The relationship cannot be determined from the information given.

75. A construction company purchased a total of 47 pieces of equipment for a total value of $2,730,000. The loaders cost $50,000 each, the dozers cost $60,000 each, and the scrapers cost $75,000 each.

In addition, tires had to be purchased for the equipment. A total of 132 tires were purchased. The loaders require 4 tires each, the dozers require zero, and the scrapers require 6 tires each. How many dozers were purchased?

(A) 18

(B) 21

(C) 6

(D) 8

(E) 14

76.

$$y \geq 6$$

Quantity A	**Quantity B**
$\dfrac{10 + y}{8}$	$\dfrac{y - 12}{\frac{2}{3}}$

(A) Quantity A is greater.

(B) Quantity B is greater.

(C) The two quantities are equal.

(D) The relationship cannot be determined from the information given.

77. Three pipes take 24 minutes, 6 minutes and 12 minutes respectively to fill a tank. If these pipes are turned on at the same time, find the most accurate range of time within which the pipes will fill the tank.

(A) 7.1 to 9 minutes

(B) 1 to 3 minutes

(C) More than 9 minutes

(D) 5.1 to 7 minutes

(E) 3.1 to 5 minutes

78. Five locomotives are in a race. Characteristics of the locomotives are provided below:

Train	Locomotive Weight (tons)	Coefficient of friction between train and rails	Base Locomotive Speed (feet per second)
Train A	100	0.80	70
Train B	85	0.90	80
Train C	115	0.75	65
Train D	90	0.85	75
Train E	95	0.90	80

The speed of each train is reduced by the following formula:

Reduction in speed $\left(\frac{ft}{s}\right)$ =[Locomotive weight (tons)](Coefficient of Friction)(0.1)

The locomotives begin the race at full speed, except for Train B, which has a mechanical malfunction and cannot start. After 2 minutes Train B is able to run and immediately attains full speed. The locomotives continue running for another 6 minutes. At this point, Train C uses a lubricant to reduce the coefficient of friction to 0.3, and Train D has a mechanical malfunction that reduces its base speed to 60 ft/s. The locomotives continue for another 6 minutes, at which point their traveled distance is measured. Which locomotives attained the qualifying distance of 44,500 feet?

Select all that apply.

(A) Train A

(B) Train B

(C) Train C

(D) Train D

(E) Train E

79.

$$15 \text{ more than } 5x = 79 \text{ less } 3x$$

Quantity A

The quantity of twice x subtracted from the quotient of 12 and $\frac{1}{3}$, divided by 4

Quantity B

The quantity of x squared less the product of six and x, divided by 4

(A) Quantity A is greater.

(B) Quantity B is greater.

(C) The two quantities are equal.

(D) The relationship cannot be determined from the information given.

80. The following expression is the nth term of a progression. Which is equivalent to this expression?

$$(1 + a)(1 + a^2)(1 + a^4)(1 + a^8) \ldots (1 + a^{2^n})$$

(A) $\dfrac{(1 - a^n)}{(1 - a)}$

(B) $\dfrac{\left(1 + a^{2^n}\right)}{(1 - a)}$

(C) $\dfrac{(1 - a^{2n})}{(1 + a)}$

(D) $\dfrac{(1 - a^{2^{(n+1)}})}{(1 + a^n)}$

(E) $\dfrac{(1 - a^{2^{(n+1)}})}{(1 - a)}$

Answers and Explanations

Level: Easy

1. **Subtopic: Quadratic Equations**

   The correct answer is (B).

   If we multiply both sides of the equation by 2, we get $x^2 + 7x + 6 = 6$, which can be rearranged into standard quadratic form: $x^2 + 7x = 0$

   This can be factored as: $(x)(x + 7) = 0$, so $x = 0$ or -7.

   The correct answer is (B).

2. **Subtopic: Inequalities and Roots**

   The correct answer is (D).

   First, we solve Inequality 1:

   $4(x + 2) \leq 2(x + 5) + 14$

   $4x + 8 \leq 2x + 10 + 14$

   $2x \leq 16$

   $x \leq 8$

   Then we solve Inequality 2:

   $\sqrt{16 - 8y + y^2} \leq 9$

   $\sqrt{(4 - y)^2} \leq 9$

   The square root of a square expression will always be a positive number, so we can write this inequality as:

   $|4 - y| \leq 9$

   $-9 \leq 4 - y \leq 9$

   $-13 \leq -y \leq 5$

   We multiply with (-1) so the inequality sign changes:

   $13 \geq y \geq -5$

   Any number equal to, or less than, 8 is a solution of the first inequality, while for the second inequality the solutions are numbers equal to, or greater than, -5 and less than, or equal to, 13.

   This means that 13 for instance is a solution for Inequality 2, which is greater than any solution of Inequality 1. However, in another example, 6 is a solution of Inequality 2, which is less than some solutions of Inequality 1 (8 for instance).

   The relationship cannot be determined without further information and (D) is the correct answer.

3. **Subtopic: Exponential Equations and Quadratic Equations**

   The correct answer is -2.

   Multiplying by 64, we get $4^{y^2} = (64)2^{-y}$

   Substituting $4 = 2^2$ and $64 = 2^6$ in the given equation results in

   $(2^2)^{y^2} = (2^6)(2^{-y})$

   Applying the law of Sequential Exponents, we have

   $2^{2y^2} = 2^{6-y}$

Since the bases are equal and the numbers are equal, the indices must be the same.

Hence

$2y^2 = 6 - y$

$2y^2 + y - 6 = 0$

Expanding the middle term, we have

$2y^2 - 3y + 4y - 6 = 0$

$y(2y - 3) + 2(2y - 3) = (y + 2)(2y - 3) = 0$

$y + 2 = 0$ and $2y - 3 = 0$

Thus $y = -2$ and $y = \frac{3}{2} = 1\frac{1}{2}$

Since $y < |y|$, it implies that y must be negative, thus, $y = -2$

4. **Subtopic: Quadratic Equations**

The correct answer is (B).

$(x - 5)(x + 6) = 0 \rightarrow x = 5$ or $x = -6$

If $x = 5$, then $x - 6 = 5 - 6 = -1$

If $x = -6$, then $x - 6 = -6 - 6 = -12$

In both the cases $x - 6$ is less than zero.

5. **Subtopic: Algebraic Expressions and Equations**

The correct answer is (B).

If we square both sides of the equation, we get $z^2 = 8zs - 16s^2$.

We can now put the quadratic in standard form $z^2 - 8zs + 16s^2 = 0$ and factor it as $(z - 4s)^2 = 0$.

Since $z - 4s = 0$, $z = 4s$.

6. **Subtopic: Algebraic Expressions**

The correct answer is (C).

$a \, @ \, b = a^2 + ab - 10$. Therefore, $2 \, @ \, 3 = 2^2 + (2)(3) - 10 = 4 + 6 - 10 = 10 - 10 = 0$

7. **Sub topic: Inequalities**

The correct answers are (B) and (E).

$-4 \leq x - 2 \leq 4$

Add 2 to all sides and simplify.

$-2 \leq x \leq 6$

Multiply all sides by -1.

$-2 \geq x \geq -6$

8. **Sub topic: Quadratic Equations**

The correct answer is (B).

$@2 = 2^2 - 11 = 4 - 11 = -7$ and $\#3 = 3^2 - 3 + 11 = 9 - 3 + 11 = 17$.

Therefore, $(@2)(\#3) = (-7)(17) = -119$

$@3 = 3^2 - 11 = 9 - 11 = -2$ and $\#2 = 2^2 - 2 + 11 = 4 - 2 + 11 = 13$.

Therefore, $(\#2)(@3) = (-2)(13) = -26$

As $-26 > -119$ so, Quantity B is greater than Quantity A.

9. **Sub topic: Quadratic Equations**

   The correct answers are (A) and (D).

   Any quadratic equation of the form $ax^2 + bx + c = 0$ will have real and equal roots if its discriminant $b^2 - 4ac = 0$.

   In the given equation, $x^2 - kx + 9 = 0$, $a = 1$, $b = -k$ and $c = 9$.

   Therefore, $b^2 - 4ac = k^2 - 4(9)(1) = k^2 - 36$.

   For the roots of the given equation to be real and equal, $k^2 - 36 = 0$ or $k^2 = 36$ or $k = 6$ or $k = -6$.

10. **Sub topic: Inequalities**

    The correct answer is (A).

    $4x - 10 \geq x + 8$

    $3x \geq 18$

    $x \geq 6$

11. **Sub topic: Inequalities**

    The correct answer is (D).

    In order to answer the question, we must compare w and y.

    From the given conditions it is possible that w could be less than y. For example, w could be 1.305 and y could be 100. It is also possible that w could be greater than y. For example, w could be 1.310 and y could be 1.305. Thus, it is not possible to determine definitively whether w is lesser or greater than y.

12. **Sub topic: Operations on Algebraic Expressions**

    The correct answer is (D).

    To simplify the expression, we need to substitute a, b, c, d and e with the appropriate value and then simplify the expression.

    $a = 5, b = 2, c = 3, d = -8$, and $e = 10$

    $a - b + c - d - e$

    $= (5) - (2) + (3) - (-8) - (10) = 5 - 2 + 3 + 8 - 10 = (5 + 3 + 8) - 2 - 10 = 16 - 12 = 4$

13. **Sub topic: Equations**

    The correct answers are (B) and (C).

    Since, $x^2 - 2x - 15 = 0$, then $(x - 5)(x + 3) = 0$, so $x = 5$ or $x = -3$. Since $x > 0$, then $x = 5$.

    (A) $5^2 - 6(5) + 9 = 25 - 30 + 9 = 4$ which is not 0.

    (B) $5^2 - 7(5) + 10 = 25 - 35 + 10 = 0$

    (C) $5^2 - 10(5) + 25 = 25 - 50 + 25 = 0$

    (D) $5^2 + 6(5) + 9 = 25 + 30 + 9 = 64$ which is not 0.

    (E) $5^2 + 7(5) + 10 = 25 + 35 + 10 = 70$ which is not 0.

(F) $5^2 + 10(5) + 25 = 25 + 50 + 25 = 100$ which is not 0.

So, the correct options are (B) and (C).

14. **Sub topic: Inequalities**

The correct answer is (A).

The best approach of solving such problems is picking a number. Since, p is a positive fraction less than 1 let's pick a value for it say $\frac{1}{9}$.

$\frac{1}{9^2} = \frac{1}{81}$ and $\frac{1}{(9+1)^2} = \frac{1}{10^2} = \frac{1}{100}$.

As, $\frac{1}{81}$ is greater than $\frac{1}{100}$ so clearly $\frac{1}{p^2}$ is greater than $\frac{1}{(p+1)^2}$.

15. **Sub topic: Algebraic Expressions**

The correct answer is (C).

When the r cards are distributed, there are 8 left over, so the number of cards distributed is $r-8$. Divide the number of cards distributed by the number of people. Since there are s people, each will receive $\frac{r-8}{s}$ cards.

Another approach is to pick numbers. Let $r = 58$ and $s = 10$; if $58 - 8$ or 50 cards were distributed evenly among 10 people, each would receive 5 cards. Plug the values you picked for r and s into the answer choices to see which ones give you 5:

(A) $\frac{s}{8-r} = \frac{10}{8-58} = -\frac{1}{5}$, Eliminate

(B) $\frac{r-s}{8} = \frac{58-10}{8} = 6$, Eliminate

(C) $\frac{r-8}{s} = \frac{58-8}{10} = 5$, Works!

(D) $s - 8r = 10 - (8 \times 58) = -454$, Eliminate.

(E) $rs - 8 = (58 \times 10) - 8 = 572$. Eliminate.

Since (C) is the only answer choice that gives you 5, it is the correct answer. But be sure to check all the answer choices when picking numbers.

16. **Sub topic: Algebraic Expressions**

The correct answer is (B).

$\frac{2F-5}{2} = F - \frac{5}{2}$ and $\frac{4F-1}{4} = F - \frac{1}{4}$.

Now $\frac{5}{2} = 2.5$ and $\frac{1}{4} = 0.25$.

Clearly $F - 2.5$ is smaller than $F - 0.25$ as $F > 0$.

17. **Sub topic: Linear Equations**

The correct answer is (A).

Write the expression in mathematical terms, solve for x and compare.

15 more than $5x = 55$ is equivalent to $15 + 5x = 55$.

$15 + 5x = 55$ Original equation

$5x = 40$ Subtract 15

$x = 8$ Divide by 5

Quantity A: 11

Quantity B: $x = 8$

The quantity of A is greater than the quantity of B.

18. Sub topic: Coordinate Geometry

The correct answer is (D).

Here is another question testing your understanding of the coordinate graph. To find the area of the rectangle, we must express the dimensions using x and y. The width of the rectangle is simply y, because the point (x, y) is located y units above the x-axis. The length of the rectangle is $x - 2$ because it runs from point 2 to point x, parallel to the x– axis. Since width is y and length is $x - 2$, the area is $y(x - 2)$.

19. Sub topic: Algebraic Expressions

The correct answers are (A), (B) and (C). $\left(\dfrac{x}{x}\right)(x + 1)$

$$y = \frac{1}{x} - \frac{1}{x+1} = \frac{x+1-x}{x(x+1)} = \frac{1}{x(x+1)}$$

$$= \frac{\frac{1}{x}}{\left(\frac{x}{x}\right)(x+1)} = \frac{\frac{1}{x}}{x+1}$$

$$= \frac{\frac{1}{x^2}}{\left(\frac{x}{x^2}\right)(x+1)} = \frac{\frac{1}{x^2}}{\frac{1}{x}(x+1)} = \frac{\frac{1}{x^2}}{1+\frac{1}{x}}$$

20. Sub topic: Algebraic Expressions

The correct answer is 5 seconds.

The effective speed that will cover the distance in between the two vehicles is $68 + 30 = 98\ mph$.

Converted to mi/s:

$$98\ mph = \frac{98mi}{3600s} = \frac{3}{100}mi/s$$

Converting the distance to *miles*:

$$795\ \text{feet} = \frac{792ft}{5280ft/mile} = \frac{3}{20}miles$$

$$\text{Time taken} = \frac{\frac{3}{20}}{\frac{3}{100}} = \frac{3}{20} \times \frac{100}{3} = 5\ s$$

21. Sub topic: Algebraic Expressions

The correct answer is (C).

Try to write the information given in a mathematical statement.

Employees in Company A $= x$.

Thrice the employees in Company A $= 3x$.

20 less than thrice the employees in Company A $= 3 - 20$.

85% of 20 less than thrice the employees in Company A $= \left(\frac{85}{100}\right)(3x - 20) = 0.85(3x - 20)$

Therefore, employees in Company B $= 0.85(3x - 20)$

22. **Sub topic: Algebraic Expressions**

    The correct answer is (B).

    You are given $a - 1 = b$, so Quantity A can be rewritten as $(a - 1)^2$. Don't assume that the quantities are equal though. In fact, $(a - 1)^2$ is not equal to $a^2 - 1$.

    $a^2 - 1$ factors to $(a + 1)(a - 1)$. Quantity A can be expressed as $(a - 1)(a - 1)$. Since you know that $a > 1$, you can factor an $(a - 1)$ from each quantity. This gives you $(a - 1)$ in Quantity A and $(a + 1)$ in Quantity B, so Quantity B is greater.

23. **Sub topic: Algebraic Expressions**

    The correct answer is (B).

    For this question, the safest way –as usual– is to try choices rather than to reason algebraically. Plugging in the choices for n, we get the following results:

    (A)$< 0 >= \frac{0 + 1}{0 - 1} = \frac{1}{-1} = -1$

    (B)$< 2 >= \frac{2 + 1}{2 - 1} = \frac{3}{1} = 3$

    (C)$< 3 >= \frac{3 + 1}{3 - 1} = \frac{4}{2} = 2$

    (D)$< 4 >= \frac{4 + 1}{4 - 1} = \frac{5}{3} = 1\frac{2}{3}$

    (E)$< 5 >= \frac{5 + 1}{5 - 1} = \frac{6}{4} = \frac{3}{2} = 1\frac{2}{3}$

    Choice (B) has the greatest value, so that must be the correct answer.

24. **Sub topic: Inequalities and Linear Equations**

    The correct answer is (D).

    Since no information is given directly about x or y, we cannot determine the relationship. Do not assume that since $x = -y$, y will be greater than $-y$ and thus greater than x. It is possible that y is a negative number, in which case x is a positive number and greater than y. Also, x and y could both be equal to zero.

25. **Sub topic: Inequalities**

    The correct answer is (D).

    Always be sure to plug in twice for Quantitative Comparison questions. You need to plug in numbers for p that are between 3 and 1. If $p = 2$, then Quantity A is 1 and Quantity B is 1. Since the quantities can be equal, you can cross out choices A and B. Now plug in a weird number. If $p = 1.5$ then Quantity A is .75 and Quantity B is .875. The quantities are no longer equal, so you can get more than one result. That means the answer must be D.

26. **Sub topic: System of Equations**

    The correct answer is 7.

Math procedure	Strategy/Explanation
$x^2 - 2 = 2x + 1$ $x^2 - 2x - 3 = 0$	When two curves intersect, they will have a common value of y. Therefore, set the right sides of the two equations equal, and simplify.
$(x - 3)(x + 1) = 0$ $x = 3, x = -1$	Factorize and solve to obtain $x = 3, x = -1$.
$y(3) = 2(3) + 1 = 7$ $y(-1) = 2(-1) + 1 = -1$	Use the simpler equation to compute y-values for $x = 2$, and for $x = -1$. The positive value of $y = 7$

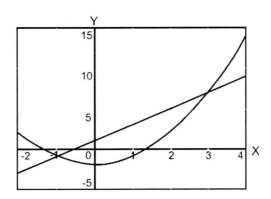

27. **Sub topic: Linear Equations**

    The correct answer is (A).

    $$x - \frac{-1}{4}x + 15 = 105$$

    $$x = 120 > 105$$

28. **Sub topic: Inequalities**

    The correct answer is (A).

    Rewriting the entry in Quantity A, we obtain $\frac{n^2 + 2}{n} = n + \frac{1}{n}$ thus, the problem becomes a comparison between $\frac{2}{n}$ in Quantity A and $\frac{1}{n}$ in Quantity B. Since $n > 0$, the entry in Column A is greater.

29. **Sub topic: Operations on Algebraic Expressions**

    The correct answers are (A), (C) and (E).

    Simplify the given expressions:

    $$K = \left(\frac{2}{3}\right)\left(\frac{3}{2} + a\right)$$

    (1) $K = \left(\frac{2a+3}{3}\right)$

    $$L = \left(\frac{3}{4}\right)\left(\frac{4}{3} + b\right)$$

    (2) $L = \left(\frac{3b+4}{4}\right)$

    $$M = \left(\frac{a}{b}\right)\left(\frac{3}{5} + 3\right)$$

(3) $M = \left(\frac{18a}{5b}\right)$

$K + L = \left(\frac{2a + 3}{3}\right) + \left(\frac{3b + 4}{4}\right)$

$K + L = \left(\frac{8a + 9b + 24}{12}\right)$

$12(K + L) = 12\left(\frac{8a + 9b + 24}{12}\right)$

$= 8a + 9b + 24$

$L + M = \left(\frac{3b + 4}{4}\right) + \left(\frac{18a}{5b}\right)$

$L + M = \left(\frac{15b^2 + 20b + 72a}{20b}\right)$

$K + M = \left(\frac{2a + 3}{3}\right) + \left(\frac{18a}{5b}\right)$

$= \left(\frac{10ab + 15b + 54a}{15b}\right)$

$L - K = \left(\frac{3b + 4}{4}\right) - \left(\frac{2a + 3}{3}\right)$

$= \left(\frac{9a - 8b}{12}\right)$

30. **Sub topic: Linear Equations**

The correct answer is (A).

The problem can be worked out using simultaneous equations, but that is not the most efficient way of solving it. For that reason, we will set up the equation (for the "aficionados"), but we will not actually solve for x and y. Let x be the number of shirts costing $13 and y the number costing $10.

$x + y = 16$

$13x + 10y = 187$

Final solution: $x = 9$ and $y = 7$

We have omitted the detailed calculations because there is a simpler method. Let us assume, for the sake of argument, that the two quantities are equal-that is, that the man bought equal numbers of both types of shirts. If we are correct in assuming that he bought eight $13 shirts and eight $10 shirts, then $(8 \times 13) + (8 \times 10)$ ought to equal $187.When we do the multiplication, we get the result $184. That tells us our original assumption of equal numbers was incorrect and, further, that the answer to the question is not (C). We should then make a second assumption, but should we assume that he bought more expensive shirts than we first guessed, or fewer? A moment of reflection will show that we should adjust our initial assumption to include a greater number of expensive shirts, for only by increasing that number will we add to the $184 which was the result of our original assumption. So, we would next assume-again for the purposes of argument-that the man bought nine $13 shirts and only seven $10 shirts. But at this point we have already solved the problem! We do not need to know the precise ratio, e.g., whether 9:7, 10:6, 11:5, 12:4, 13:3, 14:4, or 15:1; we have already determined that the ratio is one of those listed, and so it must be the case that Quantity A is greater.

31. **Sub topic: Coordinate Geometry**

The correct answer is (B).

We know that if a line is represented as $y = mx + c$ then m defines the slope of the line.

Writing the given equation of the straight line in the similar format we get,

$2y + 3x - 5 = 0$

$2y = -3x + 5$

$y = \left(-\dfrac{3}{2}\right)x + 5$

So, the slope of the given line is $-\dfrac{3}{2}$ which is smaller than $\dfrac{3}{2}$

The correct answer is (B).

Level: Medium

32. **Sub topic: Functions**

The correct answer is (B).

Since $f(x) = ax^4 - 5x^2 + ax - 5$,

$f(b) = ax^4 - 5x^2 + ax - 5$

$= ab^4 - 5b^2 + ab - 5$

$f(-b) = ax^4 - 5x^2 + ax - 5$

$= a(-b)^4 - 5(-b)^2 + a(-b) - 5$

$= ab^4 - 5b^2 - ab - 5$

Therefore, $f(b) - f(-b) = ab^4 - 5b^2 + ab - 5 - (ab^4 - 5b^2 - ab - 5) = 2ab$

Alternatively, we could have recognized that the only term of the function that will be different for $f(b)$ than for $f(-b)$ is "ax."The other three terms are all unaffected by the sign of the variable.More succinctly, $f(b) - f(-b)$ must equal $ab - (-ab) = 2ab$.

The correct answer is (B).

33. **Sub topic: Algebraic Expressions**

The correct answers are (B), (C) and (E).

Choose a number for x and determine the elements of each set. Let $x = 3$, for example. Then

$A = \{(-1 + 3 + 9), (1 - 3 + 9), (1 + 3 + 9)\}$

$B = \{(-1 + 9 + 27), (1 - 9 + 27), (1 + 9 - 27)\}$

Simplify the expressions in each set.

$A = \{11, 7, 13\}$

$B = \{35, 19, -17\}$

Now, check the statements one by one against these sets.

A. The greatest element of A is 13 and the least element of B is -17. Since 13 is not greater than -17, so (A) is false.

B. The greatest element of A, 13, is greater than the least element of B, -17; so (B) is true.

C. The greatest element of A, 13, is less than greatest element of B, 35. So, (C) is true.

D. Find the average of the elements of each set.

Average of A = M $= \dfrac{\left(-1 + x + x^2\right) + \left(1 - x + x^2\right) + \left(1 + x + x^2\right)}{3}$

$= \dfrac{3x^2 + x + 1}{3}$

Average of B = N = $\dfrac{\left(-1 + x^2 + x^3\right) + \left(1 - x^2 + x^3\right) + \left(1 + x^2 + x^3\right)}{3}$

$= \dfrac{3x^2 + x^2 + 1}{3}$

Next, compare two averages.

$\dfrac{3x^2 + x + 1}{3} \boxed{?} \dfrac{3x^3 + x^2 + 1}{3}$

$3x^2 + x + 1 \boxed{?} 3x^3 + x^2 + 1$

$3x^2 + x \boxed{?} 3x^3 + x^2$

$x(3x + 1) \boxed{?} x^2(3x + 1)$

$x \boxed{?} x^2$

Since the square of any real number greater than 1 is greater than the number itself, so we replace $\boxed{?}$ with $<$. That is, $x < x^2$. Thus, the statement (E) is true.

$x = x^2$ only when $x = 1$. So, answer (F) is incorrect.

Choice (G) cannot be true, since Option (E) disproves it.

34. **Sub topic: Functions**

The correct answer is (A).

First, we need to find the inverse of $f(x)$ and $g(x)$.

$f(x) = 3x - 15$

In order to find its inverse, we need to solve $y = 3x - 15$ for y

$3x = y + 15$

$x = \dfrac{y + 15}{3}$

$f^{-1}(x) = \dfrac{x + 15}{3}$

$g(x) = (x + 3)^2 + 3 \text{ for } x \geq -3$

In order to find its inverse, we need to solve $y = (x + 3)^2 + 3$ for $y \geq 3$

$y - 3 = (x + 3)^2$

$\sqrt{y - 3} = x + 3$

$x = \sqrt{y - 3} - 3$

$g^{-1}(x) = \sqrt{x - 3} - 3$

$f^{-1}(-3) = \dfrac{-3 + 15}{3} = 4$

$g^{-1}(4) = \sqrt{4 - 3} - 3 = -2$

4 is greater than -2. So, the left column is greater than the right column and (A) is the correct answer.

35. **Sub topic: Linear Equation, Algebraic Expressions**

The correct answer is 5.

Place x over 1 to form a fraction on the right side.

$\dfrac{5x^2 + ax + b}{3x^2 + 7x + 5} = \dfrac{x}{1}$

Cross multiply and simplify.

$x(3x^2 + 7x + 5) = 5x^2 + ax + b$

$3x^3 + 7x^2 + 5x = 5x^2 + ax + b$

Subtract $5x^2$, ax, and b from each side, and factor.

$3x^3 + 7x^2 + 5x - 5x^2 - ax - b = 5x^2 + ax + b - 5x^2 - ax - b$

$3x^3 + 2x^2 + 5x - ax - b = 0$

$3x^3 + 2x^2 + (5 - a)x - b = 0$

$3x^3 + 2x^2 - b = 0$(given in the problem)

$(5 - a)x = 0$

Divide each side by x knowing that we are given $x \neq 0$.

$5 - a = 0$

$a = 5$

36. **Sub topic: System of Equations**

The correct answer is (B).

$x + y = 8$ and $x + z = 11$. Therefore, $x + y - (x + z) = 8 - 11 = -3$ or $z - y = 3$

$z - y = 3$ and $y + z = 7$. Therefore, $z - y + (y + z) = 3 + 7$ or, $2z = 10$ or $z = 5$.

Checking $z - y = 3$ and $z = 5$. Therefore, $y = 2$.

$x + y = 8$ and $y = 2$. Therefore, $x = 6$.

So, $x + y - z = 6 + 2 - 5 = 3$.

37. **Sub topic: Functions**

The correct answers are (A), (C) and (E).

Function (A) is the symmetric of the given function around the y-axis. Replacing x by $-x$ in the given equation results in (A). So, (A) is a correct answer.

(C) This function, in fact, is equivalent of the given function. Multiplying both sides of the given function results in (C). Thus, (C) is a correct answer.

(E) This function is the transformation of the given function $\dfrac{1}{3}$ unit to the top.

38. **Sub topic: Inequalities**

The correct answer is (A).

$k = 3$. Therefore, from $h + k < 7$ we get $h + 3 < 7 \rightarrow h < 4$.

$2h < 8$

$g + 2h < 8 + g$

$12 < 8 + g$

$g > 4$

Now, $g + 2h = 12 \rightarrow g + 2(\text{Less Than } 4) = 12 \rightarrow g + (\text{Less Than } 6) = 12 \rightarrow g = 12 - (\text{Less Than } 6) \rightarrow g = (\text{Greater Than } 6) \rightarrow g > 6$.

39. **Sub topic: Inequalities**

The correct answer is (A).

Simplify the inequalities, so that all the inequality symbols point in the same direction. Then, line up the inequalities as shown. Finally, combine the inequalities.

$y < x, x < 7$, and $-4 < y$ can be written together as $-4 < y < x < 9$.

Now as x and y each cannot be equal to 9 and so the maximum value of $x + y < 18$. The largest prime number smaller than 18 is 17. Hence, the largest prime number that can be equal to $x + y$ is 17.

40. **Sub topic: Functions**

The correct answer is (C).

To determine the number of roots in the equation, set $f(x) = 0$ and use the determinant ($b^2 - 4ac$) to determine the number of roots. If the determinant is negative, there are no real roots. If the determinant is zero, then there is exactly one real root, and if the determinant is positive, there are two real roots.

Quantity A:

$0 = 2x^2 - 3x + 1$

$a = 2, b = -3, c = 1$

Determinant$= b^2 - 4ac = (-3)^2 - 4(2)(1) = 1$

2 real roots

Quantity B:

$0 = x^2 - 7x - 8$

$a = 1, b = -7, c = -8$

Determinant $= b^2 - 4ac = (-7)^2 - 4(1)(-8) = 81$

2 real roots

Both have two real roots, so the answer is C.

41. The correct answer is 100.

52% of all employees or in other words 52% of $150 = 78$ employees contribute to the plan.

If S employees are in the $35 +$ age group, then 63% of S or 0.63S contribute.

There are 150-S employees in the 25-35 age group and 30% of these i.e. $0.3(150 - S)$ contribute. Thus $0.63S + 0.3(150 - S) = 78$. Solving we get $S = 100$.

42. **Sub topic: Quadratic Equations**

The correct answer is (C).

$x^2 - 6x - 27 = 0 \rightarrow (x + 3)(x - 9) = 0 \rightarrow x = -3$ or $x = 9$.

$y^2 - 6y - 40 = 0 \rightarrow (y + 4)(y - 10) = 0 \rightarrow y = -4$ or $y = 10$.

Therefore, the maximum value of $x - y = 9 - (-4) = 13$ and hence, maximum value of $2(x + y) = 2 \times 13 = 26$.

43. **Sub topic: Functions**

The correct answers are (B), (C), (D) and (F).

In order to find the domain of a rational function, we need to turn the denominator expression equal to zero.

Rational function:

$$f(x) = \frac{x^3 - 9x}{\sqrt{3x^2 - 6x - 9}}$$

Denominator expression $= 0$

$\sqrt{3x^2 - 6x - 9} = 0$

Square both sides:

$3x^2 - 6x - 9 = 0$-----dividing the equation by 3

$x^2 - 2x - 3 = 0$

Factoring the quadratic equation to find the zeroes of the equation:

$x^2 - 3x + x - 3 = 0$

$x(x - 3) + 1(x - 3) = 0$

$(x - 3)(x + 1) = 0$

$x - 3 = 0, x + 1 = 0$

$x = 3, x = -1$

This means that the given rational function becomes equal to zero at $x = 3$ and $x = -1$

Thus, the domain of the function is all the values of x except 3 and -1.

Options B, C, D and F are correct.

44. Sub topic: Algebraic Expressions and Inequalities

The correct answer is (B).

Set up an unknown comparison of the two expressions and simplify.

$\dfrac{10+y}{8} \boxed{?} y$	Initial comparison
$10 + y \boxed{?} 8y$	Multiply by 8
$10 \boxed{?} 7y$	Subtract y
$\dfrac{10}{7} \boxed{?} y$	Divide by 7

Since we know that $y \geq 6$ then we can say $\dfrac{10}{7} > y.$ Now that we have determined the correct inequality for the equation $\dfrac{10}{7} > y$ we must reverse our step from above to determine if the inequality sign remains the same.

$\dfrac{10}{7} > y$	Last Comparison
$10 > 7y$	Multiply by 7
$10 + y > 8y$	Add y
$\dfrac{10 + y}{8} > y$	Divide by 8

As each step is reversed the inequality sign remains unchanged.

Thus, Quantity B is greater than Quantity A.

45. Sub topic: System of Equations

The correct answer is (C).

$x^2 - 6x - 27 = 0 \rightarrow (x + 3)(x - 9) = 0 \rightarrow x = -3$ or $x = 9$.

$y^2 - 6y - 40 = 0 \rightarrow (y + 4)(y - 10) = 0 \rightarrow y = -4$ or $y = 10$.

Therefore, the minimum value of $x + y = (-3) + (-4) = -7$.

46. Sub topic: Linear inequalities

The correct answers are (C), (D), (E), (F), (G), (H)and (I).

First solve the equation for b.

$2x - 3b = 0$

$2x = 3b$

$\dfrac{2x}{3} = b$

Then by substitution, the inequality $b < 2$ becomes

$\dfrac{2x}{3} < 2$

$x < \left(\dfrac{3}{2}\right)(2)$

$x < 3$

So, x is valid for all values less than 3.

47. Sub topic: Quadratic Functions

The correct answer is (B).

Set up an unknown comparison of the two expressions and simplify.

$8x - 5 \text{ ? } x^2 + 16$ Initial comparison

$-5 \text{ ? } x^2 + 16 + 8x$ Subtract $8x$

$-5 \text{ ? } (x - 4)^2$ Factor the perfect square

Since we know that $(x - 4)^2$, like any square, must be positive we can say $-5 < (x - 4)^2$. Now that we have determine the correct inequality for the equation $8x - 5 \text{ ? } x^2 + 16$, we must reverse our step from above to determine if the inequality sign remains the same.

$-5 < (x - 4)^2$ Last comparison

$-5 < x^2 + 16 + 8x$ Expand the square

$8x - 5 < x^2 + 16$ Add $8x$

As each step is reversed the inequality sign remains unchanged.

Thus, Quantity B is greater than Quantity A.

48. Sub topic: Functions

The correct answer is (D).

According to the question, the "ampersand function" is only applicable to three-digit numbers. The function takes the hundreds, tens and units digits of a three-digit number and applies them as exponents for the bases 3, 5, and 7 respectively, yielding a value which is the product of these exponential expressions.

Let's illustrate with a few examples:

$*223* = (3^2)(5^2)(7^3)$

$*348* = (3^3)(5^4)(7^8)$

According to the question, the three-digit number f must have the digits of rst, since $*f* = (3^r)(5^s)(7^t)$.

If $*g* = (25)(*f*)$

$*g* = (25)(3^r)(5^s)(7^t)$

$*g* = (5^2)(3^r)(5^s)(7^t)$

$*g* = (3^r)(5^{s+2})(7^t)$

g is also a three-digit number, so we can use the *g* value to identify the digits of *g*:

hundreds $= r$, tens $= s + 2$, units $= t$.

All of the digits of *f* and *g* are identical except for the tens digits. The tens digit of *g* is two more than that of *f*, so $g - f = 20$.

49. **Sub topic: Functions**

The correct answer is 1.30.

Math procedure	Strategy/Explanation
$g(2) = \dfrac{2}{1+2} = \dfrac{2}{3}$	Compute $g(2)$
$f\left(\dfrac{2}{3}\right) = 1 + \left(\dfrac{2}{3}\right)^3 = 1.2963$	Compute $f[g(2)] = f\left(\dfrac{2}{3}\right)$
$f\left(\dfrac{2}{3}\right) \approx 1.30$	Use 2 decimal place accuracy

50. The correct answers are (C), (F), (G), (I) and (J).

The table below shows all possibilities for the algebraic signs of *x*,*y*, and *z*. Those satisfying $xy > 0$ are checked in the fourth column of the chart, and those satisfying $yz < 0$ are checked in the fifth column of the chart.

x	y	z	$xy > 0$	$yz < 0$
+	+	+	✓	
+	+	−	✓	✓
+	−	+		✓
+	−	−		
−	+	+		
−	+	−		✓
−	−	+	✓	✓
−	−	−	✓	

The table below shows only the possibilities that satisfy both $xy > 0$ and $yz < 0$. Noting that the expression in answer choice (E) is the product of the squares of three non-zero numbers, which is always positive.

			(A)	(B)	(C)	(D)	(E)	(F)	(G)	(H)	(I)	(J)
x	y	z	xyz	xyz^2	xy^2z	xy^2z^2	$x^2y^2z^2$	x^2yz	$-x^2y^2z^2$	x^2yz^2	$x(-y)z^2$	$-(xyz^2)$
+	+	−	−	+	−	+	+	−	−	+	−	−
−	−	+	+	+	−	−	−	−	−	−	−	−

51. The correct answers are (A), (D) and (E).

Since *x* is real $x + \dfrac{1}{x} \geq 1$ and the given expression is at least 1. Alternatives A, D & E are all < 1 andthese are the values that the expression does not take.

52. **Sub topic: Quadratic Equations**

    The correct answer is (D).

    Select choices for x and determine the value of $y - 10$ and compare. $y = 3x^2 + 8x - 10$

    When $x = 0$, $y = 3(0)^2 + 8(0) - 10 = -10$ and $y - 10 = -10 - 10 = -20$.

    In this case Quantity A is greater.

    When $x = 1$, $y = 3(1)^2 + 8(1) - 10 = 3 + 8 - 10 = 1$ and $y - 10 = 1 - 10 = -9$.

    In this case Quantity A is greater.

    When $x = 2$, $y = 3(2)^2 + 8(2) - 10 = 12 + 16 - 10 = 18$ and $y - 10 = 18 - 10 = 8$.

    In this case Quantity B is greater.

    Since different results were obtained the correct answer is D, the relationship cannot be determined based on the information given.

53. **Sub topic: Applications**

    The correct answers are (A), (C) and (E).

    Let C be x then B will be $\dfrac{2x}{3}$ and A will be $\dfrac{4x}{15}$.This means that $\dfrac{4x}{15} + \dfrac{2x}{3} + x = 620x = 320.7$

    The share of A will be $4 \times \dfrac{320.7}{15} = 86$

    The share of B will be $2 \times \dfrac{320.7}{3} = 213$

    The share of C will be 321.

54. **Sub topic: System of Equation**

    The correct answer is (A).

    To determine the value of $7x + 10y$, we need to solve the system of equations for x and y using the linear combination or elimination method.

    $2(-5x + 2y = 9)$

    $1(3x - 4y = -4)$

    $-10x + 4y = 18$

    $3x - 4y = -4$

    $-7x = 14$

    $x = -2$

    Substituting $x = -2$ in the first equation i.e. $-5x + 2y = 9$, we get:

    $-5(-2) + 2y = 9$

    $10 + 2y = 9$

    $2y = -1$

    $y = -\dfrac{1}{2}$

    Therefore, $(x, y) = \left(-2, -\dfrac{1}{2}\right)$

    To solve for $7x + 10y$, plug the values of x and y into the equation.

$$7(-2) + 10\left(-\frac{1}{2}\right)$$
$$= -14 - 5$$
$$= -19$$

The answer is (A).

55. **Sub topic: Graphs of Functions**

The correct answers are (B) and (D).

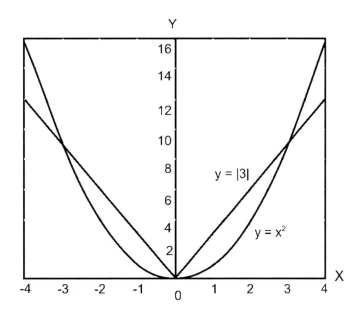

When the curves intersect, the values of y are equal.

$|3x| = x^2$

Case 1:

$|3x| = x^2 \rightarrow x(x - 3) = 0 \rightarrow x = 0,3$

Intercepts: $(0, 0), (3, 9)$

Case 2:

$-|3x| = x^2 \rightarrow x(x + 3) = 0 \rightarrow x = 0,-3$

Intercepts: $(0, 0), (-3, 9)$

56. **Sub topic: Quadratic Functions**

The correct answer is (D).

To determine the quadratic equation with those roots, we need to work backwards.

If $x = 5$, then we will write an equation equal to 0. The new equation will be $x - 5 = 0$, therefore $x - 5$ is a factor.

For $x = \frac{2}{3}$, repeat the process, and we get $3x = 2$. Writing an equation equal to 0 results in $3x - 2 = 0$, therefore a second factor is $3x - 2$.

Multiply the two factors using FOIL to find the resulting polynomial. Multiply by -1 to ensure that the parabola opens downwards.

$f(x) = -1(x - 5)(3x - 2) = -1(3x^2 - 2x - 15x + 10) = -1(3x^2 - 17x - 10) = -3x^2 + 17x - 10$

57. **Sub topic: Quadratic Equations**

The correct answers are (A), (B) and (D).

Case 1: Use positive value of $|x^2 - x + 1| = x^2 - x + 1$

$x^2 - x + 1 = 2x - 1$

$x^2 - 3x + 2 = 0 \rightarrow (x - 1)(x - 2) = 0$

$x = 1, 2$

Case 2: Use negative value of $|x^2 - x + 1| = -x^2 + x - 1$

$-x^2 + x - 1 = 2x - 1$

$x^2 + x = 0 \rightarrow x(x + 1) = 0$

$x = 0, -1$

58. **Sub topic: Inequalities**

The correct answer is (D).

Try values for the variables.

If $x = 2$ and $y = 1$, then 2 in Quantity A is greater than $\dfrac{1}{2}$ in Quantity B.

But, if $x = -1$ and $y = -2$, then $\dfrac{1}{2}$ in Quantity A is less than 2 in Quantity B.

Since more than one relationship is possible, choice (D) is correct.

59. **Sub topic: Quadratic Functions**

The correct answer is (D).

$f(x) = 2x^2 - 5x$ and $g(x) = x^2 + x - 3$

Find the value of $(f \times g)(-2) - [f(3) + g(2)]$

$(f \times g)(-2)$: means the same as $f(g(-2))$.

First calculate $g(5)$ then find f at that answer.

$g(-2) = (-2)^2 + (-2) - 3$

$g(-2) = 4 + (-2) - 3$

$g(-2) = 4 - 5$

$g(-2) = -1$

$f(-1) = 2(-1)^2 - 5(-1)$

$f(-1) = 2(1) - 5(-1)$

$f(-1) = 2 - (-5)$

$f(-1) = 7$

$f(3)$:

$f(3) = 2(3)^2 - 5(3)$

$f(3) = 2(9) - 5(3)$

$f(3) = 18 - (15)$

$f(3) = 3$

$g(2)$:

$g(2) = (2)^2 + (2) - 3$

$g(2) = 4 + (2) - 3$

$g(2) = 3$

$(f \times g)(-2) - [f(3) + g(2)]$

$7 - (3 + 3) = 1$

60. Sub topic: Inequalities

The correct answer is (D).

Since x^2 is a positive fraction less than 1, its positive square root, x, must also be a fraction less than 1, which you are told is positive. When a positive fraction less than 1 is squared, the result is positive fraction smaller than the original. Therefore, $x^2 < x$. For example, $\left(\frac{1}{2}\right)^2 < \frac{1}{2}$, since $\left(\frac{1}{2}\right)^2 = \frac{1}{4}$, so in Quantity A you are subtracting a positive value from 1, and in Quantity B you are subtracting a larger positive value from 1, so Quantity A must be greater.

61. Sub topic: System of Equation

The correct answer is (E).

With algebraic answer choices, we should plug in numbers. Let $x = y = 2$, which makes $z = 4$. Plugging these values into the choices, we'd get the following:

[Yes] (A) $2(2) + 2(2) = 2(4)$

[Yes] (B) $2 - 2 = 0$

[Yes] (C) $2 - 4 = 2 - 4$

[Yes] (D) $2 = \frac{4}{2}$

[No] (E) $4 - 2 = 2(2)$

62. **Sub topic: System of Equation**

The correct answers are (A), (B), (C), and (D).

Math Procedure	Strategy
Jack: 8A + 5P + 6O = 8.70...(1) Cindy: 10A + 4P + 3O = 7.95...(2) Sarah: 5A + 7P + 8O = 8.90...(3)	Let A, P, O represent prices for apple, pear, and orange respectively. Jack purchases 8 apples, 5 pears, and 6 oranges for $8.70 Cindy purchases 10 apples, 4 pears, and 3 oranges for $7.95. Sarah purchases 5 apples, 7 pears, and 8 oranges for $8.90.
10A + 4P + 3O – (10A + 14P + 16O = 7.95 – (2) (8.90) 10P + 13O = 9.85	Multiply equation (3) by 2, and subtract from equation (2), to obtain 10P + 13O = 9.85 (4)
Multiply (1) by 5 to obtain 40A + 25P + 30O = (5) (8.70) Multiply (3) by 8 to obtain 40A + 56P + 64O = (8) (8.90)	Multiply equation (1) by 5, multiply equation (4) by 8, and subtract to obtain, 40A + 25P + 30O − (40A + 56P + 64O) = (5) (8.70)– (8)(8.90) 31P + 34O = 27.70
From (4): 31(0.985 − 1.3O) + 34O = 27.70 6.3O = 2.835 O = 0.45 Now compute P = 0.985 – 1.3O = 0.985 − .585 = 0.40 10A = 7.95 − 4P − 3O = 7.95 − 1.60 − 1.35 = 5 A = 0.50	From (3), P = 0.985 − 1.3O Therefore, substitute into (4), and solve for O Now compute P = 0.985 − 1.3O After obtaining P and O, substitute into equation (2) and solve for A. Solution: A = $0.50, P = $0.40, O = $0.45.

Answers: (A), (B), (C), (D).

63. **Sub topic: Inequalities**

The correct answer is (D).

Try $x = y = 2$. Then Quantity A $= y^x = 2^2 = 4$. Quantity B $= y^{x+1} = 2^3 = 8$, making Quantity B greater. But if $x = 2$ and $y = \frac{1}{2}$, Quantity A $= \left(\frac{1}{2}\right)^2 = \frac{1}{4}$ and Quantity B $= \left(\frac{1}{2}\right)^3 = \frac{1}{8}$. In this case, Quantity A is greater than Quantity B, so the answer is (D).

64. The correct answer is 0.613.

Math Procedure	Strategy/Explanation
$4\$9 = \dfrac{\sqrt{4}}{\sqrt{4}+\sqrt{9}} = \dfrac{2}{5}$	Compute $4\$9$ and simplify.
$1\$\left(\dfrac{2}{5}\right) = \dfrac{\sqrt{1}}{\sqrt{1}+\sqrt{\frac{2}{5}}} = 0.6126$	Compute $1\$\left(\dfrac{2}{5}\right)$ and simplify
$1\$\left(\dfrac{2}{5}\right) \approx 0.613$	Use 3 decimal place accuracy.

65. **Sub topic: Linear Equations**

The correct answer is (A).

First, we solve the first equation for a in terms of b:

$\dfrac{(3a+2b)}{(7a+4b)} = \dfrac{15}{32}$; $(3a+2b) \times 32 = 15 \times (7a+4b)$ or $96a + 64b = 105a + 60b$ or $4b = 9a$; $a = \dfrac{4b}{9}$

Now substitute the expression for a into the second equation:

$\dfrac{(3a+b)}{7b} = \left(\dfrac{\frac{3\times4b}{9}+b}{7b}\right) = \left(\dfrac{\frac{4b}{3}+b}{7b}\right) = \dfrac{7b}{(3\times7b)} = \dfrac{1}{3}$

66. **Sub topic: Inequalities**

The correct answer is (A).

It is given that $c = d + 2$. Quantity A asks for the value of $c^2 - d^2$, while Quantity B asks for the value of $4d$. Solve for the value in Quantity A first, in terms of d, by substituting the given information for c in $c^2 - d^2$. Then, $(d+2)^2 - d^2 = (d^2 + 2d + 2d + 4) - d^2 = 4d + 4$. Now look again at Quantity B: $4d$. Is $4d + 4$ greater than $4d$? To compare, set up an inequality: $4d + 4 > 4d$. See if this inequality is true by solving for d. $4d + 4 - 4d > 4d - 4d$; so, $4 > 0$. Since this is true in every instance, $4d + 4$ must be greater than $4d$ no matter what value d takes on.

67. **Sub topic: Quadratic Equations**

The correct answers are (B) and (C).

The intercepts occur when the values of y are equal i.e. from the intersection of curves. (Geometry)

$x^2 - x + 4 = 4x - 1$

$x^2 - 5x + 5 = 0$

$x = \dfrac{1}{2}\left[5 \pm \sqrt{25 - 20}\right] = \dfrac{1}{2}\left(5 \pm \sqrt{5}\right)$

$x = 3.62$, or $x = 1.38$

Therefore (A) is false, (B) is true, (C) is true, (D) is false, (E) is false.

68. **Sub topic: Linear Equations**

The correct answer is (B).

There's one box that's in both rows -the one in the middle with value $\frac{2}{9}$.

In fact, we have

$\frac{1}{3} + \frac{2}{9} + y$ in the horizontal row,

$x + \frac{2}{9} + \frac{4}{5}$ in the vertical row, and we are comparing x and y.

Since $\frac{2}{9}$ is the part of both rows, we can throw it out.

So, we have $\frac{1}{3} + y = \frac{4}{5} + x$.

Since $\frac{4}{5}$ is greater, the number we add to $\frac{4}{5}$ has to be less than the number we add to $\frac{1}{3}$ for the sums to be the same.

Hence, x must be less than y. The answer is (B).

69. **Sub topic: System of Equations**

The correct answers are (A) and (D).

The $31.50 in bills and $3.50 in pennies is subtracted from the total $50. The remaining amount = $15.00

Let q = number of quarters, d = number of dimes, n = number of nickels (3 unknowns).

$n = 3q$

$d = n + 3 \rightarrow d = 3q + 3$

$0.25q + 0.1d + 0.05n = 15$

$0.25q + 0.1(3q + 3) + 0.05(3q) = 15$

$0.7q + 0.3 = 15 \rightarrow q = 21$

$n = 63, d = 66$

Details:

$n = 3q$(there are three times as many nickels as quarters)

$d = n + 3$(there are three more dimes than nickels)

$0.25q + 0.1d + 0.05n = 15$(these are the quarters, dimes, and nickels that make up $15.00)

We used the substitution $d = 3q + 3$, because$d = n + 3 = 3q + 3$.

Sum of nickels and dimes = $(63)(0.05) + (66)(0.10) = \$9.75$.

70. **Sub topic: Exponents**

The correct answer is (D).

When in doubt, you must plug in at least twice for quantitative comparison questions. Since x can be 1, you should start by trying $x = 1$. In that case, Quantity A equals $1^{(1+2)}$, or 1^3, which is 1. Quantity B equals $(1 + 2)^1$, or 3^1, which is 3. Quantity B is greater. What if $x = 2$? In that case, Quantity A equals2^{2+2} or 2^4, which is 16. Quantity B equals $(2 + 2)^2$, or 4^2, which is 16. So, the quantities can be equal. You can get more than one result, so the answer is D.

71. **Sub topic: Algebraic Expressions**

The correct answer is (A).

Multiply each side of the given equation by $(m + n)$.

$(m + n)(m - n) = (m + n)$

Find the product on the left using conjugate identity $a^2 - b^2 = (a + b)(a - b)$.

$m^2 - n^2 = m + n$

Subtract m from and add n^2 to each side.

$m^2 - n^2 - m + n^2 = m + n - m + n^2$

Combine the like terms.

$m^2 - m = n + n^2$

Factor each side.

$m(m - 1) = n(n + 1)$

Thus, (A) is the correct answer.

Level: Difficult

72. **Sub topic: Functions**

The correct answer is (E).

We change the equation $y = 2x^2 - 16x + 29$ into its vertex form using completing square method.

$y = 2x^2 - 16x + 29 = 2(x^2 - 8x) + 29$

$= 2(x^2 - 8x + 16) + 29 - 32$

$= 2(x - 4)^2 - 3$

The vertex is at $(4, -3)$.

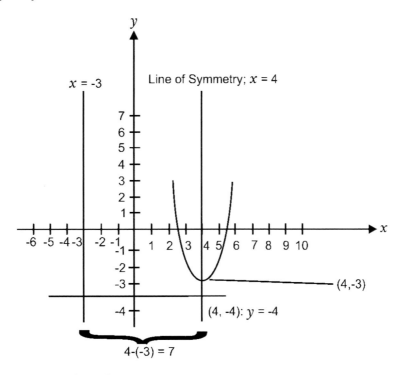

The line of symmetry passes through $x = 3$.

The shortest distance is along the horizontal line. Since the line of symmetry $x = 3$ and $x = -3$ are vertical lines in opposite sides of the y-axis, the shortest distance between them is $4 - (-3) = 4 + 3 = 7$ units.

73. **Sub topic: Algebraic Expressions**

The correct answers are (A) and (F).

We are given

$m - n = 1$, where $m \neq -n$ or $m + n \neq 0$

Multiply each side by $(m + n)$. We can multiply by $m + n$ because it is nonzero.

$(m + n)(m - n) = (m + n)$

Find the product on the left using the conjugate identity $a^2 - b^2 = (a + b)(a - b)$.

$m^2 - n^2 = m + n$

Subtract m from and add n^2 to each side. Then, cancel out the opposite terms

$m^2 - m = n^2 + n$

Factor each side

$m(m - 1) = n(n + 1)$

Thus, (A) is a correct answer.

(F)$\dfrac{1}{mn^2} - \dfrac{1}{m^2n} + 1 = \dfrac{1 + m^2n^2}{m^2n^2}$

$\dfrac{m - n + m^2n^2}{m^2n^2} = \dfrac{1 + m^2n^2}{m^2n^2}$

$m - n + m^2n^2 = 1 + m^2n^2$

$m - n = 1$

Therefore, (F) is correct.

74. **Sub topic: System of Equations**

The correct answer is (A).

To determine which quantity is greater, we need to solve the equations for both x and y using linear combination or elimination methods.

$1(-5x + 12y = 18) i.e. -5x + 12y = 18$

$2(2x - 6y = -11) i.e. 4x - 12y = -22$

Add equations together to solve for x

$-x = -4$ or $x = 4$

Solve for y by plugging in -7 for x:

$2(4) - 6y = -11$

$8 - 6y = -11$

$-6y = -17$

$y = \dfrac{17}{6}$

Now to compare the two quantities:

Quantity A:

$(x)(y) = (4)\left(\dfrac{17}{6}\right) = \dfrac{28}{3}$

Quantity B:

$(x) + (y) = (4) + \left(\dfrac{17}{6}\right) = \dfrac{41}{6}$

The answer is A.

75. **Sub topic: System of Equations**

The correct answer is (A).

In order to solve the problem, three equations need to be constructed. The first involves the number of pieces of equipment, which is known to be 47.

Loaders $= a$, Dozers $= b$, and Scrapers $= c$:

$a + b + c = 47$

Next, an equation can be constructed based on the known total cost and known cost per item:

$\$50,000a + \$60,000b + \$75,000c = \$2,730,000$

Reduced is: $10a + 12b + 15c = 546$

Finally, an equation can be constructed based on the known tire quantities:

$4a + 0b + 6c = 132$

Now that we have three equations, we can solve for variables and substitute:

$4a + 0b + 6c = 132 \rightarrow 4a = 132 - 6c \rightarrow a = 33 - \dfrac{3}{2}c$

$a + b + c = 47 \rightarrow 33 - \dfrac{3}{2}c + b + c = 47 \rightarrow b = 14 + \dfrac{1}{2}c$

$10a + 12b + 15c = 546 \rightarrow 10\left(33 - \dfrac{3}{2}c\right) + 12\left(14 + \dfrac{1}{2}c\right) + 15c = 546$

$330 - 15c + 168 + 6c + 15c = 546 \rightarrow 6c = 48 \rightarrow c = 8$

$4a + 0b + 48 = 132 \rightarrow 4a = 84 \rightarrow a = 21$

$b = 47 - 21 - 8 = 18$

The answer is (A).

76. **Sub topic: Inequalities**

The correct answer is (B).

Set up an unknown comparison of the two expressions and simplify.

$\dfrac{10 + y}{12}\ \boxed{?}\ \dfrac{y - 1}{3}$ Initial comparison

$10 + y\ \boxed{?}\ 12\left(\dfrac{y-1}{3}\right)$ Multiply by 12

$10 + y\ \boxed{?}\ 4(y - 1)$

$10 + y\ \boxed{?}\ 4y - 4$

$y\ \boxed{?}\ 4y - 14$ Subtract 10

$-3y\ \boxed{?}\ -14$ Subtract 4y

$y\ \boxed{?}\ 4\dfrac{2}{3}$ Divide by -3

Since we know that $y \geq 6$ then we can say $y > 4\dfrac{2}{3}$. Now that we have determined the correct inequality for the $y > 4\dfrac{2}{3}$, we must reverse our steps from above to determine if the inequality sign remains the same.

$y > 4\dfrac{2}{3}$ Last Comparison

$-3y < -14$ Multiply by -3 (change sign)

$y < 4y - 14$ Add 4y

$10 + y < 4y - 4$ Add 10

$$\frac{10 + y}{12} < \frac{4y - 4}{12} \qquad \text{Divide by 12}$$

$$\frac{10 + y}{12} < \frac{y - 1}{3} \qquad \text{Simplify}$$

As each step is reversed the inequality sign changes once, when both sides are multiplied by -3.

77. Sub topic: Applications

The correct answer is (E).

The pipes can fill $\frac{1}{24}, \frac{1}{6}$ and $\frac{1}{12}$ of the tank individually, per minute.

If they are turned on at the same time, they take fill $\frac{1}{24} + \frac{1}{6} + \frac{1}{12} = \frac{7}{24}$ of the tank in one minute.

To be full, it takes $\frac{24}{7} = 3.43$ minutes, which falls within the range of 3.1 to 5 minutes.

78. Sub topic: Applications

The correct answers are (A) and (E).

Start by determining the adjusted speed of the locomotives:

Reduction in speed $\left(\dfrac{ft}{s}\right)$ =[Locomotive weight(tons)](Coefficient of Friction)(0.1)

Train	Base Locomotive Speed (feet per second)		Locomotive Weight (tons)		Coefficient of friction between train and rails		Reduced Locomotive Speed (feet per second)
Train A	70		100		0.80		62
Train B	80		85		0.90		72.4
Train C	65	$-$	115	$\times$	0.75	$\times\ 0.1 =$	56.4
Train D	75		90		0.85		67.4
Train E	80		95		0.90		71.5

All the locomotives travel at this speed for 120 seconds (2 minutes).Distance is determined by multiplying the speed by the time. Note that Train B had a mechanical malfunction and did not run during this duration:

Train	Reduced Locomotive Speed (feet per second)		Time (seconds)		Distance Travelled (feet)
Train A	62				7,440
Train B	0				-
Train C	56.4	$\times$	120	$=$	6,768
Train D	67.4				8,088
Train E	71.5				8,580

Train B is fixed, and all locomotives continue for another 300 seconds (5 minutes):

Train	Reduced Locomotive Speed (feet per second)		Time (seconds)		Distance Travelled (feet)		Previous Distance Travelled (feet)		Cumulative Distance Travelled (feet)
Train A	62				18,600		7,440		26,040
Train B	72.4				21,720		-		21,720
Train C	56.4	×	300	=	16,920	+	6,768	=	23,688
Train D	67.4				20,220		8,088		28,308
Train E	71.5				21,450		8,580		30,030

At this point, the friction coefficient on Train C changes to 0.3, so its reduced speed becomes $65 - (115 \times 0.3 \times 0.1) = 61.6$ feet per second. Train D has a mechanical malfunction that reduces its base speed to 60 feet per second, so its reduced speed become $60 - (90 \times 0.85 \times 0.1) = 52.4$ feet per second. The trains travel for another 5 minutes.

Train	Reduced Locomotive Speed (feet per second)		Time (seconds)		Distance Travelled (feet)		Previous Distance Travelled (feet)		Cumulative Distance Travelled (feet)
Train A	62				18,600		26,040		44,640
Train B	72.4				21,270		21,720		42,540
Train C	61.6	×	300	=	18,480	+	23,688	=	42,168
Train D	52.4				15,720		28,308		44,028
Train E	71.5				21,450		30,030		51,480

79. **Sub topic: Inequalities**

The correct answer is (A).

Write the expression in mathematical terms, solve for x and compare.

15 more than $5x = 79$ less $3x$ is equivalent to $15 + 5x = 79 - 3x$.

$15 + 5x = 79 - 3x$	Original equation
$5x = 64 - 3x$	Subtract 15.
$8x = 64$	Add $3x$.
$x = 8$	Divide by 8

Quantity A: The quantity of twice x subtracted from the quotient of 12 and $\frac{1}{3}$, divided by 4. $(x = 8)$

$\left\{ \frac{12}{\frac{1}{3}} - 2(8) \right\} \div 4$	Original equation
$= \{36 - 2(8)\} \div 4$	Division in ( )
$= \{36 - 16\} \div 4$	Multiplication in ( )
$= \{20\} \div 4$	Subtraction in ( )
$= 5$	Division

Quantity B: The quantity of x squared less the product of six and x, divided by 4. ($x = 8$)

$= \dfrac{8^2 - (6)(8)}{4}$ Original equation

$= \dfrac{64 - (6)(8)}{4}$ Exponents in numerator

$= \dfrac{64 - 48}{4}$ Multiplication in numerator

$= \dfrac{16}{4}$ Subtraction in numerator

$= 4$ Division

Compare:

$5 > 4$

The quantity of A is greater than the quantity of B.

80. **Sub topic: Algebraic Expressions**

The correct answer is (E).

Denote the term by P. Multiply and divide P by $(a - 1)$.

$$P = \frac{(1-a)(1+a)(1+a^2)(1+a^4)(1+a^8)....(1+a^{2n})}{(1-a)}$$

$$= \frac{(1-a^2)(1+a^2)(1+a^2)(1+a^4)(1+a^8)....(1+a^{2n})}{(1-a)}$$

$$= \frac{(1-a^4)(1+a^4)(1+a^8)....(1+a^{2n})}{(1-a)}$$

$$= \frac{(1-a^8)(1+a^8)....(1+a^{2n})}{(1-a)}$$

$$= \frac{(1-a^{16})....(1+a^{2n})}{(1-a)}$$

$$= \frac{(1-a^{2n})}{(1-a)}$$

Chapter 5

Geometry Practice Questions

This chapter consists of *81 Geometry* practice questions. The questions cover all the question types as explained in Chapter 2 and are segregated into 3 levels of difficulty - Easy, Medium and Difficult. You may choose to start solving the Easy questions first and then move on to higher levels of difficulty or solve the questions in any random order. You will find answers and detailed explanations towards the end of this chapter.

Level: Easy

1.

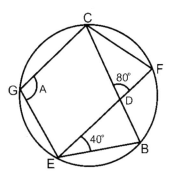

Select all the statements that best give the measure of ∠A.

Select all that apply.

(A) between 80° and 100°

(B) between 100° and 130°

(C) between 50° and 80°

(D) between 90° and 125°

(E) between 130° and 150°

(F) between 70° and 100°

(G) between 91° and 115°

2.

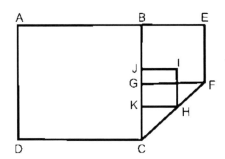

A side of the square ABCD is twice as a side of the square BEFG, and H is the midpoint of CF. Also, IJKH is a square. If the area of IJKH is 9, what is the area of ABCD?

(A) 122

(B) 132

(C) 144

(D) 120

(E) 76

3.

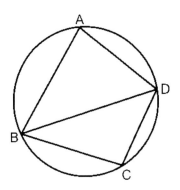

$m\angle ABC= 80°$ and BD is the circle's diameter.

Quantity A	**Quantity B**
$m\angle BAD$	$m\angle ADC-10°$

(A) Quantity A is greater.

(B) Quantity B is greater.

(C) The two quantities are equal.

(D) The relationship cannot be determined from the information given.

4.

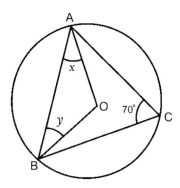

Select the statements that give the correct measure of ∠x.

Select all that apply.

(A) between 25° and 30°

(B) between 16° and 30°

(C) between 22° and 42°

(D) between 15° and 30°

(E) between 25° and 30°

(F) between 11° and 19°

(G) between 21° and 27°

5.

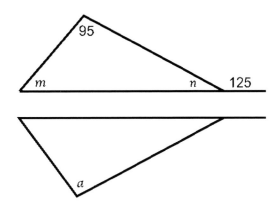

In the above figure, the sum of two angles at the end of the horizontal side of the upper triangle is greater than the sum of the corresponding angles in the lower triangle. Which statement is true?

(A) $a = 90°$

(B) $a < 85°$

(C) $a > 85°$

(D) $a < 95°$

(E) $a > 95°$

6.   Which title best represents X in the table?

Name of quadrilateral	X	Four sides
Kites	Yes	Yes
Trapezoids	No	Yes

(A) Two pairs of consecutive congruent sides

(B) Two pairs of opposite angles congruent

(C) Four congruent sides

(D) Congruent diagonals

(E) Sum of all angles is 180°

7.

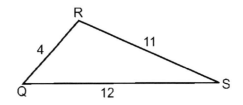

Quantity A	**Quantity B**
The area of triangle QRS	The perimeter of triangle QRS

(A) Quantity A is greater.

(B) Quantity B is greater.

(C) The two quantities are equal.

(D) The relationship cannot be determined from the information given.

8.

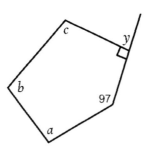

Determine the value of $a + b + c + y$.

 degrees

9.

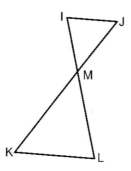

Which of the following is true if IJ ∥ KL? ?

Select all that apply.

(A) ∠JIM ≅ ∠MKL

(B) ∠IMJ ≅ ∠LMK

(C) $\dfrac{IM}{ML} = \dfrac{JM}{MK}$

(D) ΔKLM ≅ ΔJIM

(E) ∠IJK ≅ ∠LKM

(F) $\dfrac{KL}{IJ} = \dfrac{JM}{KM}$

10. How many different pentagons can be drawn inside a hexagon?

(A) 3

(B) 4

(C) 5

(D) 6

(E) 7

11.

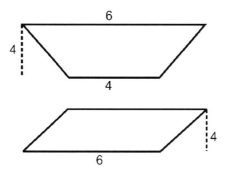

Quantity A   **Quantity B**

The area of the trapezoid   The area of the parallelogram

(A) Quantity A is greater.

(B) Quantity B is greater.

(C) The two quantities are equal.

(D) The relationship cannot be determined from the information given.

12. The diameter of a circle is $2\sqrt{2}m$. The diameter of another circle having 8 times the area of the first circle is:

       ⎡⎯⎯⎯⎯⎯⎯⎯⎤
       ⎣⎯⎯⎯⎯⎯⎯⎯⎦m

13. A field is of a square shape. If total expense of building fence around it is $1600 at rate of $5 per meter. What will be the perimeter and length of one side of the field?

Select all that apply.

(A) 40m

(B) 80m

(C) 100m

(D) 320m

(E) 350m

(F) 370m

14.

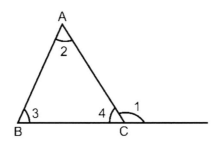

ABC is a triangle and ∠1 is 124° and ∠2 is 46° then ∠3 & ∠4 will be?

Select all that apply.

(A) 46°

(B) 56°

(C) 78°

(D) 124°

(E) 132°

15.

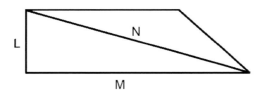

Quantity A

The length of line N

Quantity B

The sum of the lengths of lines M and L

(A) Quantity A is greater.

(B) Quantity B is greater.

(C) The two quantities are equal.

(D) The relationship cannot be determined from the information given.

16. In a regular polygon, the exterior angle has a measure of 12°. What type of polygon is it?

(A) Dodecagon

(B) 15-gon

(C) 20-gon

(D) 25-gon

(E) 30-gon

17. Five disks have circumferences π, 10π, 12π, 20π, and 50π. Label the disks A, B, C, D, E, respectively. Which disc(s) would fit into a hoop with area 470 units^2?

Select all that apply.

(A) A

(B) B

(C) C

(D) D

(E) E

18.

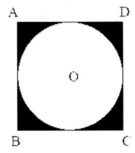

In the figure above ABCD is a square and a circle with center O touches its four sides internally. If radius of the circle is 5 meters, then what will be the area of shaded region? Provide the answer up to two significant digits in the answer box.

19. Length of a rectangle is 3cm less than the double of the width. If perimeter of the rectangle is 96cm then what will be its width and length?

Select all that apply.

(A) 15cm

(B) 17cm

(C) 27cm

(D) 31cm

(E) 34cm

20. Point A is located at $(-3, -11)$ and Point B is located at $(4, 13)$. What is the length of line segment AB?

(A) $4\sqrt{15}$

(B) 5

(C) 17

(D) 24

(E) 25

21.

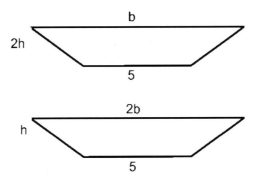

<table>
<tr><td><u>Quantity A</u></td><td><u>Quantity B</u></td></tr>
<tr><td>The area of the top trapezoid</td><td>The area of the bottom trapezoid</td></tr>
</table>

(A) Quantity A is greater.

(B) Quantity B is greater.

(C) The two quantities are equal.

(D) The relationship cannot be determined from the information given.

22. Let m_1 and m_2 be the slopes of two lines. The lines will be perpendicular to each other if one of the following is satisfied.

Select all that apply.

(A) $m_1 m_2 = 1$

(B) $m_1 = m_2$

(C) $m_1 m_2 = -1$

(D) $m_1 = -m_2$

(E) $m_1 m_2 + 1 = 0$

23.

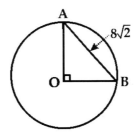

In the diagram above, if the hypotenuse of the right triangle is $8\sqrt{2}$, what is the area of the shaded region?

(A) $16\pi - 32$

(B) $16\pi - 32\sqrt{2}$

(C) 32π

(D) $64\pi - 32$

(E) $64\pi - 32\sqrt{2}$

24.

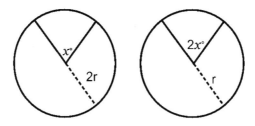

Quantity A	**Quantity B**
The area of the sector in the left circle	The area of the sector in the right circle

(A) Quantity A is greater.

(B) Quantity B is greater.

(C) The two quantities are equal.

(D) The relationship cannot be determined from the information given.

25. What is the surface area of a sphere with the same radius as the side of a square with a perimeter of 32?
$SA_{sphere} = 4\pi r^2$

(A) 16π

(B) 32π

(C) 64π

(D) 256π

(E) 1024π

26.

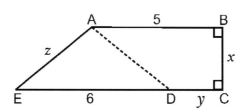

Select statements that are true for the figure shown above:

Area of $\Delta AED = 12$

Select all that apply.

(A) $x = 4.5$

(B) $x = 4$

(C) $z = 5$

(D) $z = 6$

27.

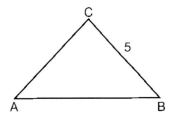

If the perimeter of ΔABC is 16, what is its area?

(A) 8

(B) 9

(C) 10

(D) 12

(E) 15

28.

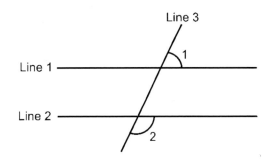

L_1 and L_2 are two lines parallel to each other and L_3 cuts through both these lines as shown in the figure above. If angle 1 is 45°, then what will the measure of angle 2 be in degrees?

Write your answer in the answer box.

29.

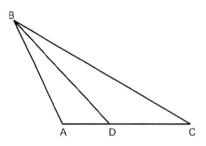

Note: Figure not drawn to scale.

In the preceding figure, AB = AD and BD = CD. If ∠C measures 19°, what is the measure of ∠A in degrees?

(A) 75

(B) 94

(C) 104

(D) 114

(E) 142

30.

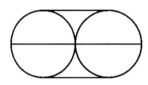

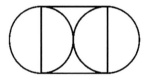

Both circles have radius, *r*.

Quantity A	**Quantity B**
The area above the horizontal line in the top figure	The area within the shaded square in the bottom figure

(A) Quantity A is greater.

(B) Quantity B is greater.

(C) The two quantities are equal.

(D) The relationship cannot be determined from the information given.

Level: Medium

31.

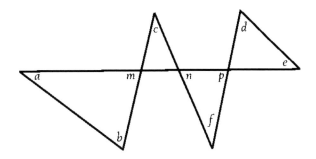

What will be the value of $a + b + c + f + d + e$, if $m + n + p$ is 200°?

(A) 420°

(B) 360°

(C) 340°

(D) 320°

(E) 280°

32.

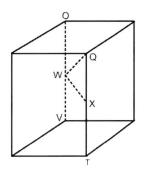

W and X are the midpoints of OV and QT, respectively.

Quantity A	**Quantity B**
QW	*WX*

(A) Quantity A is greater.

(B) Quantity B is greater.

(C) The two quantities are equal.

(D) The relationship cannot be determined from the information given.

33. The points $A(0,0)$, $B(0, 5p - 2)$, and $C(2p + 2, 4p + 6)$ form a triangle. If $\angle ABC = 90°$, what is the area of $\triangle ABC$?

    Select all that apply.

    (A) Area of $\triangle ABC$ is < 250

    (B) Area of $\triangle ABC$ is < 300

    (C) Area of $\triangle ABC$ is > 300

    (D) Area of $\triangle ABC$ is < 350

    (E) Area of $\triangle ABC$ is > 380

    (F) Area of $\triangle ABC$ is > 420

34.

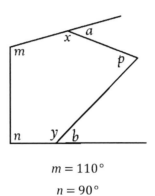

$$m = 110°$$
$$n = 90°$$

Quantity A	**Quantity B**
$a + b$	$90°$

(A) Quantity A is greater.

(B) Quantity B is greater.

(C) The two quantities are equal.

(D) The relationship cannot be determined from the information given.

35.

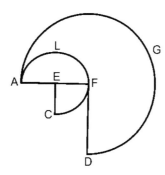

In the figure above, E and F are the centers of the circular curves (portions of circles). ALF is a semicircle, and EFC is a quadrant of a circle. Also, quadrant AFD is cut-out of the larger circle. If the arc CF measures 3π, what is the perimeter of the figure AGDFLA?

(A) 20π + 8

(B) 12π + 8

(C) 16π + 6

(D) 22π + 12

(E) 24π + 12

36. If the number of diagonals in a polygon is 54, identify the statement that best gives the number of sides of the polygon.

Select all that apply.

(A) between 9 and 13

(B) between 8 and 10

(C) between 10 and 14

(D) between 13 and 15

(E) between 6 and 8

(F) between 7 and 11

(G) between 13 and 17

37.

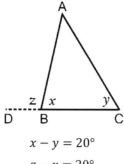

$$x - y = 20°$$
$$z - x = 20°$$

Quantity A

Measure of ∠BAC

Quantity B

40°

(A) Quantity A is greater.

(B) Quantity B is greater.

(C) The two quantities are equal.

(D) The relationship cannot be determined from the information given.

38. A metallic sheet of paper whose shape is a sector of 60° is extracted from a circle of diameter 18 inches. If the sector is used to make a cone, what would be the approximate volume of the cone?

(A) 95 cubic inches

(B) 191 cubic inches

(C) 21 cubic inches

(D) 185 cubic inches

(E) 50 cubic inches

39.

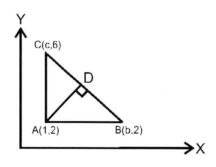

ΔABC is an isosceles right triangle with hypotenuse BC. AD is perpendicular to BC. Points A, B and C are defined by their coordinates. What is the length of AD?

(A) $4\sqrt{2}$

(B) $2\sqrt{2}$

(C) $3\sqrt{2}$

(D) 2

(E) 3

40. If each interior angle of a regular polygon is given to be 135° in measure, select the statements that best give the sum of all interior angles in the polygon.

    Select all that apply.

    (A) between 900° and 1000°

    (B) between 900° and 1240°

    (C) between 810° and 900°

    (D) between 1000° and 1240°

    (E) between 1100° and 1240°

    (F) between 700° and 1000°

    (G) between 1200° and 1380°

41.

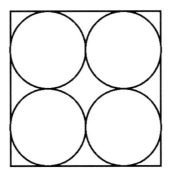

Figure not drawn to scale

In the figure above, four identical circles with equal diameters are enclosed in a square with an area of 256, each circle touches the edges of other circles and the square as shown.

Quantity A	Quantity B
The total area of the grey region	$300-50\pi$

    (A) Quantity A is greater.

    (B) Quantity B is greater.

    (C) The two quantities are equal.

    (D) The relationship cannot be determined from the information given.

42. A ΔABC is defined by the points with the following coordinates: A(2, $2\sqrt{3}$), B(4,0) and C(0,0). What is the $m\angle$BAC?

    (A) 30°

    (B) 45°

    (C) 60°

    (D) 75°

    (E) 90°

43.

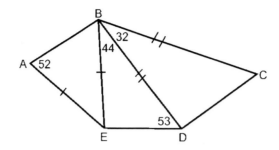

Which of the following statements are true regarding the figure above?

Select all that apply.

(A) AB is the longest side of ∆ABE.

(B) BE is the shortest side of ∆EBD.

(C) ∠EBD = 44°

(D) ∆BED is an isosceles triangle.

(E) ∠BCD = 78°

(F) The sum of all interior angles of the pentagon is 720°

(G) BD is the longest side of ∆BCD

44.

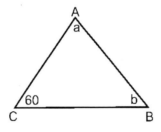

Figure not drawn to scale

In the ∆ABC above, AC > AB and ∠c = 60°

<table>
<tr><td>Quantity A</td><td>Quantity B</td></tr>
<tr><td>Length of AB</td><td>Length of BC</td></tr>
</table>

(A) Quantity A is greater.

(B) Quantity B is greater.

(C) The two quantities are equal.

(D) The relationship cannot be determined from the information given.

45.

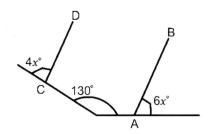

In the above figure given that AB ∥ CD, *x* is,

(A) 8.33

(B) 12.5

(C) 13

(D) 26

(E) 50

46. If area and perimeter of a rectangular region are $24cm^2$ and $20cm$ respectively. Then length and width in *cm* will be?

Select all that apply.

(A) 2 *cm*

(B) 3 *cm*

(C) 4 *cm*

(D) 6 *cm*

(E) 8 *cm*

(F) 12 *cm*

47.

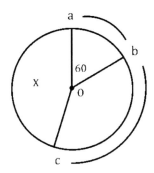

Figure not drawn to scale

In this figure, the radius of the circle is 4, the length of *arc bc* is 3π

Quantity A	**Quantity B**
Area X	$\dfrac{21\pi}{3}$

(A) Quantity A is greater.

(B) Quantity B is greater.

(C) The two quantities are equal.

(D) The relationship cannot be determined from the information given.

48.

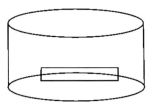

A cylinder container has a height of 4 cm and a radius of 3 cm; a metallic rectangular solid object has a length of 2 cm, width of 1 cm and height of 3 cm. This object rests on the bottom of the container and is completely covered by the cylinder as shown above (not drawn to scale). Now, you are trying to pour in 2 liters of orange juice into the cylinder from an old container. 1liter = $(10cm)^3 = 1000cm^3$

Quantity A	**Quantity B**
The total amount of juice fits into the cylinder	The total amount of juice remains in the old container

(A) Quantity A is greater.

(B) Quantity B is greater.

(C) The two quantities are equal.

(D) The relationship cannot be determined from the information given.

49.

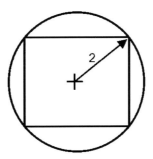

A square is inscribed inside a circle whose radius = 2, as shown in the figure. Determine, to 2 decimal places, the area of the shaded region.

```

```

50.

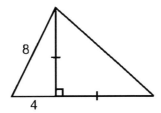

What is the area of the above triangle?

(A) 16 units^2

(B) 22.5 units^2

(C) 30 units^2

(D) $8\sqrt{3} + 24$ units^2

(E) $8\sqrt{3} + 6$ units^2

51.

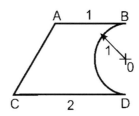

Select all the statements that are true about the figure.

In the figure shown above, lines AB and CD are parallel.

Select all that apply.

(A) Shaded area > 1.25

(B) Perimeter of shaded area < 8

(C) Shaded area < 1.5

(D) Perimeter > 8

52.

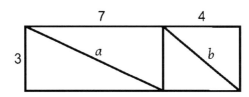

In the above diagram, the sum $a + b$ is equal to:

(A) $5 + \sqrt{58}$

(B) $16 + \sqrt{2}$

(C) 14

(D) $\dfrac{25}{3}$

(E) $17 + 3\sqrt{6}$

53.

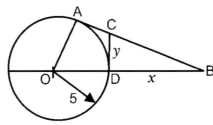

Select statements that are true for the figure shown above:

AB is tangent to the circle at point A

CD is tangent to the circle at point D

Circle has radius = 5

Length of AB = 12

Select all that apply.

(A) $x = 7$

(B) $x = 8$

(C) $y = 3$

(D) $y = \frac{10}{3}$

Questions 54 and 55 are based on the following diagram.

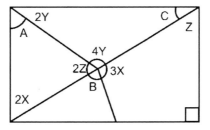

54.

Figure not drawn to scale

Quantity A	**Quantity B**
X	22

(A) Quantity A is greater.

(B) Quantity B is greater.

(C) The two quantities are equal.

(D) The relationship cannot be determined from the information given.

55.

Quantity A	**Quantity B**
$A + B + C$	$3(A + C) - B + 2X - 8Y$

(A) Quantity A is greater.

(B) Quantity B is greater.

(C) The two quantities are equal.

(D) The relationship cannot be determined from the information given.

56. A triangle has vertices at $(-10, 9)$, $(-2, 3)$ and $(-2, 13)$. What is the perimeter of the triangle after a scale factor of $\frac{3}{4}$?

(A) $15 + 3\sqrt{5}$

(B) $18\sqrt{5}$

(C) $20 + 4\sqrt{5}$

(D) 24

(E) $24\sqrt{5}$

57.

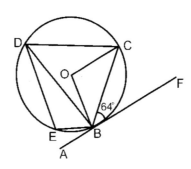

In the above figure, O is the center of the circle, AF is the tangent line to the circle at B and $\angle CBF = 64°$. Find the size of $\angle COB$.

(A) $232°$

(B) $128°$

(C) $116°$

(D) $64°$

(E) $32°$

58.

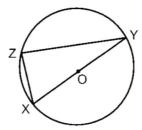

In circle O above, XY is a diameter, OX = 8.5, and YZ = 15. What is the area of ΔXYZ in square units?

(A) 40

(B) 60

(C) 120

(D) 127.5

(E) 180

59.

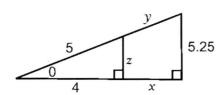

Select statements that are true for the figure shown above:

Select all that apply.

(A) $x + y < 7$

(B) $x > 3$

(C) $y < 4$

(D) x and y cannot be determined

60. What is the area of rhombus with a perimeter of 40 and a diagonal of 10?

(A) $50\sqrt{3}$

(B) 100

(C) $100\sqrt{3}$

(D) 200

(E) 400

61.

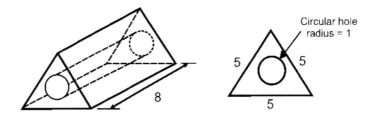

A circular hole that has a radius of 1 is bored through a triangular prism. Determine the percentage remaining from the original volume of the prism.

(A) 65%

(B) 68%

(C) 71%

(D) 75%

(E) 78%

62.

The ratio of the sum of interior angles of polygons A and B is 4:5. The sum of their sides is 13.

Quantity A	**Quantity B**
A sixth of the interior ∠A	A seventh of the interior ∠B

(A) Quantity A is greater.

(B) Quantity B is greater.

(C) The two quantities are equal.

(D) The relationship cannot be determined from the information given.

Level: Difficult

63.

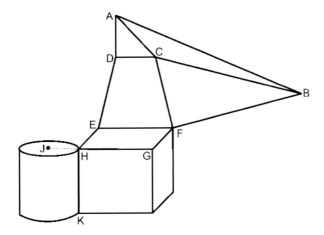

Given the above figure, determine the circumference of circle J.

∠ABC = 10

∠EFB = 165

∠CAB = 25

Area of CDEF = 33.4

BF = 10

AC = 5

AD = 3

EH = 5

The volume of the cube = 150

The volume of the cylinder = 20π

64.

Given the segments MN, NP, and PD, only points M, D, and N are collinear.

D is the midpoint of MN.

Quantity A

DN − PM

Quantity B

PD

(A) Quantity A is greater.

(B) Quantity B is greater.

(C) The two quantities are equal.

(D) The relationship cannot be determined from the information given.

65.

CB is twice AC, and AD is twice BD. How many distinct points, besides the points A, B, C, and D, are needed to represent the midpoints of all the possible segments formed by points A, B, C, and D?

(A) One

(B) Three

(C) Four

(D) Five

(E) Six

66.

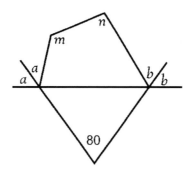

Quantity A   **Quantity B**

$m + n$ 180°

(A) Quantity A is greater.

(B) Quantity B is greater.

(C) The two quantities are equal.

(D) The relationship cannot be determined from the information given.

67.

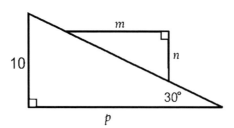

What will be the value of $p\left(\dfrac{m}{n}\right)$ in the figure above, if the horizontal legs of the triangles are parallel?

(A) 45

(B) 40

(C) 30

(D) 32

(E) 22

68.

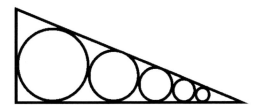

Figure NOT drawn to scale:

In this figure, five circles are fully encased in a triangle as shown above (they do not have to touch the sides of the triangle). The circles have radii of 16,8,4,2, and 1 respectively. The grey regions measure a total of 679π, the base of the triangle measures 34π.

Quantity A	**Quantity B**
The height of this triangle	60

(A) Quantity A is greater.

(B) Quantity B is greater.

(C) The two quantities are equal.

(D) The relationship cannot be determined from the information given.

69.

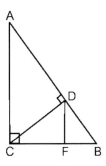

$\triangle ABC$ is a right triangle, as is $\triangle ADC$ and $\triangle DBC$. What is the length of the line DF if $AC = 14$ and $\angle CAB = 35°$?

70.

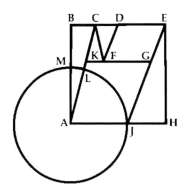

Given:

JH = 4

BC = 2.68

ABEH is a square

DEGF is a parallelogram

∠DCF = 77.9°

CF = 3.86

CD = 2.32

What is the area of the grey shaded region?

(A) 14.3

(B) 8.7

(C) 3.7

(D) 4.8

(E) 12.5

71.

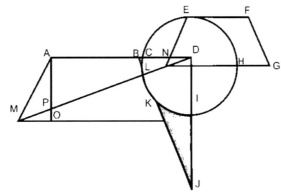

Given the figure above, and the following values:

AP = 4, PM = 3, ∠AMP = 45°, EF = 5, GN = 8, Area of EFGN = 26

What is the approximate area of the shaded region?

(A) 35

(B) 13

(C) 22

(D) 15

(E) 24

72.

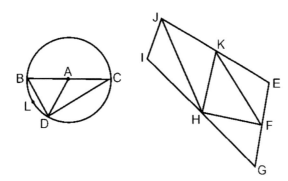

Length of arc BLD = 5.24   Length of line AD = 5

Length of line JK = 7.5   Length of line HF = 7.48

Length of line HG = 9.06   Length of line KE = 7.5

Length of line KF = 10.34

Measure of ∠EKF = 27.03°   Measure of ∠FHG = 33.51°

Quantity A   **Quantity B**

Area of ΔBCD   Area of ΔJHI

(A) Quantity A is greater.

(B) Quantity B is greater.

(C) The two quantities are equal.

(D) The relationship cannot be determined from the information given.

73.

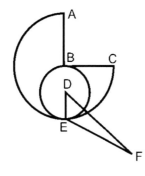   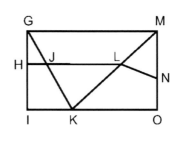

Given:

∠DEF = 120°;DF = 12;∠EDF = 50°;GM = 24;JL = 13.7;HI = 8

Area GJLM = 113.1;∠GJH = 60°;NO = 5.52;∠MNL = 70°

The area of which shapes is greater than the shaded area?

Select all that apply.

(A) GKI

(B) MLN

(C) JLK

(D) GJH

(E) KLNO

74.

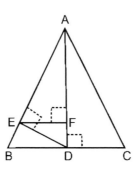

ABC is an equilateral triangle with side = 6.

Quantity A	**Quantity B**
EF	$\dfrac{5}{2}$

(A) Quantity A is greater.

(B) Quantity B is greater.

(C) The two quantities are equal.

(D) The relationship cannot be determined from the information given.

75.

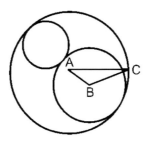

Given AB = 2, BC = 4, ∠ACB = 20°, A is the center of the large circle, B is the center of the medium circle, the area of the shaded region is 35% of the area of the large circle and the radius of the medium circle is 75% larger than the radius of the smaller circle, what is the approximate radius of the medium circle?

(A) 19

(B) 79

(C) 50

(D) 4

(E) 27

76.

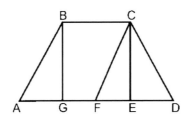

ABCD is an isosceles trapezoid with AD = 2s and AB = BC = CD. BG and CE are perpendicular to AD. F marks the middle of line segment AD (AF = FD) and $m\angle ADC = 60°$

Quantity A	**Quantity B**
$\dfrac{\text{Perimeter of } \Delta\text{CFD}}{\text{Perimeter of rectangle BCEG}}$	$5 - 3\sqrt{3}$

(A) Quantity A is greater.

(B) Quantity B is greater.

(C) The two quantities are equal.

(D) The relationship cannot be determined from the information given.

77. A circle passes through the points A, B and C whose coordinates are $(6, -8)$, $(3, -9)$ and $(3, 1)$ respectively. Which of the following statements are true for the given circle?

    Select all that apply.

    (A) The circle passes through a point D whose coordinates are $(-4, 3)$.

    (B) The radius of the circle is 5 units.

    (C) A point whose coordinates are $(4, 1)$ lies inside the circle.

    (D) The circumference of the circle is 56.52 units.

    (E) The coordinates of the center of the circle are $(3, -4)$.

    (F) The area of the circle is 78.5 units.

78.

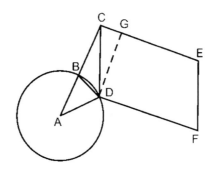

    Given:

    Length of arc BD = 7, Area of CDFE = 358.3, CE = 24, CE||FD, $\angle BDF = 154°$, $\angle DCE = 72°$, $\angle CBD = 110°$

    What is the area of the sector ABD?

    (A) 314

    (B) 30

    (C) 18

    (D) 34

    (E) 24

79.

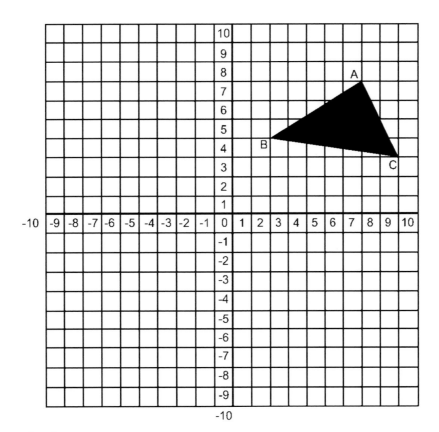

Given the above triangle:

The triangle is to undergo a reflection over the following transformations, in this order:

- Reflection over the y-axis

- Translation of $(x, y) \rightarrow (x - 1, y - 5)$

- Rotation of $90°$ about the origin $(0,0)$

What is the area of the ΔBCB'?

80.

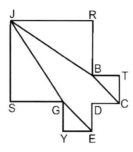

Two smaller congruent squares are attached to the larger square at the bottom right corner. Measures of sides of the larger and smaller squares are $m + n$ and $m - n$, respectively. What is the area of BCDEGJ?

(A) $2m(m - 2n)$

(B) $2m(m - n)$

(C) $2m(2m - n)$

(D) $2m(m + 2n)$

(E) $2m(m + n)$

81.

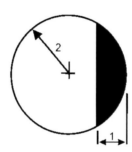

Determine the area of the shaded portion of the circle, with 1 decimal place accuracy.

Answers and Explanations

Level: Easy

1. **Sub topic: Triangles**

   The correct answers are (B) and (D).

   In the figure, $\angle CDF$ and $\angle EDB$ are vertically opposite angles. Therefore, they are of equal measure.

   $\angle CDF = \angle EDB = 80°$

   Consider ΔDEB.

   $\angle EDB = 80°$ and $\angle DEB = 40°$

   Since the three angles of a triangle add to give 180°,

   $\angle DBE = 180° - 40° - 80°$

   $= 180° - 120°$

   $= 60°$

   Consider the cyclic quadrilateral GEBC. Opposite angles of a quadrilateral add to 180°.

   $\angle CGE + \angle CBE = 180°$

   $\angle A + \angle CBE = 180°$

   $\angle A = 180° - 60° = 120°$

   Among the options, statements B and D give the measure of $\angle A$ correctly.

2. **Sub topic: Quadrilaterals**

   The correct answer is (C).

   Since two sides of the squares BEFG and IJHK have common portion on their left sides, then their horizontal sides are parallel. It follows that KH and GF are parallel. On the other hand, KH is drawn from the midpoint of CF. These two conditions imply that KH bisects the other side as well. This conclusion relies on the following principle:

   If a segment joining two midpoints of sides in a triangle is parallel to the other side and is one-half this side. Also, if a segment drawn from the midpoint of a side parallel to the second side, then it bisects the third side.

   So, using the principle

   (1) $KH = \dfrac{GF}{2}$

   The area of IJKH is given as 9. Taking square root of the area gives the measure of a side as 3. That is,

   (2) KH = 3

   Replace (2) in (1)

   $3 = \dfrac{GF}{2}$

   Cross multiply this equation.

   (3) GF = 6

   Since BEFG is a square, it implies BG = GF. Applying (3) to this equation gives us

   (4) BG = 6

We are given a side of the square ABCD as twice as a side of the square BEFG. This means that BC is as twice as BG or CG, or G is the midpoint of BC. That is,

(5) BC = 2BG

Replace the value of BG from (4) in (5) and simplify.

BC = 2(6)

BC = 12

Then

Area of square ABCD = (BC)

$= (12)^2$

$= 144$

So, the correct answer is (C).

3. **Sub topic: Circles**

   The correct answer is (C).

   The opposite angles in a quadrilateral inscribed in a circle are supplementary.

   That means that $m\angle ABC + m\angle ADC = 180°$

   $m\angle ADC = 180° - 80° = 100°$

   $m\angle ADC - 10° = 100° - 10° = 90°$

   If BD is the circle's diameter − ΔBAD and ΔBCD are both right angle triangles with the hypotenuse being BD − $m\angle BAD = 90°$

   $m\angle ADC - 10° = m\angle BAD = 90°$, hence the correct answer is (C).

4. **Sub topic: Circles/Triangles**

   The correct answers are (B) and (D).

   By the property of circles, we know that the angle formed at the center is twice the angle formed at the circumference. Therefore $\angle AOB = 2 \times \angle ACB$

   Hence, $\angle AOB = 2 \times 70° = 140°$

   OB and OA are the radii of the circle.

   OB = OA

   Hence, ΔOAB is an isosceles triangle and $\angle OAB = \angle OBA$

   By the triangle sum property, $\angle OAB + \angle OBA + \angle AOB = 180°$

   But, $\angle OBA = \angle OAB$

   Hence, $\angle OAB + \angle OAB + 140° = 180°$

   $2 \times \angle OAB = 180° - 140°$

   $\angle OAB = 20° = \angle OBA$

   Therefore, the value of the $\angle x$ is 20°.

   Among the options, statements B and D give the current measure of $\angle x$.

5. **Sub topic: Triangles**

   The correct answer is (E).

   In a triangle, the exterior angle is equal to the sum of two remote interior angles. Applying this principle to the exterior angle of the upper triangle, we obtain

$125 = m + 95$

Subtract 95 from each side, and simplify

$m = 125 - 95$

$m = 30°$

The sum of interior angles in any triangle is 180°. In the upper triangle,

$m + n + 95 = 180$

Replace the value of m in this equation and solve for n.

$30 + n + 95 = 180$

$n + 125 = 180$

$n + 125 - 125 = 180 - 125$

$n = 55$

Thus, the sum of two angles at the end of the horizontal side of the upper triangle is $m + n = 55 + 30 = 85$. We are given, the sum of the corresponding angles to these angles in the lower triangle less than 85. Denote these angles by x and y. Then

$m + n > x + y$

$(1)\ 85 > x + y$

Using the angle sum postulate in the lower triangle

$a + x + y = 180$

Subtract a from each side of this equation and cancel out the opposite sides.

$a + x + y - a = 180 - a$

$(2)\ x + y = 180 - a$

Replace the equivalent of $x + y$ from (2) in (1)

$85 > 180 - a$

Add $(a - 85)$ to each side of this equation and simplify.

$85 + a - 85 > 180 - a + a - 85$

$a > 95$

6. **Sub topic: Quadrilaterals**

   The correct answer is (A).

   By definition, a quadrilateral is a kite if and only if it has two pairs of consecutive congruent sides. Further, only one pair of opposite angles is congruent, not both.

   A trapezoid may have exactly one pair of consecutive congruent sides. In the special case of an isosceles trapezoid, the base angles are congruent.

   Neither kites nor trapezoids have four congruent sides or congruent diagonals. The sum of all angle is not 180^0 in kites and trapezoids.

   Hence, the title X can only be 'Two pairs of consecutive congruent sides'.

7. The correct answer is (B).

   B. First, draw a line segment from point R perpendicular to QS. This is the altitude of triangle QRS, and it must be less than 4. The formula for the area of a triangle is $\frac{1}{2} \times$ base $\times$ height. The base is 12, and if the height were 4, the area would be 24. Since the height is actually less than 4, the area must be less than 24. You don't have to find the actual value of area, though. Whatever the area is, the perimeter (the sum of all this sides) is 27. Quantity B is bigger regardless of the exact value of Quantity A.

8. **Sub topic: Polygons**

The correct answer is 443°.

We know the formula to determine the sum of interior angles of a polygon is $(S = (n - 2)180)$

Number of sides in a Pentagon $= 5$

Sum of interior angles $= (5 - 2)180 = 3(180) = 540°$

Now we have the following equation:

$a + b + c + 97 + 90 = 540$

$a + b + c + 187 = 540$

$a + b + c = 353$

To calculate the value of y:

$90 + y = 180$

$y = 90$

Now we can calculate the value of the expression.

$a + b + c + y = 353 + 90 = 443°$

The sum is 443°.

9. **Sub topic: Triangles/Lines & Angles**

The correct answers are (B), (C) and (E).

If IJ ∥ KL, then we have two similar triangles. To determine which angles are similar, we need to match the corresponding angles when we write the similarity statement.

Since the intersection of the two lines form a point of intersection at M, we know ∠IMJ ≅ ∠LMK because they are vertical angles. Statement B is true.

Since IJ ∥ KL, we also know that the sets of alternate interior angles are also congruent.

The two pairs of alternate interior angles are: ∠JIM ≅ ∠KLMand. ∠IJM ≅ ∠LKM This means that statement A is false and statement E is true. Now we can write a similarity statement: ΔKLM∼ΔJIM

Statement D is false because it states that the two triangles are congruent not similar.

Since two triangles are similar, we know the sides are proportional between the two triangles.

If we compare the top triangle to the bottom triangle: $\dfrac{KL}{JI} = \dfrac{LM}{IM} = \dfrac{KM}{JM}$

If we compare the bottom triangle to the top triangle: $\dfrac{JI}{KL} = \dfrac{IM}{LM} = \dfrac{JM}{KM}$

Statement C is true and has a correctly written proportion. Statement F is false because the proportion is incorrectly written.

The true statements are B, C, E.

10. **Sub topic: Polygons**

The correct answer is (C).

Draw a hexagon and see how many pentagons can be drawn inside the hexagon.

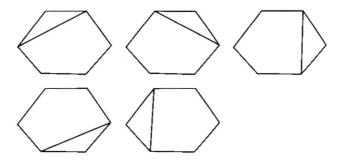

5 different pentagons can be made out of a hexagon.

The answer is C.

11. **Sub topic: Quadrilaterals**

The correct answer is (B).

The area of the trapezoid $= \dfrac{4(4 + 6)}{2} = 20$.

The area of the parallelogram $= 4 \times 6 = 24$.

12. **Sub topic: Circles**

The correct answer is 8m.

The area of a circle is πr^2. Area varies as the square of the radius. If the area becomes 8 times, the radius, and thus the diameter, becomes $\sqrt{8}$ times or $2\sqrt{2}$ times. The diameter of another circle having 8 times the area of the first circle becomes $2\sqrt{2} \times 2\sqrt{2} = 8$m.

13. **Sub topic: Polygons**

The correct answers are (B) and (D).

Total length of the fence will be $\dfrac{1600}{5} = 320$ meters.

This will equal to the perimeter of the square field, so length of one side will be $\dfrac{320}{4} = 80$ meters.

14. **Sub topic: Triangles/Lines & Angles**

The correct answers are (B) and (C).

∠1 and ∠4 are supplementary angles then ∠4 will be $180° − 124° = 56°$.

As sum of all three angle of a triangle is 180^0 then ∠3 will be $180° − (56° + 46°) = 78°$

15. **Sub topic: Triangles**

The correct answer is (B).

The sum of any two sides must be greater than the third side to form a triangle. Since LMN forms a triangle, M + L > N.

16. **Sub topic: Polygons**

The correct answer is (E).

The sum of the exterior angles of a polygon is $360°$. N represents the number of sides in the polygon. A represents the angle measure of one exterior angle.

AN = 360

(12)(N) = 360

N = 30

Therefore, the polygon is a 30-gon.

The answer is (E).

17. **Sub topic: Circles**

The correct answers are (A), (B), (C) and (D).

Find the radius of each disc using the formula: $C = 2\pi r$

A: $\pi = 2\pi r \rightarrow r = \frac{1}{2}$ B: $10\pi = 2\pi r \rightarrow r = 5$ C; $12\pi = 2\pi r \rightarrow r = 6$

D: $20\pi = 2\pi r \rightarrow r = 10$ E: $50\pi = 2\pi r \rightarrow r = 25$

Find the area of each disc using the formula: $A = \pi r^2$

A: $A = \pi\left(\frac{1}{2}\right)^2 = \frac{\pi}{4} \approx 0.79$ B: $A = \pi(5)^2 = 25\pi \approx 78.54$ C: $A = \pi(6)^2 = 36\pi \approx 113.1$

D: $A = \pi(10)^2 = 100\pi \approx 314.16$ E: $A = \pi(25)^2 = 625\pi \approx 1,963.46$

The answers are A, B, C, D.

18. **Sub topic: Circles**

The correct answer is $21 m^2$.

Length of each side of the square is equal to the diameter of the radius that is

Area of square will be $10 \times 10 = 100 \ m^2$

Area of the circle will be $3.142 \times 52 = 78.55 \ m^2$

Area of shaded region = Area of square − Area of the circle = $21.45 \ m^2$, which in two significant digits is 21.

19. **Sub topic: Polygons**

The correct answers are (B) and (D).

Let width $= x$

Then length $= 2x - 3$

Perimeter $= 2(x + 2x - 3) = 6x - 6$

According to the condition,

$6x - 6 = 96$

$x = 17$cm

Width $= 17$cm and length $= 31$cm

20. **Sub topic: Coordinate Geometry**

The correct answer is (E).

The distance formula, derived from the Pythagorean theorem, is $d = \sqrt{(x_1 - x_2)^2 + (y_1 - y_2)^2}$, where

$x_1 - x_2$ and $y_1 - y_2$ are the lengths of the legs of the right triangle and d is the length of the hypotenuse.

The difference in x-values is $-3 - 4 = -7$

The difference in y-values is $-11 - 13 = -24$

At this point you may realize that $7 - 24 - 25$ is a Pythagorean triple and d is thus equal to 25. Otherwise, substitute these values in the formula and solve for d.

$$d = \sqrt{(-7)^2 + (-24)^2}$$

$$d = \sqrt{49 + 576}$$

$$d = \sqrt{625}$$

$$d = 25$$

21. **Sub topic: Quadrilaterals**

    The correct answer is (A).

    The area of the top figure is $\dfrac{2h(b+5)}{2} = hb + 5h$.

    The area of the bottom figure is $\dfrac{h(2b+5)}{2} = hb + \left(\dfrac{5}{2}\right)h$.

    So, the correct answer is (A).

22. **Sub topic: Lines & Angles**

    The correct answer is (C).

    The slope of a line perpendicular to the line of slope m is $-\dfrac{1}{m}$

23. **Sub topic: Triangles/Circles**

    The correct answer is (D).

    Find the area of the triangle and subtract it from the area of the circle to find the area of the shaded region.

    Area of the triangle:

    Since leg OB and OA are also radii we know they are equal. An isosceles right triangle is a $45° - 45° - 90°$ triangle. The ratio of the sides of an isosceles triangle is $1:1:\sqrt{2}$, thus we know the length of the OB and OA are 8.

    $$A_{triangle} = \dfrac{bh}{2} = \dfrac{(8)(8)}{2} = \dfrac{64}{2} = 32$$

    The radius of the circle is the length of OB and OA: $r = 8$

    $$A_{circle} = \pi r^2 = \pi \times 8^2 = 64\pi$$

    Area of shaded region:

    $64\pi - 32$

24. **Sub topic: Circles**

    The correct answer is (A).

    The area of the left sector is $\left(\dfrac{x}{2}\right)(2r)^2 = 2r^2x$.

    The area of the right one is $\left(\dfrac{2x}{2}\right)r^2 = r^2x$

25. **Sub topic: Quadrilaterals/Three-Dimensional Figures**

    The correct answer is (D).

Because the sides of a square are equal you can determine the length of the side by dividing the perimeter by 4, $32 \div 4 = 8$. The SA of a sphere with a radius of 8 is:

$$SA_{sphere} = 4\pi r^2$$

$$SA_{sphere} = 4\pi \times 8^2$$

$$SA_{sphere} = 4\pi(64)$$

$$SA_{sphere} = 256\pi$$

26. **Sub topic: Triangles/Quadrilaterals**

    The correct answers are (B) and (C).

    Area of $\Delta AED = 12 = \frac{1}{2}(6)(x) \rightarrow x = 4$

    $z^2 = 3^2 + 4^2 \rightarrow z = 5$

27. **Sub topic: Triangles**

    The correct answer is (D).

    To find the area you need to know the base and height. If the perimeter is 16, then $AB + BC + AC = 16$; that is, $AB = 16 - 5 - 6 = 5$. Since $AB = BC$, this is an isosceles triangle. If you drop a line from a vertex B to AC, it will divide the base in half. This divides up the triangle into two smaller right triangles:

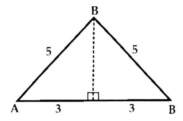

    These right triangles each have one leg of 3 and a hypotenuse of 5; therefore, they are $3 - 4 - 5$ right triangles. So, the missing leg (which is also the height of ΔABC) must have length 4. We now know that the base of ABC is 6 and the height is 4, so the area is $\frac{1}{2} \times 6 \times 4$, or 12, answer choice (D).

28. **Sub topic: Lines & Angles**

    The correct answer is 135°.

    Angles 1 and 2 are supplementary angles, if $\angle 1$ is 45° then $\angle 2 = 180° - 45° = 135°$

29. **Sub topic: Triangles**

    The correct answer is (C).

    $BD = CD$, $\angle CBD = \angle C = 19°$

    Therefore, $\angle BDC = 180° - (\angle CBD + \angle C)$

    $= 180° - (19° + 19°)$

    $= 180° - 38° = 142°$

    Then $\angle BDA = 180° - \angle BDC = 180° - 142° = 38°$

    Since $AB = AD$, $\angle ABD = \angle BDA = 38°$

Therefore, $\angle A = 180° - (\angle BDA + \angle ABD)$

$= 180° - (38° + 38°)$

$= 180° - 76° = 104°$

The correct answer is C.

30. **Sub topic: Circles**

The correct answer is (B).

The top figure contains two half-circles, as well as section a, as below. The bottom figure contains two half-circles, section a, and section b as below. The correct answer is B.

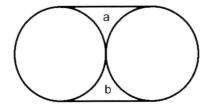

Level: Medium

31. **Sub topic: Angles/Triangles**

The correct answer is (D).

Apply the Angle Sum Postulate to each triangle.

(1) $a + m + b = 180°$

m and n are vertical angles with respect to two angles of the second triangle from left. So, we can replace the two unknown angles in the second triangle from the left with their vertical equivalents m, and n

(2) $c + m + n = 180°$

The sum of the interior angles in the third triangle from the left is expressed below:

(3) $n + p + f = 180°$

In the triangle to the right, one angle is vertical to p. Thus, the sum of the interior angles for this triangle will be as follows:

(4) $d + p + e = 180°$

Add (1) through (4).

$a + m + b + c + m + n + n + p + f + d + p + e = 180° + 180° + 180° + 180°$

(5) $a + b + c + d + e + f + 2(m + n + p) = 720°$

Replace the given value of $(m + n + p) = 200$ in this equation and simplify.

$a + b + c + d + e + f + 2(200) = 720°$

$a + b + c + d + e + f + 400 = 720°$

$a + b + c + d + e + f + 400 - 400 = 720° - 400°$

$a + b + c + d + e + f = 320°$

32. **Sub topic: Triangles**

The correct answer is (A).

Consider the plane whose boundaries are limited to OQ, QT, TV, and OV. This plane is a rectangle in which W

and *X* are the midpoints of two opposite sides.

Since the midline *WX* joins the midpoints of two opposite sides it is perpendicular to both sides; that is, angle *QXW* measures 90°. Now, we proceed to investigate the feature of the right Δ*QWX*. We know that in any right triangle the hypotenuse is longer than any leg. In this triangle, *WQ* is the hypotenuse and *WX* is a leg; therefore, *QW* is longer than *WX* and *QW* > *WX*.

The correct answer choice is (A).

33. **Sub topic: Polygons**

The correct answers are (C) and (D).

Let us plot all the points on the coordinate plane.

The point A is the origin on the coordinate plane.

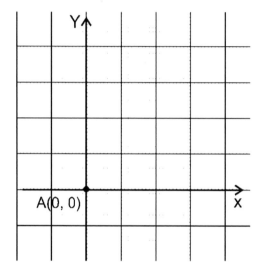

The point B has its *x* coordinate = 0, that shows it lies somewhere on the *y*-axis.

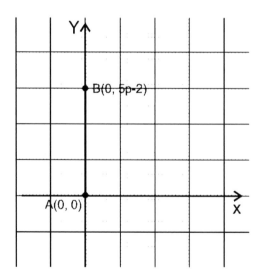

∠ABC = 90°, then ΔABC will look like:

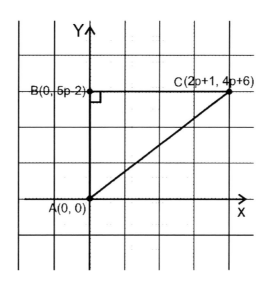

Since line BC is horizontal, the y coordinates of point B and C will be equal.

$5p - 2 = 4p + 6$

$5p - 4p = 6 + 2$

$p = 8$

Substituting the value of p to find the coordinates of B and C:

$B(0, 5p - 2)$

y coordinate of B $= 5 \times 8 - 2 = 40 - 2 = 38$

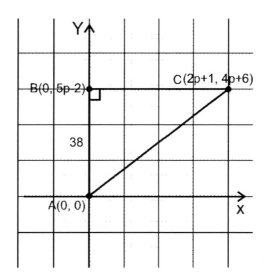

Similarly, $C(2p + 2, 4p + 6)$

x coordinate of C $= 2 \times 8 + 2 = 16 + 2 = 18$

y coordinate of C $= 4 \times 8 + 6 = 32 + 6 = 38$

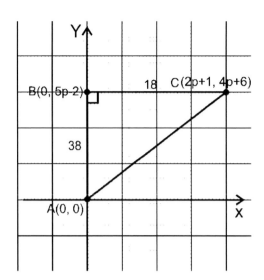

Area of Triangle $= \dfrac{base \times height}{2}$

Area of $\angle ABC = \dfrac{18 \times 38}{2} = 9 \times 38 = 342$

Options C and D are correct.

34. **Sub topic: Lines & Angles/Polygons**

The correct answer is (D).

In the figure

$x + a = 180°$

$y + b = 180°$

Adding these equations, we obtain

$x + y + a + b = 180° + 180° = 360°$

Having the value of $x + y$, then we can find $a + b$ using the equation above. To find $x + y$ as the sum of the measures of two interior angles of a pentagon, we need the sum of the measures of the other interior angles, m, n, and p. The given statements provide the values of m and n. The value of p is still unknown. Thus, to solve the problem, the given conditions are not sufficient. So, the correct answer choice is (D).

35. **Sub topic: Circles**

The correct answer is (E).

From the figure, we realize that CF is an arc from a circle whose diameter is AF and whose center is at E. The circumference of the circle E is four times the length of the arc CF according to the given fact. If we multiply the length of arc CF by 4, it gives us the circumference of the circle E.

Circumference of Circle E = 4[Length of arc (CF)]

$= 4(3\pi)$

$= 12\pi$

If we divide the circumference of the circle E by π, the result is the diameter of the circle.

Diameter of Circle E $= \dfrac{12\pi}{\pi}$

$= 12$

Now, we have a diameter of the circle E, then we can calculate the length of the semicircle ALF.

Length of Semicircle ALF $= \dfrac{\text{Circumference of Circle E}}{2}$

$= \dfrac{\pi(12)}{2}$

$= 6\pi$

The radius of the circle F is equal to the diameter of the circle E. Thus,

Radius of Circle F = AF

Doubling AF gives a diameter of the circle F.

Diameter of Circle F = 2(AF)

$= 2(12)$

$= 24$

Having a diameter of the circle F, calculate its circumference.

Circumference of Circle F $= \pi(24)$

$= 24\pi$

Length of the arc AGD is $\dfrac{3}{4}$ the circumference of the circle F. Therefore,

Length of arc AGD $= \dfrac{3}{4}(24\pi)$

$= 18\pi$

From the given figure,

Perimeter of the figure AGDFLA = Length of arc AGD + DF + Length of Semicircle ALF

Replace the measure of each arc in the equation above, knowing that DF is a radius of the circle F and is found to be 12.

Perimeter of the figure AGDFLA $= 18\pi + 12 + 6\pi$

$= 24\pi + 12$

36. **Sub topic: Polygons**

The correct answers are (A) and (C).

In a polygon with 'n' vertices, the number of lines that can be drawn is given by

$$n_{C_2} = \dfrac{n(n-1)}{2}$$

In any polygon, a diagonal is a straight line which does not connect adjacent vertices. In a polygon with 'n' vertices, there are 'n' lines connecting adjacent vertices.

Hence, the number of diagonals in any polygon $= \dfrac{n(n-1)}{2} - n$

$\dfrac{n^2 - 3n}{2} = 54$

$n^2 - 3n = 108$

$n^2 - 3n - 108 = 0$

$(n-12)(n+9) = 0$

$n - 12 = 0 \text{ or } n + 9 = 0$

$n = 12 \text{ or } n = -9$

$n = -9$ is inadmissible. Hence, the polygon has 12 sides.

Among the options, statements A and C give the number of diagonals of the polygon.

37. **Sub topic: Lines & Angles/Triangles**

    The correct answer is (C).

    Let's use both statements. Here are the given statements:

    $x - y = 20°$

    $z - x = 20°$

    Add the equations and cancel the opposite terms.

    (1) $z - y = 40°$

    From the figure, using the property of exterior angle in a triangle

    (2) $z = m\angle A + y$

    Subtract y from each side of (2).

    (3) $m\angle A = z - y$

    Replace the value of $z - y$ from (A1) in (3).

    $A = 40°$

38. **Sub topic: Three-Dimensional Figures**

    The correct answer is (C).

    Length of the arc of the sector = the circumference of the base of the cone

    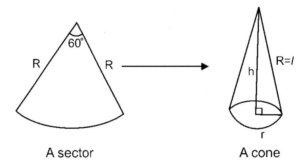

    A sector   A cone

    Taking R to be the radius of the circle where the sector is extracted and r to be the radius of the base of the cone, we have

    Length of the arc of the sector = the circumference of the base of the cone

    That is,

    $$\frac{60}{360} \times \pi \times 2R = \pi \times 2r$$

    Dividing both sides by 2π, we have

    $$r = \frac{60}{360}R = \frac{60}{360} \times 9 = \frac{3}{2} \text{inches}$$

    The radius of the sector = the slant height of the cone

    The perpendicular height h, slant height l, and the radius of the cone r forms a right-angle triangle where the slant height is the hypotenuse.

    Using the Pythagorean Theorem, perpendicular height $= \sqrt{9^2 - 1.5^2} = \sqrt{78.75} = 8.874$

    Volume $= \left(\frac{1}{3}\right) \times \pi \times \left(\frac{3}{2}\right)^2 \times 8.874 = 20.909 \approx 21$ cubic inches

39. **Sub topic: Coordinate Geometry**

The correct answer is (B).

ΔABC is an isosceles right triangle with hypotenuse $BC \rightarrow AC$ and AB are perpendicular

AB has a slope of 0 (slope $= \dfrac{(2-2)}{(b-1)} = \dfrac{0}{(b-1)} = 0) \rightarrow AB$ is parallel to x-axis

$\rightarrow AC$ must be parallel to y-axis $\rightarrow C(c, 6) = C(1, 6)$ because c must be 1 to match with $A(1,2)$

ΔABC is isosceles with hypotenuse $BC \rightarrow AC = AB$

We use the coordinates of the points and the definition of the distance between the points, to rewrite the above as:

$$\sqrt{(1-c)^2 + (2-6)^2} = \sqrt{(b-1)^2 + (2-2)^2} \rightarrow \sqrt{(1-1)^2 + 16} = \sqrt{(b-1)^2}$$

$b - 1 = 4 \rightarrow b = 5$

$AC = AB = 4$

Using the same the definition of the distance between the points:

$$BC = \sqrt{(b-c)^2 + (2-6)^2} = \sqrt{(5-1)^2 + 16} = \sqrt{2 \times 16} = 4\sqrt{2}$$

AD is perpendicular to $BC \rightarrow$ Area of ΔABC can be calculated as $\dfrac{(AD \times BC)}{2}$ but because the triangle is also a right

triangle the Area is also equal to $\dfrac{AB \times AC}{2} \rightarrow AD = \dfrac{AB \times AC}{BC}$

$AD = \dfrac{(4 \times 4)}{4\sqrt{2}} = \dfrac{4}{\sqrt{2}} = 2\sqrt{2}.$

40. **Sub topic: Polygons**

The correct answers are (B) and (D).

The measure of each interior angle of a regular polygon $= \dfrac{(n-2) \times 180°}{n}$

Hence,

$\dfrac{(n-2) \times 180°}{n} = 135°$

$\dfrac{(n-2)}{n} = \dfrac{135°}{180°}$

$\dfrac{(n-2)}{n} = \dfrac{3}{4}$

$4(n-2) = 3n$

$4n - 3n = 8$

$n = 8$

Therefore, the number of sides is 8.

The sum of all the interior angles of a regular polygon $= (n-2) \times 180°$

We have $n = 8$

Hence, $(8-2) \times 180°$

$= 6 \times 180°$

$= 1080°$

Among the options, statements B and D give the sum of all interior angles in the polygon.

41. **Sub topic: Circles**

The correct answer is (B).

First, we need to find the measurement of the four sides of the square. The side length is the square root of 256 is 16. Then, according to the figure, this is also the sum of the diameters of two circles, which means the diameter of each circle is $\frac{1}{2} \times 16 = 8$ and the radius is 4. Next, we find the area of each circle: $A = r^2\pi = 4^2\pi = 16\pi$. The total area of the four circles is $4 \times 16\pi = 64\pi$. Therefore, the area of the grey regions is the difference between the area of the square and the areas of the circles: $256 - 64\pi \approx 54.94$. This is smaller than $300 - 50\pi, \approx 142.92$.

This means B is the correct answer.

42. **Sub topic: Coordinate Geometry**

The correct answer is (C).

One approach would be to calculate the slopes of lines AB and AC to see if their product equals -1 in which case the lines would be perpendicular

The slope of AB is $\dfrac{2\sqrt{3} - 0}{2 - 4} = -\sqrt{3}$

The slope of AC is $\dfrac{2\sqrt{3} - 0}{2 - 0} = -\sqrt{3}$

The product of the slopes is -3, which means the lines cannot be perpendicular. Option E is definitely wrong.

Next, we can calculate the length of the triangle sides to see if that gives a helpful indication.

$AB = \sqrt{(4 - 2)^2 + (0 - 2\sqrt{3})^2} = \sqrt{4 + 12} = 4$

$AC = \sqrt{(0 - 2)^2 + (0 - 2\sqrt{3})^2} = \sqrt{4 + 12} = 4$

$BC = \sqrt{(4 - 0)^2 + (0 - 0)^2} = \sqrt{16 + 0} = 4$

$AB = AC = BC$

$\triangle ABC$ is equilateral; all angles in $\triangle ABC = 60°$, including $\angle BAC$, which is answer (C).

43. **Sub topic: Triangles/Polygons**

The correct answers are (A), (C) and (G).

In the polygon ABCDE, we have a pentagon. The sum of the interior angles in a polygon is dictated by the following equation. $S = (n - 2)180$

Number of sides in a Pentagon = 5

Sum of interior angles = $(5 - 2)180 = 3(180) = 540°$

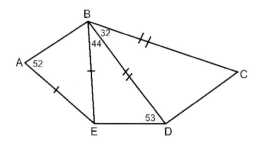

To determine if the statements are true, we need to first find the missing angles.

ΔABE is an isosceles triangle, so therefore ∠ABE is also 52°. The sum of the interior angles in the triangle should equal180°Now we can calculate the ∠AEB.

∠EAB + ∠ABE + ∠BEA = 180°

52° + 52° + ∠BEA = 180°

104° + ∠BEA = 180°

∠BEA = 76°

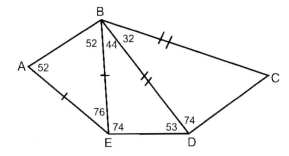

ΔBCD is also an isosceles triangle. Therefore ∠BCDand ∠BDC are congruent.

∠DBC + ∠BDC + ∠BCD = 180°

32° + ∠BDC + ∠BCD = 180°

∠BDC + ∠BCD = 148°

∠BDC = 74°

∠BCD = 74°

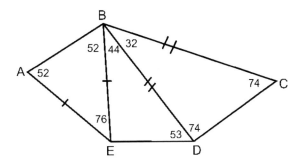

Now we can find the missing angle: ∠BED

∠BED + ∠EDB + ∠DBE = 180°

∠BED + 53° + 44° = 180°

∠BED + 97° = 180°

∠BED = 83°

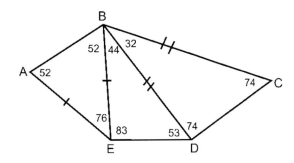

Now we can address the statements:

A. AB is the longest side of ΔABE.

This statement is true because the angle opposite is the largest angle in the triangle.

B. BE is the shortest side of ΔEBD.

This statement is false because this side is opposite the 53°angle, and there is a smaller angle in the triangle.

C. ∠EBD = 44°

This statement is true.

D. ΔBED is an isosceles triangle.

ΔBED is not an isosceles triangle because all three sides are different lengths.

E. ∠BCD = 78°

This statement has been proven false.

F. The sum of all interior angles of the pentagon is 720°.

This statement is false.

G. BD is the longest side of ΔBCD.

This statement is true. It is one of the longest sides of the triangle. It is the side opposite the greatest angle in the triangle.

44. **Sub topic: Triangles**

The correct answer is (A).

In order to solve this question, you would need to know some rules of triangles and use logical reasoning. First, we know right way ∠a + ∠b + 60 = 180. We also know the triangles is not an equilateral or an isosceles triangle since AC > AB, and c = 60. This means that ∠b must be greater than ∠c = 60.So, we can eliminate choice (C). Since ∠b > 60 angle a must be less than 60. The rule of triangles states that, the side opposite the largest angle is the longest side, and the side opposite the smallest angle is the shortest side. Therefore BC, AB, AC are the sides of the triangle in order of smallest to largest and the correct answer is A.

Note: The difficulty with this question is, without knowing these properties of triangles, student would think it is not determinable.

45. **Sub topic: Lines & Angles**

The correct answer is (C).

As a rule, for all geometry questions it may be necessary to either redraw the diagram/ add lines/labels etc. We are aware of rules for parallel & transverse lines. Thus, we will have to create a similar situation. This is achieved by drawing a line EF which is parallel to both AB & CD as shown. Now ∠CEF = 4*x*°(Corresponding angles, CD ∥ EF, CE is the transverse) and ∠AEF = 6*x*°. Thus 130° = 10*x*° and *x* =13

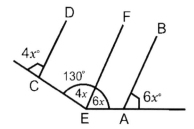

Note: If we do not pay close attention to the fact that AEC is NOT a straight line we may be tempted to say 6*x*° = 180−130, and *x* = 8.33 OR 4*x*° =180−130, and *x* = 12.5. Once again it always helps to redraw the diagram provided to you. Remember it may not be the best representation of what you need.

46. **Sub topic: Polygons**

The correct answers are (C) and (D).

Let x be the width and y be the length

Perimeter $= 2x + 2y = 20$

$x = 10 - y$

Area $= xy = 24$

Putting the value of x

$y(10 - y) = 24$

$10y - y^2 = 24$

$y^2 - 10y + 24 = 0$

$(y - 6)(y - 4) = 0$

Length will be 6 cm and width will be 4 cm.

47. **Sub topic: Circles**

The correct answer is (A).

To solve this question, we need to know how to find the angle given the arc length and how to calculate area given the angle. Since the radius is 4, the diameter is 8 and the circumference of the circle is 8π. Therefore, ratio of arc $\dfrac{BOC}{Cir} = \dfrac{3\pi}{8\pi} = \dfrac{3}{8}$, which means $\dfrac{\angle BOC}{360°} = \dfrac{3}{8} \times 360 = \dfrac{3}{8} = 135°$. Therefore, $\angle AOB + \angle BOC = 135 + 60 = 195$, and $\angle AOC = 360 - 195 = 165°$. The ratio of X to the total area of the circle is $\dfrac{165}{360}$ or $\dfrac{11}{24}$. The total area of the circle is $A = r^2\pi = 4^2\pi = 16\pi$ and the area of $X = \dfrac{11}{24} \times 16\pi = \dfrac{22\pi}{3}$, which is larger than $\dfrac{21\pi}{3}$.

Therefore, the correct answer is A.

48. **Sub topic: Three-Dimensional Figures**

The correct answer is (B).

To solve this problem, we need to find out the volume of the cylinder container and the volume of the rectangular object. To find the volume of the container, we use the given equation $V = r^2\pi h = 3^2\pi(4) = 9\pi(4) = 36\pi \text{cm}^3$. The volume of the rectangular object is $V = lwh = 2 \times 1 \times 3 = 6\text{cm}^3$. This means the cylinder can now hold a maximum of $36\pi\text{-}6$ cm^3 of juice, which is approximately $113.04 - 6 = 107.04\text{cm}^3$. 2 liters $= 2000\text{cm}^3$. Since the cylinder can hold about 107.04 cm^3, there will be 92.96 cm^3 remaining in the old container. Therefore, (B) is the correct answer.

49. **Sub topic: Triangles**

The correct answer is 4.57.

From geometry, we know that the diagonals of an inscribed square are diameters of the circumscribed circle.

So, in the right ΔABC, AC$= 2(2) = 4$. Using the Pythagorean Theorem,

$(AB)^2 + (BC)^2 = (AB)^2 + (AB)^2 = 4^2 = 16$

$2(AB)^2 = 16$

$AB = \sqrt{8}$

The area of the square ABCD $= \left(\sqrt{8}\right)^2 = 8$

On the other hand, Area of circle $= \pi(2^2) = 4\pi$

Shaded area $= 4\pi - 8 \approx 4.57$(to 2 decimal places).

50. **Sub topic**: **Triangles**

The correct answer is (D).

In the figure we are going to use the ratios of the sides of a 30°-60°-90° triangle, which is $x : x\sqrt{3} : 2x$

The smaller triangle has a side length of 4 and a hypotenuse of 8.

4:h:8

$x : x\sqrt{3} : 2x$

The value of x is 4 in this triangle. Therefore, the height of the triangle is $4\sqrt{3}$. The length of the base is $4 + 4\sqrt{3}$

If we use the formula for the area of triangle, we can calculate the area of the triangle.

$A = \dfrac{1}{2}bh = \dfrac{1}{2}\left(4 + 4\sqrt{3}\right)\left(4\sqrt{3}\right)$

$A = \dfrac{1}{2}\left(16\sqrt{3} + 16\sqrt{9}\right) = \dfrac{1}{2}\left(16\sqrt{3} + 48\right)$

$A = 8\sqrt{3} + 24$

The answer is D.

51. **Sub topic**: **Triangles/Quadrilaterals/Circles**

The correct answers are (A), (C) and (D).

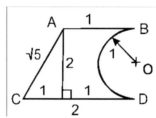

$\overline{AC} = \sqrt{1^2 + 2^2} = \sqrt{5}$

Height of trapezoid ABDC = diameter of semicircle = 2

Area of trapezoid ABDC $= \dfrac{1}{2}(2 + 1)(2) = 3$

Area of semicircle $= \left(\dfrac{1}{2}\right)\pi$

Shaded area $= 3 - \dfrac{\pi}{2} = 1.429$

Perimeter of shaded area $= \sqrt{5} + 2 + \pi + 1 = 8.38$

Answers: (A), (C), (D)

52. **Sub topic**: **Triangles**

The correct answer is (A).

$b = \sqrt{4^2 + 3^2} = \sqrt{25} = 5$

$a = \sqrt{7^2 + 3^2} = \sqrt{58}$

The correct answer is (A), $5 + \sqrt{58}$

53. **Sub topic: Circles/Triangles**

The correct answers are (B) and (D).

Because AB is tangent to the circle, $\angle OAB = 90°$. Similarly, $\angle ODC = 90°$,

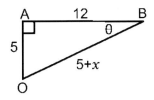 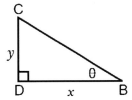

$(5 + x)^2 = 5^2 + 12^2 \rightarrow 5 + x = \sqrt{169} = 13 \rightarrow x = 8$

$\tan(\theta) = \dfrac{5}{12} = \dfrac{y}{8} \rightarrow y = \dfrac{10}{3}$

Answers: (B), (D)

54. **Sub topic: Lines & Angles/Triangles**

The correct answer is (A).

In order to solve this question, we need to figure out what conditions are given first. There are three triangles encased in this rectangle, each one has sum of internal angles of $180°$.

Since 2X and Z are alternate interior angles to the diagonal that bisects the rectangle, they are congruent, and $2X = Z$. We also know that $C = 90 - Z$ and $2Z + 4Y = 180$ because they create a straight angle, therefore, $Z = 90 - 2Y$

Then, we can find the measurement of A, where:

$A = 180 - 2X - 2Z$ and $A = 90 - 2Y \rightarrow 2Y = 90 - A$

$A = 180 - 2X - 4X = 180 - 6X$, substitute this into:

$2Y = 90 - (180 - 6X) = -90 + 6X = 6X - 90, \rightarrow Y = 3X - 45$

The sum of the interior angles in the upper triangle has an equation of $2Y + 4Y + C = 180$, therefore, $180 = 2Y + 4Y + 90 - Z \rightarrow 180 = 6Y + 90 - (90 - 2Y) \rightarrow 180 = 8Y \rightarrow Y = 22.5$

Now that we know the value of Y we can find the value of X

$22.5 = 3X - 45 \rightarrow 3X = 67.5 \rightarrow X = 22.5$

Since $22.5 > 22$, the correct answer is A.

55. **Sub topic: Triangles/Lines & Angles**

The correct answer is (A).

To solve this problem, you would need

$2X = Z$ because they are alternate interior angles.

$B = 360 - 2Z - 3X - 4Y \rightarrow B = 360 - 4X - 3X - 4Y \rightarrow B = 360 - 7X - 4Y$

$A + 2X + 2Z = 180$, substitute 2X into Zx we get $A = 180 - 6X$

$C = 90 - Z \rightarrow C = 90 - 2X$

Therefore, $A + B + C = 180 + 360 + 90 - 6X - 7X - 4Y - 2X \rightarrow A + B + C = 630 - 15X - 4Y$

$3(A + C) - B + 2X - 8Y = 3(180 + 90 - 6X - 2X) - B + 2X - 8Y$

$3(A + C) - B + 2X - 8Y = 3(270 - 8X) - (360 - 7X - 4Y) + 2X - 8Y$

$3(A + C) - B + 2X - 8Y = 810 - 24X - 360 + 7X + 4Y + 2X - 8Y$

$3(A + C) - B + 2X - 8Y = 450 - 17X \mp 4Y + 2X$

$3(A + C) - B + 2X - 8Y = 450 - 15X - 4Y$

$630 - 15X - 4Y > 450 - 15X - 4Y$

Therefore, $A + B + C > 3(A + C) - B + 2X - 8Y$ and A is the correct answer.

56. **Sub topic: Coordinate Geometry**

The correct answer is (A).

First draw the triangle.

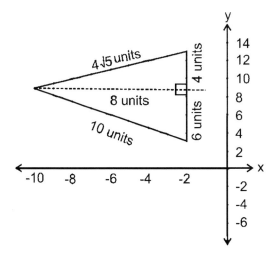

From the diagram it is easy to see that the length of the base is 10 units and the length of the height is 8 units. The height splits the triangle into two right triangles. Looking at the bottom right triangle one can see that the base of this half is 6 units and the height is 8 units, so the hypotenuse is 10 units as 6-8-10 is a Pythagorean triple. If this fact is not memorized the distance formula can be used to determine the length of the hypotenuse.

The distance formula, derived from the Pythagorean theorem, is $d = \sqrt{(x_1 - x_2)^2 + (y_1 - y_2)^2}$, where $(x_1 - x_2)$ and $(y_1 - y_2)$ are the lengths of the legs of the right triangle and d is the length of the hypotenuse.

$d = \sqrt{(8)^2 + (6)^2}$

$d = \sqrt{100}$

$d = 10$ units

Looking at the top right triangle one can see that the base is 4 and the height is 8. Using the distance formula, the length of the hypotenuse is

$d = \sqrt{(8)^2 + (4)^2}$

$d = \sqrt{80}$

$d = 4\sqrt{5} \; units$

The perimeter of the triangle is $10 + 10 + 4\sqrt{5} = 20 + 4\sqrt{5}$

After a scale factor of $\frac{3}{4}$, the perimeter becomes

$(20 + 4\sqrt{5}) \times \frac{3}{4} = 15 + 3\sqrt{5}$

57. **Sub topic**: **Circles**

The correct answer is (B).

Since AF is the tangent to the circle at B and BC is a chord of the circle from the point of contact of the circle with the tangent. Therefore, BC divides the circle into two segments called opposite segments.

∠CDB = CBF = 64° (Angle subtended by a chord in the opposite segment)

∠COB = 2 (∠CDB) = 2 × 64°= 128° (Angles at the circumference and at the center subtended on one side of the common chord)

Thus, the obtuse ∠COB = 128°

The other possibility is the reflex ∠360° − 128° = 232°

58. **Sub topic**: **Triangles/Circles**

The correct answer is (B).

∠XYZ is inscribed in a semicircle and is therefore a right angle.

Therefore, ΔXYZ is a right triangle and the Pythagorean Theorem states

$(XY)^2 = (XZ)^2 + (YZ)^2$

$(17)^2 = (XZ)^2 + (15)^2$ (XY is a diameter)

$289 = (XZ)^2 + 225$

$289 - 225 = (XZ)^2$

$(XZ)^2 = 64$

$XZ = \sqrt{64}$

$XZ = 8$

Area of ΔXYZ $= \dfrac{1}{2}bh$

$= \dfrac{1}{2}(8)(15) = 60$

The correct answer is B.

59. **Sub topic**: **Triangles**

The correct answers are (A), and (C).

From the Pythagorean Theorem $z = \sqrt{5^2 - 4^2} = 3$

Since the triangles are similar, we can calculate the variables using ratios:

$\dfrac{5.25}{4 + x} = \dfrac{3}{4} \rightarrow 3(4 + x) = (4)(5.25) \rightarrow x = 3$

$\dfrac{5.25}{5 + y} = \dfrac{3}{5} \rightarrow 3(5 + y) = (5)(5.25) \rightarrow y = 3.75$

Answers: (A), (C)

60. **Sub topic**: **Quadrilaterals**

The correct answer is (A).

Because the perimeter of the rhombus is 40, each side has length 10. Because the diagonals of a rhombus are perpendicular and bisect each other.

$x^2 + 5^2 = 10^2$

$$x^2 + 25 = 100$$

$$x^2 = 75$$

$$x = \sqrt{75}, x = 5\sqrt{3}.$$

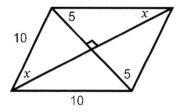

The area of a quadrilateral with perpendicular diagonals d_1 and d_2 is

$$= \frac{1}{2}d_1.d_2$$

$$= \frac{1}{2}(10)(10\sqrt{3})$$

$$= 50\sqrt{3}.$$

61. **Sub topic: Three-Dimensional Figures**

The correct answer is (C).

Math Procedure	Strategy
Height of equilateral triangular base $= \sqrt{5^2 - 2.5^2} = 4.33$	From Pythagorean Theorem, $\sqrt{(2a)^2 - a^2} = h$
Area of triangular base $= \frac{1}{2}(5)(4.33) = 10.825$	Area of triangle (Geometry)
Area of circular hole $= \pi$	Area of circle (Geometry)
Remaining area $= 10.825 - \pi = 7.684$ % remaining area (or volume) $= 100\frac{7.684}{10.825} =$ 70.98%	*Note:* The lengths of the prism and the circular bore are the same and therefore the percentage of area and volume are the same.

The correct answer is C.

62. **Sub topic: Polygons**

The correct answer is (A).

The sum of interior angles of a polygon is given by $180(n - 2)$ where n is the number of sides.

Let the polygons A and B have x and y sides respectively, then

$$180(x - 2) : 180\,(y - 2) = 4 : 5 \text{ or } \frac{x - 2}{y - 2} = \frac{4}{5}$$

$$5x - 10 = 4y - 8$$

$$5x - 4y = 2\ldots\ldots\ldots\ldots(i)$$

The sum of the sides is 13, implies $x + y = 13$.

Multiplying $x + y = 13$ by 4, we get $4x + 4y = 52$..........(ii)

Adding (i) to (ii) we get

$9x = 54$

$x = 6 ; y = 7$

The interior angle of A $= \dfrac{180(6-2)}{6} = 120°$

The interior angle of B $= \dfrac{180(7-2)}{7} = 128.57°$

Quantity A $= \dfrac{1}{6} \times 120 = 20° > \dfrac{1}{7} \times 128.57° = 18.37° = $ QuantityB

Level: Difficult

63. **Sub topic**: **Three-Dimensional Figures/Triangles/Polygons**

    The correct answer is 4π.

    Start by solving for the length of CD, which is 4, since ACD is a right triangle.

    Next, find the length of BC using the law of sines:

    $\dfrac{\sin BAC}{BC} = \dfrac{\sin ABC}{AC} \rightarrow \dfrac{\sin 25}{BC} = \dfrac{\sin 10}{5}$

    BC = 12.16

    Since BCF is a right triangle, we can solve for CF:

    $(CF)^2 + (10)^2 = (12.16)^2 \rightarrow CF = 6.91$

    We can draw a right triangle to find the height of the trapezoid:

    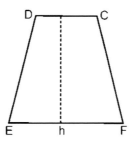

    We know ∠EFB to be 165°.Therefore, subtracting 90° (∠BFC), ∠EFC is 75°.

    $\sin 75 = \dfrac{h}{6.92} \rightarrow h = 6.68$

    Using the area of trapezoid, we can find EF:

    $33.4 = \dfrac{4 + EF}{2}(6.68) \rightarrow 10 = 4 + EF \rightarrow EF = 6$

    We know the volume of the cube to be 150, therefore:

    $5 \times 6 \times HK = 150 \rightarrow HK = 5$

    We know the volume of the cylinder to be 20π, therefore:

    $20\pi = \pi r^2 5 \rightarrow r = 2; d = 4;$ circumference$= 4\pi$

    The answer is 4π.

64. **Sub topic**: **Lines & Angles/Polygons**

    The correct answer is (B).

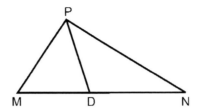

Since M, D, and N are collinear due to the statement (1) and D is the midpoint of MN by statement (2), then the segment MN is a straight-line segment, where D is an internal point between M and N, as shown in the graph below. Since only M, N, and D are given collinear in (1), therefore P is not on MN. Draw PM and PN. We know that in a triangle, the sum of two sides is greater than the third side. Hence, in ΔPDM,

(1) PD + PM > MD

Statement (2) indicates that

(2) DN = MD

Replacing DN for MD from (2) in (1), we get

$DN < PD + PM$ or PD $> DN -$ PM

Therefore, the proper answer choice is (B).

65. **Sub topic: Lines & Angles**

The correct answer is (B).

These are the distinct segments on AB:

AC, AD, AB, CD, CB, BD

We are given

(1) BC = 2AC

(2) 2BD = AD

Applying the Segment Addition Postulate to the segments included in the equations above using the figure, we have

BD + CD = 2AC

2BD = AC + CD

Add these equations sides by side.

BD + CD + 2BD= 2AC + AC + CD

CD + 3BD = CD + 3AC

Subtract CD from each side and cancel out the opposite terms.

CD + 3BD − CD = CD + 3AC − CD

3BD = 3AC

(3) BD = AC

Replace the equivalent of BD from this equation in (2).

2AC = AD

This equation indicates that C is the midpoint of AD. Thus, we do not need any extra point to label the midpoint of AD, and we can remove AD from the list of segments we provided at the beginning of the solution. So, we now have the following list of segments to look for their midpoints.

AC, AB, CD, CB, BD

Replacing the equivalent of AC from (3) in (1).

BC = 2BD

This indicates that D is the midpoint of BC. That is, we do not need extra point to label the midpoint of CD; so, we can take out BC from the list of the segments above.

AC, AB, CD, BD

AB and CD share a midpoint since AC = BD. Therefore, we can remove either AB or CD from the list.

AC, AB, BD

There is no point on the figure that represents the midpoint of any of these segments. So, to mark the midpoints of these segments, we need three points. Therefore, (B) is the correct answer.

66. **Sub topic: Triangles/Polygons**

The correct answer is (B).

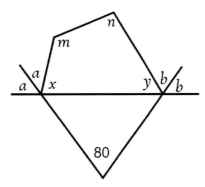

Angles a and b are vertical with two angles of the triangle. Using the angle sum postulate in a triangle, we obtain

$a + b + 80 = 180°$

Subtract 80 from each side of this equation and combine numbers on each side.

$a + b + 80 - 80 = 180° - 80°$

(1) $a + b = 100°$

In any quadrilateral, the sum of the interior angles is 360°. Applying this rule to the quadrilateral above the horizontal line we obtain

$m + n + x + y = 360°$

Subtract $x + y$ from each side of this equation and cancel out the opposite terms.

$m + n + x + y - (x + y) = 360° - (x + y)$

(2) $m + n = 360° - (x + y)$

The sum of the angles formed above the horizontal line around each point of intersection is 180. Thus,

(3) $x + a + a = 180°$

(4) $y + b + b = 180°$

Subtract $2a$ from each side of (3) and subtract $2b$ from each side of (4).

$x + a + a - 2a = 180° - 2a$

$y + b + b - 2b = 180° - 2b$

Combine the like terms on the left side of each equation.

$x = 180° - 2a$

$y = 180° - 2b$

Add these equations side by side and then factor out 2 on the right side.

(5) $x + y = 360° - 2(a + b)$

Replace (1) in (5).

(6) $x + y = 360 - 2(80) = 200°$

In any quadrilateral, the sum of the interior angles is 360°.

(7) $m + n + x + y = 360°$

Replace (6) in (7) and solve for $(m + n)$.

$m + n + 200 = 360°$

$m + n = 360° - 200°$

$= 160°$

Answer: (B).

67. **Sub topic: Triangles**

The correct answer is (C).

Since the horizontal angles of the triangles are parallel, therefore, the angle measures 30° in lower triangle and the corresponding angle in the upper triangle are alternate interior angles and are equal.

We know that two right triangles are similar if they have a pair of equal angles. Therefore, the two right triangles are similar. Write the proportion among the ratios of sides in the triangles.

$(1) \dfrac{m}{p} = \dfrac{n}{10}$

We know that if one of the angles is a right triangle is 30°, then the opposite leg is one-half the hypotenuse. So, in the larger triangle, the hypotenuse is $2 \times 10 = 20$. The other acute angle in each triangle is 60° since $30° + 60° + 90° = 180°$.

In a right triangle, the leg opposite 60° angle is $\dfrac{\sqrt{3}}{2}$, times the hypotenuse. So, in the larger triangle

$p = \dfrac{\sqrt{3}}{2}(20) = 10\sqrt{3}$

Replace the value of p in (1).

$(2) \dfrac{m}{10\sqrt{3}} = \dfrac{n}{10}$

Multiply each side by $\dfrac{10\sqrt{3}}{n}$

$\left(\dfrac{10\sqrt{3}}{n}\right)\left(\dfrac{m}{10\sqrt{3}}\right) = \left(\dfrac{10\sqrt{3}}{n}\right)\left(\dfrac{n}{10}\right)$

Reduce the product of fractions on each side.

$\dfrac{m}{n} = \sqrt{3}$

Replace the known values in $p\dfrac{m}{n}$, and simplify.

$p\left(\dfrac{m}{n}\right) = 10\sqrt{3}(\sqrt{3}) = 10(3) = 30$

68. **Sub topic: Triangles/Circles**

The correct answer is (C).

We need to find the area of all the circles using the equation $A = \pi r^2$

Circle 1: $A = \pi(16^2) = 256\pi$

Circle 2: A $= \pi(8^2) = 64\pi$

Circle 3: A $= \pi(4^2) = 16\pi$

Circle 4: A $= \pi(2^2) = 4\pi$

Circle 5: A $= \pi^2$

Total area of circles: $(256 + 64 + 16 + 4 + 1)\pi = 341\pi$

Now, we can find the total area of the triangle, which is the total areas of the circle + the grey regions= $(341 + 679)\pi = 1020\pi$.

To find the height, we use the equation for area of triangle: A $= \left(\frac{1}{2}\right)bh \rightarrow 1020\pi = \left(\frac{1}{2}\right)34\pi h \rightarrow h = 60$, so these quantities are equal, and the correct answer is C.

69. **Sub topic: Triangles**

The correct answer is 4.606.

First, the sine of $\angle$CAB can be used to determine the length of line CD.

$\sin\angle CAB = \frac{opposite}{hypotenuse}$.Line AC forms the hypotenuse in $\triangle$ACD, and the value is known, AC $= 14$. The angle of CAD is also known as 35°.

To solve: $\sin 35° = \frac{CD}{14}$

CD $= 0.5735 \times 14 = 8.03$.

Since the value of the $\angle$CAD is known as 35°, and $\angle$ADC is a right angle, $\angle$ACD $= 180° - 90° - 35° = 55°$.

Since ACB is a right angle, the value of $\angle$BCD $= 90° - 55° = 35°$.

The length of DF can now be found using the sine of $\angle$BCD.

To solve: $\sin 35° = \frac{DF}{8.03}$

DF $= 0.5735 \times 8.03 = 4.606$.

70. **Sub topic: Triangles/Quadrilaterals/Circles**

The correct answer is (B).

Find the value of DF:

$(DF)^2 = 2.32^2 + 3.86^2 - 2 \times 2.32 \times 3.86 \times \cos 77.9° \rightarrow DF = 4.07$

Now find $\angle$CDF:

$\frac{\sin 77.9}{4.07} = \frac{\sin CDF}{3.86} \rightarrow \angle CDF = 68.02° \rightarrow \angle EDF = 111.08° \rightarrow \angle DEG = 68.02° = \angle EJH$

$\tan 68.02 = \frac{EH}{4} \rightarrow EH = 9{,}91 \rightarrow$ radius of circle A $= 9.91 - 4 = 5.91 = AJ$

$\tan \angle BAC = \frac{2.68}{9.91} \rightarrow \angle BAC = 15.13°$

$AC^2 = 9.91^2 + 2.68^2 \rightarrow AC = 10.27$

The area of the square is 9.91^2, or 98.21

The area of the trapezoid ACEH is:

$\text{Area}_{ACEH} = \frac{7.23 + 9.91}{2}9.91 = 84.93$

The area of the sector ALM is:

$$\text{Area}_{ALM} = \frac{15.13}{360}\pi(5.91)^2 = 4.61$$

Area of shaded sector = 98.21 − 84.93 − 4.61 = 8.67 ≈ 8.79.76~9.8.

71. **Sub topic: Triangles/Quadrilaterals/Circles**

The correct answer is (C).

Determine the value of ∠APM using the Law of Sines:

$$\frac{\sin \angle AMP}{AP} = \frac{\sin \angle MAP}{PM} \rightarrow \frac{\sin 45}{4} = \frac{\sin \angle MAP}{3}$$

$$\frac{3\sqrt{2}}{8} = \sin \angle MAP \rightarrow \angle MAP \sim 32°, \text{ therefore } \angle APM = 180 - 45 - 32 = 130°$$

∠MPO equals 180° − 103°, or 77°, which means that ∠PMO equals 180° − 90° − 77° = 13°, therefore ∠BDL also equals 13°.

The next step is determining the radius of the circle. Since the area of EFGN is known, along with the lengths of EF and GN, we can use the area of a trapezoid to find the distance from E to D, which is also the radius of the circle.

$$\text{Area EFGN} = \frac{EF + GN}{2}ED$$

$$26 = \frac{5 + 8}{2}ED \rightarrow \frac{26}{6.5} = ED = 4$$

Since we now know the radius, we can determine the area of the sector CDI:

$$\text{Area CDI} = \frac{1}{4}\pi r^2 = \frac{\pi 16}{4} = 4\pi$$

Now find the area of the ΔBDJ:

First, find the length of the side BD by using the cosine of ∠BDL:

$$\cos \angle BDL = \frac{DL}{DB} \rightarrow \cos 13° = \frac{4}{DB} \rightarrow DB = \frac{4}{0.97} \sim 4$$

Since the ∠DBL = DBJ is known to be 77°, and the length of DB is known, we can use the tangent function to find the length of DJ:

$$\tan \angle DBJ = \frac{DJ}{DB} \rightarrow \tan 77° = \frac{DJ}{4} \rightarrow DJ = (4)(4.33) = 17.3$$

The area of ΔBDJ is therefore:

$$\text{Area } \Delta BDJ = \frac{1}{2}(DB)(DJ) = \frac{(17.3)(4)}{2} = 34.6 \sim 35$$

The area of the shaded sector is therefore:

$$35 - 4\pi \sim 22$$

72. **Sub topic: Triangles/Circles**

The correct answer is (D).

First, find the area of ΔBCD:

Length of arc BLD = $5.24 = 2(AD)\pi\left(\frac{\angle BAD}{360}\right) \rightarrow \angle BAD = 60°$

Since ABD is an equilateral triangle, BD = 5 and CD is found by:

$$\tan 60 = \frac{CD}{5} \rightarrow CD = 8.66$$

Area of ΔBCD = 0.5 × 5 × 8.66 = 21.65

Next, find the lengths of lines FG and EF using the Law of Cosines:

$(EF)^2 = 7.5^2 + 10.34^2 - 2(7.5)(10.34) \cos 27.03 \to EF = 5.15$

$(FG)^2 = 7.48^2 + 9.06^2 - 2(7.48)(9.06) \cos 33.51 \to FG = 5$

Find the angles EFK and GFH:

$\dfrac{\sin 33.51}{5} = \dfrac{\sin GFH}{9.06} \to \angle GFH = 90°$

$\dfrac{\sin 27.03}{5.15} = \dfrac{\sin EFK}{7.5} \to \angle EFK = 41.44° \to \angle HFK = 48.56°$

Next, find the length of line KH using the Law of Cosines:

$(KH)^2 = 7.48^2 + 10.34^2 - 2(7.48)(10.34) \cos 48.56 \to KH = 7.78$

Find the $\angle FKH$:

$\dfrac{\sin 48.56}{7.78} = \dfrac{\sin FKH}{7.48} \to \angle FKH = 46.12° \to \angle JKH = 106.85°$

Next, find the length of line JH using the Law of Cosines:

$(JH)^2 = 7.5^2 + 7.78^2 - 2(7.5)(7.78) \cos 106.85 \to JH = 12.27$

At this point we could find angles KJH, KHJ and JHI, but would not have enough information to solve for the area of ΔJHI. The relationship cannot be determined from the information given.

73. **Sub topic: Triangles/Polygons/Circles/ Lines & Angles**

The correct answers are (A), (C) and (E).

First, since GM and JL are known, we can find the length of GH, which is the same height as the trapezoid GJLM:

Area GJLM $= \dfrac{GM + JL}{2} GH$

$113.1 = \dfrac{24 + 13.7}{2} GH$

$GH = 6$

HJ is found using:

$\tan GJH = \dfrac{GH}{HJ}$

$\tan 60 = \dfrac{6}{HJ}$

$HJ = 3.46$

The area of ΔGHJ is $3.46 \times 6 \times 0.5 = 10.38$

The length of IK is found using proportions for similar triangles:

$\dfrac{IK}{JH} = \dfrac{IG}{HG}$

$\dfrac{IK}{3.46} = \dfrac{14}{6}$

$IK = 8.07$

The area of ΔGKI is $8.07 \times 14 \times 0.5 = 56.5$

$(GK)^2 = (14)^2 + (8.07)^2$

$GK = 16.16$

We can find the length of side KM using the law of cosines:

$(KM)^2 = (GK)^2 + (GM)^2 - 2 \times GK \times GM \times \cos KGM$

KM = 21.2

KO = 24 − 8.07 = 15.93

$$\frac{\sin KGM}{KM} = \frac{\sin GMK}{GK}$$

$$\frac{\sin 60}{21.2} = \frac{\sin GMK}{16.16}$$

∠GMK = 41.3°

∠KMO = 48.7°

∠MKO = 41.3°

Therefore, ∠MLN = 61.3°

The area of triangle

KOM = 0.5 × 15.93 × 14 = 111.51

Therefore, the area of ΔJLK = (24 × 14) − 56.5 − 111.51 − 113.1 = 54.89.

MN = 14 − NO = 14 − 5.52 = 8.48

$$\frac{\sin 61.3}{8.48} = \frac{\sin 48.7}{LN}$$

LN = 7.26

Area ΔMLN = $\frac{1}{2}$(LN)(MN) sin 70 = 28.93

Area of KLNO= 111.51 − 28.93 = 82.58

∠DFE = 10°; $\frac{\sin 10}{DE} = \frac{\sin 120}{12}$

DE = 2.4

Radius of circleD = π(2.4)² = 18.09

Radius of circleB = 0.75π(4.8)² = 54.28

Shaded area = 54.28 − 18.09 = 36.19

The area of which shapes is greater than that of the shaded area?

The answers are A, C and E.

74. **Sub topic: Triangles**

The correct answer is (B).

ABC is an equilateral triangle and AD is perpendicular to BC.

AD is the height and it splits the ΔABC into two right angle triangles (ΔABD and ΔADC) with identical areas which are equal to half of the area of ΔABC.

As per the formula for the area of an equilateral triangle, the area of ΔABC = $AC^2 \times \frac{\sqrt{3}}{4}$

$$= 6^2 \times \frac{\sqrt{3}}{4} = 9\sqrt{3}$$

The area of ΔABD = $\frac{DE \times AB}{2} = \frac{DE \times 6}{2} = DE \times 3$

We established that the area of ΔABD is also half of the area of ΔABC.

$$DE \times 3 = \frac{9\sqrt{3}}{2}$$

$$DE = \frac{9\sqrt{3}}{2 \times 3} = \frac{3\sqrt{3}}{2} = \frac{\sqrt{27}}{2}$$

Alternatively, if you do not remember the formula for the area of an equilateral triangle, you can still arrive at the correct result by using the Pythagorean Theorem (as long as you remember the formula for the area of a triangle).

ΔADC has a right angle → you can apply the Pythagorean Theorem

$AC^2 = AD^2 + DC^2$

$AD^2 = AC^2 - DC^2 = 6^2 - 3^2 = 36 - 9 = 27$

$AD = \sqrt{27}$

From here you can calculate the area of ΔABC as $\dfrac{AD \times AC}{2}$ and then follow the same steps as in the first solution.

Now that you know DE and AD, you can calculate AE applying Pythagoras' theorem in ΔADE

$AD^2 = AE^2 + DE^2$

$AE^2 = AD^2 - DE^2 = 27 - \dfrac{27}{4} = \dfrac{81}{4}$

$AE = \dfrac{9}{2}$

We can see that Δs ABD and AEF are similar. The ratio AE:AB is therefore equal to the ratio EF:BD. The ratio is $\left(\dfrac{9}{2}\right) : 6 \to EF = \dfrac{9}{4}$ which is less than $\dfrac{5}{2} \to$ the right column is greater than the left column, hence (B) is the correct answer.

75. Sub topic: Circles

The correct answer is (C).

Determine the radius of the large circle using the Law of Sines:

$\dfrac{\sin \angle BAC}{BC} = \dfrac{\sin \angle ACB}{AB} \to \dfrac{\sin \angle BAC}{4} = \dfrac{\sin 20}{2}$

$\sin \angle BAC = 2\sin 20$

The measure of ∠BAC is approximately 43°, which means that ∠ABC is 117°.

$\dfrac{\sin 117}{AC} = \dfrac{\sin 20}{2} \to AC \sim 5$

The area relationship is:

Area of shaded section $= 0.35(\pi(\text{large radius})^2) = \pi(\text{large radius})^2 - \pi(1.75 \times \text{small radius})^2 - \pi(\text{small radius})^2$

$0.35(25\pi) = 25\pi - \pi(1.75 \times \text{small radius})^2 - \pi(\text{small radius})^2$

$0.35(25) = 25 - (1.75 \times \text{small radius})^2 - (\text{small radius})^2$

$(1.75 \times \text{small radius})^2 + (\text{small radius})^2 = 16.25$

$(1.75 + 1)(\text{small radius})^2 = 16.25 \to \text{small radius}^2 = 5.9$

Small radius $= \sqrt{5.9} = 2.43$

Medium radius $= 2.43 \times 1.75 = 4.25 \sim 4$

76. Sub topic: Quadrilaterals/Triangles

The correct answer is (A).

Let $AB = BC = CD = x$

CE is perpendicular to AD→ΔCED is right angled

Also, $m\angle ADC = 60° \rightarrow \cos(\angle ADC) = \frac{ED}{CD} \rightarrow \cos(60°) = \frac{ED}{CD} \rightarrow \frac{1}{2} = \frac{ED}{CD} \rightarrow ED = \frac{CD}{2}$

$ED = \frac{x}{2}$

The ABCD trapezoid is isosceles $m\angle DAB = m\angle ADC$

We can apply the same logic/calculations in $\triangle BGA$ as we applied in $\triangle CED \rightarrow AG = \frac{AB}{2} = \frac{x}{2}$

BCEG is a rectangle$\rightarrow GE = BC = x$

$AB = AG + GE + ED$ and we were told that $AB = 2s \rightarrow 2s = \frac{x}{2} + x + \frac{x}{2} \rightarrow 2s = 2x \rightarrow x = s$

In $\triangle CFD$: $FD = CD = s$ and we also know that $m\angle ADC = 60°$

$\triangle CFD$ is an equilateral triangle $\rightarrow FD = CD = CF = s \rightarrow$ Perimeter of $\triangle CFD = 3s$

In the right angled $\triangle CED$ we can calculate CE:

$\sin(\angle ADC) = \frac{CE}{CD} \rightarrow \sin(60°) = \frac{CE}{CD} \rightarrow \frac{\sqrt{3}}{2} = \frac{ED}{s} \rightarrow CE = \frac{s\sqrt{3}}{2}$

Perimeter of rectangle $BCEG = 2BC + 2CE = 2s + s\sqrt{3} = s(2 + \sqrt{3})$

$$\frac{\text{Perimeter of } \triangle CFD}{\text{Perimeter of rectangle } BCEG} = \frac{3s}{s(2+\sqrt{3})} = \frac{3}{(2+\sqrt{3})} = \frac{3(2-\sqrt{3})}{(2+\sqrt{3})(2-\sqrt{3})} = \frac{3(2-\sqrt{3})}{4-3} = 6 - 3\sqrt{3}$$

$6 - 3\sqrt{3}$ is greater than $5 - 3\sqrt{3} \rightarrow$ the left column is greater than the right column and (A) is the correct answer

77. **Sub topic: Coordinate Geometry**

The correct answers are (B), (E) and (F).

Let the coordinates of the center, O of the circle be (x, y)

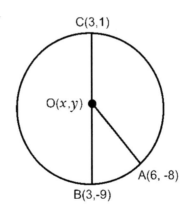

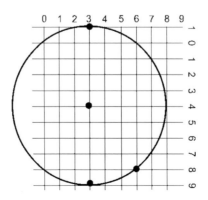

OA, OB and OC are the radii of the circle.

OA = OB = OC

Coordinates of A are $(6, -8)$ and coordinates of O are (x, y)

Length OA can be calculated using the distance formula:

$$\sqrt{(x_2 - x_1) + (y_2 - y_1)}$$

OA = $\sqrt{(6 - x)^2 + (-8 - y)^2}$

Coordinates of B are $(3, -9)$ and coordinates of O are (x, y)

OB = $\sqrt{(3 - x)^2 + (-9 - y)^2}$

Since OA = OB, then OA² = OB²

$(6 - x)^2 + (-8 - y)^2 = (3 - x)^2 + (-9 - y)^2$

$36 + x^2 - 12x + 64 + y^2 + 16y = 9 + x^2 - 6x + 81 + y^2 + 18y$

Subtracting x^2 and y^2 from both sides:

$100 - 12x + 16y = 90 - 6x + 18y$

$10 - 6x - 2y = 0$---- multiplying the equation by -1

$6x + 2y - 10 = 0$

$6x + 2y = 10$----- dividing the equation by 2

$3x + y = 5$------- equation 1

Similarly, OB = OC and OB^2 = OC^2

Coordinates of B are $(3, -9)$ and coordinates of O are (x, y)

Coordinates of C are $(3, 1)$ and coordinates of O are (x, y)

OB = $\sqrt{(3 - x)^2 + (-9 - y)^2}$

OC = $\sqrt{(3 - x)^2 + (1 - y)^2}$

OB^2 = OC^2

$(3 - x)^2 + (-9 - y)^2 = (3 - x)^2 + (1 - y)^2$ ------ Subtracting $(3 - x)^2$ from both sides

$(-9 - y)^2 = (1 - y)^2$

$81 + y^2 + 18y = 1 + y^2 - 2y$----- Subtracting y^2 from both sides

$80 + 20y = 0$

$20y = -80$

$y = -4$

Substituting the value of y in equation 1:

$3x + y = 5$

$3x + (-4) = 5$

$3x = 9$

$x = 3$

Coordinates of the center of the circle are $(3, -4)$.

OA = $\sqrt{(6 - x)^2 + (-8 - y)^2}$

Substituting the value of x and y:

OA = $\sqrt{(6 - 3)^2 + \left(-8 - (-4)\right)^2}$

$= \sqrt{(3)^2 + (-8 + 4)^2}$

$$= \sqrt{9 + (-4)^2}$$

$$= \sqrt{9 + 16}$$

$$= \sqrt{25} = 5 \text{ units}$$

The radius of the circle is 5 units.

The area of the circle $= \pi r^2 = 3.14 \times 5 \times 5 = 78.5$ units

The circumference of the circle $= 2\pi r = 2 \times 3.14 \times 5 = 31.4$ units

Options B, E and F are correct.

78. **Sub topic: Triangles/Quadrilaterals/Circles**

The correct answer is (D).

Since CDFE is a parallelogram, the area $= bh$.

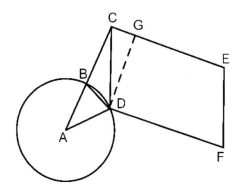

Since we know the area, we can find DG:

$358.3 = 24GD \rightarrow GD = 14.9$

Since $\angle DCE = 72°$,

$\sin 72 = \dfrac{14.9}{CD} \rightarrow CD = 15.67$

Since CDFE is a parallelogram, and we know that $\angle DCE = 72°$, we can find the $\angle CDF$:

$\angle CDF = 180° - 72° = 108°$

Since $\angle BDF = 154°$, $\angle CDB = 46°$. Since $\angle CBD = 110°$, $\angle BCD = 24°$

BD can be found by:

$\dfrac{\sin 24}{BD} = \dfrac{\sin 110}{15.67} \rightarrow BD = 6.78$

Since $180° - \angle CBD = 70°$, ABD is an isosceles triangle, and we know that $\angle BAD = 40°$ we can find the radius of the circle:

$\dfrac{\sin 40}{6.78} = \dfrac{\sin 70}{\text{radius}} \rightarrow \text{radius} = 9.9$

Area of the sector $= \dfrac{40}{360}(9.9)^2 \pi \rightarrow 34.2$

The answer is D.

79. **Sub topic: Geometric Transformations**

The correct answer is 25.

First, reflect the triangle over the y-axis by applying the following to each point:$(x, y) \rightarrow (-x, y)$

The points become: $(2, 4) \rightarrow (-2, 4)$; $(7, 7) \rightarrow (-7, 7)$; $(9, 3) \rightarrow (-9, 3)$

The following is obtained:

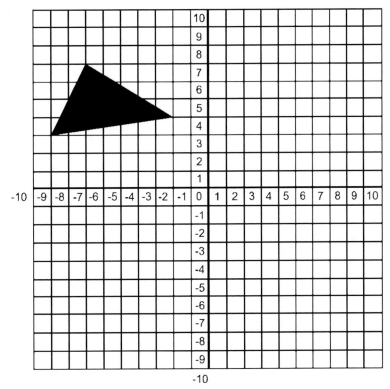

Next, the points are translated by applying the following to each point:$(x, y) \rightarrow (x - 1, y - 5)$

The points become: $(-2, 4) \rightarrow (-3, -1)$; $(-7, 7) \rightarrow (-8, 2)$; $(-9, 3) \rightarrow (-10, -2)$:

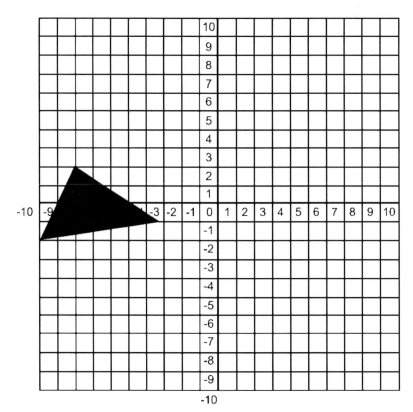

Finally, the triangle is rotated 90° about the origin:

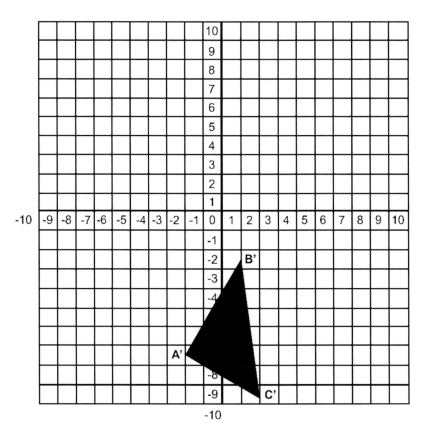

The ΔBCB' is now shown:

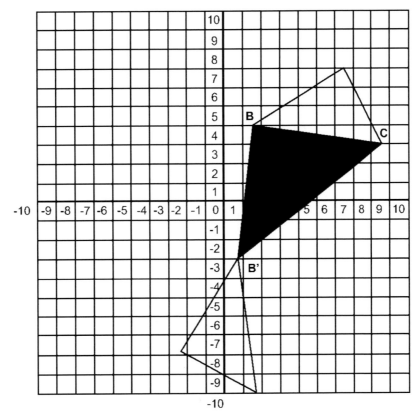

Find the distances of the lines using the formula: distance $= \sqrt{(x_2 - x_1)^2 + (y_2 - y_1)^2}$

$BC = \sqrt{(9-2)^2 + (3-4)^2} = 7.07$

$BB' = \sqrt{(1-2)^2 + (-3-4)^2} = 7.07$

$B'C = \sqrt{(9-1)^2 + (3--3)^2} = 10$

We can use the law of cosines to find the angle of BCB':

$\cos BCB' = \dfrac{[(BC)^2 + (B'C)^2 - (BB')^2]}{2 \times BC \times B'C} = 0.707 \rightarrow \angle BCB' = 45° = \angle BB'C$

Since this is a right triangle, we can find the area using: $\dfrac{1}{2} \times 7.07 \times 7.07 = 25$

The answer is 25.

80. **Sub topic: Triangles**

The correct answer is (B).

From the figure, we notice that SG is the difference between a side of the larger square and a side of the smaller square. Similarly, BR is the difference between a side of the larger square and a side of a smaller square. Using the given lengths

$SG = BR = (m + n) - (m - n)$

$= 2n$

(1) Area of the right $\triangle JSG$ = Area of the right $\triangle JBR$

$= \dfrac{(m + n)(2n)}{2}$

$$= n(m+n)$$

(2) Area of ΔBCT = Area of ΔGYE = $\frac{1}{2}(m-n)^2$

(3) Area of the entire shape = $2(m-n)^2 + (m+n)^2$

Subtract twice (1) and twice (2) from (3). The result is the area of *BCDEGJ*.

Area of BCDEGJ = $2(m-n)^2 + (m+n)^2 - 2\left[\frac{1}{2}(m-n)^2\right] - 2n(m+n)$

$= 2(m-n)^2 + (m+n)^2 - (m-n)^2 - (2n)(m+n)$

$= (m-n)^2 + (m+n)^2 - (2n)(m+n)$

$= m^2 - 2mn + n^2 + m^2 + 2mn + n^2 - 2mn - 2n^2$

$= 2m^2 - 2mn$

$= 2m(m-n)$

81. **Sub topic: Circles/Triangles**

The correct answer is .0.4.

From the geometry, we can determine that $\sin(\theta) = \frac{1}{2}$, or $\theta = 30°$.

The area of the triangle = $(\sqrt{3})(1) = \sqrt{3}$

Area of entire circle (with 360^0 angle about the center) = $\pi(2^2) = 4\pi$

Area of arc of circle (with 300^0 angle about the center) = $\frac{300}{360}(4\pi) = \frac{10}{3}\pi$

Area of shaded portion of circle = (Area of entire circle) − (Area of arc, shaded grey) − (Area of triangle, shaded white)

$= 4\pi - \frac{10}{3}\pi - \sqrt{3} = 0.3623 \approx 0.4$ (with 1 decimal place accuracy)

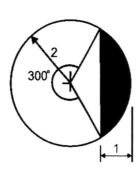 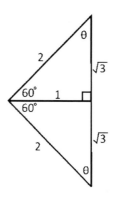

The correct answer is 0.4.

Chapter 6

Data Analysis Practice Questions

This chapter consists of *80 Data Analysis* practice questions. The questions cover all the question types as explained in Chapter 2 and are segregated into 3 levels of difficulty - Easy, Medium and Difficult. You may choose to start solving the Easy questions first and then move on to higher levels of difficulty or solve the questions in any random order. You will find answers and detailed explanations towards the end of this chapter.

Level: Easy

For Questions1 to 3, refer to the bar graph below.

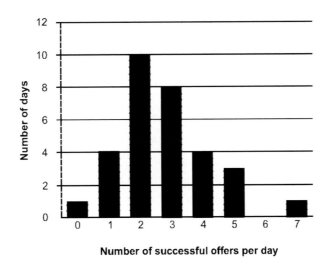

Number of successful offers per day

Michael keeps track of the number of successful product offers he makes per day. The graph above represents Michael's data for the past month.

1. What is the probability that Michael will make 7 successful offers in any given day? (Round off to 3 decimal places)

    (A) 0.143

(B) 0.125

(C) 0.100

(D) 0.032

(E) 0.169

2. What is the probability that Michael will make 2 or 3 successful offers on a given day? (Round off to 3 decimal places)

(A) 0.083

(B) 0.323

(C) 0.581

(D) 0.600

(E) 0.815

3. Find the probability that Michael makes at least 1 successful offer on a given day. (Round off to 3 decimal places)

(A) 0.968

(B) 0.677

(C) 0.419

(D) 0.032

(E) 0.017

Questions 4 to 6 are based on the following table.

Destination	North America	Europe	Asia
Number of males	55	72	23
Number of females	48	60	17

The table above shows the results of the survey conducted in an international airport where travelers were asked of their flight destinations.

4. A traveler is chosen at random. What is the probability that this traveler is going to Asia? (Answer in fraction)

```
┌──────────┐
│          │
└──────────┘
┌──────────┐
│          │
└──────────┘
```

5. A traveler is selected at random. Find the probability that the traveler is a female going to Europe. (Answer in fraction)

```
┌──────────┐
│          │
└──────────┘
┌──────────┐
│          │
└──────────┘
```

6. A traveler is selected at random. What is the probability that this traveler is a male, given that he is going to North America? (Answer in fraction)

For Questions 7 and 8, refer to the following Venn diagram.

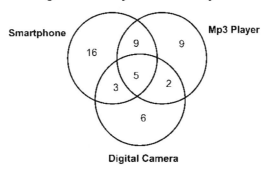

A group of 50 children aged 8 to 15 years old were interviewed and asked whether they own any smart phone, MP3 player or digital camera. The results of the survey were presented in a Venn Diagram as shown above.

7. If a child owns a smart phone, what is the probability that he also owns an MP3 player?

(A) $\frac{9}{16}$

(B) $\frac{7}{8}$

(C) $\frac{14}{33}$

(D) $\frac{9}{33}$

(E) $\frac{1}{8}$

8. Two children are chosen at random. Find the probability that both of them own only a digital camera.

(A) 0.012

(B) 0.014

(C) 0.098

(D) 0.125

(E) 0.001

Questions 9 and 10 are based on the following table.

The following table lists the unemployment rates for all states of the United States based on data from the Bureau of Labor Statistics. Answer the following questions regarding the table:

2013 State Unemployment Rates *

State	Jan	Feb	Mar	Apr	May	June	July
Alabama	6.9	7.2	7.2	6.9	6.8	6.5	6.3
Alaska	6.7	6.5	6.2	6.0	5.9	6.1	6.3
Arizona	8.0	7.9	7.9	7.9	7.8	8.0	8.0
Arkansas	7.2	7.2	7.2	7.1	7.3	7.3	7.4
California	9.8	9.6	9.4	9.0	8.6	8.5	8.7
Colorado	7.3	7.2	7.1	6.9	6.9	7.0	7.1
Connecticut	8.1	8.0	8.0	8.0	8.0	8.1	8.1
Delaware	7.2	7.2	7.3	7.2	7.2	7.3	7.4
D.C.	8.6	8.6	8.5	8.5	8.5	8.5	8.6
Florida	7.8	7.7	7.5	7.2	7.1	7.1	7.1
Georgia	8.7	8.6	8.4	8.2	8.3	8.6	8.8
Hawaii	5.2	5.2	5.1	4.9	4.7	4.6	4.5
Idaho	6.3	6.2	6.2	6.1	6.2	6.4	6.6
Illinois	9.0	9.5	9.5	9.3	9.1	9.2	9.2
Indiana	8.6	8.7	8.7	8.5	8.3	8.4	8.4
Iowa	5.0	5.0	4.9	4.7	4.6	4.6	4.8
Kansas	5.5	5.5	5.6	5.5	5.7	5.8	5.9
Kentucky	7.9	7.9	8.0	7.9	8.1	8.4	8.5
Louisiana	5.9	6.0	6.2	6.5	6.8	7.0	7.0
Maine	7.3	7.3	7.1	6.9	6.8	6.8	6.9
Maryland	6.7	6.6	6.6	6.5	6.7	7.0	7.1
Massachusetts	6.7	6.5	6.4	6.4	6.6	7.0	7.2
Michigan	8.9	8.8	8.5	8.4	8.4	8.7	8.8
Minnesota	5.6	5.5	5.4	5.3	5.3	5.2	5.2
Mississippi	9.3	9.6	9.4	9.1	9.1	9.0	8.5
Missouri	6.5	6.7	6.7	6.6	6.8	6.9	7.1
Montana	5.7	5.6	5.6	5.5	5.4	5.4	5.3
Nebraska	3.8	3.8	3.8	3.7	3.8	4.0	4.2
Nevada	9.7	9.6	9.7	9.6	9.5	9.6	9.5
New Hampshire	5.8	5.8	5.7	5.5	5.3	5.2	5.1
New Jersey	9.5	9.3	9.0	8.7	8.6	8.7	8.6
New Mexico	6.6	6.8	6.9	6.7	6.7	6.8	6.9
New York	8.4	8.4	8.2	7.8	7.6	7.5	7.5
North Carolina	9.5	9.4	9.2	8.9	8.8	8.8	8.9
North Dakota	3.3	3.3	3.3	3.3	3.2	3.1	3.0
Ohio	7.0	7.0	7.1	7.0	7.0	7.2	7.2
Oklahoma	5.1	5.0	5.0	4.9	5.0	5.2	5.3
Oregon	8.4	8.4	8.2	8.0	7.8	7.9	8.0
Pennsylvania	8.2	8.1	7.9	7.6	7.5	7.5	7.5
Puerto Rico	14.6	14.5	14.2	13.7	13.4	13.2	13.5
Rhode Island	9.8	9.4	9.1	8.8	8.9	8.9	8.9
South Carolina	8.7	8.6	8.4	8.0	8.0	8.1	8.1
South Dakota	4.4	4.4	4.3	4.1	4.0	3.9	3.9
Tennessee	7.7	7.8	7.9	8.0	8.3	8.5	8.5
Texas	6.3	6.4	6.4	6.4	6.5	6.5	6.5
Utah	5.4	5.2	4.9	4.7	4.6	4.7	4.6
Vermont	4.7	4.4	4.1	4.0	4.1	4.4	4.6
Virginia	5.6	5.6	5.3	5.2	5.3	5.5	5.7
Washington	7.5	7.5	7.3	7.0	6.8	6.8	6.9
West Virginia	7.4	7.3	7.0	6.6	6.2	6.1	6.2
Wisconsin	7.0	7.2	7.1	7.1	7.0	6.8	6.8
Wyoming	4.9	4.9	4.9	4.8	4.6	4.6	4.6

Source: Bureau of Labor Statistics

* Preliminary figures provided by BLS in its monthly updates

9. Based on the data presented in the table, what percentage of the states and other locations saw a decline of 0.8% or greater (in percentage points) between January 2013 to July 2013?

    (A) 3%

    (B) 6%

    (C) 9%

    (D) 12%

    (E) 15%

10. Florida has a population of 19.32 million. How many people are unemployed in May 2013 assuming only 65% of the population can legally work?

   (A) 0.89 million people

   (B) 1.32 million people

   (C) 3.56 million people

   (D) 8.91 million people

   (E) 12.5 million people

Questions 11 and 12 are based on the following chart.

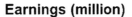

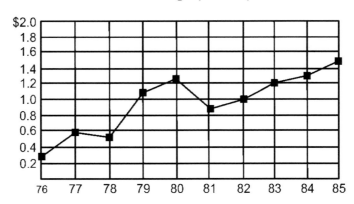

11. From 1977 to 1983, inclusive, what was the amount of the greatest increase in earnings from one year to the next?

   (A) $1,000,000

   (B) $1,200,000

   (C) $3,00,000

   (D) $6,00,000

   (E) $750,000

12. For years 1981 to 1985, inclusive, average earnings of Company *K* were approximately

   (A) $1,180,000

   (B) $720,000

   (C) $880,000

   (D) $920,000

   (E) $998,000

Questions 13 and 14are based on the following data.

One Day Summary of Activity			
Stock symbol	**Closing Price($)**	**Volume (1,000's)**	**Change in Price**
Arx	53.25	869.45	$2\frac{3}{4}$
Bim	41.4	4110.392	$2\frac{11}{16}$
Csf	27.84	36.411	$-1\frac{1}{8}$
Mbd	96.33	599.994	$-3\frac{1}{2}$
Nys	11.11	546.362	$\frac{1}{4}$
Qug	22.28	8.13	$1\frac{7}{16}$
Tvk	81.15	3146.633	$\frac{3}{8}$

13. What was the opening price for *Mbd*?

    (A) $27.52

    (B) $92.83

    (C) $96.33

    (D) $99.70

    (E) $99.83

14. How many stocks closed at a higher price than the stock with the greatest amount of activity for the day?

    (A) 1

    (B) 2

    (C) 3

    (D) 4

    (E) 5

Questions 15 and 16 are based on the following chart.

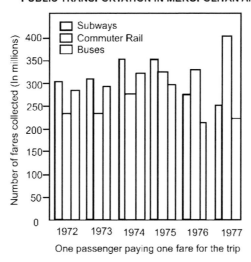

PUBLIC TRANSPORTATION IN MEROPOLITAN AREA

15. From 1972 to 1977, inclusive the total number of fares collected for subways was approximately how many millions?

    (A) 1,100
    (B) 1,300
    (C) 1,500
    (D) 1,700
    (E) 1,800

16. From 1975 to 1977, the number of fares collected for subway dropped by approximately what percent?

    (A) 15
    (B) 25
    (C) 35
    (D) 9
    (E) 90

Questions 17 and 18 are based on the following diagram.

The expenditures and the income of College M have been shown below:

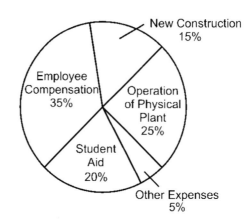

**BUDGET INFORMATION FOR
COLLEGE M IN A YEAR**

OUTLAYS*

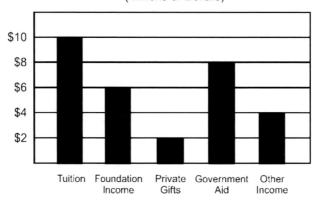

INCOME**
(Millions of Dollars)

**Includes all expenditure
**Includes all Source of income
NOTE: Outlays = Income*

17. For the year shown, College M spent how much money on the operation of its physical plant?

    (A) $2,500,000

    (B) $4,000,000

    (C) $7,500,000

    (D) $8,000,000

    (E) $9,500,000

18. For the year shown, what percentage of College M's income came from foundation income?

    (A) 6%

    (B) 20%

    (C) 25%

    (D) 33%

    (E) 60%

Questions 19 to 22 are based on the following chart.

Average snowfall during previous year at South Haven's ski resort

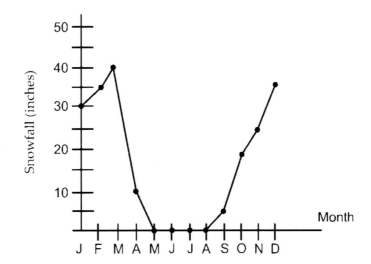

19. How many months averaged at least twice the snowfall of October?

    (A) 1

    (B) 2

    (C) 3

    (D) 4

    (E) 5

20. Which month had $\frac{2}{3}$ less snowfall than December?

    (A) March

    (B) April

    (C) September

    (D) October

    (E) November

21. What percentage drop in snowfall occurred between March and April?

(A) 300%

(B) 30%

(C) 400%

(D) 25%

(E) 75%

22. What was the average amount of snowfall from January through May?

(A) 24 inches

(B) 30 inches

(C) 23 inches

(D) 28 inches

(E) 15inches

Questions 23 to 26 are based on the following diagram.

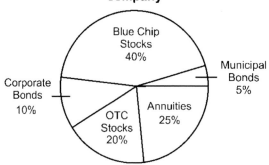

Distribution(%) of earnings of a company

23. What percentage of earning is not invested in stocks?

(A) 20%

(B) 40%

(C) 60%

(D) 80%

(E) 85%

24. If $3,000 was invested last month, what amount went into annuities?

(A) $2,250

(B) $1,500

(C) $1,200

(D) $750

(E) $600

25. How much more money was invested in annuities than in corporate bonds if a total of $10,000 was invested?

    (A) $1,500

    (B) $2,500

    (C) $1,000

    (D) $8,500

    (E) $3,500

26. Which sector had $800 invested in it from $4,000 earnings?

    (A) OTC Stocks

    (B) Corporate Bonds

    (C) Blue Chip Stocks

    (D) Municipal Bonds

    (E) Annuities

Level: Medium

Questions 27 to 31 are based on the following diagram.

Periodic table is a tabular arrangement of chemical elements based on the order of their atomic numbers. The elements are grouped in two ways in the periodic table:

Period: Each horizontal row of elements is called a period.

Group: Each column of the periodic table is called a group.

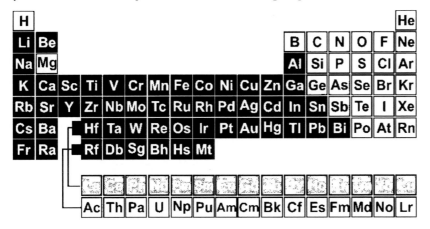

The reaction rates for elements are different. But all follow the following rules:

1. In each column or group, elements are more reactive from bottom to top.

2. In each row or period, elements are more reactive from left to the right.

27. Which elements are certainly more reactive than "*Cd*?"

    (A) *Ge, Se, N*

    (B) *Ta, N, Pb*

    (C) *Pa, Ta, Rn*

    (D) *Rn, Mn, Mg*

    (E) *Mg, Tb, Gd*

28. Which elements are certainly less reactive than "*Ru?*"

    (A) *He, Ta, Xe*

    (B) *Zr, La, He*

    (C) *Ta, Na, Cr*

    (D) *La, Th, Ba*

    (E) *Ba, Cl, Si*

29. Identify the elements *a* and *b* such that a is more reactive and *b* is less reactive than "*Au.*"

    (A) *a: Pt* and *b: Li*

    (B) *a: At* and *b: Fr*

    (C) *a: Li* and *b: Cr*

    (D) *a: At* and *b: Pt*

    (E) *a: Ar* and *b: Np*

30. Which list shows the given elements in a descending order of reactivity?

    (A) *F, Zn, Os, Ac*

    (B) *F, Ge, Co, He*

    (C) *Ta, Tb, Ba, Kr*

    (D) *Ta, He, Sg, Zr*

    (E) *Sg, Cl, Pa, Mg*

31. Which list shows the given elements in an ascending order of reactivity?

    (A) *Fe, Tc, Fr, Be*

    (B) *Pt, P, Lu, Al*

    (C) *Ra, Sg, Fe, P*

    (D) *Al, K, Pb, Cu*

    (E) *P, Pb, Br, Ca*

Questions 32 to 35 are based on the following graph.

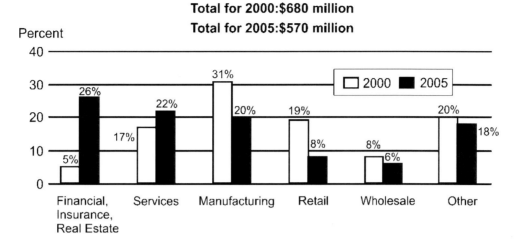

Corporate Support for Philanthropic Causes by sector in 2000 and 2005

Total for 2000:$680 million

Total for 2005:$570 million

32. What was the total contribution in 2005(approx. in million dollars) by the corporate sectors that decreased their support for Philanthropic causes from 2000 to 2005?

    (A) 150 million dollars

    (B) 200 million dollars

    (C) 250 million dollars

    (D) 300 million dollars

    (E) 350 million dollars

33. Find the average amount contributed by those sectors who contributed more than $100 million each to the Philanthropic Causes in both 2000 and 2005?

    (A) $114 million

    (B) $238.6 million

    (C) $263.13 million

    (D) $324.8 million

    (E) $342.6 million

34. Of the Financial, Insurance and Real Estate Sector's 2005 contribution to Philanthropic Causes, one-third went for rebuilding homes lost due to Hurricane Katrina and one fourth of the remainder went to providing medical aid to the injured. Approximately how many million dollars more did the Financial, Insurance and Real Estate Sector contribute towards rebuilding homes that year than to providing medical aid?

    (A) $20 million

    (B) $25 million

    (C) $30 million

    (D) $35 million

    (E) $40 million

35. Financial, Insurance and Real Estate Sector showed a steep increase in contribution for philanthropic causes between 2000 and 2005. If the government excluded this industry and calculated, what would be the average change in contribution of all the other industries, calculated to the nearest integer?

    (A) −30%
    (B) −31%
    (C) −32%
    (D) −33%
    (E) −34%

Questions 36 to 39 are based on the following diagram.

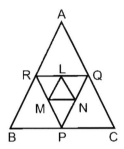

The midpoints of the sides of a ΔABC are joined to form a new ΔPQR. The midpoints of the ΔPQR so formed are joined to form another ΔLMN.

36. Which of these is the ratio of the perimeter of ΔABC to the perimeter of ΔLMN?

    (A) 1 : 3
    (B) 3 : 1
    (C) 1 : 4
    (D) 4 : 1
    (E) 1 : 16

37. If ΔABC were a right-angled triangle right angled at B such that AB = x and BC= y, then which of these would have been the area of ΔLMN?

    (A) $\frac{1}{2}xy$

    (B) $\frac{1}{4}xy$

    (C) $\frac{1}{8}xy$

    (D) $\frac{1}{16}xy$

    (E) $\frac{1}{32}xy$

38. If following the above pattern, n triangles are formed, which of these is the ratio of the area of innermost triangle to the outermost triangle?

    (A) $1 : n$

    (B) $n : 1$

    (C) $1 : n^2$

    (D) $n^2 : 1$

    (E) $1 : 4^n$

39.

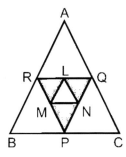

    If the $\triangle ABC$ were an equilateral triangle having side length x units, which of these is area of the shaded region?

    (A) $\dfrac{3\sqrt{3}}{64} x^2$

    (B) $\dfrac{\sqrt{3}}{16} x^2$

    (C) $\dfrac{\sqrt{3}}{64} x^2$

    (D) $\dfrac{5\sqrt{3}}{64} x^2$

    (E) $\dfrac{3\sqrt{3}}{16} x^2$

For Questions 40 and 41, refer to the figure below.

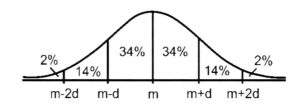

The figure above shows the bell curve or normal distribution curve with mean, *m*, and standard deviation, *d*. The percentages given refer to the approximate probability under the specified area. For example, the probability of an event occurring that is between the mean (*m*) and +1 standard deviation away from the mean (*m* + *d*) is 34%.

In a certain district, the heights of 1,000 high school students are normally distributed with a mean of 165 cm and standard deviation of 3 cm.

40. If a high school student is selected at random, what is, approximately, the probability that the student's height is less than 162 cm?

  (A) 14%

  (B) 16%

  (C) 34%

  (D) 56%

  (E) 84%

41. A high school student selected at random will have any of the following heights:

  I.   Less than 159 cm

  II.   Between 159 cm and 162 cm

  III. Between 162 cm and 165 cm

  IV.   Between 165 cm and 168 cm

  V.   Between 168 cm and 171 cm

  VI.   More than 171 cm

  Which of the following pairs have equal probabilities? Select all such pairs.

  (A) I and VI

  (B) II and V

  (C) III and IV

  (D) II and IV

For Questions 42 and 43, refer to the following chart.

A city relay race is run on a rectangular course, with a runner switch occurring at each angle. The graph below charts the speeds and times of each runner in one of the teams competing. Examine the graph and answer the questions below.

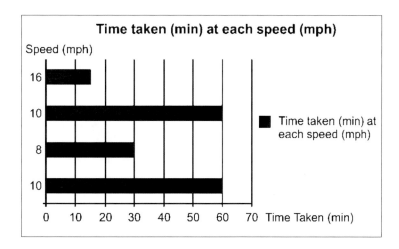

42. What is the area of the course? What is the perimeter of the course?

    (A) 40 sq. miles, 20 miles

    (B) 40 sq. miles, 28 miles

    (C) 50 sq. miles, 25 miles

    (D) 60 sq. miles, 24 miles

    (E) The answer cannot be determined given the information in the chart.

43. Assume the course is parallelogram and the information in the graph is otherwise the same. If you attempted to answer the same question as in previous question, how would your answer change in comparison to above?

    (A) No change

    (B) Same area, different perimeter

    (C) The area cannot not be determined given the information in the chart, same perimeter

    (D) Same area, the perimeter cannot be determined

    (E) Neither area nor perimeter can be determined given the information in the chart

Questions 44 to 47 are based on the following chart.

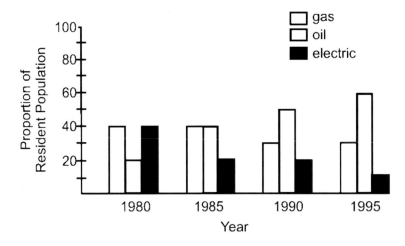

Heating Methods utilized by residents of Region X

44. What year or years had the greatest increase in oil usage by residents from one set of years to the next?

    (A) 1980

    (B) 1985

    (C) 1990

    (D) 1995

    (E) 1990 and 1995

45. What is the mean percent of residents who use oil as their main heating source?

    (A) 42.5%

    (B) 35%

    (C) 22.5%

    (D) 50%

    (E) 37.5%

46. If 50,000 residents make up Region X, how many more residents chose oil heat over electric heat in 1995?

    (A) 5,000

    (B) 15,000

    (C) 25,000

    (D) 30,000

    (E) 55,000

47. What percentage of gas consumers from 1985 switched to alternative heating method in 1990?

    (A) 10%

    (B) 25%

    (C) 50%

    (D) 75%

    (E) 100%

Questions 48 to 51 are based on the following chart.

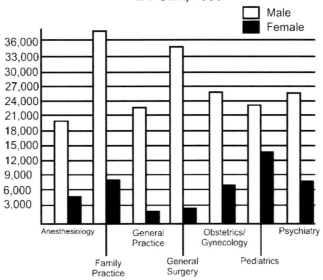

U.S. PHYSICIANS IN SELECTED SPECIALTIES BY SEX, 1986

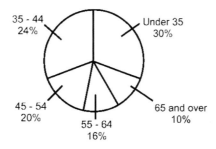

GENERAL SURGERY PHYSICIANS BY AGE, 1986

48. In 1986, the lowest ratio of males to females was observed in which speciality of physicians?

    (A) Family practice

    (B) General surgery

    (C) Obstetrics/gynecology

    (D) Pediatrics

    (E) Psychiatry

49. In 1986, approximately how many general surgery physicians were between the ages of 45 and 54, inclusive?

    (A) 5,440

    (B) 6,300

    (C) 7,350

    (D) 7,800

    (E) 8,900

50. If in 1986 all the family practice physicians represented 7.5 percent of all the physicians in the United States, approximately how many physicians were there total?

   (A) 300,000

   (B) 360,000

   (C) 430,000

   (D) 485,000

   (E) 570,000

51. Calculate the approximate number of male general surgery physicians under the age of 35, considering the female general surgery physicians (under 35) represent 3.5% of all the general surgery physicians.

   (A) 9,200

   (B) 9,800

   (C) 10,750

   (D) 11,260

   (E) 11,980

Questions 52 and 53 are based on the following Diagram.

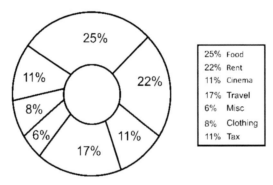

Distribution of expenses

52. Which of the following items amounts to the same expenditure as on food?

   (A) Tax, clothing and miscellaneous

   (B) Travel, cinema and miscellaneous

   (C) Cinema and travel

   (D) Rent and miscellaneous

   (E) Rent and cinema

53. A reduction of 2% in taxation enables him to increase his expenditure by one per cent on each of the items, cinema and travel. Then a ratio of 1:2:3 is maintained on the expenditures incurred on which of the following items.

    (A) Travel, miscellaneous and cinema

    (B) Miscellaneous, cinema and travel

    (C) Miscellaneous, tax and clothing

    (D) Miscellaneous, travel and cinema

    (E) None of the above

Level: Difficult

Questions 54 to 60 are based on the following table.

The following table illustrates the number of enrollments in different classes of a college during a semester. Additionally, assume that there is no student who takes both Chemistry and Algebra classes.

Courses	Number of Students
Number of students who took Algebra	28
Number of students who took Geometry	47
Number of students who took Physics	42
Number of students who took Chemistry	46
Total number of students who took either Algebra, Geometry, or Physics	87
Number of students who took either Chemistry, Physics, or Geometry	102
Number of students who took Algebra and Geometry	11
Number of students who took Algebra and Physics	12
Number of students who took Geometry and Physics	12
Number of students who took Geometry and Chemistry	13
Number of students who took Chemistry and Physics	12

54. How many students did enrol in all Algebra, Geometry, and Physics classes?

55. What is the number of students who enrolled in all Chemistry, Geometry, and Physics classes?

56. How many students did enrol in Geometry and Physics classes only?

    (A) 11

    (B) 10

    (C) 7

    (D) 5

    (E) 3

57. What is the number of students who enrolled in Chemistry and Geometry classes only?

    ```
    ┌──────────────┐
    │              │
    └──────────────┘
    ```

58. What is the total number of students who enrolled either in Geometry class or in Chemistry class only?

    ```
    ┌──────────────┐
    │              │
    └──────────────┘
    ```

59. What is the total number of students who enrolled either in Chemistry class or in Algebra class only?

    (A) 56
    (B) 59
    (C) 66
    (D) 67
    (E) 74

60. What is the total number of students who enrolled either Geometry class or Physics class only?

    (A) 77
    (B) 65
    (C) 56
    (D) 49
    (E) 45

Questions 61 to 64 are based on the following graph.

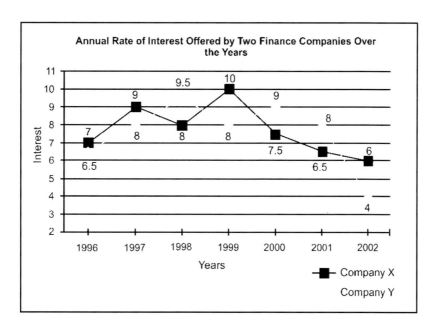

Company X and Y (both finance companies) announce a fixed interest rate for their investors as shown in the line graph above. This interest rate changes every year depending on the banks rate of interest and variation in country's economy.

61. An investor invests two different amounts in the two companies' X and Y in the year 1999. If the ratio of the amounts earned from the two companies at the end of 1999 is 2:1. Find the ratio of the amounts invested in the two companies.

   (A) 27:55
   (B) 21:34
   (C) 43:54
   (D) 55:27
   (E) 34:21

62. An investor invests $10,000 in both the companies in 1996. He then keeps reinvesting the amount he gets at the end of each year in the same company. Find the difference of the amounts that he gets at the end of the year 2000 from the two companies.

   (A) $1039.17
   (B) $39.17
   (C) $68.34
   (D) $1068.17
   (E) $139.17

63. $45 was partly invested in Company X and the other part was invested in Company Y in the year 2000 for 1-year. The total interest at the end of the year was $3.75 million. How much of the $45 million was invested in Company Y?

    (A) $20 million

    (B) $25 million

    (C) $40 million

    (D) $15 million

    (E) $12 million

64. A person A invested a certain amount in Company X in the year 1996 and continued to stay invested till 2002. Another person B invested the same amount in Company Y in the same year 1996. He doubled the amount invested in 2000 and allowed it to stay invested till 2002 in Company Y. What is the increased percentage in interest that B earned over A during the period 1996 to 2002?

    (A) 52%

    (B) 53%

    (C) 54%

    (D) 55%

    (E) 56%

Questions 65 to 68 are based on the following diagram.

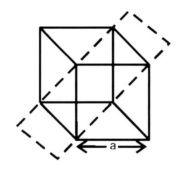

The above image shows a metallic cube whose edge measures *a* units.

65. If the cube shown above is sliced into two parts by a plane along its diagonal, which of these is the surface area of each part so formed?

    (A) $3a^2$

    (B) $12a^2$

    (C) $\sqrt{2a^2}$

    (D) $3 + \sqrt{2a^2}$

    (E) $(3 + \sqrt{2})a^2$

66. If the cube shown were hollow and is sliced into two parts by a plane along its diagonal, which of these is the correct ratio of the total surface area of each part to the surface area of the original cube?

    (A) $1:1$

    (B) $1:2$

    (C) $2:1$

    (D) $6:3+\sqrt{2}$

    (E) $3+\sqrt{2}:6$

67. If instead of a plane along the diagonal, the cube is sliced into 4 parts by two perpendicular planes passing through the centre of the cube, which of these is the ratio of the surface area of the original cube to the total surface area of the 4 parts so formed?

    (A) $1:4$

    (B) $4:1$

    (C) $1:1$

    (D) $1:2$

    (E) $2:1$

68. If two planes, one along each diagonal, slice the cube into 4 parts, which of these is the surface area of each part so formed?

    (A) $\left(\frac{3}{2}+\sqrt{2}\right)a^2$

    (B) $\frac{3}{2}a^2$

    (C) $\left(\frac{3\sqrt{2}}{2}\right)a^2$

    (D) $(3+\sqrt{2})a^2$

    (E) $\left(\frac{3+z\sqrt{2}}{2}\right)a^2$

For Questions 69 and 70, refer to the following diagram.

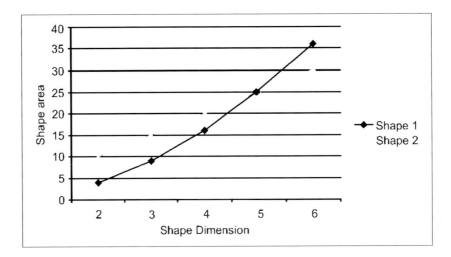

In the above chart, the change in the area of two shapes is charted as *one* of their dimensions is changed. The other dimensions, if the shape has any, are unchanged unless they depend on the changed dimension. All shapes involved are quadrilaterals.

69. What possible shapes could Shape 2 be?

    Select all that apply.

    (A) A rectangle

    (B) A square

    (C) A parallelogram

    (D) A trapezoid

    (E) The answer cannot be determined from the information given

70. What possible shapes could Shape 1 be?

    Select all that apply.

    (A) A rectangle

    (B) A square

    (C) A parallelogram

    (D) A trapezoid

    (E) The answer cannot be determined from the information given

Questions 71 to 73 are based on the following chart.

US PLANE CRASHES
(Total passenger miles in billions)

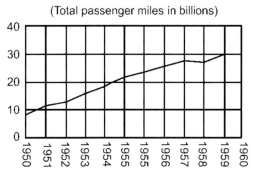

(Deaths per 100 million passenger miles)

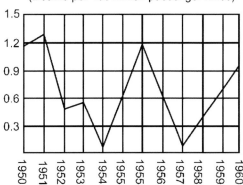

71. All of the following statements can be inferred from the information provided in the graphs EXCEPT:

   (A) The highest rate of passenger deaths per mile traveled during the period covered by the graphs occurred in 1951.

   (B) The largest yearly increase in deaths per mile traveled occurred in the period 1954 to 1955.

   (C) The rate of passenger deaths per mile traveled was approximately the same in 1954 and 1957.

   (D) Total passenger miles traveled approximately tripled between 1951 and 1959.

   (E) The percentage increase in deaths per 100 million passenger-miles was constant for 1958, 1959, and 1960.

72. In which year did the longest uninterrupted period of increase in the rate of passenger deaths per mile traveled finally end?

   (A) 1951

   (B) 1953

   (C) 1955

   (D) 1957

   (E) 1960

73. The greatest number of fatalities was recorded in which year?

    (A) 1960

    (B) 1957

    (C) 1955

    (D) 1953

    (E) 1951

Questions 74 to 78are based on the following data.

Average Undergraduate Budgets, 1998-99						
Sector	**Tuition & Fees**	**Books & Supplies**	**Room & Board**	**Transportation**	**Other Expenses**	**Total Expenses**
2-year Public Resident	1600	620	*	*	*	N/A
Commuter	1,600	620	2,000	1,000	1,200	6,420
2-year Private Resident	7,300	660	4,600	550	1,000	14,110
Commuter	7,300	660	2,200	880	1,200	12,240
4-year Public Resident	3,250	660	4,500	600	1,400	10,140
Commuter	3,250	660	2,100	1,000	1,500	8,510
Out-of-State	8,400	6600	4,500	600	1,400	15,560
4-year Private Resident	14,500	670	5,800	550	1,000	22,520
Commuter	14,500	670	2,100	860	1,200	19,330

74. If a commuter decides to attend a two-year private college instead of a two-year public college, she can expect her total expenses to be

    (A) Approximately the same

    (B) Almost twice as much

    (C) Almost thrice as much

    (D) Slightly less

    (E) There is not enough information to determine the amount

75. How much more does a resident attending a two-year private college pay for room and board than a commuter does?

    (A) $330

    (B) $2,200

    (C) $2,400

    (D) $3,700

    (E) $6,800

76. Approximately what percent of a four-year public college commuter's total expenses are for transportation?

    (A) 4%

    (B) 6%

    (C) 8%

    (D) 12%

    (E) 15%

77. Approximately what percent of a four-year private resident's college budget is used to pay non-tuition and fee expenses?

    (A) 16%

    (B) 20%

    (C) 24%

    (D) 28%

    (E) 36%

78. Tuition and fees and room and board account for approximately what percent of two-year public college commuters' expenses?

    (A) 44%

    (B) 52%

    (C) 56%

    (D) 62%

    (E) 68%

Question 79 is based on the following table.

Diameter of heart (in mm)	120	121	122	123	124	125
Number of persons	5	9	14	8	5	9

79. The median of the given frequency distribution is :

    (A) 122 mm

    (B) 122.25 mm

    (C) 123 mm

    (D) 122.5 mm

    (E) 122.75 mm

Question 80 is based on the following table.

Class interval	3-6	6-9	9-12	12-15	15-18	18-21	21-24
Frequency	2	5	21	23	10	12	3

80. The mode of the above frequency distribution is

(A) 11.5

(B) 12.4

(C) 12

(D) 11.8

(E) 12.27

Answers and Explanations

Level: Easy

1. **Sub topic**: **Data Interpretation with Probability**

   The correct answer is (D).

   First, identify the total number of days Michael recorded his successful offers. Adding the number of days represented by the bars from the graph, the total number of days is 31. Michael makes 7 successful offers on 1 out of 31 days. Hence, the probability is $\frac{1}{31} = 0.032258 \cong 0.032$.

2. **Sub topic**: **Data Interpretation with Probability**

   The correct answer is (C).

   The event of making 2 successful offers is mutually exclusive from the event of making 3 successful offers. The bars on the graph represent 31 days. Therefore, the number of days for each event can be read from the bar graph, and the probabilities can be added together.

   P(2 offers) + P(3 offers)$= \frac{10}{31} + \frac{8}{31} = \frac{18}{31} = 0.58065 \cong 0.581$.

3. **Sub topic**: **Data Interpretation with Probability**

   The correct answer is (A).

   The probability of having at least 1 successful offer is the complement (or opposite) of having 0 offers on a day. Therefore, the equation for this is:

   P(at least 1 offer) $= 1 -$ P(no offer)

   P(at least 1 offer) $= 1 - \frac{1}{31} = 1 - 0.032 = 0.968$

4. **Sub topic**: **Probability**

   The correct answer is $\frac{8}{55}$.

   There is a total of 275 travelers who participated in the survey. There are 40 people traveling to Asia (23 + 17). Hence, the probability is $\frac{40}{275} = \frac{8}{55}$.

5. **Sub topic**: **Probability**

   The correct answer is. $\frac{12}{55}$.

   There is a total of 275 travelers who participated in the survey. The number of females going to Europe is 60. Hence, the probability is $\frac{60}{275} = \frac{12}{55}$.

6. **Sub topic**: **Probability**

   The correct answer is $\frac{55}{103}$.

This is a conditional probability question. There are 55 males going to North America, and there are a total of (55 + 48 = 103) people going to North America. Since the condition is that the traveler is going to North America, the probability that the traveler is a male is 55 out of 103, or $\frac{55}{103}$.

7. **Sub topic: Probability**

    The correct answer is (C).

    This is a conditional probability question. The total number of children who own a smart phone is $16 + 9 + 5 + 3 = 33$ children. Out of the 33 children, those who also own an MP3 player are $9 + 5 = 14$ children. Hence, the probability is $\frac{14}{33}$.

8. **Sub topic: Probability**

    The correct answer is (A).

    There are 6 children who own only a digital camera. Choosing two children is a simultaneous event without replacement. Hence, the probability can be solved as follows:

    P(2 children with only digital camera)$= \frac{6}{50} \times \frac{5}{49} = \frac{30}{2450} = 0.01224 \cong 0.012$.

9. **Sub topic: Numerical Methods**

    The correct answer is (E).

    There is a total of 52 locations in the table. We need to calculate the number of areas that saw a decline of 0.8% or greater from the list of areas by calculating the difference in the unemployment rates.

    The following locations had a decline of 0.8% or more:

California	9.8	9.6	9.4	9.0	8.6	8.5	8.7
Mississippi	9.3	9.6	9.4	9.1	9.1	9.0	8.5
New Jersey	9.5	9.3	9.0	8.7	8.6	8.7	8.6
New York	8.4	8.4	8.2	7.8	7.6	7.5	7.5
Puerto Rico	14.6	14.5	14.2	13.7	13.4	13.2	13.5
Rhode Island	9.8	9.4	9.1	8.8	8.9	8.9	8.9
Utah	5.4	5.2	4.9	4.7	4.6	4.7	4.6
West Virginia	7.4	7.3	7.0	6.6	6.2	6.1	6.2

    There are 8 locations that fit this description. The percentage of locations that had a change of 0.8% is:

    $\frac{8}{52} \times 100 = 0.15 \times 100 = 15\%$

    Therefore, the answer is E.

10. **Sub topic: Numerical Methods**

    The correct answer is (A).

    Florida has a population of 19.32 million, but only 65% of those are allowed to legally work. So, to determine the number of people that can legally work,

    $(19.32 \times 10^6)(0.65) = 12.56 \times 10^6 = 12.56$ million

Based on the chart, the unemployment rate is 7.1% for Florida during the month of May.

So, we multiply 12.56 million by 7.1% to get the number of unemployed in Florida.

$(12.56 \times 10^6)(0.071) = 0.892 \times 10^6 = 0.89$ million

11. **Sub topic: Graphical Methods**

   The correct answer is (D).

   The greatest increase occurred from 1978 to 1979. It was:

   1979 Earnings − 1978 Earnings = 1.1 – 0.5 = 0.6 million = $600,000.

12. **Sub topic: Graphical Methods**

   The correct answer is (A).

   Just calculate the average: (0.9 + 1.0 + 1.2 + 1.3 + 1.5) ÷ 5 = 5.9 ÷ 5 = 1.18 = $1,180,000.

13. **Sub topic: Numerical Data Description**

   The correct answer is (D).

   The opening price is found by subtracting the change in price from the closing price of stock.

   The change in price for *Mbd* stock is $-3\frac{1}{2}$ or −$3.50.

   The closing price for *Mbd* stock is $96.33.

   The opening price, then is 96.33 − (−3.50) = 96.33 + 3.50 = $99.83.

14. **Sub topic: Numerical Data Description**

   The correct answer is (C).

   The stock with the greatest amount of activity is the stock with the greatest volume. *Blm* stock had the greatest amount of activity on this particular day. Its closing price is $41.40. Three stocks have closing prices greater than $41.40 *(Arx, Mbd,* and *Tvk).*

15. **Sub topic: Graphical Data Description**

   The correct answer is (E).

   This is just a matter of adding up the total fares collected for subways in the six years:

1972	300 million
1973	310 million
1974	350 million
1975	350 million
1976	275 million
1977	(250 million)/(1835 million)

16. **Sub topic: Graphical Data Description**

   The correct answer is (C).

The number of fares collected in 1975 was \$350 million, and the number of fares collected in 1977 was \$250 million. The number of fares dropped by \$100 million, but we are looking for the rate, or percentage, of decrease. So, we set our fraction up, difference over starting amount, $\frac{100}{350} = 28.6\%$, which is closest to 25%.

17. **Sub topic: Graphical Data Description**

The correct answer is (C).

To answer this question, you must first determine the total number of dollars in the budget. This can be done by adding together the various sources of income shown in the bar graph:

\$10 + \$6 + \$2 + \$8 + \$4 = \$30 (millions of dollars).

From the pie chart, we learn that 25%,$\frac{1}{4}$ or of this \$30 million was allocated tooperation of thephysical plant,$\frac{1}{4}$ of \$30 million is \$7,500,000.

18. **Sub topic: Graphical Data Description**

The correct answer is (B).

Income from the foundation accounted for \$6 million of the total of \$30 million, and

$\frac{6}{30} = \frac{1}{5} = 20\%$.

19. **Sub topic: Graphical Description**

The correct answer is (D).

The snowfall that accumulated in October was approximately 15 inches. Twice that amount is 30 inches, the months that averaged at least 30 inches, including 30 inches, were January, February, March, and December, for a total of 4 months.

20. **Sub topic: Graphical Description**

The correct answer is (B).

December had about 30 inches of snow. Two-thirds this amount is $30 \times \frac{2}{3} =20$ inches.

The month that had $\frac{2}{3}$rd less or 20 inches less snow than December's 30 inches must have had 10 inches of snow. Find the mark on the graph corresponding to 10 inches. Looking across that point in the horizontal direction, only month April had that amount.

21. **Sub topic: Graphical Description**

The correct answer is (E).

The amount of snow that fell in March was about 40 inches. The amount of snow that fell in April was about 10 inches. From March to April, the drop-in snowfall is 40 − 10 = 30 inches. The drop-in snowfall divided by the original amount of snowfall gives the percentage drop between the two months. So,

(30 inch drop)/(40 inches originally)$= \frac{3}{4} =75$ percent

22. **Sub topic: Graphical Description**

The correct answer is (C).

To find the average amount of snowfall, add up the amount of snowfall for each month in the given range, and divide that sum by the total number of months. From January to May, the amount of snowfall, respectively, was $30 + 35 + 40 + 10 + 0 = 115$ inches. Since the range includes a total of 5 months, the average snowfall is $\frac{115}{5} = 23$ inches.

23. Sub topic: Graphical Data Description

The correct answer is (B).

Stocks include Blue Chip and OTC. Together, these make up $40 + 20 = 60$ percent of the distribution. Be careful when answering this question. What is being asked for is the amount not being invested in stocks. $100 - 60 = 40$ percent of investments are not put into stocks.

24. Sub topic: Graphical Data Description

The correct answer is (D).

The percentage of earnings going towards Annuities is 25 percent. The dollar amount is $\$3000 \times 25\,\% = \$750$, which is choice (D).

25. Sub topic: Graphical Data Description

The correct answer is (A).

If a total of $\$10,000$ is invested, 25 percent or $\$2,500$ is put into Annuities and 10 percent or $\$1,000$ is put into Corporate Bonds. The difference between these two amounts is $\$2,500 - \$1,000 = \$1,500$.

26. Sub topic: Graphical Data Description

The correct answer is (A).

To find the sector with $\$800$ from a $\$4,000$ investment, find the percentage 800 is of 4,000. The correct answer is 0.2 or 20 percent. From the pie chart, only OTC Stocks make up 20 percent of the distribution.

Level: Medium

27. Sub topic: Graphical Methods

The correct answer is (A).

Remake: To make comparison of the rates of reactivity of the elements, we use the sign $\prec$. The element next to the dent side of the sign has higher rate of reactivity than the element on the corner side of the sign. [This is different from the inequality sign in algebra.].

For example, if $H \succ Pb$, then it means that the rate of reactivity of H is higher than rate of reactivity of Pb, and vice versa. That is, $Pb \prec H$ means that the rate of reactivity of Pb is lower than the rate of the reactivity of H.

From Group 14: $Ge \succ Sn$,

From Period 5: $Sn \succ Cd$

Comparing the above inequalities results in

(1) $Ge \succ Cd$

From Group 16: $Se \succ Te$

From Period 5: $Te \succ Cd$

So,

(2) $Se > Cd$

From Group 15: $N > Sb$

From Period 5: $Sb > Cd$

So,

(3) $N > Cd$

The relationships (1)-(3) indicate that Ge, Se, and $N > Cd$

28. **Sub topic: Graphical Methods**

The correct answer is (D).

From Group 8: $Ru > Os$

From Period 6: $Os > La$

Comparing the above inequalities results in

(1) $Ru > La$

From Group 8: $Ru > Hs$

From Period 7: $Hs > Th$

So,

(2) $Ru > Th$

From Group 8: $Ru > Os$

From Period 7: $Os > Ba$

So,

(3) $Ru > Ba$

The relationships (1)-(3) indicate that $Ru > La$, Th, and Ba.

29. **Sub topic: Graphical Methods**

The correct answer is (E).

From Group 18: $Ar > Rn$

From Period 6 $Rn > Au$

So,

(1) $Ar > Au$. That is **a** = Au

From Group 8, Periods 6 and 7, we see that $Np < Hs < Os < Au$

(2) $Au > Np$, That is $b = Np$

30. **Sub topic: Graphical Methods**

The correct answer is (A).

From group 17: $F > Br$

From period 4: $Br > Zn$

So,

(1) $F > Zn$

From group 12: $Zn > Hg$

From period 6: $Zn > Os$

So,

(2) $Zn > Os$

From group 8: $Os > Pm$

From period 7: $Pm > Np$

So,

$Os > Np$

Comparing (1)-(3) results in $F > Zn > Os > Np$

31. **Sub topic: Graphical Methods**

The correct answer is (C).

From period 7: $Ra < Sg$

So,

(1)$Ra < Sg$

From period 6: $Sg < Hs$

From group 8: $Hs < Fe$

Therefore,

(2)$Sg < Fe$

From period 4: $Fe < As$

From group 15: $As < P$

So,

(3)$Fe < P$

Comparing (1)-(3) results in $Ra < Sg < Fe < P$

32. **Sub topic: Graphical Methods**

The correct answer is (D).

The corporate sectors that decreased their support for Philanthropic causes from 2000 to 2005 are: Manufacturing, Retail, Wholesale and Others.

The total contribution by the Corporate Sectors towards Philanthropic Causes in the year 2005 was $570 million.

Amount contributed by the Manufacturing Sector in 2005 = 20% of 570 million

$= \frac{20}{100} \times 570 = \$114$ million

Amount contributed by the Retail Sector in 2005 = 8% of 570 million

$= \frac{8}{100} \times 570 = \$45.6$ million

Amount contributed by the Wholesale Sector in 2005 = 6% of 570 million

$= \frac{6}{100} \times 570 = \$34.2$ million

Amount contributed by the Other Sectors in 2005 = 18% of 570 million

$= \frac{18}{100} \times 570 = \$102.6$ million

The total amount contributed by these four sectors towards Philanthropic Causes in the year 2005 = 114 + 45.6 + 34.2 + 102.6 = \$296.4 million = \$300 million approximately.

Option D is correct.

33. **Sub topic: Graphical Methods**

    The correct answer is (C).

    Amount contributed by the Finance, Insurance and Real Estate Sector in:

    Year 2000 = $\frac{5}{100}$ × 680 = \$34 million

    Year 2005 = $\frac{26}{100}$ × 570 = \$148.2 million

    Amount contributed by the Service Sector in:

    Year 2000 = $\frac{17}{100}$ × 680 = \$115.6 million

    Year 2005 = $\frac{22}{100}$ × 570 = \$125.4 million

    Amount contributed by the Manufacturing Sector in:

    Year 2000 = $\frac{31}{100}$ × 680 = \$210.8 million

    Year 2005 = $\frac{20}{100}$ × 570 = \$114 million

    Amount contributed by the Retail Sector in:

    Year 2000 = $\frac{19}{100}$ × 680 = \$129.2 million

    Year 2005 = $\frac{8}{100}$ × 570 = \$45.6 million

    Amount contributed by the Wholesale Sector in:

    Year 2000 = $\frac{8}{100}$ × 680 = \$54.4 million

    Year 2005 = $\frac{6}{100}$ × 570 = \$34.2 million

    Amount contributed by the Other Sectors in:

    Year 2000 = $\frac{20}{100}$ × 680 = \$136 million

    Year 2005 = $\frac{18}{100}$ × 570 = \$102.6 million

    We see that three sectors (Service, Manufacturing and Other) contributed more than \$100 million in both 2000 and 2005.

    Total amount contributed by the Service Sector in both years = 115.6 + 125.4 = \$241 million

    Total amount contributed by the Manufacturing Sector in both years = 210.8 + 114 = \$324.8 million

    Total amount contributed by the Other Sectors in both years = 136 + 102.6 = \$238.6 million

    Average amount contributed by these three sectors = $\frac{241 + 324.8 + 238.6}{3}$ = \$263.13 million

34. **Sub topic: Graphical Methods**

    The correct answer is (B).

    Financial, Insurance and Real Estate Sector's 2005 contribution to Philanthropic Causes

    = $\frac{26}{100}$ × 570 = \$148.2 million

Amount given for re-building homes $= \frac{1}{3} \times 148.2 = \$49.40$ million

Amount remaining $= 148.2 - 49.40 = \$98.80$ million

Amount given for providing medical aid $= \frac{1}{4} \times 98.8 = \$24.7$ million

Amount spent on rebuilding homes– Amount spent on medical aid

$= 49.40 - 24.70 = \$24.7$ million $= \$25$ million approximately.

Option B is correct.

35. **Sub topic: Graphical Methods**

The correct answer is (D).

Draw a table of the figures.

	Year	Financial, Insurance and Real Estate	Services	Manufacturing	Retail	Wholesale	Others
680	2000	34	115.6	210.8	129.2	54.4	136
570	2005	148.2	125.4	114	45.6	34.2	102.6
Increase/Decrease		335.88%	8.48%	−45.92%	−64.71%	−37.13%	−24.56%

Excluding the Financial, Insurance, and Real Estate industries, the average change in contribution works out to −33%.

36. The correct answer is (D).

Perimeter of ΔABC = AB + BC + CA = P1 (Say)

Given that the points P, Q and R are the midpoints of the sides of the ΔABC.

Remember, in a triangle, the line joining the centers of the 2-sides of a Δ is parallel to the 3rdside.

So, $PQ = \frac{1}{2}AB$

$QR = \frac{1}{2}BC$

$RP = \frac{1}{2}CA$

So, the perimeter of $\Delta PQR = PQ + QR + RP = P_2$ (Say)

$P_2 = \frac{1}{2}(AB + BC + CA)$

$P_2 = \frac{1}{2}P_1 \dots (1)$

Similarly, the points L, M and N are the mid points of the sides of the ΔPQR.

So, in the same way as above we can obtain that,

Perimeter of ΔLMN, $P_3 = \frac{1}{2}$(Perimeter of ΔPQR)

$P_3 = \frac{1}{2}P_2 \dots (2)$

Substituting the value of P_2 from the equation (1) in equation (2), we get

$P_3 = \frac{1}{2}\left(\frac{1}{2}P_1\right)$

$P_3 = \frac{1}{4}P_1$

$\dfrac{P_1}{P_3} = \dfrac{4}{1}$

So, the ratio of the perimeter of the $\triangle$ABC to the perimeter of $\triangle$LMN is 4:1.

Hence option D is correct.

37. The correct answer is (E).

    Given that $\triangle$ABC is a right-angled triangle and the points P, Q and R are the midpoints of the sides of the $\triangle$ABC.

    $ar\triangle ABC = \dfrac{1}{2}xy$ .... (1)

    Remember, in a triangle, the line joining the centers of the 2- sides of a $\triangle$ is parallel to the 3rd side and half of it.

    So, PQ $= \dfrac{1}{2}$ AB

    $\dfrac{PQ}{AB} = \dfrac{1}{2}$

    QR $= \dfrac{1}{2}$ BC

    $\dfrac{QR}{BC} = \dfrac{1}{2}$

    RP $= \dfrac{1}{2}$ CA

    $\dfrac{RP}{CA} = \dfrac{1}{2}$

    Thus, $\dfrac{PQ}{AB} = \dfrac{QR}{BC} = \dfrac{RP}{CA} = \dfrac{1}{2}$

    So, by SSS Similarity Criteria, $\triangle$ABC ~$\triangle$PQR.

    The ratio of the areas of two similar triangles is equal to the square of the ratio of their corresponding sides.

    $\dfrac{ar\triangle PQR}{ar\triangle ABC} = \left(\dfrac{1}{2}\right)^2$

    $\dfrac{ar\triangle PQR}{ar\triangle ABC} = \dfrac{1}{4}$

    $ar\triangle PQR = \dfrac{1}{4} ar\triangle ABC$

    $ar\triangle PQR = \dfrac{1}{4}\left(\dfrac{1}{2}xy\right)$[From equation (1)]

    $ar\triangle PQR = \dfrac{1}{8}xy$ ....(2)

    Similarly, in $\triangle$PQR,L, M and N are the mid points of the sides RQ, RP and PQ respectively.

    So, as above, we may get,

    $ar\triangle LMN = \dfrac{1}{4} ar\triangle PQR$

    $ar\triangle LMN = \dfrac{1}{4}\left(\dfrac{1}{8}xy\right)$[From equation (2)]

    $ar\triangle LMN = \dfrac{1}{32}xy$

    Hence option E is correct.

38. The correct answer is (E).

Given that the points P, Q and R are the midpoints of the sides of the ΔABC.

Remember, in a triangle, the line joining the centers of the 2- sides of a Δis parallel to the 3rd side.

So, $PQ = \frac{1}{2}AB$

$\frac{PQ}{AB} = \frac{1}{2}$

$QR = \frac{1}{2}BC$

$\frac{QR}{BC} = \frac{1}{2}$

$RP = \frac{1}{2}CA$

$\frac{RP}{CA} = \frac{1}{2}$

Thus, $\frac{PQ}{AB} = \frac{QR}{BC} = \frac{RP}{CA} = \frac{1}{2}$

This process is followed *n* times to create *n* triangles. Each time the side of the triangle gets halved.

Let XYZ be the innermost (nth) triangle.

So, as above, we may obtain

$\frac{XY}{AB} = \frac{YZ}{BC} = \frac{ZX}{CA} = \frac{1}{2}$

Since the corresponding sides of the ΔABC and ΔXYZ are in the same ratio, the triangles will be similar, by Side-Side-Side similarity.

The ratio of the areas of two similar triangles is equal to the square of the ratio of their corresponding sides.

$\frac{ar\Delta XYZ}{ar\Delta ABC} = \left(\frac{1}{2^n}\right)^2$

$\frac{ar\Delta XYZ}{ar\Delta ABC} = \frac{1}{4^n}$

So, the ratio of the area of innermost ΔXYZ to the outermost ΔABC is $1:4^n$.

Hence option E is correct.

39. The correct answer is (A).

Given that ΔABC is an equilateral triangle whose side measures *x* units.

Area of equilateral triangle $= \frac{\sqrt{3}}{4}(\text{side})^2$

Area of ΔABC $= \frac{\sqrt{3}}{4}x^2$

Given that the points P, Q and R are the midpoints of the sides of the ΔABC.

Remember, in a triangle, the line joining the centers of the 2- sides of a Δis parallel to the 3rd side.

So, $PQ = \frac{1}{2}AB$

$\frac{PQ}{AB} = \frac{1}{2}$

$QR = \frac{1}{2}BC$

$\frac{QR}{BC} = \frac{1}{2}$

$$RP = \frac{1}{2}CA$$

$$\frac{RP}{CA} = \frac{1}{2}$$

Thus, $\frac{PQ}{AB} = \frac{QR}{BC} = \frac{RP}{CA} = \frac{1}{2}$

Since the corresponding sides of the ΔABC and ΔPQR are in the same ratio, the triangles will be similar, by Side-Side-Side similarity.

The ratio of the areas of two similar triangles is equal to the square of the ratio of their corresponding sides.

$$\frac{ar\Delta PQR}{ar\Delta ABC} = \left(\frac{1}{2}\right)^2$$

$$\frac{ar\Delta PQR}{ar\Delta ABC} = \frac{1}{4}$$

$$ar\Delta PQR = \frac{1}{4}ar\Delta ABC$$

$$ar\Delta PQR = \frac{1}{4}\left(\frac{\sqrt{3}}{4}\right)x^2$$

$$ar\Delta PQR = \frac{\sqrt{3}}{16}x^2$$

Similarly, we can prove that,

$$ar\Delta LMN = \frac{1}{4}ar\Delta PQR$$

$$ar\Delta LMN = \frac{\sqrt{3}}{64}x^2$$

From the given figure we can observe that,

Area of the shaded region = Area of ΔPQR − Area of ΔLMN

$$= \frac{\sqrt{3}}{16}x^2 - \frac{\sqrt{3}}{64}x^2$$

$$= \frac{3\sqrt{3}}{64}x^2$$

Hence option A is correct.

40. **Sub topic: Data Interpretation with Statistics**

The correct answer is (B).

Given that $m = 165$ and $d = 3$, $162cm = 165 - 3 = m - d$. Looking at the graph above, the sections on the bell curve to the left of $m - d$ represent the probabilities of 14% and 2%, which add up to 16%.

41. **Sub topic: Data Interpretation with Statistics**

The correct answers are (A), (B), and (C).

Each event above has the following probabilities:

I.   Less than 159 = 2%

II. Between 159 and 162 = 14%

III. Between 162 and 165 = 34%

IV. Between 165 and 168 = 34%

V.　Between 168 and 171 = 14%

VI.　More than 171 = 2%

By observation, I and VI are equal, II and V are equal, and III and IV are equal. II and IV are not equal.

42. **Sub topic: Graphical Methods**

The correct answer is (B).

The first runner has a speed of 10 mph and runs for 60 min. This is precisely one hour, so the first side length is 10 miles. The second runner has a speed of 8 mph and runs for 30 min. This is a half hour, so he runs 4 miles. Taking these two sides and length and width we know that the area is $4 \times 10 = 40$ square miles. Also, as this is a rectangle, the other two sides mirror these two sides, and so the perimeter is $10 + 4 + 10 + 4 = 28$ miles. The answer is B.

43. **Sub topic: Graphical Methods**

The correct answer is (C).

The perimeter would be the same, as we have information for all four sides. However, the area of a parallelogram cannot be determined from the length of its sides alone, so the answer is C.

44. **Sub topic: Graphical Methods**

The correct answer is (B).

Find the proportion of oil usage by residents for each of the given years. In 1980, 20% used oil; in 1985, 40% used oil; in 1990, 50% used oil; and in 1995, 60% used oil. The greatest increase was from 20% to 40%, which occurred in 1985.

45. **Sub topic: Graphical Methods**

The correct answer is (A).

Mean refers to the average. To find the average sum all percentage of oil usage from the given years and divide by the number of given years. The average is

$$\frac{20 + 40 + 50 + 60}{4} = \frac{170}{4} = 42.5\%.$$

46. **Sub topic: Graphical Methods**

The correct answer is (C).

The proportion of residents who used oil heat in 1995 was 60%. The proportion that used electric heat that year was 10%. The percentage difference between these two types of heating methods is 50%; 50% of 50,000 is 25,000.

47. **Sub topic: Graphical Methods**

The correct answer is (B).

The percentage of gas consumers in 1985 was 40%. In 1990, gas consumers made up 30% of the population. So 10% of the gas users from 1985 changed to alternative heating methods in the following time frame.

48. **Sub topic: Graphical Methods**

The correct answer is (D).

We're looking for the lowest ratio of males to females, so we have to get the smallest number of males and the largest number of females. Skimming the bar graphs, we can see that in pediatrics the female graph and the male graph are closer than any of the others. Pediatrics is (D), the correct answer.

49. **Sub topic: Graphical Methods**

The correct answer is (C).

To refer to ages of physicians, we need to find the slice of the pie that goes 45 to 54. It's 20 percent, but 20 percent of what? We're not looking for a percent; we're looking for a number of doctors. For general surgery the male bar goes up to about 35,000 and the female bar goes up to about 2,000- about 37,000 total. So, 20 percent of 37,000 is the number of general surgery physicians between ages 45 and 54, inclusive. What's 20 percent of 37,000, or $\frac{1}{5}$ of 37,000? Well, let's see, $\frac{1}{5}$ of 35,000 is 7,000, $\frac{1}{5}$ of 2,000 is 400, making 7,400.(C) is 7,350, the correct answer.

50. **Sub topic: Graphical Methods**

The correct answer is (E).

We'll have to find the total number of family practice physicians, which represents 7.5 percent of all the physicians in the United States, then we can find 100 percent of that number. The male bar of family practice physicians goes just over 36,000, so we'll say it's 36,000 plus. The number of females goes just over 6,000 so we'll call that 6,000 plus, so we have about 43,000 altogether. This is 7.5 percent of all the physicians. 7.5 percent is awkward—it's three-quarters of 10 percent, which is $\frac{3}{4} \times \frac{1}{10}$ or $\frac{3}{40}$. So, 43,000 is $\frac{3}{40}$ of the total number of doctors. To change 43,000 into the number of total physicians we multiply it by $\frac{40}{3}$.

Think of it this way: we have an equation now, $\frac{3}{40}$ of the number were looking for, we'll call it N. The number of physicians, equals 43,000. We want to get N by itself, so we have to get rid of that $\frac{3}{40}$.So, we multiply by the reciprocal,$\frac{40}{3}$, andthat leaves us with N by itself on the left. But the hard part is multiplying $\frac{40}{3} \times 43,000$.

What's $\frac{40}{3}$? It's $13\frac{1}{3}$and that's easier to multiply. 13×43 is 559 so $13 \times 43,000$ is$559\,000$ — you look at your choices and estimate. Only one is close to 559,000−(E), 570,000, and we are going to add on to that, so (E) is the correct answer.

51. **Sub topic: Graphical Methods**

The correct answer is (B).

How many male general surgeon physicians were under 35 years old? The pie chart breaks down general surgery physicians by age, so be working with it. And, since we're looking for a number of general surgery physicians, we know that we're going to have to find the total number of general surgery physicians, then break it down according to the percentages on the pie chart. We're told the number of female general physicians in the under-35 category represented 3.5 percent of all the general surgery physicians What this does is break that slice of the pie for under-35 into two smaller slices, one for men under 35 and one for women under 35. Now we know that the whole slice for under-35-year-olds is 30 percent of the total and we are just being told that the number of females under 35 is 3.5 percent of the total. So, the between 30 percent and 3.5 percent must be the men in the under-35 category, which leaves 26.5 percent, which we have to multiply by the total number of general surgery physicians. We figured out in that there were 37,000 total general surgery physicians, and 26.5 percent of those are men under 35. What's 26.5 percent of 37,000? One-quarter of 37,000 is 9,250 and that's very close to (A), but remember we've still got another 1.5 percent to go. One percent of 37,000 is 370 and half of that, or 5 percent will be 185, so if you add 370 and 185 to 9,250 you end up with a total of 9,805 which is very close to (B), the correct answer.

52. **Sub topic: Graphical Methods**

The correct answer is (A).

Tax, Clothing and miscellaneous $= 11 + 8 + 6 = 25\% = \frac{1}{4}th$ of his income which is the expenses on food.

53. **Sub topic: Graphical Methods**

The correct answer is (B).

After reduction of 2% in tax: $11\% - 2\% = 9\%$. Increase of 1% each on cinema and travel amount to 12% on cinema and 18% on travel.

Level: Difficult

54. **Sub topic: Set Theory**

The correct answer is 5.

Number of students enrolled in all three classes =

[Number of students enrolled in Algebra, Geometry, or Physics] +

[Number of students enrolled both Algebra and Geometry] +

[Number of students enrolled both Geometry and Physics] +

[Number of students enrolled both Algebra and Physics] −[Number of students in Algebra] −

[Number of students in Geometry] −[Number of students in Physics]

$= 87 + 11 + 12 + 12 - 28 - 47 - 42 = 5$

55. **Sub topic: Set Theory**

The correct answer is 4.

Number of students enrolled in all three classes =

[Number of students enrolled in Chemistry, Geometry, or Physics] +

[Number of students enrolled both Chemistry and Geometry] +

[Number of students enrolled both Geometry and Physics] +

[Number of students enrolled both Chemistry and Physics]−

[Number of students in Chemistry] −[Number of students in Geometry] −[Number of students in Physics]

$= 102 + 13 + 12 + 12 - 46 - 47 - 42 = 4$

56. **Sub topic: Set Theory**

The correct answer is (E).

[Number of students enrolled Algebra + Geometry + Physics, Chemistry + Geometry + Physics, or Physics + Geometry] $= 12$

Subtracting the sum of [Algebra + Geometry + Physics] +[Chemistry + Geometry + Physics] $= 5 + 4 = 9$ from this number gives the answer $12 - 9 = 3$.

57. **Sub topic: Set Theory**

    The correct answer is 9.

    Number of students enrolled chemistry + geometry only =

    [Number of students enrolled chemistry + geometry] −

    [Number of students enrolled chemistry + geometry + physics]= 13 − 4 = 9

58. **Sub topic: Set Theory**

    The correct answer is 45.

    Number of students taking Chemistry = 46

    Number of students taking only chemistry = 46 − [Those taking only geometry and chemistry] − [Those taking chemistry and physics] = 46 − 9 − 12 = 25 (note, none is taking algebra with chemistry)

    Number of students taking Geometry = 47

    Number of students taking only Geometry = 47 − [Those taking geometry and chemistry] − [Those taking geometry and physics but not chemistry] − [Those taking geometry and algebra but neither chemistry nor physics]

    Note that, [Those taking geometry and physics but not chemistry] = [Those taking geometry and physics] − [Those taking geometry and physics and chemistry] = 12 − 4 = 8 (this includes, students who may or may not take algebra)

    Note that, [Those taking geometry and algebra but neither chemistry nor physics] = [Those taking geometry and algebra] − [Those taking geometry and algebra and physics] = 11 − 5 = 6 (this automatically excludes any chemistry students since, taking algebra implicitly means not taking chemistry)

    Hence, Number of students taking only Geometry = 47 − 13 − 8 − 6 = 20. Final Answer is 25 + 20 = 45

59. **Sub topic: Set Theory**

    The correct answer is (E).

    [Number of students enrolled in Chemistry or Algebra] = 46 + 28 = 74

60. **Sub topic: Set Theory**

    The correct answer is (A).

    [Number of students enrolled either physics class or geometry class, NOT algebra or chemistry class] =

    [Number of students in Geometry class] + [Number of students in Physics class] − [Number of students in both classes] = 47 + 42 − 12 = 77

61. **Sub topic: Graphical Methods**

    The correct answer is (D).

    Let the amount invested in Company X = x

    And, the amount invested in Company Y = y

    Rate of interest given by Company X in 1999 = 8%

    Rate of interest given by Company Y in 1999 = 10%

    Interest per annum is calculated by $= \dfrac{P \times r \times t}{100}$ where,

    P is amount invested

    r is rate of interest

t is the time period

Interest earned on \$$x$ at 8% interest $= \dfrac{x \times 8 \times 1}{100} = \$\dfrac{8x}{100}$

Amount earned in 1999 on \$$x$ at 8% interest $= \dfrac{8x}{100} + x = \$\dfrac{108x}{100}$

Interest earned on \$$y$ at 10% interest $= \dfrac{y \times 10 \times 1}{100} = \$\dfrac{10y}{100}$

Amount earned in 1999 on \$$y$ at 10% interest $= \dfrac{10y}{100} + y = \$\dfrac{110y}{100}$

Ratio of amounts earned from X and Y $= \dfrac{108x}{100} : \dfrac{110y}{100} = \dfrac{108x}{100} \times \dfrac{100}{110y} = \dfrac{108x}{110y} = \dfrac{54x}{55y}$

It is given that the ratio of amounts earned was 2:1

Hence, $\dfrac{54x}{55y} = \dfrac{2}{1}$

$\dfrac{x}{y} = \dfrac{110}{54} = \dfrac{55}{27} = 55 : 27$

Option D is correct.

62. **Sub topic: Graphical Methods**

The correct answer is (C).

To calculate the amount earned by investing \$10,000 in company X:

Amount invested in Company X in 1996 = \$10,000

Interest earned in 1996 $= \dfrac{10,000 \times 7 \times 1}{100} = \$700$

Amount earned in 1996 = 10,000 + 700 = \$10,700

Amount invested in Company X in 1997 = \$10,700

Interest earned in 1997 $= \dfrac{10,700 \times 9 \times 1}{100} = \$963$

Amount earned in 1997 = 10,700 + 963 = \$11,663

Amount invested in Company X in 1998 = \$11,663

Interest earned in 1998 $= \dfrac{11,663 \times 8 \times 1}{100} = \$933.04$

Amount earned in 1998 = 11,663 + 933.04 = \$12,596.04

Amount invested in Company X in 1999 = \$12,596.04

Interest earned in 1999 $= \dfrac{12,596.04 \times 10 \times 1}{100} = \$1,259.60$

Amount earned in 1999 = 12,596.04 + 1,259.60 = \$13,855.64

Amount invested in Company X in 2000 = \$13,855.64

Interest earned in 2000 $= \dfrac{13,855.64 \times 7.5 \times 1}{100} = \$1,039.17$

Amount earned in 2000 = 13,855.64 + 1,039.17 = \$14,894.81

To calculate the amount earned by investing \$10,000 in company Y:

Amount invested in Company Y in 1996 = \$10,000

Interest earned in 1996 $= \dfrac{10,000 \times 6.5 \times 1}{100} = \$650$

Amount earned in 1996 = 10,000 + 650 = \$10,650

Amount invested in Company Y in 1997 = \$10,650

Interest earned in 1997 $= \frac{10{,}650 \times 8 \times 1}{100} = \$852$

Amount earned in 1997 $= 10{,}650 + 852 = \$11{,}502$

Amount invested in Company Y in 1998 = $11,502

Interest earned in 1998 $= \frac{11{,}502 \times 9.5 \times 1}{100} = \$1{,}092.69$

Amount earned in 1998 $= 11{,}502 + 1{,}092.69 = \$12{,}594.69$

Amount invested in Company Y in 1999 = $12,594.69

Interest earned in 1999 $= \frac{12{,}594.69 \times 8 \times 1}{100} = \$1{,}007.58$

Amount earned in 1999 $= 12{,}594.69 + 1{,}007.58 = \$13{,}602.27$

Amount invested in Company Y in 2000 = $13,602.27

Interest earned in 2000 $= \frac{13{,}602.27 \times 9 \times 1}{100} = \$1{,}224.20$

Amount earned in 2000 $= 13{,}602.27 + 1{,}224.20 = \$14{,}826.47$

Difference in the amounts earned at the end of the year 2000 from the two companies

$= 14{,}894.81 - 14{,}826.47 = \$68.34$

Option C is correct.

63. **Sub topic: Graphical Methods**

    The correct answer is (B).

    Let the amount invested in Company X be x

    Then the amount invested in Company Y = $\$(45{,}000{,}000 - x)$

    Interest earned on $\$x$ at 7.5% in the year 2000 $= \frac{x \times 7.5 \times 1}{100} = \frac{\$7.5x}{100}$

    Interest earned on $\$(45{,}000{,}000 - x)$ at 9% in the year 2000 $= \frac{(45{,}000{,}000 - x) \times 9 \times 1}{100}$

    $= \frac{405{,}000{,}000}{100} - \frac{9x}{100}$

    $= 4{,}050{,}000 - \frac{9x}{100}$

    Total interest earned $= \frac{7.5x}{100} + 4{,}050{,}000 - \frac{9x}{100} = 4{,}050{,}000 - \frac{1.5x}{100}$

    Total interest earned in the year 2000 = $3.75 million

    $3{,}750{,}000 = 4{,}050{,}000 - \frac{1.5x}{100}$

    $\frac{1.5x}{100} = 4{,}050{,}000 - 3{,}750{,}000$

    $\frac{1.5x}{100} = 300{,}000$

    $x = \frac{300{,}000 \times 100}{1.5} = \$20{,}000{,}000$

    Amount invested in Company X = $20,000,000

    Amount invested in Company Y = $45,000,000 - 20,000,000 = $25,000,000

    Option B is correct.

64. **Sub topic: Graphical Methods**

The correct answer is (C).

Consider that A invested $100 in Company X.

The amount earned during the period 1996 to 2002 is,

$$\$100 \times \frac{1}{100} \times (7 + 9 + 8 + 10 + 7.5 + 6.5) = \$48$$

A would have earned $48 over the entire period.

B invests $100 in Company Y.

During the period 1996 to 1999, B would have earned

$$\$100 \times \frac{1}{100} \times (6.5 + 8 + 9.5 + 8) = \$32$$

In 2000, he doubles the investment to $200.

In the period 2000 to 2002, B would have earned

$$\$200 \times \frac{1}{100} \times (9 + 8 + 4) = \$42$$

Total interest earned by B = $74

Increased interest earned over A = $74− $48 = $26.

Hence, the percentage increase $= \dfrac{\$26}{\$48} = 54\%$

65. The correct answer is (E).

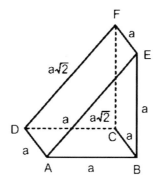

From the figure above, we can see that, each part now has 5 surfaces.

Note that △ABE is a right triangle.

So, $AE^2 = AB^2 + BE^2$ (Pythagorean Theorem)

$AE^2 = a^2 + a^2$

$AE^2 = 2a^2$

$AE = \sqrt{2a}$

Area of face ABE $= \frac{1}{2} \times a \times a = \frac{1}{2}a^2$

Area of face DCF $= \frac{1}{2} - a - a = \frac{1}{2}a^2$

Area of face ABCD $= a - a = a^2$

Area of face CBEF $= a - a = a^2$

Note that the new surface AEFD formed along the diagonal is a rectangle of dimensions $\sqrt{2a}$ and a.

So, area of face AEFD $= \sqrt{2a} \times a = \sqrt{2a}$

So, the surface area of each part will be

$$S = \frac{1}{2}a^2 + \frac{1}{2}a^2 + a^2 + \sqrt{2}a^2$$

$$S = (3 + \sqrt{2})a^2$$

So, option E is correct.

66. The correct answer is (A).

Surface area of given cube $= 6a^2$

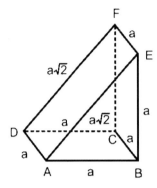

From figure observe that ∆ABE is right triangle.

So, $AE^2 = AB^2 + BE^2$..............(Pythagorean Theorem)

$AE^2 = a^2 + a^2$

$AE^2 = 2a^2$

$AE = \sqrt{2}a$

Since the cube is hollow, each of the two parts will have only 4 faces (AEFD will not be a face).

Area of face ABE $= \frac{1}{2} \times a \times a = \frac{1}{2}a^2$

Area of face DCF $= \frac{1}{2} \times a \times a = \frac{1}{2}a^2$

Area of face ABCD $= a \times a = a^2$

Area of face CBEF $= a \times a^2 = a^2$

Surface area of each part $= \frac{1}{2}a^2 + \frac{1}{2}a^2 + a^2 + a^2 = 3a^2$

But, since the cube is hollow, it will have inner and outer surface areas.

So, total surface area of each part $= 2 \times 3a^2 = 6a^2$

So, ratio of surface area of each part to the surface area of original cube will be $\frac{6a^2}{6a^2} = 1:1$

Hence, option A is correct.

67. The correct answer is (C).

Surface area of given cube $= 6a^2$

When this cube is sliced into 4 parts by perpendicular planes passing through the centre of the cube, we get 4 new cubes.

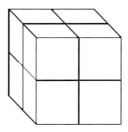

The length of the edge for each of the new cube will be $\dfrac{a}{2}$

So, surface area of new cube $= 6\left(\dfrac{a}{2}\right)^2$

Therefore, surface area of 4 new cubes $= 4\times 6 \times \left(\dfrac{a}{2}\right)^2$

$= 4 \times 6 \times \dfrac{a^2}{4} = 6a^2$

So, the ratio of surface area of the original cube to the total surface area of 4 new cubes is $\dfrac{6a^2}{6a^2}$ or $1:1$.

Hence, option C is correct.

68. The correct answer is (A).

When two planes cut along the diagonals, 4 prisms are formed.

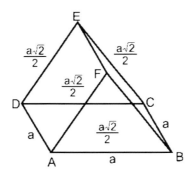

From the figure above, we can see that, each of the 4 parts is a triangular prism and has 5 surfaces. Also note that AF is half the diagonal of a face of the cube.

So, AF $= \dfrac{a\sqrt{2}}{2}$. Note that ΔAFB is a right triangle whose sides measure $\dfrac{a\sqrt{2}}{2}, \dfrac{a\sqrt{2}}{2}$ and a.

Area of face ABF $= \dfrac{1}{2} \times \dfrac{a\sqrt{2}}{2} \times \dfrac{a\sqrt{2}}{2} = \dfrac{a^2}{4}$

Similarly, area of face DEC $= \dfrac{a^2}{4}$

Area of face AFED $= \dfrac{a\sqrt{2}}{2} \times a \dfrac{a\sqrt{2}}{2} \times a = \dfrac{\sqrt{2}}{2}a^2$

Similarly, area of face BCEF $= \dfrac{\sqrt{2}}{2}a^2$

Area of face ABCD $= a \times a = a^2$

So, the surface area of each part will be

$S = \dfrac{a^2}{4} + \dfrac{a^2}{4} + \dfrac{\sqrt{2}}{2}a^2 + \dfrac{\sqrt{2}}{2}a^2 + a^2$

$$S = \frac{a^2}{4} + \sqrt{2}a^2 + a^2$$

$$S = \frac{3a^2}{2} + \sqrt{2}a^2$$

$$S = \left(\frac{3}{2} + \sqrt{2}\right)a^2$$

So, option A is correct.

69. **Sub topic: Quadrilaterals**

The correct answers are (A), (C), and (D).

The area of this shape is in direct proportion to the dimension. The area formulas for trapezoid, parallelogram, and rectangle all fit this description. The formula for squares does not. The answers are A, C, and D.

70. **Sub topic: Quadrilaterals**

The correct answer is (B).

The area increases as a square of the dimension. Only a square fits this description. The answer is B.

71. **Sub topic: Graphical Data Description**

The correct answer is (E).

Looking at the two charts, we see that the upper one, representing the total passenger miles, shows a smooth increase, generally speaking, while the lower one shows large changes. Since the lower one is deaths per passenger-mile, the sharp changes in the rate must be from sharp changes in the number of deaths. (A) is inferable since the highest level reached by the line on the lower graph was approximately 1.3, in 1951. (B) is also inferable. The largest jump in the line on the lower graph for a one-year period occurred in the period 1954-1955. (C) is also inferable. The two low points on the line of the lower graph occurred in 1954 and 1957; both were approximate. (D) is inferable: 10 to 30. But (E) is not inferable. Remember not to confuse absolute numbers and percent increase.

72. **Sub topic: Graphical Data Description**

The correct answer is (E).

The question stem asks about the longest, not the most severe or greatest increase. Although the largest increase ended in 1955, the longest increase lasted from 1956 until 1960. The word "finally" is also a clue.

73. **Sub topic: Graphical Data Description**

The correct answer is (A).

It would be counter-productive to spend a lot of time computing the actual number of deaths for each of the five years mentioned. Instead, a rough estimate will suffice. At first glance, it appears that the only reasonable possibilities are 1951, 1955, and 1960, since the fatality rate (lower graph) is at least approximately equal in those years. Now, it is absolutely critical to realize that, though the fatality rate in 1951 was higher than the fatality rate in 1960 (1.3 compared with 1.0), there were three times as many miles traveled in 1960 as in 1951. Similarly, though the fatality rate was higher in 1955 than it was in 1960 (1.2 compared with 1.0), there were 50% more miles traveled in 1960 than in 1955. This reasoning shows that the greatest numbers of fatalities occurred in 1960. Even though the fatality rate that year was not as high as those for 1955 and 1951, this was more than offset by the greater number of passenger-miles traveled. Of course, a longer method of attack is to actually do a rough calculation for each:

(A) 1960: $\dfrac{1}{100 \text{ million}} \times 30 \text{ billion} = 300$

(B) 1957: $\dfrac{1}{100 \text{ million}} \times 25 \text{ billion} = 25$

(C) 1955: $\dfrac{1.2}{100 \text{ million}} \times 20 \text{ billion} = 240$

(D) 1953: $\dfrac{0.6}{100 \text{ million}} \times 15 \text{ billion} = 90$

(E) 1951: $\dfrac{1.3}{100 \text{ million}} \times 10 \text{ billion} = 120$

74. The correct answer is (B).

   The total expenses for a commuter at a two-year public college are $6,420, while the total expenses for a commuter at a two-year private college are $12,240. The best answer is, thus, "almost twice as much."

75. The correct answer is (C).

   A resident attending a two-year private college pays $4,600, while a commuter pays $2,200. The difference is $4,600 − $2,200 = $2,400.

76. The correct answer is (D).

   The transportation expenses are $1,000 out of a total of $8,510 to $8,500 gives us an approximate answer of

   $$\frac{1000}{8500} \times 100\% = \frac{10}{85} \times 100\% \approx 11.7\% \approx 12\%$$

77. The correct answer is (E).

   The easiest way to do this problem is to find what percent tuition and fees represent and subtract this percentage from 100%.

   $$\frac{14{,}500}{22{,}520} \times 100\% \approx 64\%$$

   Therefore, the percent spent on non-tuition and fee expenses is 100% − 64% = 36%.

78. The correct answer is (C).

   The total tuition and fees and room and board expenses are $1,600 + $2,000 = $3,600. The total expenses are $6,420 ≈ $6,400. Thus, the percent is

   $$\frac{3{,}600}{6{,}400} \times 100\% = \frac{9}{16} \times 100\% \approx 56\%$$

79. The correct answer is (A).

   The given table may be presented as:

Diameter of heart (in mm)	Number of persons	Cumulative frequency
120	5	5
121	9	14
122	14	28
123	8	36
124	5	41
125	9	50

Here $n = 50$.

So $\dfrac{n}{2} = 25$ & $\dfrac{n}{2} + 1 = 26$.

Median $= \dfrac{1}{2}\left(25^{\text{th}} \text{ term} + 26^{\text{th}} \text{ term}\right) = \dfrac{(122 + 122)}{2} = 122$. [Because both lie in that row whose c.f. is 28]

80. The correct answer is (B).

Maximum frequency is 23. So, modal class is 12-15.

Because $L_1 = 12$, $L_2 = 15$, $f = 23$, $f_1 = 21$ and $f_2 = 10$.

Because Mode

$$L_1 + \dfrac{f - f_1}{2f - f_1 - f_2}(L_1 - L_2) = 12 + \dfrac{(23 - 21)}{(46 - 21 - 10)}(15 - 12) = 12.4$$

Chapter **7**

Exercise #1

Questions: 20 | Time: 30 minutes

This Exercise includes *20 practice questions*. The questions cover all the question types as explained in Chapter 2 and may fall into any of the following categories - Arithmetic, Algebra, Geometry or Data Analysis. You will find answers and detailed explanations towards the end of this chapter.

1. The second term of a geometric progression is $\frac{2}{9}$. If the fourth term is $\frac{8}{81}$, find the sum of the first three terms and that of the first seven terms.

    Select all that apply.

    (A) $\frac{2059}{2187}$

    (B) $\frac{2}{27}$

    (C) $\frac{2059}{6561}$

    (D) $\frac{64}{2187}$

    (E) $\frac{7}{27}$

    (F) $\frac{19}{27}$

2.　Given the following data:

$$\frac{4a}{23} + 15b = 3d$$

$$\frac{c}{17} + 5a = 32$$

$$2b + \frac{8e}{3} = 15c$$

$$15d + 2a = \frac{1,414}{23}$$

The value of e in terms of b is:

(A)　$46 + \frac{4,507,222b}{85,281}$

(B)　$\frac{4,242 - 5,175b}{198}$

(C)　$-\frac{632,145}{88} - \frac{6,588,521b}{85,288}$

(D)　$\frac{245b}{32} + \frac{1,232,003}{17}$

(E)　$-\frac{23,033}{23} + \frac{4,587b}{29,334}$

3. There are three runners in a race.

    The base velocities of the runners are known as:

    Runner A = 18 feet/second

    Runner B = 16 feet/second

    Runner C = (Runner A's velocity multiplied by 3) − (Runner B's velocity multiplied by 2).

    Runner D = 15 feet/second

    Runner E = 12 feet/second

    In addition, the runner's velocities are affected by efficiency multipliers based on their diet and preparation for the race.

    The multipliers at the start of this race are:

    Runner A = 75% effective

    Runner B = 80% effective

    Runner C = 70% effective

    Runner D = 70% effective

    Runner E = 95% effective

    The race begins, with the runner's attaining their speeds immediately after the starting gun sounds. After 1 minute, Runner C stops immediately to tie a shoe, while the other racers continue on. After 20 seconds runner C rejoins the race. Two minutes after Runner C rejoins the race, the runners grab energy drinks from a roadside stand without slowing their pace, and thirty seconds later their efficiency multipliers change to the following:

    Runner A = 75% effective

    Runner B = 80% effective

    Runner C = 70% effective

    Runner D = 70% effective

    Runner E = 95% effective

    The race continues another 4 minutes and a whistle is blown, ending the race. What is the approximate average distance in feet covered by the runners?

    (A) 5,640

    (B) 5,830

    (C) 7,300

    (D) 6,400

    (E) 7,035

4.

The arithmetic mean of a, b, c and 24 is M, and the arithmetic mean of a, b, c, and d, is N. The arithmetic mean of b, c, d, and 24 is (M + N).

Quantity A	**Quantity B**
$d - a$	4N

(A) Quantity A is greater.

(B) Quantity B is greater.

(C) The two quantities are equal.

(D) The relationship cannot be determined from the information given.

5.

Two salespeople bought TV sets for resale from different wholesalers. Susan made a profit of 24% after selling the TV set at $148.80, while Christina sold her TV at a loss of 4% less than the percent of Susan's profit, or $96.00 total.

Quantity A	**Quantity B**
The buying price of Susan	The buying price of Christina

(A) Quantity A is greater.

(B) Quantity B is greater.

(C) The two quantities are equal.

(D) The relationship cannot be determined from the information given.

6. The sides of an isosceles triangle are 3, 3 and 5. What is the area of the triangle?

(A) 15

(B) $\dfrac{15}{2}$

(C) $\dfrac{15}{4}$

(D) $\dfrac{15}{8}$

(E) 16

7.

Let $x < 0, y > 0$ and $|x| > y$.

Quantity A	**Quantity B**
$\dfrac{2x^2 + y}{2y + x^3 + 3}$	$\dfrac{x + 2y^2}{2y + x^2 + 3}$

(A) Quantity A is greater.

(B) Quantity B is greater.

(C) The two quantities are equal.

(D) The relationship cannot be determined from the information given.

Questions 8 and 9 are based on the following data:

Number of reported cases of AIDS in Bangkok has increased each year since 1991. The two bars for each year represent the number of cases diagnosed respectively in the first and second half of the year. The following table gives the fatality percentages among the cases corresponding to each half year. Most of patients who were diagnosed before 1996 as having AIDS have already died.

Percentage of AIDS cases Resulted in Death

	1991	1992	1993	1994	1995	1996	1997
1st Half	92	89	90	83	80	70	47
2nd Half	93	89	89	83	77	58	33

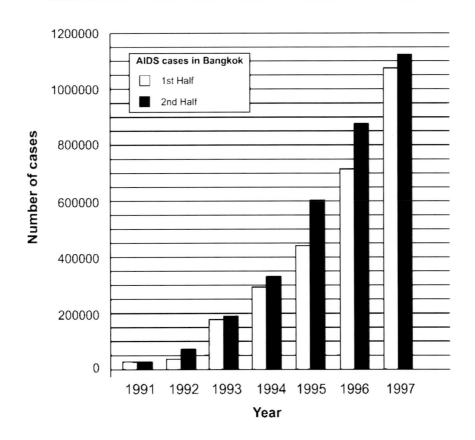

8. The approximate percentage increase of the reported cases in the first half of 1997 as compared to the second half of 1995 is

    (A) 90

    (B) 95

    (C) 70

    (D) 83

    (E) 93

9. In 1994 the increase in the number of reported cases in the second half of the year as compared to the first half is

    (A) 150000

    (B) 75000

    (C) 50000

    (D) 100000

    (E) 125000

10. At the grocery store, an apple costs $1.34, an orange costs $0.47, and a banana costs $0.19. How much did Helen pay for 5 apples, 3 oranges, and 7 bananas?

    (A) $7.70

    (B) $9.44

    (C) $10.56

    (D) $11.74

    (E) $30.00

11.

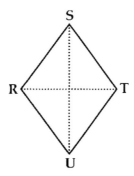

    The diagram above shows rhombus RSTU. If $\angle RST = 5x - 14$ and $\angle UST = 2x + 4$, what is the value of x?

    (A) 2.5

    (B) 4

    (C) $5\frac{1}{3}$

    (D) 18

    (E) 22

12.

A boat takes equal time to cover 0.6 miles downstream and 0.4 miles upstream.

Quantity A

Speed of the boat in still water

Quantity B

Time taken by the boat to cover 1.2 miles downstream in the same river

(A) Quantity A is greater.

(B) Quantity B is greater.

(C) The two quantities are equal.

(D) The relationship cannot be determined from the information given.

13.

$$2x + 4y - 2z = 5t$$

$$4y - 2z - t = 6x$$

$$15x - y + 7z = 13t$$

$$13z - 2y = 36x - 6t - 8$$

Quantity A

$4x - 3y + t$

Quantity B

$3t - 2y - z$

(A) Quantity A is greater.

(B) Quantity B is greater.

(C) The two quantities are equal.

(D) The relationship cannot be determined from the information given.

14. 8, 9, 12, 17, 24 ...

In the preceding sequence, a certain pattern determines each of the subsequent numbers. What is the next number in the sequence?

(A) 41

(B) 35

(C) 33

(D) 30

(E) 29

15. If the volume and the total surface area of a cube are equal, how long must the edge of the cube be?

(A) 2 units

(B) 3 units

(C) 4 units

(D) 5 units

(E) 6 units

16. 150 regular size chocolate bars include 10 lbs. of sugar total. When promotional size bars are made 20% more sugar is needed. How many pounds of sugar will be required to make 250 promotional size chocolates?

| |lbs

17.

Tank A has an inlet pipe that allows a steady incoming flow of 45 gallons per minute (gpm); the outlet on Tank A allows a continuous exit flow of 10 gallons per minute. Tank B has an inlet pipe that allows a steady incoming flow of 60 gallons per minute and allows a continuous exit flow of 15 gallons per minute. The valves on the inlet pipes are opened simultaneously and the water begins to flow into the tanks. After 20 minutes of operation, two leaks start in the sides of Tank B. Leak A has a flow of 23 gallons per minute, which spills to the floor. Leak B is draining 14 gallons per minute of water back into Tank A and draining 11 gallons per minute onto the floor. 25 minutes after the leaks started, Leak B is repaired, but Leak A continues to drain. The inlet pipes are allowed to run for another 15 minutes and then the flow is shut off.

Quantity A	**Quantity B**
Amount of water in Tank A	Amount of water in Tank B

(A) Quantity A is greater.

(B) Quantity B is greater.

(C) The two quantities are equal.

(D) The relationship cannot be determined from the information given.

18.

Andrew tells David, "If you give me $100 then I will have twice the money that you have". David, in turn tells Andrew, "If you give me $10, I shall have six times the amount you have".

Quantity A	**Quantity B**
Original amount with Andrew + Original amount with David	Original amount with David + Amount borrowed from Andrew

(A) Quantity A is greater.

(B) Quantity B is greater.

(C) The two quantities are equal.

(D) The relationship cannot be determined from the information given.

19.

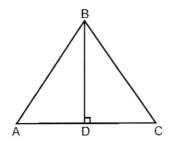

Note: Figure not drawn to scale.

In the preceding figure, BD ⊥ AC, AB =34, BD = 30, and BC = 34. What is the length of AC?

(A) 8

(B) 18

(C) 30

(D) 32

(E) 34

20.

It is given that
$$\frac{b+6}{4b^2} + \frac{3}{2b^2} = \frac{b+4}{8b^2}$$

Quantity A
$$\frac{b+6}{4b^2}$$

Quantity B
$$\frac{b+4}{8b^2}$$

(A) Quantity A is greater.

(B) Quantity B is greater.

(C) The two quantities are equal.

(D) The relationship cannot be determined from the information given.

Answers and Explanations

1. **Topic: Arithmetic**

    Sub topic: Progressions

    The correct answers are (A) and (F).

    The nth term of a geometric progression is given by $a_n = ar^{n-1}$ where the letters have their usual meaning.

    The second term $ar = \frac{2}{9}$, the fourth term is $ar^3 = \frac{8}{81}$

    Therefore $\frac{ar^3}{ar} = \frac{8}{81} \times \frac{9}{2}$

    $r^2 = \frac{4}{9}; r = \frac{2}{3}$

    The common ratio is $\frac{2}{3}$

    The first term $a = \frac{2}{9} \times \frac{3}{2} = \frac{1}{3}$

    The first, second and third term is $\frac{1}{3}, \frac{2}{9}$ and $\frac{2}{9} \times \frac{2}{3} = \frac{2}{27}$

    The sum of the first three terms is $\frac{1}{3} + \frac{2}{9} + \frac{4}{27} = \frac{19}{27}$

    Using the formula for the first n terms, $S_n = \frac{a(1-r^n)}{1-r}$, we have,

    $$S_7 = \frac{\frac{1}{3}\left(1 - \frac{2^7}{3^3}\right)}{1 - \frac{2}{3}} = \frac{2059}{2187}$$

    The correct answers are A and F.

2. **Topic: Algebra**

    Sub topic: Linear Equations

    To find the value of e, equation substitution must be used. Use the fourth equation and solve for d:

    $$15d = \frac{1414}{23} - 2a \rightarrow d = \frac{1414}{23 \times 15} - \frac{2a}{15} \rightarrow d = \frac{1414}{345} - \frac{2a}{15}$$

    Substitute d into the first equation to obtain b in terms of a:

    $$\frac{4a}{23} + 15b = 3\left(\frac{1414}{345} - \frac{2a}{15}\right) \rightarrow \frac{4a}{23} = \frac{4242}{345} - \frac{6a}{15} - 15b$$

    $$\frac{4a}{23} + \frac{6a}{15} = \frac{4242}{345} - 15b \rightarrow \frac{60a}{345} + \frac{138a}{345} = \frac{4242}{345} - 15b \rightarrow \frac{198a}{345} = \frac{4242}{345} - 15b$$

    $$a = \frac{\left(\frac{4242}{345} - 15b\right)345}{198} \rightarrow a = \frac{4,242 - 5,175b}{198}$$

    Now use the third equation to determine c:

    $$\frac{c}{17} = 32 - 5\frac{4,242 - 5,175b}{198} \rightarrow \frac{c}{17} = 32 - \frac{21,210 - 25,875b}{198}$$

    $$c = 544 - \frac{360,570 - 439,875b}{198}$$

    Finally, substitute using the third equation:

$$2b + \frac{8e}{3} = 15c \rightarrow 2b + \frac{8e}{3} = 15\left(544 - \frac{360{,}570}{198} - \frac{439{,}875b}{198}\right)$$

$$\frac{8e}{3} = 8{,}160 - \frac{5{,}408{,}550}{198} - \frac{6{,}598{,}125b}{198} - 2b \rightarrow 8e = 24{,}480 - \frac{16{,}225{,}650}{198} - \frac{19{,}794{,}375b}{198} - 6b$$

$$e = 3{,}060 - \frac{16{,}225{,}650}{1{,}584} - \frac{19{,}794{,}375b}{1{,}584} - \frac{3b}{4}$$

$$e = \frac{4{,}847{,}040}{1{,}584} - \frac{16{,}225{,}650}{1{,}584} - \frac{19{,}794{,}375b}{1{,}584} - \frac{1{,}188b}{1{,}584}$$

$$e = -\frac{632{,}145}{88} - \frac{19{,}795{,}563b}{1{,}584} \rightarrow e = -\frac{632{,}145}{88} - \frac{6{,}588{,}521b}{85{,}288}$$

The answer is C.

3. **Topic: Arithmetic**

    Sub topic: Time and Distance

    The correct answer is (B).

    First, determine the adjusted velocities of the runners at the start of the race:

    Runner A = 18 feet/second × 0.75 = 13.5

    Runner B = 16 feet/second × 0.80 = 12.8

    Runner C = [(18 × 3) − (16 × 2)] × 0.70 = 15.4

    Runner D = 15 feet/second × 0.70 = 10.5

    Runner E = 12 feet/second × 0.95 = 11.4

    The distances covered by the runners for the first 60 seconds (1 minute) are determined by multiplying the velocity by the elapsed time, Velocity * 60:

Runner	Distance (ft)
A	810
B	768
C	924
D	630
E	684

At 80 seconds since the start, all runners have progressed except runner C, who stopped to tie a shoe. The distances calculated during this 20 seconds are added to the previous:

Runner	Distance (ft)
A	1080
B	1024
C	924
D	840
E	912

Note that runner C is at the same distance.

The runners then continue for another 150 seconds before the energy drinks kick in and their rates change.

The distance covered at this point is:

Runner	Distance (ft)
A	3105
B	2944
C	3234
D	2415
E	2622

The new velocities starting from this point are:

Runner	Base Velocity	Multiplier	Adjusted Velocity
A	18	0.6	10.8
B	16	0.8	12.8
C	22	0.6	13.2
D	15	0.9	13.5
E	12	0.95	11.4

This race continues for 240 seconds and then stops. The final distances are:

Runner	Distance (ft)
A	5697
B	6016
C	6402
D	5655
E	5358

The average distance covered is:

$$\frac{5,697 + 6,016 + 6,402 + 5,655 + 5,358}{5} = 5825.6 \sim 5,830$$

4. **Topic: Algebra**

   Sub topic: Algebraic Expressions

   The correct answer is (C).

   $(1) a + b + c + 24 = 4M$

   $(2) a + b + c + d = 4N$

   Subtract.

   $(3) 24 - d = 4M - 4N$

   $(4) b + c + d + 24 = 4M + 4N$

   Subtract (2) from (4).

   $(5) 24 - a = 4M$

   Subtract (3) from (5).

   $d - a = 4N$

5. **Topic: Arithmetic**

   Sub topic: Profit & Loss

   The correct answer is (C).

   Susan's selling price = $148.80 to get a profit of 24%

   Buying price percentage = 100% and

   Selling price = % buying price + % profit = 100 + 24 = 124%

   Susan's buying price = $\frac{100}{124} \times \$148.80 = \$120.00$

   Christina's selling price = $96 to get a loss of 24% − 4% = 20%

   Buying price percentage = 100% and

   Selling price = % buying price − % loss = 100 − 20 = 80%

   Christina's buying price = $\frac{100}{80} \times 96 = \$120$

   Therefore, the two quantities are equal; the correct option is C.

6. **Topic: Geometry**

   Sub topic: Triangles

   The correct answer is (C).

   The area of an isosceles triangle with equal sides $a = 3$ and the third side $b = 5$ is given by $\frac{b}{4}\sqrt{4a^2 - b^2}$

   Therefore,

   $\text{Area} = \frac{5}{4} \times \sqrt{(4(3)^2 - (5)^2)}$

   $= \frac{5}{4} \times \sqrt{(36 - 25)}$

   $= \frac{5}{4} \times 3$

   $= \frac{15}{4}$

7. **Topic: Algebra**

   Sub topic: Inequalities

   The correct answer is (A).

   Since $x < 0$, $x^2 > 0$ Given that $|x| > y$, $x^2 > y^2$ and $2x^2 > 2y^2$

   Since $x < 0$, $y > 0$, $x < y$ hence $2x^2 + y > 2y^2 + x$.

   $x < 0$ implies that $x^3 < 0 > x^2$, thus $2y + x^3 + 3 < 2y + x^2 + 3$

   Therefore, Quantity A $= \frac{2x^2 + y}{2y + x^3 + 3} > \frac{x + 2y^2}{2y + x^2 + 3} = $ Quantity B

8. **Topic: Data Analysis**

   The correct answer is (D).

   Number of reported cases in the first half of 1997 = 1100000

   Number of reported cases in the second half of 1995 = 600000

   Increase as a percentage

$$= \frac{1100000 - 600000}{600000} \times 100$$

$$= \frac{5 \times 100}{6} = 83.3\% \cong 83\%$$

9. **Topic: Data Analysis**

The correct answer is (C).

In 1994, the number of cases reported in the first half = 250000 and the number of cases reported in the second half = 300000. Hence, the increase = 50000.

10. **Topic: Arithmetic**

Sub topic: Quadratic Functions

The correct answer is (A).

Helen bought 5 apples, 3 oranges and 7 bananas. Each apple costs $1.34. Each orange costs $0.47. Each banana costs $0.19.

To calculate the total that Helen paid, we need to calculate how much Helen paid for each kind of fruit and then add the totals together.

Based on this table, Helen paid $9.44 for the fruit. The answer is B.

Items	Cost per Item	Number of Items	Total cost for Item
Apples	$1.34	5	5 × $1.34 = $6.70
Oranges	$0.47	3	3 × $0.47 = $1.41
Banana	$0.19	7	7 × $0.19 = $1.33
			$9.44

11. **Topic: Geometry**

Sub topic: Quadrilaterals

The correct answer is (E).

The diagonals of the rhombus bisect the angles. The measure of ∠RST is thus twice the measure of ∠UST. Use this relationship to create an equation and solve for x.

$\angle RST = 2(\angle UST)$

$5x - 14 = 2(2x + 4)$

$5x - 14 = 4x + 8$

$x - 14 = 8$

$x = 22$

12. **Topic: Arithmetic**

Sub topic: Boat & Stream

The correct answer is (D).

Let x be the speed of the boat in still water and y be the speed of the stream

Effective speed downstream $= x + y$

Distance travelled = 0.6 miles

Time taken $= \dfrac{0.6}{x + y}$

Effective speed upstream $= x - y$

Distance travelled $= 0.4$

Time taken $= \dfrac{0.4}{x - y}$

Thus $\dfrac{0.6}{x + y} = \dfrac{0.4}{x - y}$

Thus $0.6x - 0.6y = 0.4x + 0.4y$

$0.2x = y$

Thus $x = 5y$

Quantity A: $5y$

Quantity B: $\dfrac{1.2}{5y + y} = \dfrac{1.2}{6y} = \dfrac{1}{5y}$

For $y > 1, \dfrac{1}{5y} < 5y$

For $0 < y < 0.2, \dfrac{1}{5y} > 5y$

Therefore, the relationship cannot be determined from the information given.

13. **Topic: Algebra**

   Sub topic: Algebraic Expressions

   The correct answer is (B).

   Use substitution to solve the equations:

   Use the first formula:

   $t = \dfrac{2x + 4y - 2z}{5}$

   Use the second formula:

   $4y - 2z - \left(\dfrac{2x + 4y - 2z}{5} \right) = 6x$

   $20y - 10z - 2x - 4y + 2z = 30x \rightarrow 16y - 8z = 32x$

   $y = 2x + \dfrac{1}{2}z$

   Use the third formula:

   $15x - \left(2x + \dfrac{1}{2}z \right) + 7z = 13 \left(\dfrac{2x + 4\left(2x + \frac{1}{2}z\right) - 2z}{5} \right)$

   $75x - 10x - \dfrac{5}{2}z + 35z = 13 \left(2x + 4\left(2x + \dfrac{1}{2}z\right) - 2z \right)$

   $65x + \dfrac{65}{2}z = 13\,(10x) \rightarrow \dfrac{65}{2}z = 65x$

   $x = \dfrac{1}{2}z$

   Use the fourth formula:

   $13z - 2y = 36x - 6t - 8$

$$13z - 2\left(2\left(\frac{1}{2}z\right) + \frac{1}{2}z\right) = 36\left(\frac{1}{2}z\right) - 6\left(\frac{2\left(\frac{1}{2}z\right) + 4\left(2\left(\frac{1}{2}z\right) + \frac{1}{2}z\right) - 2z}{5}\right) - 8$$

$$13z - 2\left(z + \frac{1}{2}z\right) = 36\left(\frac{1}{2}z\right) - 6\left(\frac{z + 4\left(z + \frac{1}{2}z\right) - 2z}{5}\right) - 8$$

$$13z - 3z = 18z - 6\left(\frac{z + 6z - 2z}{5}\right) - 8$$

$$10z = 18z - 6\left(\frac{5z}{5}\right) - 8$$

$$10z = 18z - 6z - 8$$

$$2z = 8 \rightarrow z = 4$$

By substitution into other formulas:

$x = 2$

$y = 6$

$t = 4$

Quantity A $= 4x - 3y + t = 8 - 18 + 4 = -6$;

Quantity B $= 3t - 2y - z = 12 - 12 - 4 = -4$

The answer is: Quantity B is greater.

14. **Topic: Arithmetic**

The correct answer is (C).

In the series 8, 9, 12, 17, 24

$9 - 8 = 1$

$12 - 9 = 3$

$17 - 12 = 5$

$24 - 17 = 7$

Therefore, the difference between the next term and 24 must be 9, or

$x - 24 = 9$

$x = 33$

Therefore, the next term in the series must be 33.

15. **Topic: Geometry**

Sub topic: Three-Dimensional Figures

The correct answer is (E).

Let x equal the length of a side of the cube. The volume $v = x^3$, and the surface area $s = 6x^2$, Therefore, $x = 6$.

16. **Topic: Algebra**

The correct answer is 20lbs.

If 150 promotional size chocolates are made they need $10 \times 1.2 = 12$ lbs. of sugar. (1.2 represents a quantity increased by 20% in decimal form). Using simple ratio proportion,

$$\frac{12}{150} = \frac{x}{250}$$

$x = 20$

17. **Topic: Arithmetic**

The correct answer is (C).

Start by finding the volume of water in Tank A:

During the first 20 minutes, the cumulative volume is (Flow In − Flow Out) × Duration = (45 gpm − 10 gpm) × 20 minutes = 700 gallons. At 20 minutes, Tank B begins to leak and adds 14 gallons per minute to the inflow into Tank A. This continues for 25 minutes, so the flow during this time is: (45 gpm+ 14 gpm – 10 gpm) × 25 minutes = 1,225 gallons. The leak is then fixed, and flow continues as normal for 15 minutes: (45 gpm − 10 gpm) × 15 = 525 gallons. Total in this tank is 2,450 gallons.

Finding the volume of water in Tank B:

During the first 20 minutes, the cumulative volume is (Flow In − Flow Out) × Duration = (60 gpm − 15 gpm) × 20 minutes = 900 gallons. At 20 minutes, Tank B begins to leak a total of 48 gpm. This continues for 25 minutes, so the flow during this time is: (60 gpm − 48 gpm − 15 gpm) × 25 minutes = 275 gallons. Then only Leak A is continuing for 15 minutes: (60 gpm− 23 pgm − 10 gpm) × 15 = 1,275 gallons. Total in this tank is 2,450 gallons.

The answer is: The two quantities are equal.

18. **Topic: Algebra**

Sub topic: System of Equations

The correct answer is (A).

The original amount with Andrew = \$$x$

The original amount with David = \$$y$

If Andrew gives \$10, then the amount left with Andrew = \$$(x - 10)$

If David gives \$100, then the amount left with David = \$$(y - 100)$

Andrew tells David, "If you give me \$100 then I will have twice the money that you have".

$x + 100 = 2(y - 100)$

$x + 100 = 2y - 200$

$x = 2y - 200 - 100$

$x = 2y - 300 \text{(Equation 1)}$

David, in turn tells Andrew, "If you give me \$10, I shall have six times the amount you have".

$y + 10 = 6(x - 10)$

$y + 10 = 6x - 60$

$y = 6x - 60 - 10$

$y = 6x - 70 \text{(Equation 2)}$

Substituting the value of x from equation 1 in equation 2:

$y = 6(2y - 300) - 70$

$y = 12y - 1800 - 70$

$y = 12y - 1870$

$1870 = 12y - y$

$11y = 1870$

$y = \dfrac{1870}{11} = \$170$

Substituting the value of y in equation 1:

$x = 2(170) - 300$

$x = 340 - 300$

$x = \$40$

Original amount with Andrew $= \$40$

Original amount with David $= \$170$

<u>Quantity A</u>: Sum of the original amount with Andrew and the original amount with David $= 40 + 170 = \$210$

<u>Quantity B</u>: Sum of the original amount with David and the amount borrowed from Andrew $= 170 + 10 = \$180$

Quantity A is greater.

19. **Topic: Geometry**

    Sub topic: Triangles

    The correct answer is (D).

    Since $AB = BE = 34$, $\triangle ABC$ is an isosceles triangle and altitude BD will bisect AC. Since $\triangle BDC$ is right triangle, use the Pythagorean Theorem, which says

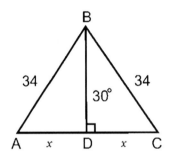

$$(BC)^2 = (BD)^2 + (CD)^2$$

$(34)^2 = (30)^2 + x^2$

$1,156 = 900 + x^2$

$x^2 = 1,156 - 900$

$x^2 = 256$

$x = \sqrt{256} = 16$

Therefore, $CD = 16 = AD$

$AC = AD + DC$

$16 + 16$

$=32$

20. **Topic: Algebra**

    Sub topic: Algebraic Expressions

    The correct answer is (B).

    $$\frac{b+6}{4b^2} + \frac{3}{2b^2} = \frac{b+4}{8b^2}$$

    $$\frac{b+6}{4b^2} + \frac{3}{2b^2} - \frac{b+4}{8b^2} = 0$$

$\left(\dfrac{b+6}{4b^2}\right) \times 2 + \left(\dfrac{3}{2b^2}\right) \times 4 - \left(\dfrac{b+4}{8b^2}\right) = 0$ Make denominators the same.

$\left(\dfrac{2b+12}{8b^2}\right) + \left(\dfrac{12}{8b^2}\right) - \left(\dfrac{b+4}{8b^2}\right) = 0$

$\dfrac{2b + 12 + 12 - b - 4}{8b^2} = 0$

$\dfrac{b + 20}{8b^2} = 0$

$b + 20 = 0$ Cross multiplying $8b^2$ and 0

$b = -20$

Quantity A: $\dfrac{b+6}{4b^2}$ Substituting the value of b

$\dfrac{-20 + 6}{4 \times (-20)^2} = \dfrac{-14}{4 \times 400} = \dfrac{-14}{1600} = -0.00875$

Quantity B: $\dfrac{b+4}{8b^2}$ Substituting the value of b

$\dfrac{-20 + 4}{8 \times (-20)^2} = \dfrac{-16}{8 \times 400} = \dfrac{-16}{3200} = -0.005$

Quantity B is bigger.

This page is intentionally left blank

Chapter **8**

Exercise #2

Questions: 20 | Time: 30 minutes

_____

This Exercise includes _20 practice questions_. The questions cover all the question types as explained in Chapter 2 and may fall into any of the following categories - Arithmetic, Algebra, Geometry or Data Analysis. You will find answers and detailed explanations towards the end of this chapter.

1. In integer whose cube root is also an integer is called a perfect cube. i.e., $216, 343, 512$ are perfect cubes as their cube roots will be 6, 7 and 8 respectively. Which of the below options shall not necessarily be a perfect cube, assuming integers m and n are perfect cubes?

   (A) $8m$

   (B) mn

   (C) $mn + 216$

   (D) $-m$

   (E) $(m - n)^9$

2. The length and the width of a rectangle is 10cm and 8cm respectively, if the side of a square is 6cm, find the ratio of the area of the rectangle to that of the square.

   (A) $\frac{20}{9}$

   (B) $\frac{3}{1}$

   (C) $\frac{10}{3}$

   (D) $\frac{3}{2}$

   (E) $\frac{5}{3}$

3.

Distinct positive integers *a*, *b*, and *c* are given. M is the arithmetic average of *a*, *b*, and *c*.

N is the arithmetic average of the reciprocal of *a*, *b*, and *c*.

Quantity A	**Quantity B**
MN	9

(A) Quantity A is greater.

(B) Quantity B is greater.

(C) The two quantities are equal.

(D) The relationship cannot be determined from the information given.

4.

Two painting crews, Crew A and Crew B, begin the month painting houses at a new project, and they have four weeks to complete the job. Crew A has 6 painters, with an individual crew member productivity rate of 3.6 houses per 40-hour week. Crew B has 5 painters with an individual crew member productivity rate of 4.2 houses per 40-hour week. In order to finish the project on schedule Crew A decides to work overtime during the first two of the four weeks, having each painter put in an additional 10 hours per week. However, Crew A also has one of the crew members out sick for the last week. Crew B decides to bring on another crew member at the start of the third week, which boosts morale and raises their individual crew member productivity rate to 4.3 for the last two weeks. Carry numbers to 4 decimal places when doing calculations.

Quantity A	**Quantity B**
Number of houses completed by Crew 1	Number of houses completed by Crew 2

(A) Quantity A is greater.

(B) Quantity B is greater.

(C) The two quantities are equal.

(D) The relationship cannot be determined from the information given.

5.

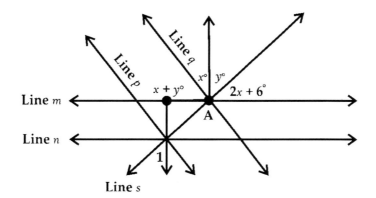

In the figure above Point A is on Line m. Line m and Line n are parallel. Line p and Line q are parallel. If $x°$ is three less than $y°$, what is the measure of $\angle 1$?

(A) 28°

(B) 31°

(C) 59°

(D) 62°

(E) Cannot be determined

6. If a store purchases several items for $1.80 per dozen and sells them at 3 for $0.85, what is the store's profit on 6 dozen of these items?

(A) $4.20

(B) $5.70

(C) $9.60

(D) $10.60

(E) $20.40

7. Andrew wants to build a new house. According to the blue-print, the length and width of the hall are $(x - 5)^2$ and $(10 + x)$ respectively and the length and the width of the library are $(x - 5)$ and $x^2 - 5$ respectively. The hall and the library are equal in area.

Which of the following statements is true?

Select all that apply.

(A) The area of the library is 196 sq. feet.

(B) The value of x is 4.5 feet.

(C) The area of hall is 304 sq. feet.

(D) The sum of the area of the hall and the library is 608 sq. feet.

(E) The value of x is 9 feet.

(F) The sum of the area of the hall and the library is 392 sq. feet.

8.

The sum of the roots of the equation $3x^2 - 5x - k(x - 2) - 2 = 0$ is -3.

Quantity A	**Quantity B**
K	The greatest root of $x^2 + 9x - 22 = 0$

(A) Quantity A is greater.

(B) Quantity B is greater.

(C) The two quantities are equal.

(D) The relationship cannot be determined from the information given.

9. Angela has nickels and dimes in her pocket. She has twice as many dimes as nickels. What is the best expression of the amount of money she has in cents if x equals the number of nickels she has?

(A) $25x$

(B) $10x + 5(2x)$

(C) $x + 2x$

(D) $5(3x)$

(E) $20(x + 5)$

10.

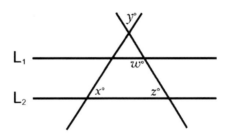

If $L_1 \parallel L_2$, $x = 60°$, and $w = 2z$, then $y + w =$?

(A) $60°$

(B) $90°$

(C) $120°$

(D) $150°$

(E) $180°$

11.

Savvy Investments bought 12 government bonds with a unit value of $300 that pay 5% interest per year. The interest payment is made every year by check. The bonds were purchased on 1st of January 2011.

On the same day when Savvy Investments purchased the bonds, it also opened a bank account with an initial amount of $4,000 that pays cumulative interest of 4% per year. On 1st of January of each of the following years, Savvy Investments would receive the interest for the bonds and pay it into the 4% bank account. No other deposits have been made and no money have been taken out.

Quantity A	**Quantity B**
The amount of interest received by the company for the bonds over the period 1st of Jan 2011 to 31st Dec 2013	The amount of interest earned by the company in the 4% cumulative interest bank account over the period 1st of Jan 2011 to 31st Dec 2013

(A) Quantity A is greater.

(B) Quantity B is greater.

(C) The two quantities are equal.

(D) The relationship cannot be determined from the information given.

12.

A cylindrical canister has the radius r and the height h. A second cylindrical canister has the same radius r as the first canister, but different height. The surface area of the second canister is twice the surface area of the first canister.

Quantity A	**Quantity B**
The volume of the second canister	The volume of a cone with the same radius r as the first canister, and with a height equal to $6h$

(A) Quantity A is greater.

(B) Quantity B is greater.

(C) The two quantities are equal.

(D) The relationship cannot be determined from the information given.

13. A reduction of 25% in the price of eggs will enable Peter to buy 4 dozen more for $9.6. What was the original price per dozen?

$☐

14. What is the area of a square inscribed in a circle whose circumference is 16π?

(A) 512

(B) 256

(C) 128

(D) 64

(E) 32

15. 6" 2" 10" 2" 5"

    Above are the measures of rainfall for five consecutive days during the winter. For the measure of those five days, which of the following is true?

    (i) The median equals the mode.

    (ii) The median equals the arithmetic mean.

    (iii) The range equals the median.

    (A) I only

    (B) II only

    (C) III only

    (D) I and II only

    (E) I and III only

16.

$$\text{Given:} \frac{n}{mn} + \frac{m}{mn} = \frac{p}{p^2 + 1} \text{ and } m + n = p^2$$

Quantity A	**Quantity B**
$p + p^3$	$mn - 1$

(A) Quantity A is greater.

(B) Quantity B is greater.

(C) The two quantities are equal.

(D) The relationship cannot be determined from the information given.

Questions 17 and 18 are based on the following diagram:

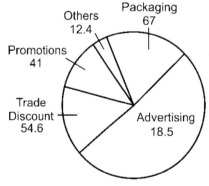

Marketing Budget for 1999

17. If the total budget is twice the present, the ratio of expenditure on packaging to trade discounts is most nearly

    (A) 5 : 6

    (B) 1.2 : 1

    (C) 1 : 2

    (D) 6 : 5

    (E) None of these

18. If the total budget is \$20 million the percentage increase in advertising expenditure over the rest is

    (A) 110%

    (B) less than 10%

    (C) more than 15%

    (D) 250%

    (E) 15%

19.

Two shaded regions are shown below: Which shaded area is larger? Use $\pi = 3.14$

Quantity A   **Quantity B**

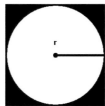 

    (A) Quantity A is greater.

    (B) Quantity B is greater.

    (C) The two quantities are equal.

    (D) The relationship cannot be determined from the information given.

20.

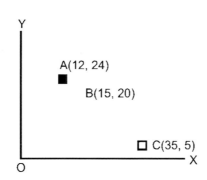

Quantity A   **Quantity B**

The square of the distance between the points A and B   The distance between the points B and C

    (A) Quantity A is greater.

    (B) Quantity B is greater.

    (C) The two quantities are equal.

    (D) The relationship cannot be determined from the information given.

Answers and Explanations

1. **Topic: Arithmetic**

    Sub topic: Integers

    The correct answer is (C).

    A perfect cube will have prime factors that are in groups of 3.

    Let us look at the options.

    Option A is $8m$. 8 is the cube of 2, and m is a cube, and so the product will also be a cube.

    Option A is mn. m is a cube and n is a cube. Hence, the product mn will also be a cube.

    Option C is $mn + 216$. mn is a cube and 216 is a cube. However, their sum need not be a cube.

    Option D is $-m$. m is a cube and hence $-m$ will also be a cube.

    Option E is$(m - n)$. $(m - n)^9 = [(m - n)^3]^3$. Hence,$(m - n)^9$will also be a cube.

2. **Topic: Geometry**

    Sub topic: Quadrilaterals

    The correct answer is (A).

    Area of the rectangle $= 10 \times 8 = 80cm^2$

    Area of the square $= 6^2 = 36cm^2$

    The ratio of the area of rectangle: square $= 80: 36$, which reduces to 20:9.

    The correct option is A.

3. **Topic: Algebra**

    The correct answer is (A).

    We know that

    $$\frac{a}{b} + \frac{b}{a} \geq 2$$

    $$\frac{a}{c} + \frac{c}{a} \geq 2$$

    $$\frac{b}{c} + \frac{c}{b} \geq 2$$

    Add both sides

    $$\frac{a}{b} + \frac{b}{a} + \frac{a}{c} + \frac{c}{a} + \frac{b}{c} + \frac{c}{b} \geq 6$$

    $$\frac{b + c}{a} + \frac{a + c}{b} + \frac{a + b}{c} \geq 6$$

    $$(1) \text{P} = \frac{b+c}{a} + \frac{a+c}{b} + \frac{a+b}{c} \geq 6$$

    On the other hand,

    $$\text{MN} = (a + b + c)\left(\frac{1}{a} + \frac{1}{b} + \frac{1}{c}\right)$$

    $$= \frac{a + b + c}{a} + \frac{a + b + c}{b} + \frac{a + b + c}{c}$$

$$= 1 + \frac{b+c}{a} + 1 + \frac{a+c}{b} + 1 + \frac{a+b}{c}$$

$$= 3 + \frac{b+c}{a} + \frac{a+c}{b} + \frac{a+b}{c} \geq 9 \text{ (Because of (1) (and the equality holds true only when } a = b = c, \text{ which is not the}$$
case)

4. **Topic: Arithmetic**

The correct answer is (C).

First, determine the productivity rates per hour:

For Crew A it is consistent through the project → 3.6 houses/40 hours = 0.09 houses per hour per crew member

For Crew B's first two weeks → 4.2 houses/40 hours = 0.105 houses per hour per crew member

For Crew B's last two weeks → 4.3 houses/40 hours = 0.1075 houses per hour per crew member

The values for each week are calculated by multiplying the numbers of crew members by the hours worked per crew member for that week by the productivity rate per hour. The following table shows the calculations:

Crew	Week	Number of workers		Productivity rate (houses per hour)		Hours worked per crew member		Houses per week	Total houses completed
A	1	6		0.09		50		27	
	2	6		0.09		50		27	93.6
	3	6		0.09		40		21.6	
	4	5	×	0.09	×	40	=	18	
B	1	5		0.105		40		21	
	2	5		0.105		40		21	93.6
	3	6		0.1075		40		25.8	
	4	6		0.1075		40		25.8	

The two quantities are equal.

5. **Topic: Geometry**

Sub topic: Lines & Angles

The correct answer is (E).

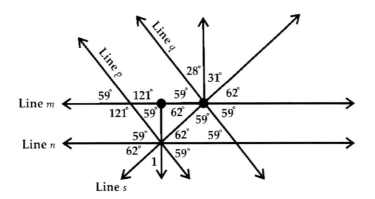

Find the measure of the angles given in terms of x and y. The sum of all four angles is 180° and $y = x + 3$.

$(x + y) + x + y + 2x + 6 = 180°$

$\{x + (x + 3)\} + x + (x + 3) + 2x + 6 = 180°$

$6x = 168°$

$x = 28°$

Now use your knowledge of angle relationships to determine the measure of ∠1. We know the sum of ∠1 and an adjacent angle are 59°, but there is no way to determine the measure of ∠1 with the given information. The answer cannot be determined.

6. The correct answer is (C).

The selling price for 1 dozen at 3 for $0.85 is $3 \times 4 = 12 = 1$ dozen $= \$0.85 \times 4 = \$3.40$

Therefore, 6 dozen will yield $\$3.40 \times 6 = \$20.40$.

The store's cost for 6 dozen at $1.80 per dozen is $\$1.80 \times 6 = \$10.80$

Therefore, the profit on 6 dozen of these items will be $\$20.40 - \$10.80$ or $\$9.60$.

7. **Topic: Geometry**

    Sub topic: Geometric Areas

    The correct answers are (C), (D) and (E).

The hall and the library are shaped like a rectangle.

The formula for calculating the area of rectangle is:

Area = Length × Width

Area of hall $= (x - 5)^2 \times (10 + x) = (x^2 - 10x + 25)(10 + x)$

$= 10x^2 - 100x + 250 + x^3 - 10x^2 + 25x$

$= x^3 - 75x + 250$

Area of library $= (x - 5) \times (x^2 - 5) = x^3 - 5x^2 - 5x + 25$

Area of hall = Area of library

$x^3 - 75x + 250 = x^3 - 5x^2 - 5x + 25$

$x^3 - x^3 + 5x^2 - 75x - 5x + 250 - 25 = 0$

$5x^2 - 70x + 225 = 0$

$x^2 - 14x + 45 = 0 \; - - - - - \text{(Dividing the equation by 5)}$

Using the quadratic formula $\dfrac{-b \pm \sqrt{b^2 - 4ac}}{2a}$ to find the value of x:

$x = \dfrac{14 \pm \sqrt{14^2 - 4 \times 1 \times (45)}}{2 \times 1}$

$x = \dfrac{14 \pm \sqrt{196 - 180}}{2}$

$$x = \frac{14 \pm \sqrt{16}}{2}$$

$$x = \frac{14 \pm 4}{2}$$

$$x = \frac{18}{2}, x = \frac{10}{2}$$

$$x = 9, x = 5$$

$x = 5$ is not correct as when we plug it in for the value of length of hall and the library, the length becomes 0, which is not possible.

Only 9 is the correct value.

Hence the area of hall $= (x - 5)^2 \times (10 + x) = (9 - 5)^2 \times (10 + 9) = 4^2 \times 19 = 16 \times 19 = 304 ft^2$

Since area of hall and library are equal, the sum of their areas is equal to $304 + 304 = 608 ft^2$

Options C, D and E are correct.

8. **Topic: Algebra**

   Sub topic: Quadratic Equations

   The correct answer is (A).

   $3x^2 - 5x - k(x - 2) - 2 = 0$ is a quadratic equation, and any quadratic equation can be written as:

   $x^2 + Sx + P = 0$ where S is the sum of the roots and P is the product of the roots. We need to bring it to this form.

   $3x^2 - 5x - k(x - 2) - 2 = 3x^2 - 5x - kx + 2k - 2 = 0$

   If we divide by 3 $\rightarrow x^2 - \frac{x(5 + k)}{3} + \frac{2(k - 1)}{3} = 0$

   We know the sum of the roots is $-3 \rightarrow -\frac{5+k}{3} = -3 \rightarrow k = 4$

   The quantity on the right is also a quadratic equation that can be factorized into $(x + 11)(x - 2) = 0$

   This means x must be either -11 or 2. So the greatest root is 2, which is less than 4.

   Hence the quantity on the left is greater, so the correct answer is A.

9. **Topic: Arithmetic**

   The correct answer is (A).

   The number of nickels that Angela has is x. Therefore, the total value of those nickels (in cents) is $5x$. Angela also has twice as many dimes as nickels, or $2x$. The total value in cents of those dimes is $2x(10)$, or $20x$. Adding together the value of the nickels and dimes gives $5x + 20x$, or $25x$.

10. **Topic: Geometry**

    Sub topic: Lines & Angles

    The correct answer is (E).

    Since $L_1 \parallel L_2$, the corresponding angles formed on lines L_1 and L_2 are equal.

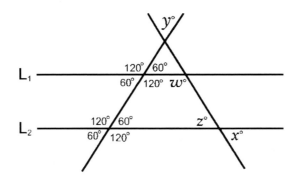

In any quadrilateral, the sum of interior degrees equals 360°. Therefore,

$\angle w + \angle z = 180°$. If $w = 2z$, $\angle w = 120°$, and $\angle z = 60°$.

Therefore,

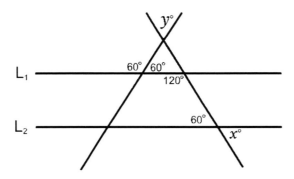

$\angle y = 60°$ (since there are 180° in a triangle). So, the sum of $y + w = 60° + 120° = 180°$.

The correct answer is E.

11. **Topic: Arithmetic**

    Sub topic: Compound Interest / Simple Interest

    The correct answer is (A).

    Notice that the quantity on the left is a simple interest question, it does not involve compound interest (clue is in the fact that the bonds are stand-alone, and the interest is paid separately by check).

    Interest for one year for one bond is: 5% × $300 = $15

    Interest for all the years (i.e. 3 years) for all the 12 bonds is: $15 × 3 × 12 = $540

    For the quantity on the right you need to take into account not only the cumulative interest, but also the additional deposits made every year:

    Year 1: interest = $4,000 × 4% = $160→ amount in the account on 12/31/2011 = $4,160

    Year 2: On 01/01/2012 the interest from the bonds was paid in → amount that earned interest in Year 2 = $4,160 + ($15 x 12) = $4,340→ interest = $4,340 × 4% = $173.6→ amount in the account on 12/31/2012 = $4,340 + $173.6 = $4,513.6

    Year 3: On 01/01/2013 the interest from the bonds was paid in → amount that earned interest in Year 3 = $4,513.6 + ($15 x 12) = $4,693.6 → interest = $4,693.6 × 4% = $187.7→ amount in the account on 12/31/2013 = $4,693.6 + $187.7 = $4,881.3

    Interest earned by the 4% bank account over the three years is: $160(Year 1) + $173.6(Year 2) + $187.7 (Year 3) = $521.3

    $540 is greater than $521.3, hence the quantity on the left is greater and the correct answer is (A).

12. **Topic: Geometry**

    Sub topic: Three-Dimensional Figures

    The correct answer is (A).

    The volume of the first cylindrical canister with radius r and height h is calculated with the formula:

    $V = \pi r^2 h$

    The surface area of the first canister is calculated with: $SA = 2\pi r^2 + 2\pi rh$

    We are told that the second canister has the same radius r and its area is twice the area of the first canister. Let h_2 be the height of the second canister.

    $2\pi r^2 + 2\pi rh_2 = 2 \times (2\pi r^2 + 2\pi rh)$

    If we divide both sides by $2\pi r$

    $r + h_2 = 2r + 2h \rightarrow h_2 = r + 2h$

    We can now substitute h_2 in the formula for calculating the second canister's volume

    Volume of the second canister $= \pi r^2(r + 2h)$

    The volume of a cone is calculated with the formula: $V = \pi$

    The volume of a cone is calculated with the formula: $V = \pi r^2 \dfrac{h}{3}$

    We are told that the cone has the same radius r as the first canister and its height $= 6h$

    Volume of the cone $= \pi r^2 \dfrac{6h}{3} = \pi r^2\, 2h$

    If we compare the volume of the second canister $\pi r^2(r + 2h)$ to the volume of the cone $\pi r^2\, 2h \rightarrow r + 2h >$ $2h \rightarrow$ the volume of the second canister is greater than the volume of the cone.

    Hence the left column is greater than the right column and (A) is the correct answer.

13. **Topic: Arithmetic**

    The correct answer is $0.8.

    Let the initial cost of eggs will be $\dfrac{\$x}{doze\,n}$

    New price is $\dfrac{\$0.75\,x}{dozen}$. In either case Peter spends $9.6 so initially he buys $\dfrac{\$9.6}{x}$ dozen eggs and now he is able to

    buy $\dfrac{\$9.6}{0.75x}$ dozen eggs for the same price, which happens to be 4 dozen more than what he bought initially.

    Expressing the statement mathematically, $4 + \dfrac{\$9.6}{x} = \dfrac{\$9.6}{0.75x}$

    This gives $x = \$0.8$

14. **Topic: Geometry**

    The correct answer is (C).

    Circumference $= \pi d$.

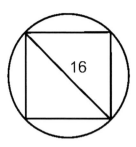

$16\pi = \pi d$

$d = 16$

Diameter of circle = diagonal of square

Area of square = $\frac{1}{2}$(product of diagonals)

$= \frac{1}{2} d_1 \times d_2$

$= \frac{1}{2}(16)(16) = 128$

Therefore, the area of the square is 128.

Alternate method: assume x for side of square.

Using Pythagorean Theorem for isosceles right triangles gives $x^2 + x^2 = 16^2$, $2x^2 = 256$, and $x^2 = 128$, which is the area of the square.

15. **Topic: Arithmetic**

The correct answer is (B).

II only. The arithmetic mean is the average (sum divided by number of items), or $6 + 2 + 10 + 2 + 5 = 25$ divided by $5 = 5$.

The median is the middle number after the numbers have been ordered: 2, 2, 5, 6, 10.

The median is 5.

The mode is the most frequently appearing number: 2.

The range is the highest minus the lowest, or $10 - 2 = 8$.

Therefore, only II is true: The median 5 equals the mean 5.

16. **Topic: Algebra**

Sub topic: Algebraic Expressions

The correct answer is (A).

Combine the fractions on the left side of the first equation as follows:

$\dfrac{n}{mn} + \dfrac{m}{mn} = \dfrac{p}{p^2 + 1}$

$\dfrac{m + n}{mn} = \dfrac{p}{p^2 + 1}$

$\dfrac{p^2}{mn} = \dfrac{p}{p^2 + 1}$

Cross-multiply.

$mnp = p^2(p^2 + 1)$

Divide each side by p.

$mn = p(p^2 + 1)$

Distribute p over the parentheses.

$mn = p^2 + p$

Since $mn = p^3 + p$, then $p^3 + p > mn - 1$. Therefore, (A) is the correct answer.

17. **Topic: Data Analysis**

The correct answer is (A).

$54.6 : 67 = 546 : 670 = 1 : 1.2$ or $5 : 6$, most nearly.

18. **Topic: Data Analysis**

The correct answer is (B).

$$\frac{185 - 175}{175} \times 100 = \frac{10}{175} \times 100 = 5.7\%.$$

i.e. excess of 'advertising' over the rest is less than 10%.

19. **Topic: Geometry**

Sub topic: Circles/Quadrilaterals

The correct answer is (B).

Let us calculate the area of the shaded region in Quantity A.

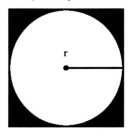

In Quantity A, a circle of radius r is inscribed in a square.

From the figure, we can see that the length of the side of the square will be the same as the diameter of the circle.

That is, side of square $= 2r$.

Area of the shaded region = Area of square $-$ Area of circle

$= (2r)^2 - \pi r^2$

$= r^2(4 - \pi)$

$= 0.86r^2$ ...(i)

Now let us find the area of the shaded region in the Quantity B.

In Quantity B, a square is inscribed inside a circle of radius r.

From the figure, we can see that the length of the diagonal of the square will be the same as the diameter of the circle.

Hence, diagonal of square $= 2r$.

side of square $= \dfrac{diagonal}{\sqrt{2}}$

$= \dfrac{2r}{\sqrt{2}}$

$= \sqrt{2}r$

Area of the shaded region = Area of circle $-$ Area of square

$= \pi r^2 - \sqrt{2}r \times \sqrt{2}r$

$= \pi r^2 - 2r^2$

$= r^2(\pi - 2)$

$= 1.14\, r^2 ...(ii)$

Comparing the two areas, we can see that Quantity B has the larger area.

20. **Topic: Geometry**

   Sub topic: Coordinate Geometry

   The correct answer is (C).

   The distance between two points is given by D$= \sqrt{dx^2 + dy^2}$ where:

   dx is the difference between the x coordinates of the points

   dy is the difference between the y coordinates of the points

   In this case:

   $AB = \sqrt{(15 - 12)^2 + (20 - 124)^2} = \sqrt{3^2 + 4^2} = \sqrt{25} = 5$

   $$(AB)^2 = 5^2 = 25$$

   $BC = \sqrt{(35 - 15)^2 + (5 - 20)^2} = \sqrt{20^2 + 15^2} = \sqrt{625} = 25$

   The left column and right column are equal($= 25$)hence the correct answer is (C).

Chapter 9

Exercise #3

Questions: 20 | Time: 30 minutes

This Exercise includes *20 practice questions*. The questions cover all the question types as explained in Chapter 2 and may fall into any of the following categories - Arithmetic, Algebra, Geometry or Data Analysis. You will find answers and detailed explanations towards the end of this chapter.

1. Given that

   $y = (x^2)^3 - 5^x$

   If $x = 4$, then the value of y will be

   ```
   ┌─────────────┐
   │             │
   └─────────────┘
   ```

2.

   A team of 3 people take 3 weeks and 2 days to complete a certain job. Every week has 6 working days and each working day is of 8 hours.

Quantity A	**Quantity B**
Number of days required to complete the job if 4 people working for 6 hours each day to complete the job	Number of days required if 5 people work to complete the job. 3 people work 8 hours a day, while 2 others work for 3 hours a day

   (A) Quantity A is greater.

   (B) Quantity B is greater.

   (C) The two quantities are equal.

   (D) The relationship cannot be determined from the information given.

3.

Two triangles are shown below. Which triangle has a larger area? Use $\sqrt{3} = 1.73$.

Quantity A   **Quantity B**

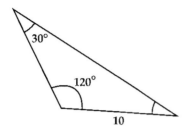   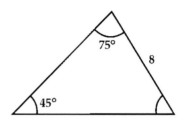

(A) Quantity A is greater.

(B) Quantity B is greater.

(C) The two quantities are equal.

(D) The relationship cannot be determined from the information given.

4. If $a > b$, and $ab > 0$, which of the following must be true?

(i) $a > 0$

(ii) $b > 0$

(iii) $\dfrac{a}{b} > 0$

(A) I only

(B) II only

(C) III only

(D) I and II only

(E) I and III only

5.

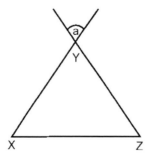

In ∆XYZ, XY = 10, YZ = 10, and ∠a = 84°. What is the degree measure of ∠Z?

(A) 96°

(B) 84°

(C) 48°

(D) 42°

(E) 24°

6. Maria plans to make sandwiches for a picnic. She has three types of bread from which to choose (rye, sourdough, and white), four types of meat from which to choose (salami, bologna, ham, and pastrami), and three types of cheese from which to choose (Swiss, cheddar, and jack). If Maria will use only one type of bread, one type of meat, and one type of cheese on each sandwich, how many different kinds of sandwiches can Maria make?

    (A) 3

    (B) 4

    (C) 10

    (D) 17

    (E) 36

7.

$$\text{Given: } \frac{x^2 + y^2}{x + y} = x + y \text{ for } x \neq -y$$

Quantity A	**Quantity B**
xy	0

(A) Quantity A is greater.

(B) Quantity B is greater.

(C) The two quantities are equal.

(D) The relationship cannot be determined from the information given.

8.

If a, b, x, and y are all > 1 satisfying $x^{\frac{2}{5}} = a^{-6}$, and $y^{\frac{2}{5}} = b^6$,

Quantity A	**Quantity B**
$(xy)^{\frac{1}{3}}$	$a^4 b^4$

(A) Quantity A is greater.

(B) Quantity B is greater.

(C) The two quantities are equal.

(D) The relationship cannot be determined from the information given.

Questions 9 and 10 are based on the following data:

	1996	1997	1998	1999	2000
Rice	1125	1752	1344	1404	1640
Maize	650	820	766	958	874
Wheat	780	795	928	750	978
Dal	1014	1162	978	1252	1360
Cotton	1777	1746	1664	1636	1542
Bajra	986	827	888	850	746

9. By what percentage is the average production of wheat less than the average production of rice?

   (A) 62.3

   (B) 71.7

   (C) 41.8

   (D) 38.6

   (E) 52.6

10. Which year did the total production see the maximum percentage increase over the previous year?

   (A) 1998

   (B) 1997

   (C) 1999

   (D) 2000

   (E) 1996

11.

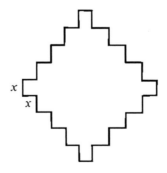

In the figure above, all lines meet at ninety-degree angle, and each segment has a length of x. What is the area of the figure in terms of x?

   (A) $25x$

   (B) $36x$

   (C) $36x^2$

   (D) $41x^2$

   (E) $41x$

12. The average of three numbers is 55. The second is more than twice the first, and the third is 4 less than three times the first. What is the largest number?

  (A) 165

  (B) 88

  (C) 80

  (D) 57

  (E) 28

13.

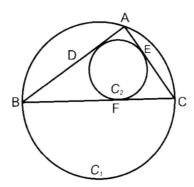

ΔABC is circumscribed by circle C_1, while all its sides are tangent to the smaller, inscribed circle C_2. The inscribed circle touches ΔABC at points D, E and F.

$m\angle BAC = 90°$, AD = 1 and CE = 2. (figure not to scale)

Quantity A	**Quantity B**
Area of circle C_1	Six times the Area of circle C_2

  (A) Quantity A is greater.

  (B) Quantity B is greater.

  (C) The two quantities are equal.

  (D) The relationship cannot be determined from the information given.

14.

$$\text{Inequality 1: } 4(x + 2) \le 2(x + 5) + 14$$

$$\text{Inequality 2: } \sqrt{16 - 8y + y^2} \le 9$$

Quantity A	**Quantity B**
x, where x is a solution of Inequality 1	y, where y is a solution of Inequality 2

  (A) Quantity A is greater.

  (B) Quantity B is greater.

  (C) The two quantities are equal.

  (D) The relationship cannot be determined from the information given.

15. If the diameter of a circle P is 40 percent of the diameter of circle Q, then the area of circle P is what percentage of the area of circle Q?

    (A) 16

    (B) 20

    (C) 40

    (D) 80

    (E) It cannot be determined from the information given.

16. x, y, and z are consecutive positive integers greater than 1, not necessarily in that order, which of the following is (are) true?

    (i)$x > z$

    (ii)$x + y > z$

    (iii)$yz < xz$

    (iv)$xy < y + z$

    (A) I only

    (B) II only

    (C) II and III only

    (D) II and IV only

    (E) III and IV only

17.

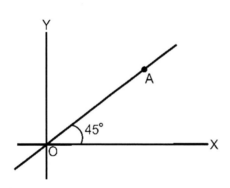

The line containing point A is rotated 90° clockwise about the origin, O.

Quantity A	**Quantity B**
The x-coordinate of point A before rotation	The x-coordinate of point A after rotation

    (E) Quantity A is greater.

    (F) Quantity B is greater.

    (G) The two quantities are equal.

    (H) The relationship cannot be determined from the information given.

18.

Point P has the coordinates $(-4, 5)$ and point Q has the coordinates $(4, -5)$ on the same rectangular coordinate plane.

Quantity A	**Quantity B**
Distance of P from origin $(0, 0)$	Distance of Q from origin $(0, 0)$

(A) Quantity A is greater.

(B) Quantity B is greater.

(C) The two quantities are equal.

(D) The relationship cannot be determined from the information given.

19. Toy train cars made of blocks of wood either 6 inches long or 7 inches long can be hooked together to make longer trains. 6 inches trains can be hooked only in pairs. Which of the following train lengths can be made by hooking together the 6-inch train cars, 7-inch train cars, or a combination of both?

Select all that apply.

(A) 30 inches

(B) 31 inches

(C) 40 inches

(D) 46 inches

(E) 38 inches

(F) 53 inches

(G) 51 inches

(H) 59 inches

20. John will be y years old x years from now. How old will he be z years from now?

(A) $y - x + z$

(B) $y + x + z$

(C) $y + x - z$

(D) $y - x - z$

(E) $x + z - y$

Answers and Explanations

1. **Topic: Algebra**

   Sub topic: Rules of Exponents

   The correct answer is 3471.

   $y = 4^6 - 5^4 = 4096 - 625 = 3471$

2. **Topic: Arithmetic**

   Sub topic: Time and Work

   The correct answer is (A).

   3 weeks and 2 days works out to 20 days.

   The total work-hours needed to complete the job $= 3 \times 20 \times 6 = 360$

   <u>Quantity A</u>

   When 4 people work for 6 hours each day, they complete 24 work-hours of the job per day.

   To complete 360 work-hours of job, they will take $\dfrac{360}{24} = 15$ days to complete the job.

   <u>Quantity B</u>

   5 people work to complete the job.

   3 people work 8 hours a day, while 2 others work for 3 hours a day

   The 3-member team completes $3 \times 8 = 24$ work-hours of job in one day.

   The 2-member team completes $2 \times 3 = 6$ work-hours of job in one day.

   Together, the team completes 30 work-hours of job in one day.

   To complete 360 work-hours of job, they will take $\dfrac{360}{24} = 15$ days to complete the job.

   Hence, Quantity A is greater than Quantity B.

3. **Topic: Geometry**

   Sub topic: Triangles

   The correct answer is (A).

   Let us calculate the area of the ΔA. Let the triangle be named ABC.

   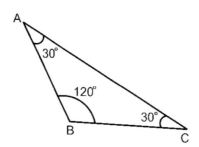

   From the figure, we can see that the third angle will also be 30°. (Angle sum property)

   ∠C = ∠B = 30°

   So, AB = BC = 10 units (In a triangle the sides opposite to equal angle are also equal.)

Draw BD perpendicular to AC.

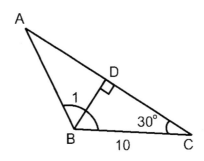

In right ΔBDC,

BD = 10 sin 30°

= 5 units.

CD = 10 cos 30°

= 5√3

As ABC is an isosceles Δ, so BD will also be a median of ΔABC.

AC = 2 CD

= 10√3 units

Area ΔABC = $\frac{1}{2}$ × 5 × 10√3

= 25√3 units²

= 43.30 units²

Now let us find the area of ΔB. Let this triangle be named PQR. Draw PS perpendicular to QR.

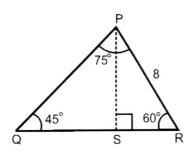

By, the angle sum property, the third angle will be 60°

In right ΔPSR

PS = 8 sin 60°

= 4√3 units

SR = 8 cos 60°

= 4units.

Similarly, In right ΔPQS

QS = PS tan 45°

= 4√3 units

Now, area ΔPQR = $\frac{1}{2}$ × 4√3 × (4 + 4√3)

= (8√3 + 24) units²

$= 37.86 \text{ units}^2$

Comparing the two areas, we can see that area $\Delta ABC > \Delta PQR$

The correct answer is (A).

4. **Topic: Algebra**

   The correct answer is (C).

   Because a and b must both be positive, or both be negative, choice C is the only answer that must be true.

5. **Topic: Geometry**

   Sub topic: Triangle

   The correct answer is (C).

   Since XY = YZ = 10, ΔXYZ is an isosceles triangle and $\angle X = \angle Z$.

   $\angle Y = 84°$ because it forms a vertical angle with the given angle

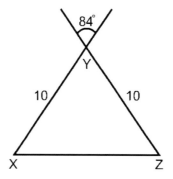

   $\angle X + \angle Y + \angle Z = 180°$

   $\angle X + 84° + \angle Z = 180°$

   $2(\angle Z) + 84° = 180°$

   $2(\angle Z) = 96°$

   $\angle Z = 48°$

   Therefore, the measure of Z = 48°

6. **Topic: Arithmetic**

   The correct answer is (E).

   Total number of different combinations ("how many different kinds") is found by multiplying the number of ways for each item. Therefore, three different breads times four different meats times three different cheeses $= 3 \times 4 \times 3 = 36$.

7. **Topic: Algebra**

   Sub topic: Equations

   The correct answer is (C).

   Place the expression on the right side over 1 to form a fraction.

   $$\frac{x^2 + y^2}{x + y} = \frac{x + y}{1}$$

   Having $x \neq -y$, which yields $x + y \neq 0$, set the cross products equal.

$(x^2 + y^2) = (x + y)(x + y)$

Expand the right side using the identity $(a + b)^2 = a^2 + 2ab + b^2$ or the FOIL method.

$x^2 + y^2 = x^2 + y^2 + 2xy$

Subtract $(x^2 + y^2)$ from each side and simplify.

$x^2 + y^2 - (x^2 + y^2) = x^2 + y^2 + 2xy - (x^2 + y^2)$

$x^2 + y^2 - x^2 - y^2 = x^2 + y^2 + 2xy^2 - x^2 - y^2$

$0 = 2xy$

$xy = 0$

Therefore, the correct answer is (C).

8. **Topic: Algebra**

   Sub topic: Exponents

   The correct answer is (A).

   First of all, we need to simply the two equations to get $x(a)$ and $y(b)$.

   In $x^{-\frac{2}{5}} = a^{-6}$, using cross multiplication, we can eliminate the minus signs and get $x^{\frac{2}{5}} = a^6$, then,

   $x = a^{6*\left(\frac{5}{2}\right)} = a^{15}$. We also have $y^{\frac{2}{5}} = b^6$, $y = b^{6*\left(\frac{5}{2}\right)} = b^{15}$.

   Therefore, $xy = a^{15}b^{15}$, and $(xy)^{\frac{1}{3}} = (a^{15}b^{15})^{\frac{1}{3}}$, which simples to $a^5 b^5$. This is greater than $a^4 b^4$ since all values of a and b are > 1.

9. **Topic: Data Analysis**

   The correct answer is (C).

   Average production of wheat

   $= \dfrac{780 + 795 + 928 + 750 + 978}{5}$

   $= \dfrac{4231}{5}$

   $= 846.2$

   Average production of rice

   $= \dfrac{(1125 + 1752 + 1344 + 1404 + 1640)}{5}$

   $= 1453$

   The required percentage $= \dfrac{1453 - 846.2}{795} \times 100 = 41.8\%$

10. **Topic: Data Analysis**

    The correct answer is (B).

	1996	1997	1998	1999	2000
Total production	5747	7102	6568	6850	7140
Percentage increase over the previous year	23.6	−7.5	4.3	4.2	-

    The answer is 1997.

11. **Topic: Geometry**

    Sub topic: Lines/Quadrilaterals Lines

    Breaking the figure into squares of sides x by adding lines gives

			1					
		2	3	4				
	5	6	7	8	9			
	10	11	12	13	14	15	16	
17	18	19	20	21	22	23	24	25
	26	27	28	29	30	31	32	
		33	34	35	36	37		
			38	39	40			
			41					

Remember that each square has area x^2. Then the total area is $41x^2$. Choices A, B, and E are not possible because area must be in square units.

12. **Topic: Arithmetic**

    Sub topic: Averages

    The correct answer is (C).

    Let x = first number, $2x + 1$ = second number, and $3x - 4$ = third number.

    Since the average of the three numbers is 55,

    $$\frac{x - (2x + 1) + (3x - 4)}{3} = 55$$

    Multiplying both sides of the equation by 3,

    $x + (2x + 1) + (3x - 4) = 165$

    $6x - 3 = 165$

    $6x - 3 + 3 = 165 + 3$

    $6x = 168$

    $\frac{6x}{6} = \frac{168}{6}$

    $x = \frac{168}{6}$

    $x = 28$ = first number

    $2x + 1 = 57$ = second number

    $3x - 4 = 80$ = third number

    Therefore, the largest number is 80.

13. **Topic: Geometry**

    Sub topic: Triangles/Circles

    The correct answer is (A).

    We know that if D and E are two points on a circle and AD and AE are tangent to the circle, then AD and AE are congruent. AD and AE are congruent, so

    $AD = AE = 1$

CE and CF are congruent, so CE = CF = 2

AC = AE + EC →AC = 3

BF and BD are congruent, so let BF = BD = x

AB = AD + BD →AB = 1 + x

BC = BF + CF →BC = x + 2

We are told that $m\angle BAC = 90°$ → ΔABC has a right angle → we can apply Pythagorean Theorem

$BC^2 = AB^2 + AC^2$

$(x + 2)^2 = (1 + x)^2 + 3^2$

$x^2 + 4x + 4 = 1 + 2x + x^2 + 9$

$2x = 6$ →$x = 3$

AB = 1 + 3 = 4

BC = 3 + 2 = 5

If $m\angle BAC = 90°$ it also means that BC is the diameter of circle C_1

BC is twice the radius of circle C_1

$$r_1 = \frac{BC}{2} = \frac{5}{2}$$

Area of circle $C_1 = \pi r_1{}^2 = \frac{25}{4}\pi$

In order to calculate Area of circle C_2, you need to remember the formula for the area of a triangle that has an incircle of radius r_2. The formula is:

Area $\Delta ABC = \frac{1}{2}(AB + BC + AC)r_2$

In this case we also know that ΔABC is a right-angle triangle, so its Area $= \frac{1}{2}(AB \times AC)$

$\frac{1}{2}(AB + BC + AC)r_2 = \frac{1}{2}(AB \times AC)$

$(4 + 5 + 3)r_2 = 4 \times 3$

$r_2 = \frac{12}{12} = 1$

Area of circle $C_2 = \pi r_2{}^2 = \pi$

Six times the Area of circle $C_2 = 6\pi$ which could also be written as $= \frac{24}{4}\pi$

$\frac{25}{4}\pi > \frac{24}{4}\pi$ →Area of circle C_1 > Six times the Area of circle C_2

The left column is greater than the right column, hence A) is the correct answer.

Note: If you do not remember the formula for the area of a triangle that has an inscribed circle, you can calculate it by splitting ΔABC into three smaller triangles using the center of the incircle C_2. The height of each of the smaller triangles will be the radius of the incircleC_2.

14. **Topic: Algebra**

Sub topic: Inequalities and Roots

The correct answer is (D).

First, we solve Inequality 1:

$4(x + 2) \le 2(x + 5) + 14$→$4x + 8 \le 2x + 10 + 14$ →$2x \le 16$→$x \le 8$

Then we solve Inequality 2:

$\sqrt{16 - 8y + y^2} \le 9 \rightarrow \sqrt{(4-y)^2} \le 9$

The square root of a square expression will always be a positive number, so we can write this inequality as:

$|4 - y| \le 9 \rightarrow -9 \le 4 - y \le 9 \rightarrow -13 \le -y \le 5$

We multiply with (-1) so the inequality sign changes:

$13 \ge y \ge -5$

Any number equal to, or less than, 8 is a solution of the first inequality, while for the second inequality the solutions are numbers equal to, or greater than, -5 and less than, or equal to, 13.

This means that 13 for instance is a solution for Inequality 2 which is greater than any solution of Inequality 1. However, in another example, 6 is a solution of Inequality 2 which is less than some solutions of Inequality 1 (8 for instance)

The relationship cannot be determined without further information and (D) is the correct answer.

15. **Topic: Geometry**

    Sub topic: Circles

    The correct answer is (A).

    The radius of circle P will also be 40% of the radius of circle Q. Because the area of any circle is πr^2, the radius will be used to compare the area of the two circles. Since

    $40\% = 0.40 = 0.4$

    and $(4)^2 = (0.16) = 16\%$

    Thus, area of circle P will be 16% of the area of circle Q.

16. **Topic: Arithmetic**

    Sub topic: Integers

    The correct answer is (B).

    Adding any two of three consecutive positive integers greater than 1 will always be greater than the other integer. Therefore, II is true. The others cannot be determined because they depend on values and/or the order of x, y, and z.

17. **Topic: Geometry**

    Sub topic: Lines & Angles/Coordinate Geometry

    The correct answer is (D).

    The relationship cannot be determined from the information given.

    If point A is at (x, y), rotating the line A by 90° clockwise will change the coordinates of point A to $(y, -x)$. Since we do not know how x and y are related, there is no way to determine which x-coordinate is greater.

    The correct answer is (D).

18. **Topic: Geometry**

    The correct answer is (C).

    The distance between two points (x_1, y_1) and (x_2, y_2) on the coordinate plane is given by $\sqrt{\{(x_2 - x_1)^2 + (y_2 - y_1)^2\}}$.

    The distance between the points $(-4, 5)$ and $(0, 0) = \sqrt{\left\{\left(0 - (-4)\right)^2 + (0 - 5)^2\right\}} = \sqrt{16 + 25} = \sqrt{41}$.

The distance between the points $(4, -5)$ and $(0, 0) = \sqrt{\left\{\left(0 - (4)\right)^2 + \left(0 - (-5)\right)^2\right\}} = \sqrt{16 + 25} = \sqrt{41}$.

The correct answer is (C).

19. **Topic: Arithmetic**

The correct answers are (B), (C), (E) and (H).

The table gives the number of train cars that need to be hooked to get the train lengths.

Total train length	No. of 6-inch trains	No. of 7-inch trains
30 inches	5	
31 inches	4	1
40 inches	2	4
46 inches	3	4
38 inches	4	2
53 inches	3	5
51 inches	5	3
59 inches	4	5

It is given that 6-inch train cars come in pairs. Options A, D, F, and G require that odd number of 6-inch train cars be hooked together. However, they can be hooked only in pairs.

Hence, the correct answers are B, C, E, and H.

20. **Topic: Arithmetic**

The correct answer is (A).

Since John will be y years from now; he is $y - x$ years old now.

Therefore, z years from now he will be $y - x + z$ years old.

This page is intentionally left blank

Chapter **10**

Exercise #4

Questions: 20 | Time: 30 minutes

This Exercise includes *20 practice questions*. The questions cover all the question types as explained in Chapter 2 and may fall into any of the following categories - Arithmetic, Algebra, Geometry or Data Analysis. You will find answers and detailed explanations towards the end of this chapter.

Questions 1 and 2 are based on the following diagram:

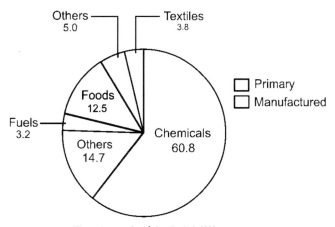

Total trade $253.1 billion

1. What percentage of the exports of primary goods in the trade flow from industrialized to developing countries will be food?

    (A) 60%

    (B) 55%

    (C) 58%

    (D) 63%

    (E) 65%

2. The difference between the values of exports of textiles and fuels from industrialized to developing countries will be

   (A) $1.5 billion

   (B) $114 billion

   (C) $2.5 billion

   (D) $114.5 billion

   (E) $2 billion

3.

There are three numbers *x, y* and *k* wherein:

$$\frac{x^2+5}{y^2}=k$$

$$k^2 + x^2 = 5y$$

$$k * y = 60$$

Quantity A	**Quantity B**
y	$\dfrac{k}{100}$

   (A) Quantity A is greater.

   (B) Quantity B is greater.

   (C) The two quantities are equal.

   (D) The relationship cannot be determined from the information given.

4. Nickels, quarters and dimes are part of a set of twenty-five coins. What is the total value of these set of coins in dollars and cents if, there are three more dimes than quarters and three-times as many dimes as nickels?

   (A) $3.65

   (B) $3.25

   (C) $2.25

   (D) $1.65

   (E) $1.25

5.

Two boats carry passengers up and down a river. The speed of the stream is 5 miles per hour.

Quantity A	**Quantity B**
Speed of Boat A if it covers 250 miles downstream and 40 miles upstream in 6 hours	Speed of Boat B if it travels 150 miles downstream and returns to the starting point in 5.5 hours

   (A) Quantity A is greater.

   (B) Quantity B is greater.

   (C) The two quantities are equal.

   (D) The relationship cannot be determined from the information given.

6.

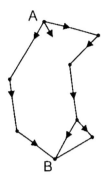

In the figure, any part from A to B must follow the connected line segments in the direction shown by the arrows. How many different paths are there from A to B?

(A) Five

(B) Six

(C) Seven

(D) Eight

(E) Nine

7. At a casino there are three tables. The payoff at the first table is 10: 1; at the second, 30: 1; and at the third, 40: 1. If a woman bets $10 at each table and wins at two of the tables, what is the difference between her maximum and minimum possible gross winnings?

(A) $200

(B) $300

(C) $400

(D) $500

(E) $600

8.

Distance from A to B is 12 *miles.*

Distance from A to C is 10 *miles.*

Quantity A   **Quantity B**

Distance from A to B   Distance from B to C

(A) Quantity A is greater.

(B) Quantity B is greater.

(C) The two quantities are equal.

(D) The relationship cannot be determined from the information given.

9. If the five vowels are repeated continuously in the pattern *a, e, i, o, u, a, e, i, o, u*, and so on, what vowel will the 327th letter be?

    (A) *a*

    (B) *e*

    (C) *i*

    (D) *o*

    (E) *u*

10.

                                      Events A and B are independent.

         Quantity A   **Quantity B**
             $P(A)$ $P\left(\dfrac{A}{B}\right)$

    (A) Quantity A is greater.

    (B) Quantity B is greater.

    (C) The two quantities are equal.

    (D) The relationship cannot be determined from the information given.

11. If $5^{x+3} = 3125$, then the value of x will be? Write your answer in the answer box.

    ┌─────────┐
    │   │
    └─────────┘

12. Gasoline varies in cost from $0.96 to $1.12 per gallon. If a car's mileage varies from 16 to 24 miles per gallon, what is the difference between the most and the least that the gasoline for a 480-mile trip will cost?

    (A) $5.12

    (B) $7.04

    (C) $11.52

    (D) $14.40

    (E) $52.80

13.

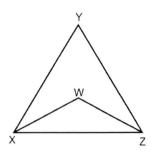

WX and WZ are angle bisectors of the base angles of isosceles ΔXYZ above. If ∠Y = 80°, what is the degree measure of ∠XWZ?

(A) 65

(B) 80

(C) 100

(D) 130

(E) 160

14.

$$n \neq 0$$
$$n \neq -\frac{1}{2}$$
$$n \neq -1$$

Quantity A

$$\frac{1}{1 + \frac{1}{1 + \frac{1}{n}}}$$

Quantity B

$$\frac{n + 1}{2n + 1}$$

(A) Quantity A is greater.

(B) Quantity B is greater.

(C) The two quantities are equal.

(D) The relationship cannot be determined from the information given.

15.

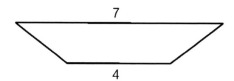

Which of the following could be the area of this trapezoid, if the height is an integer?

Select all that apply.

(A) 11

(B) 17

(C) 34

(D) $\dfrac{12}{5}$

(E) $\dfrac{17}{2}$

(F) $\dfrac{11}{2}$

(G) 33

16. If a book costs $5.70 after 40% discount, what was its original price?

(A) $2.28

(B) $6.10

(C) $7.98

(D) $9.12

(E) $9.50

17.

Quantity A	**Quantity B**
Volume of cube with side 6	Volume of rectangular prism with two dimensions less than 6

(A) Quantity A is greater.

(B) Quantity B is greater.

(C) The two quantities are equal.

(D) The relationship cannot be determined from the information given.

18.

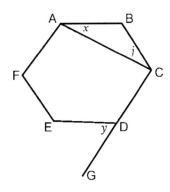

Hexagon ABCDEF is a regular hexagon.

Quantity A

$x + j$

Quantity B

y

(A) Quantity A is greater.

(B) Quantity B is greater.

(C) The two quantities are equal.

(D) The relationship cannot be determined from the information given.

19. If x is an integer and $3x + 11$ is even, which of the following must be even?

(A) x

(B) $x + 1$

(C) x^2

(D) $2x + 1$

(E) x^3

20.

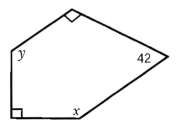

Quantity A

$2x$

Quantity B

$2y$

(A) Quantity A is greater.

(B) Quantity B is greater.

(C) The two quantities are equal.

(D) The relationship cannot be determined from the information given.

Answers and Explanations

1. **Topic: Data Analysis**

   The correct answer is (A).

   Food exports = 12.5%. 'Primary' export = 3.2 + 12.5 + 5.0 = 20.7%. As a percentage, $\frac{12.5}{20.7} \times 100 = 60.4 = 60\%$

2. **Topic: Data Analysis**

   The correct answer is (A).

   Difference = $\frac{\$(3.8 - 3.2)}{100} \times 253.1$ billion = \$1.5.

3. **Topic: Algebra**

   Sub topic: Exponents

   The correct answer is (B).

   First, we plug the second equation into the first one:

   $k^2 + x^2 = 5y$, i.e. $x^2 = 5y - k^2$ into $k = \frac{x^2 + 5}{y^2}$

   $k = \frac{5y - k^2 + 5}{y^2}$

   Multiply y^2 on both sides and using k × y =60, we get

   $60y = 5y - 5k^2 + 5$

   This simplifies into

   $-55y = 5k^2 - 5$ *or*

   $-11y = k^2 - 1$

   Then we have

   $k^2 = 1 - 11y,$

   Therefore, since $y > 0$, k^2 is less than 1. This means k is also less than 1, regardless of being negative or positive number (between 0 and 1 in order to have a square less than 1).

4. **Topic: Arithmetic**

   The correct answer is (A).

   Let n = number of nickels, $3n$ = number of dimes, and $3n - 3$ = number of quarters. Since 25 coins are in the collection,

   $n + 3n + (3n - 3) = 25$

   $7n - 3 = 25$

   $7n = 28$

   $n = 4$ nickels = \$0.20

   $3n = 12$ dimes = \$1.20

   $3n - 3 = 9$ quarters = \$2.25

   Therefore, the total value of collection is \$0.20 + \$1.20 + \$2.25 = \$3.65.

5. **Topic: Arithmetic**

   Sub topic: Boat & Stream

   The correct answer is (B).

   Let the speed of the boat be represented by s $\frac{miles}{hour}$

   Speed of the boat downstream $= (s + 5)\frac{miles}{hour}$

   Speed of the boat upstream $= (s - 5)\frac{miles}{hour}$

   <u>Quantity A</u>

   $$\frac{250}{s + 5} + \frac{40}{s - 5} = 6$$

   $$\frac{250(s - 5) + 40(s + 5)}{s^2 - 25} = 6$$

   $$250s - 1250 + 40s + 200 = 6s^2 - 150$$

   $$6s^2 - 290s + 900 = 0$$

   s can be 45 or 3.33. If the speed of the boat is less than the speed of the stream, it cannot travel upstream. Hence, s should be 45.

   Speed of the boat A is 45 $\frac{miles}{hour}$.

   <u>Quantity B</u>

   $$\frac{150}{s + 5} + \frac{150}{s - 5} = 5.5$$

   $$\frac{150(s - 5) + 150(s + 5)}{s^2 - 25} = 5.5$$

   $$150s - 750 + 150s + 750 = 5.5s^2 - 137.5$$

   $$5.5s^2 - 300s - 137.5 = 0$$

   $$s = 55 \text{ or } -\frac{5}{11}$$

   Speed cannot be negative.

   Hence, Speed of the boat B is 55 $\frac{miles}{hour}$.

   Hence, option B is the correct answer.

6. **Topic: Arithmetic**

   The correct answer is (A).

   There are three parts that start out from point A, the one on the left leads straight to point B, for one route. The middle part veers off midway, offering two routes to point B. The right path also veers off midway, offering two routes. Therefore, there are 5 routes from A to B.

7. **Topic: Arithmetic**

   The correct answer is (B).

   The maximum winning would result from winning at the tables with 40: 1 odds and 30: 1 odds. Betting $10 at the 40: 1 Table and winning result in a prize of ($10) (40) = $400. Winning at the 30: 1 Table yields ($10) (30) = $300, making the maximum possible winnings $400 + $300 = $700. The minimum winnings result from winnings at the 10: 1 table and the 30: 1 table. Winning at the 10: 1 table yields ($10) (10) = $100, making the minimum winnings $100 + $300 = $400. The difference is $700 − $400 = $300.

8. **Topic: Arithmetic**

    The correct answer is (D).

    Since we know nothing about the placement of A, B, and C, we cannot determine anything about their distances.

9. **Topic: Arithmetic**

    The correct answer is (B).

    Because each letter repeats after every five vowels, divide 327 by 5, and the remainder will determine the vowel in that place of the pattern. Since 327 ÷ 5 = 65 with a remainder of 2, indicates that the second vowel (E) will be the 327th letter.

10. **Topic: Data Analysis**

    The correct answer is (C).

    The two quantities are equal. Quantity B refers to conditional probability: the probability of an event A given an event B occurs. The formula is given as follows:

    $P(A|B) = \frac{P(A \cap B)}{P(B)}.$

    But since it is given that A and B are independent events, $P(A|B) = \frac{P(A) \times P(B)}{P(B)} = P(A).$

    Therefore, Quantity B is equivalent to Quantity A.

11. **Topic: Algebra**

    Sub topic: Rules of Exponents

    The correct answer is 2.

    First convert 3125 to an exponent with base 5.

    $5^{x+3} = 5^5$

    Now equate the exponents and solve for x

    $x + 3 = 5$

    $x = 2$

12. **Topic: Data Analysis**

    The correct answer is (D).

    The most the trip would cost is when gas costs $1.12 and the mileage is 16mph. Therefore, $1.12 \times \left(\frac{480}{16}\right) =$ $33.60. The least would be $0.96 \times \left(\frac{480}{24}\right) = $19.20. The difference is therefore $14.40.

13. **Topic: Geometry**

    The correct answer is (D).

    In isosceles ΔXYZ, ∠X =∠Z.

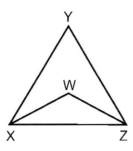

$\angle X + \angle Y + \angle Z = 180°$

$\angle X + 80° + \angle Z = 180°$

$\angle X + \angle Z = 100°$

$\angle X = \angle Z = 50°$

Since WX bisects $\angle$YXZ and WZ bisects $\angle$YZX,

$\angle YXW = \angle WXZ = \angle YZW = \angle WZX = 25°$

Therefore, on ΔXWZ,

$\angle XWZ + \angle WXZ + \angle WZX = 180°$

$\angle XWZ + 25° + 25° = 180°$

$\angle XWZ + 50° = 180°$

$\angle XWZ = 130°$

14. **Topic: Arithmetic**

    Sub topic: Fractions

    The correct answer is (C).

    Simplifying the complex fraction in column A,

    $$\cfrac{1}{1 + \cfrac{1}{1 + \frac{1}{n}}} = \cfrac{1}{1 + \cfrac{1}{\frac{n}{n} + \frac{1}{n}}} = \cfrac{1}{1 + \cfrac{1}{\frac{(n+1)}{n}}} = \cfrac{1}{1 + \cfrac{n}{n+1}}$$

    $$= \cfrac{1}{\frac{n+1}{2n+1} + \frac{n}{n+1}} = \cfrac{1}{\frac{n+1+n}{n+1}} = \cfrac{1}{\frac{2n+1}{n+1}} = \frac{n+1}{2n+1}$$

15. **Topic: Geometry**

    Sub topic: Quadrilaterals

    The correct answers are (A), (F) and (G).

    The area is $\dfrac{h(4+7)}{2}$. If h is an integer, then the area must be an integer multiple of $\dfrac{11}{2}$. Answer A would have h=2, answer F would have h=1 and answer G would have h=6.

16. **Topic: Arithmetic**

    Sub topic: Profit and Loss

    The correct answer is (E).

    Let x = original price. Then

    $x - 0.40\,x = 5.70$

$0.60x = 5.70$

$x = 9.50$

Hence, the book originally cost $9.50.

17. **Topic: Geometry**

    Sub topic: Volumes

    The correct answer is (D).

    Volume of cube with side 6 is $6 \times 6 \times 6 = 216$. Volume of rectangular prism with two dimensions less than 6 is not determinable because the third dimension is needed. Therefore, no comparison can be made.

18. **Topic: Geometry**

    Sub topic: Quadrilaterals

    The correct answer is (C).

    If Hexagon ABCDEF is a regular hexagon, all sides and angles are congruent. First, we need to determine the sum of the interior angles in the hexagon. The sum of the interior angles in a polygon is $(S = (n - 2)180)$

    Number of sides in a Hexagon $= 6$

    Sum of interior angles $= (6 - 2)180 = 4(180) = 720°$

    The measure of $\angle B$ can be calculated by dividing the sum of the interior angles by the total number of angles.

    $\angle B = \dfrac{720°}{6} = 120°$

    Now we can calculate the measure of x and j. They are both equal since the sides opposite them are equal.

    The degrees in the three angles of a triangle sum to $180°$.

    $x + j + 120 = 180°$

    $x + x + 120 = 180°$

    $2x + 120 = 180°$

    $2x = 60°$

    $x = 30°, j = 30°$

    Therefore, Quantity A is $60°$.

    For Quantity B, the interior angle is $120°$ just like all interior angles of a regular hexagon. A straight line has an angle measure of $180°$. The measure of y is $180 - 120$, so y is $60°$.

    The question can also be evaluated conceptually without calculations by using the knowledge that the interior angles B and D are equal, $x + j$ will be supplementary to B, and y will be supplementary to D. Therefore, $x + j$ must equal y.

    Both quantities are $60°$; therefore, the answer is C.

19. **Topic: Arithmetic**

    Sub topic: integers

    The correct answer is (B).

    Since the sum of two odd integers is an even integer, and $3x + 11$ is even, then $3x$ must be odd. Since the product of two odd integers is an odd integer, then x must be an odd integer. Hence $x + 1$ must be an even integer.

20. **Topic: Geometry**

    Sub topic: Quadrilaterals

    The correct answer is (D).

    First, we need to determine the sum of the interior angles in the pentagon. The sum of the interior angles in a polygon is dictated by the following equation. $(S = (n - 2)180°)$

    Number of sides in a Pentagon $= 5$

    Sum of interior angles $= (5 - 2)180 = 3(180) = 540°$

    We know all interior angles of the polygon should sum to 540°. Now we can find the measure of x and y.

    $x + y + 90 + 90 + 42 = 540°$

    $x + y + 222 = 540°$

    $x + y = 318°$

    We know that the sum of the angles is 318°, but we are unable to calculate the measure of each individual angle. The answer is D, cannot be determined.

This page is intentionally left blank

Chapter **11**

Exercise #5

Questions: 20 | Time: 30 minutes

This Exercise includes *20 practice questions*. The questions cover all the question types as explained in Chapter 2 and may fall into any of the following categories - Arithmetic, Algebra, Geometry or Data Analysis. You will find answers and detailed explanations towards the end of this chapter.

1.

Jimmy and his friends are going river rafting from Camp A to Camp B. The river has a current of 7 mph. It takes Jimmy and his friends 2 hours to paddle downstream from Camp A to Camp B and 10 hours for them to return to Camp A.

Quantity A	**Quantity B**
The amount of time it would take Jimmy and his friends to paddle from Camp A to Camp B in still water	The amount of time it will take Jimmy and his friends to paddle from Camp A to Camp B downstream with a current of 4 mph

(A) Quantity A is greater.

(B) Quantity B is greater.

(C) The two quantities are equal.

(D) The relationship cannot be determined from the information given.

2.

At a store, all shoes are being marked off 30% and all bags are marked off 25%.

Quantity A   **Quantity B**

Sale price of a pair of shoes that originally cost   Sale price of a bag that originally cost $75
$80

(A) Quantity A is greater.

(B) Quantity B is greater.

(C) The two quantities are equal.

(D) The relationship cannot be determined from the information given.

3.

In the figure above, six equilateral triangles with sides of 1 are joined to form a hexagon. A circle is then circumscribed about the hexagon. What is the area of the shaded region?

(A) $\pi - \frac{\sqrt{3}}{2}$

(B) $\pi - \frac{3\sqrt{3}}{2}$

(C) $\pi - \frac{\pi\sqrt{3}}{2}$

(D) $2\pi - 3\sqrt{3}$

(E) $2\pi - 3\sqrt{3}$

4.   For how many integers' values of x will the value of the expression $3x - 4$ be an integer greater than 4 and less than 250?

(A) 86

(B) 85

(C) 84

(D) 83

(E) 82

5. Two uniform dice marked 1 to 6 are tossed together. The probability of the total 7 in a single throw is

(A) $\dfrac{5}{36}$

(B) $\dfrac{5}{12}$

(C) $\dfrac{2}{31}$

(D) $\dfrac{1}{6}$

(E) None of these

6.

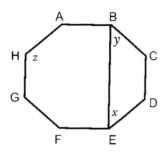

Polygon ABCDEFGH is a regular octagon.

Quantity A

$x + y$

Quantity B

$z - y$

(A) Quantity A is greater.

(B) Quantity B is greater.

(C) The two quantities are equal.

(D) The relationship cannot be determined from the information given.

7. Dolly's age is 15 years. Pinky is $\dfrac{1}{3}$ years older than Dolly's current age. How many years ago was Pinky twice as old as Dolly was then?

Write your answer in the answer box.

8.

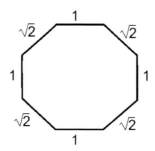

Note: - Figure not drawn to scale.

The sides of an octagon alternate in length. As pictured above, each side with Length 1 is next to a side of length $\sqrt{2}$. What is the area of the octagon?

(A) 5

(B) 6

(C) 7

(D) 8

(E) 9

9.

On January 1, 2013 Tommy deposits $3,000 dollars into a bank account that pays 6.25% interest annually compounded weekly. Tommy receives $1,346 for his birthday and deposits the entire amount into the same bank account on January 1, 2015.

Quantity A	**Quantity B**
The balance in the bank account on January 1, 2013	The change in balance between January 1, 2013 and June 1, 2018

(A) Quantity A is greater.

(B) Quantity B is greater.

(C) The two quantities are equal.

(D) The relationship cannot be determined from the information given.

10. What is the area of the square with vertices at the points $(0, 2)$, $(0, -2)$, $(2, 0)$, and $(-2, 0)$?

(A) 4

(B) 6

(C) 8

(D) 12

(E) 16

Questions 11 and 12 are based on the following chart:

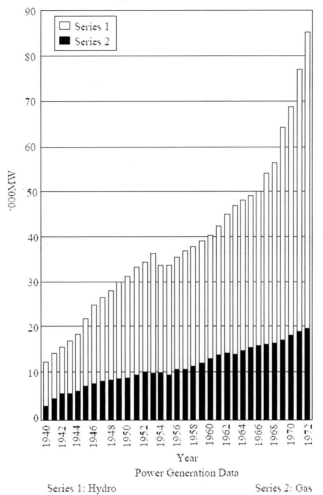

Series 1: Hydro   Series 2: Gas

11. In which of the following years was the increase maximum over the previous year in the installed capacity of hydro?

    (A) 1969

    (B) 1960

    (C) 1968

    (D) 1965

    (E) 1944

12. Number of times the installed capacity of gas decreased over the previous year is

    (A) once

    (B) twice

    (C) thrice

    (D) four times

    (E) never

13.

Quantity A	**Quantity B**
$(5.32)(0.453) - \dfrac{4.328}{0.5}$	$\dfrac{6.3452}{0.2} - (12.56)(0.45)$

(A) Quantity A is greater.

(B) Quantity B is greater.

(C) The two quantities are equal.

(D) The relationship cannot be determined from the information given.

14. A cylindrical roller 12 inches long is dipped into blue paint, and then rolled for one complete revolution over a white wall. If the area of the blue region is 48 square inches, what is the radius, in inches, of the roller?

(A) $\dfrac{2}{\pi}$

(B) $\dfrac{4}{\pi}$

(C) 2

(D) 4

(E) 2π

15.

Quantity A	**Quantity B**
$(2)^4(8)^{-\frac{2}{3}}$	$(4)^{\frac{5}{2}}(16)^{-\frac{3}{4}}$

(A) Quantity A is greater.

(B) Quantity B is greater.

(C) The two quantities are equal.

(D) The relationship cannot be determined from the information given.

16.

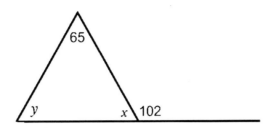

<table>
<tr><td align="center"><u>**Quantity A**</u></td><td align="center"><u>**Quantity B**</u></td></tr>
<tr><td align="center">$2x + y$</td><td align="center">$x + 2y$</td></tr>
</table>

(A) Quantity A is greater.

(B) Quantity B is greater.

(C) The two quantities are equal.

(D) The relationship cannot be determined from the information given.

17. If $(x + 1)$ times $(2x + 1)$ is an odd integer, then x must be

(A) an odd integer

(B) an even integer

(C) a prime number

(D) a compose number

(E) a negative number

18. Given that $y - x^2 + 3x + 7 = 0$

If x is a positive multiple of 5, then which of the following could be possible values of y?

Select all that apply.

(A) 3

(B) 62

(C) 173

(D) 243

(E) 333

(F) 642

(G) 1113

(H) 1563

19.

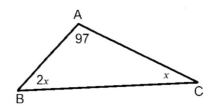

Quantity A	**Quantity B**
The length of AB	The length of AC

(A) Quantity A is greater.

(B) Quantity B is greater.

(C) The two quantities are equal.

(D) The relationship cannot be determined from the information given.

20.

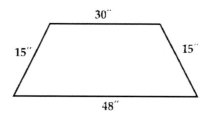

What is the area of the preceding trapezoid in square inches?

(A) 108

(B) 234

(C) 368

(D) 468

(E) 585

Answers and Explanations

1. **Topic: Arithmetic**

   Sub topic: Time and Distance

   The correct answer is (A).

   To solve this problem, we need to use the following formula:

   Distance = rate × time

   The distance between the two camps will stay the same. The rate and time will be different for the trips depending on the direction we are going on the river. We do not know the speed at which they are paddling, so this will be our x.

	Rate	Time	Distance=Rate × Time
Camp A to Camp B Downstream	$x + 7$	2	$2(x + 7)$
Camp B to Camp A Upstream	$x - 7$	10	$10(x - 7)$

   Both ways are the same distance, so now we can set both expressions equal to each other and solve the equation.

   $2(x + 7) = 10(x - 7)$

   $2x + 14 = 10x - 70$

   $84 = 8x$

   $10.5 = x$

   In still water, Jimmy and his friends are paddling at a rate of 10.5 miles per hour in the raft. Now let's start to compare Quantity A and Quantity B.

   Quantity A: Substitute the value of x into the equation to calculate the distance from Camp A to Camp B.

   Distance from Camp A to Camp B = $2(10.5 + 7) = 2(17.5) = 35$ miles.

   Now we can work backwards to calculate how long it would take to travel in still water:

   Distance = 35 miles, Rate = 10.5 mph, Time = ?

   $35 = (10.5)(t)$

   $3.3 \text{hours} = t$

   Quantity B: Distance= 35 miles, Rate = 10.5 + 4(current), Time=?

   $35 = (10.5 + 4)t$

   $35 = (14.5)t$

   $2.4 \text{ hours} = t$

   Quantity A is greater, so the answer is A.

2. **Topic: Arithmetic**

   Sub topic: Profit and Loss

   The correct answer is (B).

   We need to determine the price of each item. Shoes are 30% off and bags are 25% off. We need to multiply the original cost by the percent discount written as a decimal. Then subtract that amount from the original price.

Quantity A: Original Price = $80, discount = 30% = 0.30

Amount of Discount = $80 × 0.30 = $24

Price of item= $80 − $24 = $56

Quantity B Original Price = $75, discount= 25% = 0.25

Amount of Discount = $75 × 0.25 = $18.75

Price of item= $75 − $18.75 = $56.25

The cost of the item in Quantity B is greater; therefore, the answer is B.

3. **Topic: Geometry**

    Sub topic: Quadrilateral

    The correct answer is (B).

    To find the area of the shaded region, simply subtract the area of the hexagon from the area of the circle. The area of the circle $= \pi r^2$.

    Since the radius of the circle is 1, its area is $\pi(1)^2 = \pi$. Since you know that the area of the hexagon must be subtracted from the area of the circle or π, you can eliminate choices (D) and (E). The hexagon is composed of six equilateral triangles, so six times the area of one triangle will give you the area of the hexagon. The area of a triangle is one half base times height. The base of each triangle is 1, but you have to solve for the height. Dropping a perpendicular line from the top vertex of a triangle to its base divides it into two triangles. Since the hypotenuse of each is 1 and the other leg of each is $\frac{1}{2}$, it is a 30:60:90 right triangle and the remaining side must be $\frac{\sqrt{3}}{2}$.

    That means the area of one equilateral triangle is $\left(\frac{1}{2} \times 1 \frac{\sqrt{3}}{2}\right) = \frac{\sqrt{3}}{4}$

    So, the area of the hexagon is $6 \times \frac{\sqrt{3}}{4} = \frac{3\sqrt{3}}{2}$

    Therefore, the area of the shaded region is $\pi - \frac{3\sqrt{3}}{2}$, choice (B).

4. **Topic: Arithmetic**

    Sub topic: Integers

    The correct answer is (E).

    For the expression $3x - 4$ to be greater than 4 and less than 250,

    $4 < 3x - 4 < 250$

    Add 4,

    $4 + 4 < 3x - 4 + 4 < 250 + 4$

    $8 < 3x < 254$

    Divide by 3,

    $\frac{8}{3} < \frac{3x}{3} < \frac{254}{3}$

    $\frac{8}{3} < x < \frac{254}{3}$

    Since x is an integer, $x = 3, 4, 5...82, 83, 84$. Hence there are 82 integer values of x.

5. **Topic: Data Analysis**

   Sub topic: Probability

   The correct answer is (D).

   In a single throw with two dice, 7 can be obtained in the following 6 ways:

   $(6, 1), (1, 6), (5, 2), (2, 5), (4, 3), (3, 4)$ and total number of ways $= 6^2 = 36$

   Therefore, required probability $= \dfrac{6}{36} = \dfrac{1}{6}$

6. **Topic: Geometry**

   Sub topic: Polygons

   The correct answer is (C).

   It is given that the polygon is a regular octagon meaning that all sides and angles of the octagon are congruent. We need to determine the sum of the interior angles in an octagon. $(S = (n - 2)180°)$

   Number of sides in an Octagon $= 8$

   Sum of interior angles $= (8 - 2)180 = 6(180) = 1080°$

   The measure of one angle in the octagon can be calculated by dividing the sum of the interior angles by the total number of angles.

   Measure of one interior angle $= \dfrac{1080°}{8} = 135°$

   Therefore, z is $135°$.

   Polygon BCDE is an isosceles trapezoid. Therefore, the base angles are congruent.

   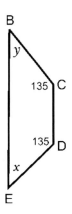

   The sum of the angles in a quadrilateral is $360°$.

   $x + y + 135 + 135 = 360°$

   $x + y + 270 = 360°$

   $x + y = 90°$

   $x = 45°$

   $y = 45°$

   Both x and y are congruent, so both are $45°$.

   Quantity A: $x + y = 45° + 45° = 90°$

   Quantity B: $z - y = 135° - 45° = 90°$

   Both quantities are $90°$.

   Therefore, the answer is (C).

7. **Topic: Algebra**

    Sub topic: Ages

    The correct answer is 10.

    Pinky will now be 20 years old since $\frac{4}{3}$ of 15 is 20.

    10 years ago, Pinky was twice as old as Dolly was since Pinky would have been 10 (20−10=10) and Dolly would have been 5 (15 − 10 = 5)

8. **Topic: Geometry**

    Sub topic: Polygons

    The correct answer is (C).

    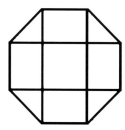

    Divide the octagon into pieces whose areas you can find. Drawing perpendiculars from the top to the bottom and from left to right breaks the figure into 5 squares and 4 right triangles, as shown above. Each of the squares has side length 1, for an area of $1^2 = 1$. Each of the right triangles is equal to half a square (they are isosceles right triangles with legs of length 1) and have an area of $\frac{1}{2}$.

    So, the total area is $5(1) + 4\left(\frac{1}{2}\right)$

    $= 5 + 2 = 7$.

9. **Topic: Arithmetic**

    Sub topic: Compound Interest

    The correct answer is (A).

    For Quantity A, there is no calculation necessary. The balance in the account on January 1, 2013 is $3,000, as stated by the first sentence of the word problem.

    To calculate the change in balance between January 1, 2013 and June 1, 2018, we have a two-step process. We first need to calculate the account balance on January 1, 2015 using the formula for compound interest:

    $P = A\left(1 + \frac{r}{n}\right)^n$, Where A is the beginning amount, r is the interest rate, n is the number of times compounded per year, and t is the time in years.

    January 1, 2013 to January 1, 2015:

    $P_1 = \$3000$

    $r = 0.0625$

    $n = 52$(number of weeks in a year)

    $t = 2$ years

    $A_1 = 3000\left(1 + \frac{0.0625}{52}\right)^{(52 \times 2)} = 3000(1.0012)^{104}$

    $= 3000(1.1328) = \$3398.40$

    Add the $1,346 to the amount and now you have the balance on January 15, 2015.

The balance is $4,744.40 on January 1, 2015.

January 1, 2015 to June 1, 2018:

$P_1 = \$4744.40$

$r = 0.0625$

$n = 52$ (number of weeks in a year)

$t = 2.5$ years (2 years and 6 months)

$A_1 = 4744.40\left(1 + \dfrac{0.0625}{52}\right)^{(52 \times 25)} = 4744.40(1.0012)^{130}$

$= 4744.40(1.1687) = \$5544.86$

The change in the account balance is the difference between $5,544.86 and $3,000 or $5544.86 − $3000.00, which is $2,544.86.

Quantity A is $3,000 and Quantity B is $2,544.86.

Therefore, Quantity A is greater.

The answer is A.

10. **Topic: Geometry**

Sub topic: Quadrilateral/Triangles

The correct answer is (C).

Make a quick sketch of the figure. You can see that each side of the square is also the hypotenuse of a right triangle. Solve for the hypotenuse of one of these triangles, say the one in the first quadrant. Each leg of the triangle falls on one of the axis, so it's easy to see that each has length 2. Two equal legs make it an isosceles right triangle. And its hypotenuse is equal to a leg times $\sqrt{2} = 2\sqrt{2}$. The area of a square is equal to a side length squared, or $(2\sqrt{2})^2 = 8$.

11. **Topic: Data Analysis**

The correct answer is (A).

In 1969 installed capacity of hydro increased from 15 thousand MW to 17 thousand MW.

12. **Topic: Data Analysis**

The correct answer is (B).

In 1954, decrease of 1 thousand MW and in 1965 decrease of 0.5 thousand MW over the previous year were observed in the installed capacity of gas.

13. **Topic: Arithmetic**

Sub topic: Numbers

The correct answer is (B).

We need to work out the values for Quantity A and Quantity B before we can determine the answer.

Quantity A: $(5.32)(0.453) - \dfrac{4.328}{0.5} = 2.40996 - 8.656 = -6.24604$

Quantity B: $\dfrac{6.3452}{0.2} - (12.56)(0.45) = 31.726 - 5.652 = 26.074$

Quantity B is greater, so B is the answer. This example can be approximated as a quick check to be sure you did not make a calculation error. Quantity A is roughly $(2 - 8)$ or -6. Quantity B is roughly $(30 - 6)$ or 24.

14. **Topic: Geometry**

The correct answer is (A).

Visualize the situation: rolling a cylindrical paint roller on the wall produces a rectangular region of blue paint, with one side of length 12. The length of its other side will be equal to the circumference of the roller. Since the area of the region is 48, the circumference must be 48 ÷ 12 = 4. Circumference equals $2\pi r$, where r is the radius. Therefore $2\pi r = 4$, $r = \dfrac{4}{2\pi} = \dfrac{2}{\pi}$.

15. **Topic: Arithmetic**

Sub topic: Exponents

The correct answer is (C).

To solve this problem, we need to use the following two properties to evaluate each expression.

- $a^{-n} = \dfrac{1}{a^n}$

- $a^{m/n} = \sqrt[n]{a^m} = \left(\sqrt[n]{a}\right)^m$

Quantity A: $(2)^4(8)^{-\frac{2}{3}} = \dfrac{(2)^4}{(8)^{\frac{2}{3}}} = \dfrac{16}{\left(\sqrt[3]{8}\right)^2} = \dfrac{16}{(2)^2} = \dfrac{16}{4} = 4$

Quantity B: $(4)^{\frac{5}{2}}(16)^{-3/4} = \dfrac{(4)^{5/2}}{(16)^{3/4}} = \dfrac{\sqrt{4^5}}{\sqrt[4]{16^3}} = \dfrac{\left(\sqrt{4}\right)^5}{\left(\sqrt[4]{16}\right)^3} = \dfrac{2^5}{2^3} = \dfrac{32}{8} = 4$

Both quantities are equal, so the answer is C.

16. **Topic: Geometry**

Sub topic: Triangles

The correct answer is (A).

To calculate the measure of x and y we need to know the following properties:

- All interior angles of a triangle have a sum of 180°.

- Two adjacent angles that form a straight line have a combined angle measure of 180°.

We can now write the following equations:

$x + 102° = 180°$

$x + y + 65 = 180°$

We can solve for x using the first equation, and then solve for y.

$x + 102 = 180°$

$x = 78°$

$78 + y + 65 = 180°$

$143 + y = 180°$

$y = 37°$

Now we can calculate Quantity A and Quantity B by substituting in the values of x and y.

Quantity A: $2x + y = 2(78) + 37 = 193°$

Quantity B: $x + 2y = 78 + 2(37) = 152°$

Quantity A is greater; therefore, the answer is A.

17. **Topic: Arithmetic**

    Sub topic: Numbers

    The correct answer is (B).

    Solve this problem by plugging in simple numbers. Start with 1, an odd integer.

    $(1 + 1)$ times $(2.1 + 1)$

    $= (2)$ times $(2 + 1)$

    $= 2.3$

    $= 6$ (not odd)

    Now, try 2, an even integer.

    $(2 + 1)$ times $(2.2 + 1)$

    $= (3)$ times $(4 + 1)$

    $= 3.5$

    $= 15$ (an odd integer)

18. **Topic: Algebra**

    Sub topic: Algebraic Expressions

    The correct answers are (A), (C), (E) and (G).

    Solving the equation $y = x^2 - 3x - 7$

x	$y = x^2 - 3x - 7$
5	3
10	63
15	173
20	333
25	543
30	803
35	1113
40	1473
45	1883
50	2343
55	2853
60	3413
65	4023

19. **Topic: Geometry**

    Sub topic: Triangles

    The correct answer is (B).

    In a triangle, the angles can be organized by the smallest angles to the largest angles. The side opposite the smallest angle is the shortest side of the triangle just as the side opposite the largest angle is the longest side.

    $\angle B > \angle C$

Therefore, the sides opposite should follow the same inequality which is AC > AB. Quantity B is greater, so the answer is B.

20. **Topic: Geometry**

    Sub topic: Quadrilaterals

    The correct answer is (D).

    Since the area of a trapezoid $= \frac{1}{2} \times h \times (b_1 + b_2)$, we need to find the altitude, h. Draw altitudes in figures as follows:

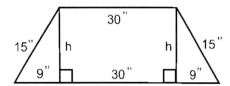

    Since the triangles formed are right triangles, use the Pythagorean Theorem, which says

    $c^2 = a^2 + b^2$

    $15^2 = 9^2 + h^2$

    $225 = 81 + h^2$

    $h^2 = 225 - 81$

    $h^2 = 144$

    $h = \sqrt{144} = 12 \; inches$

    Hence the area of the trapezoid will be

    $\frac{1}{2} \times h \times (b_1 + b_2) = \frac{1}{2} \times 12 \times (30 + 48)$

    $= (6)\,(78)$

    $= 468 \; square \; inches.$

Chapter **12**

Exercise #6

Questions: 20　|　Time: 30 minutes

This Exercise includes *20 practice questions*. The questions cover all the question types as explained in Chapter 2 and may fall into any of the following categories - Arithmetic, Algebra, Geometry or Data Analysis. You will find answers and detailed explanations towards the end of this chapter.

1. Conglomerate Corp manufactures hubcaps in 3-different factories. How many days would it take to manufacture a million hubcaps if these factories produce hubcaps in the following ratios:

   The first 2 factories can manufacture hundred-thousand hubcaps in fifteen-days while the third factory is thirty-percent faster.

   (A) 38

   (B) 42

   (C) 44

   (D) 46

   (E) 50

2. If $m^4 + n^4 = 0$, what is the value of $9m - 5n$?

   (A) 9

   (B) 5

   (C) 4

   (D) 0

   (E) −1

3.

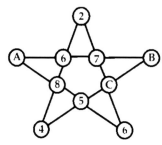

If the sums of four circles along any line segment of the star above are equal, then B =

(A) 3

(B) 4

(C) 6

(D) 7

(E) It cannot be determined from the information given.

4.

Quantity A	Quantity B

$$\frac{1}{3} \div \frac{5}{9} + \frac{2}{5} \times \frac{4}{7}$$ $$\frac{1}{3} \div \frac{5}{7} + \frac{4}{5} \times \frac{4}{7}$$

(A) Quantity A is greater.

(B) Quantity B is greater.

(C) The two quantities are equal.

(D) The relationship cannot be determined from the information given.

5.

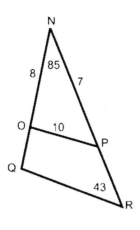

OP || QR

Quantity A	**Quantity B**
Length of QR	Length of NQ

(A) Quantity A is greater.

(B) Quantity B is greater.

(C) The two quantities are equal.

(D) The relationship cannot be determined from the information given.

6.

Quantity A	**Quantity B**
11^5	5^{11}

(A) Quantity A is greater.

(B) Quantity B is greater.

(C) The two quantities are equal.

(D) The relationship cannot be determined from the information given.

Questions 7 and 8 are based on the following chart:

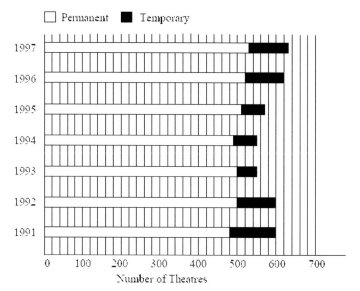

7. The average number of shows per theatre, in thousands, of the year having maximum shows is approximately

    (A) 1.5

    (B) 15

    (C) 1.2

    (D) 1.05

    (E) 1.3

8. In the seven years, how many times the number of cinema shows remained same in alternate years?

    (A) not even once

    (B) thrice

    (C) once

    (D) twice

    (E) four times

9. Tickets numbered from 1 through 50 are placed in a container, and one ticket will be selected at random. What is the probability that the ticket selected will have a number on it divisible by 3?

    (A) $\frac{1}{5}$

    (B) $\frac{1}{5}$

    (C) $\frac{3}{10}$

    (D) $\frac{8}{25}$

    (E) $\frac{1}{3}$

10.

Quantity A	**Quantity B**
Twice the area of a 5-12-13 right triangle	The area of a 5-12-13 right triangle after a scale factor of 2

(A) Quantity A is greater.

(B) Quantity B is greater.

(C) The two quantities are equal.

(D) The relationship cannot be determined from the information given.

11.

Quantity A	**Quantity B**
The interest earned on $500 after 5% interest compounded annually for six years	The interest earned on $500 after 2.5% interest compounded monthly for one year

(A) Quantity A is greater.

(B) Quantity B is greater.

(C) The two quantities are equal.

(D) The relationship cannot be determined from the information given.

12. Which of the following statements MUST be true?

I. If n^2 is even, then n^3 is even.

II. If $2n$ is even, then n is odd.

III. If n is even, then $2n - 1$ is odd.

(A) I only

(B) II only

(C) III only

(D) I and II only

(E) I and III only

13. In a certain examination 60% of the students passed in Mathematics, 74% passed in English and 18% failed in both English and Mathematics. If 416 students passed in both these subjects, then what will be the total number of students who took the exam?

(A) 740

(B) 770

(C) 800

(D) 820

(E) 840

14. In a class of 83 students, 72 are present. What percentage of the student is absent? Provide answer up to two significant digits in the answer box.

    ┌─────────────┐
    │   │
    └─────────────┘

15.

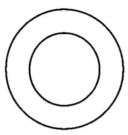

The radius of the inner circle is r, and the distance from the inner circle to the outer circle is also r.

Quantity A	**Quantity B**
The area of the unshaded portion	The area of the shaded portion

(A) Quantity A is greater.

(B) Quantity B is greater.

(C) The two quantities are equal.

(D) The relationship cannot be determined from the information given.

16.

$$x = 4, y = 20, z = -5$$

Quantity A	**Quantity B**
$z^{-3} + 2(xy)$	$(xz)^2 \div y - z$

(A) Quantity A is greater.

(B) Quantity B is greater.

(C) The two quantities are equal.

(D) The relationship cannot be determined from the information given.

17.

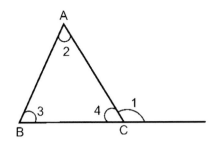

ABC is a triangle and angle 1 is 124° and angle 2 is 46° then angle 3 & 4 will be?

(A) 46°

(B) 56°

(C) 78°

(D) 124°

(E) 132°

18. Emma had some oranges, by adding $\frac{5}{3}$ of these the total became 80. How many oranges Emma had before?

(A) 40

(B) 30

(C) 35

(D) 25

(E) 20

19. Which of the following statements are false?

Select all that apply.

(A) $[7 - (5 + 4)^2 \div 3] + 10 = -10$

(B) $6^2 + [18 \div 2 \times 3 - 7] = 32$

(C) $(4 - 1)^2 + [(9 - 4)(7 - 10) - 6] = -12$

(D) $[9 \div 3^2 - 4]^2 + 10 = 35$

(E) $2^3 \times 5^2 \div 10 - 6^2 = -16$

(F) $(4^2 + 5) + [4 \times 6 \div 3 - 3^2]^5 = -21$

20.

A six-sided number cube is rolled two times.

Quantity A	**Quantity B**
The probability of rolling a number greater than 1 on the first roll and a prime number on the second roll	The probability of rolling an even number on the first roll and a factor of six on the second roll

(A) Quantity A is greater.

(B) Quantity B is greater.

(C) The two quantities are equal.

(D) The relationship cannot be determined from the information given.

Answers and Explanations

1. **Topic: Arithmetic**

   The correct answer is (D).

   First, calculate the rates of production per day. Two of the factories each make $100,000/15 \cong 6667$ hubcaps per day. The third plant makes $1.3 \times 6667 \cong 8667$ hubcaps per day. The total production rate is $8667 + 2(6667) = 22,001$ hubcaps per day. At that rare, it would take 45.5 days to produce a million hubcaps.

2. **Topic: Arithmetic**

   The correct answer is (D).

   For any numbers m and n, $m^4 \geq 0$ and $n^4 \geq 0$.

   Since $m^4 + n^4 = 0$, then both $m = 0$ and $n = 0$. Therefore $9m - 5n = (9)(0) - 5(0) = 0$.

3. **Topic: Geometry**

   The correct answer is (C).

   The full line of the numbers on the star shows you that:

   Each group of four circles must sum to $2 + 6 + 8 + 4$, or 20.

   Therefore, $A + 8 + 5 + 6 = 20$ and $A = 1$. Therefore, $1 + 6 + 7 + B = 20$

   Hence $B = 6$.

4. **Topic: Arithmetic**

   The correct answer is (B).

   Evaluate each expression for Quantity A and Quantity B to determine the answer. We are adding, subtracting, multiplying, and dividing fractions.

   - Add/Subtracting Fractions: Get a common denominator for both fractions, combine the numerators, and simplify the fraction.
   - Multiplying Fractions: Multiply straight across the numerator and denominator to obtain your answer.
   - Dividing Fractions: Keep the first fraction. Change the division to multiplication and take the reciprocal of the second fraction. Simplify.

   Quantity A: $\dfrac{1}{3} \div \dfrac{5}{9} + \dfrac{2}{5} \times \dfrac{4}{7} = \dfrac{1}{3} \times \dfrac{9}{5} + \dfrac{2}{5} \times \dfrac{4}{7} = \dfrac{9}{15} + \dfrac{8}{35} = \dfrac{63}{105} + \dfrac{24}{105} = \dfrac{87}{105}$

   Lowest common denominator is 105.

   Quantity B: $\dfrac{1}{3} \div \dfrac{5}{7} + \dfrac{4}{5} \times \dfrac{4}{7} = \dfrac{1}{3} \times \dfrac{7}{5} + \dfrac{4}{5} \times \dfrac{4}{7} = \dfrac{7}{15} + \dfrac{16}{35} = \dfrac{49}{105} + \dfrac{48}{105} = \dfrac{97}{105}$

   Lowest common denominator is 105.

   Both answers have the same denominator, but the numerator is greater in quantity B, hence the answer is B.

5. **Topic: Geometry**

   The correct answer is (A).

   Because OP || QR, we know $\triangle NQR \sim \triangle NOP$. Therefore, we can conclude the following segments are proportional.

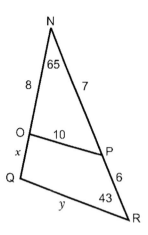

$$\frac{NQ}{NO} = \frac{QR}{OP} = \frac{NR}{NP}$$

$$\frac{8+x}{8} = \frac{y}{10} = \frac{7+6}{7}$$

$$\frac{8+x}{8} = \frac{y}{10} = \frac{13}{7}$$

To solve the following proportions, we should have two different equations that we can solve using cross multiplication.

6. **Topic: Arithmetic**

   The correct answer is (B).

   Because the five is being multiplied by itself many more times than the 11 it is a good guess to say that quantity B is greater, however, the question can be answered with authority by performing these quick calculations using the calculator. $11^5 = 161,051$ and $5^{11} = 48,828,125$

7. **Topic: Data Analysis**

   The correct answer is (A).

   The year having maximum shows is 1996. The number of theatres = 620. Number of shows = 950 thousand.
   Average $= \frac{950}{620}$ thousand = 1.5 thousand.

8. **Topic: Data Analysis**

   The correct answer is (D).

   In the seven years, 1992 and 1994 have 850000 shows each. Also, in 1993 and 1995, there are 900000 shows each. Hence the answer is 'twice'.

9. **Topic: Arithmetic**

   The correct answer is (D).

   In the set of numbers from 1 to 50 inclusive, there are 16 numbers divisible by 3: 3, 6, 9... 48. Therefore, the probability that a ticket selected will have a number divisible by 3 is $\frac{16}{50} = \frac{8}{25}$

10. **Topic: Geometry**

The correct answer is (B).

Remember that area is 2-D and a scale factor is only linear. So the area of the figures after a scale factor of 2 is the same as multiplying the original area by 2^2 or 4.

$$A = \frac{bh}{2} = \frac{(5)(12)}{2} = 30$$

Quantity A: $30 \times 2 = 60$

Quantity B: $= 30 \times 4 = 120$.

Quantity B is greater than Quantity A.

11. **Topic: Arithmetic**

The correct answer is (B).

The formula for calculating the compound interest is $A = Pr^t$ where A is the total amount of money after compounding, P is the principal or original amount, r is 1 plus the interest rate as a decimal, and t is the amount of time.

Quantity A: This quantity is compounded annually so $t = 6 \times 1$ year or 6 years

$P = 500, r = 1.05, t = 6$ years

$Pr^t = 500(1.05)^6 = 670.05$

Interest earned: $670.50 - \$500 = \$170.50$

Quantity B: This quantity is compounded monthly so $t = 12$ months $\times 1$ or 12 months

$P = 500, r = .025, t = 12\ months$

$Pr^t = 500(1.025)^{12} = 672.44$

Interest earned: $672.44 - \$500 = \$172.44$

Quantity B is greater than Quantity A.

12. **Topic: Arithmetic**

The correct answer is (E).

Let's evaluate each statement separately.

Statement I must be true: Raising an even number to a power will always result in an even number. Eliminate choices (B) and (C) since they do not include statement I.

Statement II isn't always true: If $2n = 8, n = 4$. Since this statement isn't always true, eliminate choice (D).

Statement III must be true: $2n$ will always result in an even number (whether n is odd or even) and when you subtract 1 from any even number, the result will always be an odd number.

Therefore, choice (E) is correct.

13. **Topic: Algebra**

Sub topic: Set Theory

The correct answer is (C).

Assume total number of students be 100.

Failed in Mathematics $= 100 - 60 = 40$

Failed in English $= 100 - 74 = 26$

Failed in both subjects $= 18$

Failed students in any of the subjects $= 40 + 26 - 18 = 48$

Students who pass in both the subjects $= 52$

If 52 passed, then total number of students$= 100$

If 416 passed, then total number of students $= \left(\frac{100}{52}\right) \times 416 = 800$

14. **Topic: Arithmetic**

The correct answer is 13.

Absent students $= 83 - 72 = 11$

Percentage of the absent students $= \left(\frac{11}{83}\right) \times 100 = 13.25$

Reducing up to two significant digits it will be 13.

15. **Topic: Geometry**

The correct answer is (B).

The unshaded area is πr^2.

The area of the shaded portion is$\pi(2r)^2 - \pi r^2 = 4\pi r^2 - \pi r^2 = 3\pi r^2$

16. **Topic: Arithmetic**

The correct answer is (A).

Substitute the values of $x, y,$ and z into both expressions, simplify and compare.

Quantity A:

$z^{-3} + 2(xy)$

$= (-5)^{-3} + 2(4)(20)$

$= -125 + 160$

$= 35$

Quantity B:

$(xy)^2 \div y - z$

$= [(4)(5)]^2 \div 20 - (-5)$

$= [20]^2 \div 20 - (-5)$

$= 400 \div 20 - (-5)$

$= 20 - (-5)$

$= 25$

Quantity A is greater than Quantity B.

17. **Topic: Geometry**

Sub topic: Triangles/Lines & Angles

The correct answer is (C).

Angle 1 and $\angle ACB$ are supplementary angles then $\angle ACB$ will be $180° - 124° = 56°$.

As sum of all three angle of a triangle is $180°$ then angle 3 will be $180° - (56° + 46°) = 78°$.

18. **Topic: Arithmetic**

The correct answer is (B).

Suppose the number of oranges Emma had before $= x$

Then according to the condition,

$$x + 5\frac{x}{3} = 80$$

$$3x + 5x = 240$$

$$x = 30$$

19. **Topic: Arithmetic**

Sub topic: Order of Operations

The correct answers are (B), (C) and (E).

To evaluate using order of operations, we need to use PEMDAS.

P: Parenthesis

E: Exponents

M/D: Multiplication and Division done from Left to Right.

A/S: Addition and Subtraction

Evaluate each expression to determine which statement is false.

A. $[7 - (5 + 4)^2 \div 3] + 10 = -10$

$[7 - (5 + 4)^2 \div 3] + 10$

$= [7 - (9)^2 \div 3] + 10$

$= [7 - 81 \div 3] + 10$

$= [7 - 27] + 10$

$= -20 + 10$

$= -10$

B. $6^2 + [18 \div 2.3 - 2] = 32$

$6^2 + [18 \div 2.3 - 7]$

$= 36 + [18 \div 2.3 - 7]$

$= 36 + [9.3 - 7]$

$= 36 + [27 - 7]$

$= 36 + [20]$

$= 56$

C. $(4 - 1)^2 + [(9 - 4)(7 - 10) - 6] = -12$

$(4 - 1)^2 + [(9 - 4)(7 - 10) - 6]$

$= (3)^2 + [(5)(-3) - 6]$

$= 9 + [-15 - 6]$

$= 9 + [-21]$

$= -12$

D. $[9 \div 3^2 - 4]^2 + 10 = 35$

$[9 \div 3^2 - 4]^2 + 10$

$= [9 \div 9 - 4]^2 + 10$

$$= [1 - 4]^2 + 10$$
$$= [-3]^2 + 10$$
$$= 9 + 10$$
$$= 19$$

E. $2^3 . 5^2 \div 10 - 6^2 = -16$

$$2^3 . 5^2 \div 10 - 6^2$$
$$= 8.25 \div 10 - 36$$
$$= 200 \div 10 - 36$$
$$= 20 - 36$$
$$= -16$$

F. $(4^2 + 5)[4.6 \div 3 - 3^2]^5 = -21$

$$(4^2 + 5)[4.6 \div 3 - 3^2]^5$$
$$= (16 + 5)[4.6 \div 3 - 9]^5$$
$$= (21)[24 \div 3 - 9]^5$$
$$= (21)[8 - 9]^5$$
$$= 21[-1]^5$$
$$= 21[-1]$$
$$= -21$$

20. **Topic: Data Analysis**

The correct answer is (A).

The probability of two independent events occurring is equal to the product of the individual event probabilities.

Quantity A:

Rolling a # > 1: 2, 3, 4, 5, 6 or $\dfrac{5}{6}$

Rolling a prime #: 2, 3, 5 or $\dfrac{3}{6}$. One is neither prime nor composite.

Quantity B:

Rolling an even number: 2, 4, 6 or $\dfrac{3}{6}$

Rolling a factor of six: 1, 2, 3, 5 or $\dfrac{4}{6}$

Without multiplying you can see that Quantity A, $\dfrac{15}{36}$, is greater than Quantity B, $\dfrac{12}{36}$.

The quantity of A is greater than the quantity of B.

Chapter **13**

Exercise #7

Questions: 20 | Time: 30 minutes

This Exercise includes *20 practice questions*. The questions cover all the question types as explained in Chapter 2 and may fall into any of the following categories - Arithmetic, Algebra, Geometry or Data Analysis. You will find answers and detailed explanations towards the end of this chapter.

1.

$$x \leq -1, y \geq 1, 2 < z \leq 4$$

Quantity A	**Quantity B**
$xy - z$	$xz + y$

(A) Quantity A is greater.

(B) Quantity B is greater.

(C) The two quantities are equal.

(D) The relationship cannot be determined from the information given.

2.

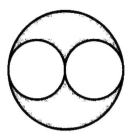

R is the radius of the large circle, and r the radius of the smaller circles.

Quantity A   **Quantity B**

The combined area of the two smaller circles   The shaded area

(A) Quantity A is greater.

(B) Quantity B is greater.

(C) The two quantities are equal.

(D) The relationship cannot be determined from the information given.

3.

Quantity A   **Quantity B**

300   26% of 960

(A) Quantity A is greater.

(B) Quantity B is greater.

(C) The two quantities are equal.

(D) The relationship cannot be determined from the information given.

4. Length of a rectangle is 3cm less than the double of its width. If perimeter of the rectangle is 96cm then what will be its width and length?

(A) 16cm & 29cm

(B) 15cm & 27cm

(C) 14cm & 25cm

(D) 13cm & 23cm

(E) 17cm & 31cm

5.   If $8^x = 128^3$, what will the value of x be?

   Select all that apply.

   (A) $\dfrac{7}{3}$

   (B) $\dfrac{5}{3}$

   (C) 5

   (D) 7

   (E) 21

6.   Which month will it be after 132 weeks of September?

   (Assume 4 weeks = 1 month)

   (A) June

   (B) August

   (C) September

   (D) October

   (E) November

7.   If Kelly received $\dfrac{1}{3}$ more votes than Mike in a student election, which of the following could have been the total number of votes cast for the two candidates?

   Select all that apply.

   (A) 12

   (B) 14

   (C) 3

   (D) 21

   (E) 8

   (F) 7

   (G) 2

   (H) 4

   (I) 16

   (J) 10

8.

a, b and c are consecutive even integers.

Quantity A	**Quantity B**
$a+b+c$	$3x + 6$

   (A) Quantity A is greater.

   (B) Quantity B is greater.

   (C) The two quantities are equal.

   (D) The relationship cannot be determined from the information given.

9.

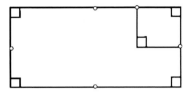

Length of the rectangle is twice as its width, and the measure of one side of the square is one half as the width of the rectangle. The perimeter of the square is 8.

<u>**Quantity A**</u>   <u>**Quantity B**</u>

Area of Rectangle   32

(A) Quantity A is greater.

(B) Quantity B is greater.

(C) The two quantities are equal.

(D) The relationship cannot be determined from the information given.

Questions 10 and 11 are based on the following chart:

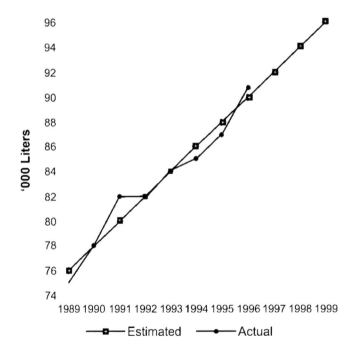

10. The average of the actual values is most nearly (in '000 liters)

(A) 83

(B) 85

(C) 79

(D) 80

(E) 81

11. The ratio of the range of actual value to the range of trend value is

    (A) 8 : 7

    (B) 7 : 8

    (C) 7 : 9

    (D) 4 : 5

    (E) 5 : 4

12. Of the total number of days in a week, what fraction of them occurs only 52 times in a leap year?

    (A) $\frac{1}{7}$

    (B) $\frac{2}{7}$

    (C) $\frac{3}{7}$

    (D) $\frac{4}{7}$

    (E) $\frac{5}{7}$

13.

The figure above is formed of two equal circles and a square. If each circle has an area of 18π, what is the perimeter of the square?

    (A) 9

    (B) 12

    (C) 18

    (D) 24

    (E) 36

14.

Two pipes T and P supply water at a rate of 1,200 cubic centimeters per minute and 2.16 liters per minute, respectively.

Quantity A	**Quantity B**
Volume of water supplied when T runs for 3 minutes continuously	Volume of water supplied when P runs for 2 minutes continuously

    (A) Quantity A is greater.

    (B) Quantity B is greater.

    (C) The two quantities are equal.

    (D) The relationship cannot be determined from the information given.

15.

Quantity A	**Quantity B**
Number of degrees in the interior angles of a pentagon	500°

(A) Quantity A is greater.

(B) Quantity B is greater.

(C) The two quantities are equal.

(D) The relationship cannot be determined from the information given.

16. What will be the smallest possible number which when divided by 5 has remainder 3 and when divided by 7 has remainder 2?

Ignore the quotients in both the cases and write the answer in answer box.

17.

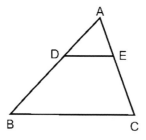

Note: - Figure not drawn to scale.

In the figure above, DE is parallel to BC and $AD = \dfrac{DB}{2}$. If the perimeter of $\triangle ABC$ is 24, what is the perimeter of $\triangle ADE$?

(A) 6

(B) 8

(C) 12

(D) 16

(E) 48

18. For which values of x is the statement $x^3 > x^2$ true?

(A) all$x$

(B) $x > 0$

(C) $x > 1$ or $x < -1$

(D) $-1 < x < 1$

(E) $x > 1$

19.

<u>Quantity A</u>	<u>Quantity B</u>
$18 \div 3 \times 6 - 2 - 3^2$	$18 + 6 \div 3 \times 2 + 2^3$

(A) Quantity A is greater.

(B) Quantity B is greater.

(C) The two quantities are equal.

(D) The relationship cannot be determined from the information given.

20. A 16-inch by 36-inchpiece of material is to be cut into equal circles, with the least amount of material left over. What is the amount of material that remains if the largest possible circles are cut from the material?

(A) $576 (\pi - 1)$

(B) $4 (144 - \pi)$

(C) 144π

(D) $144 - \pi$

(E) $144 (4 - \pi)$

Answers and Explanations

1. **Topic: Arithmetic**

    Sub topic: Numbers

    The correct answer is (D).

    Based on the above conditions, x is less than or equal to -1, so x is always a negative number. y is greater than or equal to 1, so y is always positive. z can be any positive number between 2 and 4.

    Quantity A: $xy - z = (-)(+) - (+) = (-) - (+) = -$

    Quantity A will always be negative.

    Quantity B: $xz + y = (-)(+) + (+) = (-) + (+)$

    This quantity can either be positive or negative depending on the value of x times y and z. We cannot determine which quantity is greater, xy or z. Therefore, we don't know whether the resulting number is negative or positive. The answer is D and cannot be determined based on the information given.

2. **Topic: Geometry**

    Sub topic: Circles

    The correct answer is (C).

    The two smaller circles are the same size, and so each has a diameter equal to R, and so a radius $r = \frac{R}{2}$. The combined area of the two smaller circles is $2\pi \left(\frac{R}{2}\right)^2 = \frac{\pi R^2}{2}$.

    The area of the large circle is πR^2, so the shaded portion has area $\pi R^2 - \frac{\pi R^2}{2} = \frac{\pi R^2}{2}$. The answer is C.

3. **Topic: Arithmetic**

    Sub topic: Percentage

    The correct answer is (A).

    Without using the calculator, we can quickly determine 26% of 960 by diving by four to obtain 25% and adding 1% or 9.6.

    Quantity A:

    300

    Quantity B:

    $960 \div 4 = 240; 240 + 9.6 = 249.6$

    Quantity A is greater than Quantity B.

4. **Topic: Arithmetic**

    Sub topic: Polygons

    The correct answer is (E).

    Let width $= x$

    Then length $= 2x - 3$

    Perimeter $= 2(x + 2x - 3) = 6x - 6$

    According to the condition

$6x - 6 = 96$

$x = 17\text{cm}$

width $= 17$cm and length $= 31$cm

5. **Topic: Arithmetic**

   Sub topic: Exponents and Roots

   The correct answer is (D).

   To solve, first convert $8^x = 2^{3x}$. Next, convert $128^3 = 2^{7\times3} = 2^{21}$

   Now relate the two exponents and solve for x.

   $3x = 21$

   $x = 7$

6. **Topic: Arithmetic**

   The correct answer is (A).

   $\dfrac{132}{4} = 33$ months

   $\dfrac{33}{12} = 2$years and 9 months

   9 months later from September will be June.

7. **Topic: Algebra**

   Sub topic: Applications

   The correct answers are (B), (D), and (F).

   Let M be the number of votes cast for Mike. Then Kelly received M $+ \left(\dfrac{1}{3}\right)$ M, or $\left(\dfrac{4}{3}\right)$ M votes. The total number of votes cast was therefore "votes for Mike" + "votes for Kelly" or M $+ \left(\dfrac{4}{3}\right)$ M $= \dfrac{7M}{3}$.

   Because M is number of votes, it cannot be a fraction – specifically, not a fraction with a 7 in the denominator. Therefore, the 7 in the expression $\dfrac{7M}{3}$ cannot be cancelled out. As a result, the total number of votes cast must be a multiple of 7. Among these answer choices, the multiples of 7 are (B) 14, (D) 21 and (F) 7.

8. **Topic: Arithmetic**

   Sub topic: Numbers

   The correct answer is (C).

   The values of a, b, and c differ by 2 as they are consecutive even integers. Let $a = x, b = x + 2, c = x + 4$.

   Now substitute these variables into Quantity A, simplify, and compare.

   Quantity A:

   $a + b + c$

   $x + (x + 2) + (x + 4)$

   $3x + 6$

   Quantity B:

   $3x + 6$

The quantity of A is equivalent to Quantity B.

9. **Topic: Geometry**

   Sub topic: Quadrilaterals

   The correct answer is (C).

   Use the following notation in solution process:

   m = Length of the rectangle

   n = Width of the rectangle

   a = Side of the square

   P = Perimeter of the square

   Q = Perimeter of the rectangle

   Translate the given facts in the same order listed above.

   (1) $m = 2n$

   (2) $n = 2a$

   (3) $P = 8$

   Also, using the formulas of perimeters of square and rectangle, we have

   (4) $P = 4a = 2(2a)$

   (5) $Q = 2(m + n)$

   Replace (2) and (3) in (4)

   (6) $8 = 2n$

   Divide each side by 4.

   (7) $n = 4$

   Apply (7) in (1) and simplify.

   $m = 2(4) = 8$

   Having measures of a length and a width of the rectangle, calculate its area.

   $A_{rectangle} = mn = (4)(8) = 32$

   The two quantities are equal.

10. **Topic: Data Analysis**

    The correct answer is (A).

    Total of eight actual values = $(75 + 78 + 82 + 82 + 84 + 85 + 87 + 91) = 664$. Average $= \dfrac{664}{3} = 83$.

11. **Topic: Data Analysis**

    The correct answer is (A).

    The range of actual values = $91 - 75 = 16$. The range of trend values = $90 - 76 = 14$. Ratio = 8 : 7

12. **Topic: Arithmetic**

    The correct answer is (E).

    There are 366 days in a leap year. $\dfrac{366}{52} = 7$, with a remainder of 2. Therefore, 2 of the 7 days in the week occur 53 times in a leap year, and the remaining 5 occur 52 times, so choice (E) is correct.

13. **Topic: Geometry**

    Sub topic: Circles/Quadrilaterals

    The correct answer is (D).

    When dealing with combined figures, look for pieces they have in common. If you sketch in a line connecting the centers of the circles, you'll see that it is also a diagonal of the square.

    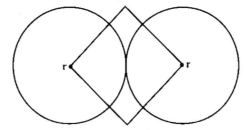

    This line is composed of a radius of each circle; since the circles are equal their radii are equal and the diagonal equals 2r. The area of a circle is 18π. So πr2 = 18π, r2 = 18 and r = $\sqrt{18}$ = $\sqrt{9}$ × $\sqrt{2}$ = 3$\sqrt{2}$. Therefore, the diagonal is 6$\sqrt{2}$.

    The diagonal is of a square is equal to a side times$\sqrt{2}$. (Since it is essential ratio of 1:$\sqrt{2}$) since the diagonal is 6$\sqrt{2}$ the side of the square must be 6. Perimeter of a square is equal to 4s = 4(6) = 24

14. **Topic: Geometry**

    The correct answer is (B).

    The rate for pipe T is $\dfrac{1200\,cm^3}{minute}$ but $1000\,cm^3 = 1\,liter$

    Hence, $\dfrac{1200\,cm^3}{minute} = \dfrac{1200\,cm^3}{1000\,cm^3\,/l}$ per minute= $1.2\,l/minute$

    Now that all rates are in liters per minute, we compute the quantities:

    Quantity A: T runs for 3 minutes, so we calculate: $\dfrac{1.2l}{min}$ × 3 min = 3.6l

    Quantity B: P runs for 2 minutes, so we calculate: $\dfrac{2.16l}{min}$ × 2 min = 4.32l

    By comparison, quantity B is greater; the correct option is B.

15. **Topic: Geometry**

    The correct answer is (A).

    To find the number of degrees in the interior angles of a pentagon, use the formula $180 \times (n - 2)$, where *n* is the number of sides. Therefore, $180 \times (5 - 2) = 180 \times 3 = 540°$

    540° > 500°

    Another method would be to draw the pentagon and break it into triangles connecting verticals (lines cannot cross), as shown here.

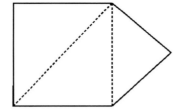

Multiplying the number of triangles (3) by 180° (degrees in a triangle) gives the same result, 540°.

16. **Topic: Arithmetic**

    The correct answer is 23.

    $x \div 5$ remainder 3

    $x \div 7$ remainder 2

    The smallest number is23.23 divided by 5 gives a quotient of 4 and a remainder of 3.23 divided by 7 gives a quotient of 3 and a remainder of 2.

17. **Topic: Arithmetic**

    Sub topic: Triangle

    The correct answer is (B).

    Since DE is parallel to BC, ∠ADE =∠ABC and ∠AED =∠ACB. Since both ΔADE and ΔABC contain A, all three of their angles are equal and they are similar. The sides of similar triangles are proportional. Since AD= $\frac{\text{DB}}{2}$, 2AD = DB

    Since AB = AD + DB,AB = 3AD, and AD= $\frac{1}{3}$AB.

    Since the perimeter ofΔABC = 24, the perimeter of ΔADE = $\frac{1}{3}(24) = 8$

18. **Topic: Arithmetic**

    The correct answer is (E).

    When $x = 0$, then $x^3 = x^2 = 0$, so choices (A) and (D) are incorrect. When x is a positive fraction, then $x^3 < x^2$;for example,$x = \frac{1}{2}, \left(\frac{1}{2}\right)^3 = \frac{1}{8} < \left(\frac{1}{2}\right)^2 = \frac{1}{4}$

    So, choice (B) is incorrect. When x is negative and x^2 is positive (a negative raised to an odd power is always negative and a negative raised to an even power is always positive), then $x^3 < x^2$ and choice (C) is therefore incorrect. Only when $x > 1$ will the inequality be true.

19. **Topic: Arithmetic**

    Sub topic: Order of Operations

    The correct answer is (B).

    To evaluate using order of operations, we need to use PEMDAS.

    P: Parenthesis

    E: Exponents

    M/D: Multiplication and Division done from Left to Right.

    A/S: Addition and Subtraction

We will evaluate each quantity.

Quantity A:

$18 \div 3 \times 6 - 2 - 3^2$

$= 18 \div 3 \times 6 - 2 - 9$

$= 6 \times 6 - 2 - 9$

$= 36 - 2 - 9$

$= 25$

Quantity B:

$18 + 6 \div 3 \times 2 + 2^3$

$= 18 + 6 \div 3 \times 2 + 8$

$= 18 + 2 \times 2 + 8$

$= 18 + 4 + 8$

$= 30$

Quantity B is greater, so the answer is B.

20. **Topic: Arithmetic**

The correct answer is (E).

The amount of material that will remain after the circles are cut out is the area of the entire piece of material, minus the total area of the circles that were cut out. The total area of the circles that were cut out will be equal to the area of one of the circles times the total number of circle.

To minimize the amount of wasted material, the diameter of the circle cut out should divide evenly into both the length and width of the cloth. Therefore, what you're really looking for is the greatest common factor of the length and width. To find the greatest common factor of 16 and 36, break down each number to its prime factorization and then multiply together all the prime factors that the two have in common. In this case, 16 and 36 share 2 prime factors of 2, so their greatest common factor is 4. Since 4 goes into 16 and 36 nine times, a total of $(4)(9) = 36$ circles with diameter of each circle is 4, its radius is 2 and the area of each circle is πr^2. Since the diameter of each circle is 4, its radius is 2 and the area of each circle is $\pi \times (2)^2 = 4\pi$. So, the material that will be left over is $(36)(16) - 36(4\pi) = 36(16 - 4\pi) = (36)(4)(4 - \pi) = 144(4 - \pi)$.

This page is intentionally left blank

Chapter **14**

Exercise #8

Questions: 20 | Time: 30 minutes

T his Exercise includes *20 practice questions*. The questions cover all the question types as explained in Chapter 2 and may fall into any of the following categories - Arithmetic, Algebra, Geometry or Data Analysis. You will find answers and detailed explanations towards the end of this chapter.

Questions 1 and 2 are based on the following data:

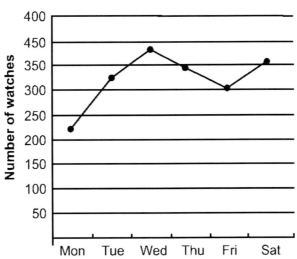

Sales of watches at a Brand X specialty store

1. What is the average number of watches sold in the specialty store per day?

(A) 327

(B) 331

(C) 329

(D) 298

(E) 281

2. The ratio of percentage increase in sales on Wednesday and percentage increase in sales on Saturday over average sales is

   (A) $1:1$

   (B) $17:13$

   (C) $13:15$

   (D) $21:17$

   (E) $17:15$

3. Which of the following ordered pairs (a, b) is NOT a member of the solution set of $2a - 3b = 6$?

   (A) $(6, 2)$

   (B) $(-3, -4)$

   (C) $(3, 0)$

   (D) $4, \dfrac{2}{3}$

   (E) $(0, 2)$

4. A circle has the same area as a square with side of length $\dfrac{1}{\pi}$. What is the diameter of the circle?

   (A) $\dfrac{1}{\sqrt{\pi}}$

   (B) $\dfrac{2}{\sqrt{\pi}}$

   (C) $\dfrac{1}{\pi\sqrt{\pi}}$

   (D) $\dfrac{1}{\pi\sqrt{\pi}}$

   (E) $\dfrac{1}{\pi^3}$

5. There are between 60 and 70 eggs in a basket. If they are counted out 3 at a time there are 2 left over, but if they are counted out 4 at a time there is 1 left over. How many eggs are in the basket?

   (A) 61

   (B) 62

   (C) 65

   (D) 68

   (E) 69

6.

Quantity A	**Quantity B**
$$\dfrac{x^7 \times y^{\frac{3}{4}}}{y^{-4} \times \left(x^{\frac{2}{3}}\right)^3 \times y^6}$$	$$\dfrac{(y^8)^{\frac{1}{2}} \times x^{\frac{1}{4}} \times y^{\frac{3}{4}}}{y^6 \times x^{-\frac{3}{4}} \times x^{-4}}$$

(A) Quantity A is greater.

(B) Quantity B is greater.

(C) The two quantities are equal.

(D) The relationship cannot be determined from the information given.

7.

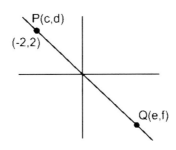

Quantity A	**Quantity B**
c	d

(A) Quantity A is greater.

(B) Quantity B is greater.

(C) The two quantities are equal.

(D) The relationship cannot be determined from the information given.

8.

The point (α, b) is on the x–axis

Quantity A	**Quantity B**
α	b

(A) Quantity A is greater.

(B) Quantity B is greater.

(C) The two quantities are equal.

(D) The relationship cannot be determined from the information given.

9. In a fraction of two positive numbers if we subtract 1 from both numerator and denominator the fraction reduces to $\frac{4}{3}$ and if we add 1 in numerator and denominator then it reduces to $\frac{9}{7}$. Write the original fraction in the answer box.

10. Ed and Lori go shopping. Ed spends $30 more than Lori in the first store and Lori spends $12 less than Ed in the second store. Which of the following must be true about Lori's total spending in the two stores compared to Ed's?

    (A) Lori spent $\frac{2}{5}$ less than Ed.

    (B) Lori spent $18 less than Ed.

    (C) Lori spent $21 less than Ed.

    (D) Lori spent $42 less than Ed.

    (E) Lori spent $42 more than Ed.

11.

    Given that, ABCD is a rectangle with sides AB and CD passing through the midpoint of the two circles. Determine the area of the shaded region in the figure above, if the value of AB is 12 and the value of AD is 16.

    (A) 120

    (B) 156

    (C) 192

    (D) 192 − 36π

    (E) 192 − 72π

12. Pam makes pies and jam pints with strawberries. This year, Pam had s grams of strawberries, of which she utilized 40% to make pies and the rest for jam pints. Each pie needs p grams of strawberries while each jam pint needs j grams. Choose the following option that gives the total jam pints Pam can make?

(A) $\dfrac{2s}{5p}$

(B) $\dfrac{2s}{5j}$

(C) $\dfrac{3s}{5j}$

(D) $\dfrac{3p}{5s}$

(E) $\dfrac{3sj}{5}$

13.
$$\left[2x + \frac{y^2 - xz}{zy + x^3}\right] \div y$$

Quantity A	**Quantity B**
$x = -3, y = 2, z = 8$	$x = 3, y = -2, z = 6$

(A) Quantity A is greater.

(B) Quantity B is greater.

(C) The two quantities are equal.

(D) The relationship cannot be determined from the information given.

14.

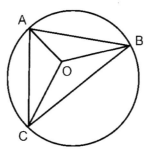

Equilateral ∆ABC is inscribed in circle O. AB=AC=CB= $8\sqrt{3}$

Quantity A	**Quantity B**
$OA + OB + OC$	24

(A) Quantity A is greater.

(B) Quantity B is greater.

(C) The two quantities are equal.

(D) The relationship cannot be determined from the information given.

15. A pair of dice is rolled. If the two numbers appearing on the dice are different, what is the probability that the sum of them is at most 4?

(A) $\frac{2}{15}$

(B) $\frac{13}{15}$

(C) $\frac{14}{15}$

(D) $\frac{1}{6}$

(E) $\frac{1}{15}$

16.

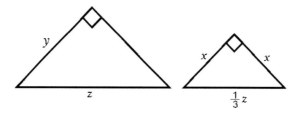

Note: - Figure not drawn to scale.

In the figures above, what is the value of y in terms of x?

(A) $\sqrt{2}x$ (approximately $1.41x$)

(B) $2x$

(C) $2\sqrt{2}x$ (approximately $2.83x$)

(D) $3x$

(E) $3\sqrt{2}x$ (approximately $4.24x$)

17.

An apartment building has 5 floors, one of which has only 2 apartments. Each of the other floor shave 4 apartments.

Quantity A	**Quantity B**
3 times the number of floors in the building	The number of apartments in the building

(A) Quantity A is greater.

(B) Quantity B is greater.

(C) The two quantities are equal.

(D) The relationship cannot be determined from the information given.

18.

Quantity A	**Quantity B**
The final cost of an item purchased for 28% off the already reduced price of 53% off the original price, with a sales tax of 6%	The final cost of an item with an original cost that is 13% more than item A purchased for a 35% discount on top of a 55% discount of the original price, with a sales tax of 8.25%

(A) Quantity A is greater.

(B) Quantity B is greater.

(C) The two quantities are equal.

(D) The relationship cannot be determined from the information given.

19. Sarah's weight is 25 pounds more than that of Tony. If together they weigh 205 pounds, what will be the weight of Sarah and Tony approximately in kilograms?

Assume 1 pound = 0.4535 kilograms

Select all that apply.

(A) 41

(B) 48

(C) 50

(D) 52

(E) 56

20.

$$\frac{m^4}{3} = 27$$

Quantity A	**Quantity B**
m	4

(A) Quantity A is greater.

(B) Quantity B is greater.

(C) The two quantities are equal.

(D) The relationship cannot be determined from the information given.

Answers and Explanations

1. **Topic: Data Analysis**

   The correct answer is (A).

   Total number of watches sold over the week

   $= 220 + 323 + 385 + 356 + 310 + 370$

   $= 1964$

   Average sales per day $= \dfrac{1964}{\text{No.of days}} = \dfrac{1964}{6} = 327$

   Please note that one must not take the number of days as 7 as clearly Sunday seems to be a holiday in this case.

2. **Topic: Data Analysis**

   The correct answer is (B).

   Percentage increase on Wednesday over average sales $= \dfrac{385 - 327}{327} \times 100$

   $= 17.7\%$

   Percentage increase on Saturday over average sales $= \dfrac{370 - 327}{327} \times 100$

   $= 13.15\%$

   The ratio $= 17.7 : 13.15 \cong 17 : 13$

3. **Topic: Algebra**

   The correct answer is (E).

   In the ordered pair $(0, 2)$, $a = 0$ and $b = 2$. For $2a - 3b$,

   $2(0) - 3(2) = 0 - 6 = -6 \neq 6$

   Therefore, the ordered pair $(0, 2)$ is not a member of the solution sets of 2a − 3b = 6.

4. **Topic: Geometry**

   The correct answer is (D).

   The formulas to use in this problem are:

   Divide both sides by π^3.

   Area of a square $= s^2$

   Area of a circle $= \pi r^2$

   Diameter $= 2r$

   Area of square of side$\left(\dfrac{1}{\pi}\right) = \left(\dfrac{1}{\pi}\right)^2 = \dfrac{1}{\pi^2}$

   We want to find radius of circle whose area equals $\dfrac{1}{\pi^2}$

   Substitute πr^2 for the area of the circle.

   Area of circle $=$ Area of square

   $\pi r^2 = \dfrac{1}{\pi^2}$ Solve for r. Multiply both side by π^2

$$\pi^2(\pi r^2) = \pi^2\left(\frac{1}{\pi^2}\right) = \pi^3 r^2 = 1$$

$$r^2 = \frac{1}{\pi^3}$$

$\sqrt{r^2} = \sqrt{\dfrac{1}{\pi^3}}$ Take square root on both the sides

$r = \dfrac{\sqrt{1}}{\sqrt{\pi^3}} = \dfrac{1}{\sqrt{\pi^2 \cdot \pi}} = \dfrac{1}{\pi\sqrt{\pi}}$ Simplify the radical $d = 2r; d = \dfrac{2}{\pi\sqrt{\pi}}$

The answer is (D).

5. **Topic: Arithmetic**

The correct answer is (C).

The integers between 60 and 70 that have a remainder of 2 when divided by 3 can be found as follows:

$61 \div 3 = 20 \text{ R1}$

$62 \div 3 = 20 \text{ R2}$

$63 \div 3 = 21 \text{ R0}$

$64 \div 3 = 21 \text{ R1}$

$65 \div 3 = 21 \text{ R2}$

$66 \div 3 = 22 \text{ R0}$

$67 \div 3 = 22 \text{ R1}$

$68 \div 3 = 22 \text{ R2}$

$69 \div 3 = 23 \text{ R0}$

Notice that remainders for a divisor of 3 can only be 0, 1, or 2.

So, when 4 is the divisor, the remainders can only be 0, 1, 2, or 3.

$60 \div 4 = 15 \text{ R0}$

$61 \div 4 = 15 \text{ R1}$

$62 \div 4 = 15 \text{ R2}$

$63 \div 4 = 15 \text{ R3}$

$64 \div 4 = 16 \text{ R0}$

$65 \div 4 = 16 \text{ R1}$

65 satisfies both conditions.

The answer is (C).

6. **Topic: Arithmetic**

The correct answer is (C).

Simplify both expressions and compare. When exponents with like bases are multiplied, the powers are added. When exponents with like bases are divided, the powers are subtracted. When exponents are raised to power, the powers are multiplied.

Quantity A:

$$\frac{x^7 \times y^{\frac{3}{4}}}{y^{-4} \times \left(x^{\frac{2}{3}}\right)^3 \times y^6}$$

$$= \frac{x^7 \times y^{\frac{3}{4}}}{y^{-4} \times x^2 \times y^6}$$

$$= \frac{x^7 \times y^{\frac{3}{4}}}{x^2 \times y^2}$$

$$= x^5 \times y^{-1\frac{1}{4}}$$

Quantity B:

$$\frac{(y^8)^{\frac{1}{2}} \times x^{\frac{1}{4}} \times y^{\frac{3}{4}}}{y^6 \times x^{-\frac{3}{4}} \times x^{-4}}$$

$$= \frac{y^4 \times x^{\frac{1}{4}} \times y^{\frac{3}{4}}}{y^6 \times x^{-\frac{3}{4}} \times x^{-4}}$$

$$= \frac{y^{4\frac{3}{4}} \times x^{\frac{1}{4}}}{y^6 \times x^{-4\frac{3}{4}}}$$

$$= y^{-1\frac{1}{4}} \times x^5 = x^5 \times y^{-1\frac{1}{4}}$$

Quantity A is equal to Quantity B.

7. **Topic: Geometry**

   Sub topic: Coordinate Geometry

   The correct answer is (B).

   Since d is above X-axis, it must be positive, and c, being to the left of the Y-axis, must be negative.

   Therefore, $c < d$ because all negatives are less than all positive.

8. **Topic: Arithmetic**

   The correct answer is (D).

   The fact the point (α, b) is on the x–axis implies that $b = 0$. It says nothing about α.

   Since α could be either positive or negative. The relationship between α and b cannot be determined.

9. **Topic: Algebra**

   Sub topic: Algebra Exercises

   The correct answer is $\frac{17}{13}$.

   Let the numerator be x and the denominator be y.

   According to the first condition $\frac{x-1}{y-1} = \frac{4}{3}$

   Solving for x

   $$x = \frac{4y - 1}{3}$$

   According to the second condition $\frac{x+1}{y+1} = \frac{9}{7}$

   Solving it

   $$7x + 7 = 9y + 9$$

Substituting the value of x in this

$$7\left(\frac{4y-1}{3}\right) + 7 = 9y + 9$$

Solve for y

$y = 13$,

Substitute back into $x = \dfrac{4y-1}{3}$ and solve for x

$$x = \frac{4(13) - 1}{3}$$

$x = 17$

This gives an original fraction of $\dfrac{17}{13}$.

10. **Topic: Arithmetic**

The correct answer is (D).

Let the amount Lori spends in each store be x. Ed spends $30 more than Lori does in the first store, or $x + 30$. In the second store, Lori spends $12 less than Ed does, so Ed spends $x + 12$. Therefore, Lori spends a total of $2x$ while Ed spends $2x + 42$, making choice (D) correct.

11. **Topic: Geometry**

The correct answer is (D).

The area of the shaded region is the area of the rectangle minus the area of one circle (the sum of the area of the two equal semi-circles). Since AB = 12 and AD = 16, the area of the rectangle is $12 \times 16 = 192$. Since AB is equal to the diameter of the circle the diameter of the circle is 12, its radius is 6 and its area is $\pi(6)2 = 36\pi$. Therefore, the area of the shaded region is $192 - 36\pi$, choice (D).

12. **Topic: Arithmetic**

The correct answer is (C).

To determine how many pints of jam Pam can make, simply divide the amount of berries set aside for jam by the number of grams required for each pint. If she uses 40 percent of the strawberries for pies, that means she has 60 percent or $\dfrac{3}{5}s$ to use for jam. Each pint requires j grams: $\dfrac{3}{5}s \div j = \dfrac{3s}{5j}$

13. **Topic: Arithmetic**

The correct answer is (B).

Substitute the values of x, y, and z into both expressions, simplify and compare.

$$\left|2x + \frac{y^2 - xz}{zy + x^3}\right| \div y$$

Quantity A: $x = -3, y = 2, z = 8$

$$\left|2(-3) + \frac{2^2 - (-3)(8)}{(8)(2) + (-3)^3}\right| \div 2$$

$$= \left|-6 + \frac{4 - (-24)}{(16) + (-27)}\right| \div 2$$

$$= \left|-6 + \frac{28}{-11}\right| \div 2$$

$= \lceil -8.54 \rceil \div 2$

$= -4.27$

Quantity B: $x = 3, y = -2, z = 6$

$$\left| 2(3) + \frac{(-2)^2 - (3)(6)}{(6)(-2) + (3)^3} \right| \div (-2)$$

$$= \left| 6 + \frac{4 - (18)}{(-12) + 27} \right| \div (-2)$$

$$= \lceil 5.06 \rceil \div (-2)$$

$$= -2.53$$

$-4.27 < -2.53$

Quantity A is less than Quantity B.

14. **Topic: Geometry**

The correct answer is (C).

Extent line CO as shown.

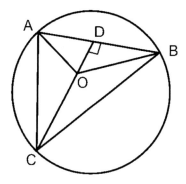

You now have ΔOBD, which is a 30°−60°−90° triangle. Since all 30°-60°-90° triangles are in proportion $1, \sqrt{3}, 2$, and since side DB = half of $8\sqrt{3}$, or $4\sqrt{3}$, side OB = 8. Therefore, OA + OB + OC = 8 + 8 + 8 = 24.

15. **Topic: Arithmetic**

The correct answer is (A).

Two dice are rolled and the number appearing on the dice are different. Consider the events P and Q such that,

S = The numbers appearing on the dice which are different.

Q = The sum of the numbers appearing on the dice which is at most 4.

S = (1, 2), (1, 3), (1, 4), (1, 5), (1, 6),

(2, 1), (2, 3), (2, 4), (2, 5), (2, 6),

(3, 1), (3, 2), (3, 4), (3, 5), (3, 6),

(4, 1), (4, 2), (4, 3), (4, 5), (4, 6),

(5, 1), (5, 2), (5, 3), (5, 4), (5, 6),

(6, 1), (6, 2), (6, 3), (6, 4), (6, 5),

$n(S) = 30$

Since the sum of the numbers is at most 4, the sum can be 2, 3 or 4.

$Q = (1, 1), (1, 2), (2, 1), (1, 3), (1, 3), (2, 2)$

Out of these we will consider the cases when the numbers on the dice are different. So, the favorable outcomes are:

$(1, 2), (2, 1), (1, 3), (3, 1)$

Or, $n(E) = 4$

So, the required probability is $P = \dfrac{n(E)}{n(S)} = \dfrac{4}{30} = \dfrac{2}{15}$

16. **Topic: Geometry**

The correct answer is (D).

Both figures are isosceles right triangles, so they are similar. Corresponding lengths of figures are proportional. Since the ratio of the hypotenuses z and $\frac{1}{3}z$ is 3: 1, the ratio of the legs must also be 3: 3. Therefore, leg y of the larger triangles must be 3 times as great as leg x of the smaller triangle, and $y = 3x$.

17. **Topic: Data Analysis**

The correct answer is (B).

This question is really not so much a matter of mathematics as just common sense. Indeed, you can probably solve it easily just by counting on your fingers (or multiplying and adding). First, Quantity A must be 15 since $5 \times 3 = 15$. As for Quantity B, since there is 1 floor with 2 apartments and 4 floors with 4 apartments, the total number of apartments in the building is 18. So, Quantity B is greater.

18. **Topic: Arithmetic**

The correct answer is (A).

Let x be the original cost of Item A. The cost of item B then becomes 113% of x or $1.13\ x$. Remember that 53% off is the same as 47% of the cost and so on.

Quantity A:

$x(0.47)(0.72)(1.06) = 0.3587$

Quantity B:

$x(1.13)(0.45)(0.65)(1.0825) = 0.3577$

Quantity A is greater than Quantity B.

19. **Topic: Arithmetic**

The correct answers are (A) and (D).

If we subtract 25 pounds from total 205, then in remaining 180 pounds, their weights are equal. So, weight of Sarah will be $90 + 25 = 115$ pounds.

In kilograms it will be $115 \times 0.4535 = 52.15$kg, it comes to approximately 52 kg.

Weight of Tony will be $205 - 115 = 90$ pounds$= 90 \times 0.4535 = 41$kg.

20. **Topic: Arithmetic**

The correct answer is (B).

If you multiply both sides by 3, you find that $m^4 = 81$. Therefore, m can equal 3 or -3. In either case, m is less than 4.

This page is intentionally left blank

Chapter **15**

Exercise #9

Questions: 20 | Time: 30 minutes

T his Exercise includes *20 practice questions*. The questions cover all the question types as explained in Chapter 2 and may fall into any of the following categories - Arithmetic, Algebra, Geometry or Data Analysis. You will find answers and detailed explanations towards the end of this chapter.

1. An amount of $620 is to be divided among three brothers A, B & C so that A gets $\frac{2}{3}$ of what B gets and B gets $\frac{2}{5}$ of what C gets. In that case, what will be the approximate share of A?

   Write your answer in the answer box.

   $ ┌──────────┐
     └──────────┘

2.

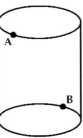

   A cylinder with a height of 5 units and radius of 2 units is showing above. Determine the longest possible distance (straight-line) between points A and B, assuming point A lies on the circumference of the top of the cylinder and point B lies on the circumference of the bottom of the cylinder.

   (A) 3

   (B) 5

   (C) 7

   (D) $\sqrt{29}$

   (E) $\sqrt{41}$

3. The average (arithmetic mean) of six numbers is 16. If five of the numbers are 15, 37, 16, 9, and 23, what is the sixth number?

(A) −20

(B) −4

(C) 0

(D) 6

(E) 16

4.

Quantity A	**Quantity B**
The number of cents in $8n$ dimes	The number of cents in $5n$ quarters

(A) Quantity A is greater.

(B) Quantity B is greater.

(C) The two quantities are equal.

(D) The relationship cannot be determined from the information given.

5.

$$x < y$$

Quantity A	**Quantity B**
$(x - y)^2$	$x^2 - y^2$

(A) Quantity A is greater.

(B) Quantity B is greater.

(C) The two quantities are equal.

(D) The relationship cannot be determined from the information given.

6.

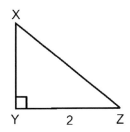

Note: Figure not drawn to scale

<u>Quantity A</u>

XY

<u>Quantity B</u>

$3\sqrt{2}$

(A) Quantity A is greater.

(B) Quantity B is greater.

(C) The two quantities are equal.

(D) The relationship cannot be determined from the information given.

7. The average (arithmetic mean) of five numbers is 8. If the average of two of these numbers is −6, what is the sum of the other three numbers?

(A) 28

(B) 34

(C) 46

(D) 52

(E) 60

8.

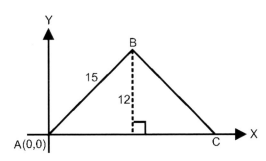

In the figure above, side AB of ΔABC contains which of the following points

(A) $(3, 2)$

(B) $(3, 5)$

(C) $(4, 6)$

(D) $(4, 10)$

(E) $(6, 8)$

9. Win : loss ratio of a basketball team is 3:1. After they won 6-straight games, the ratio changed to 5:1. How many games did the team win before it won the 6-straight games.

    (A) 3

    (B) 6

    (C) 9

    (D) 15

    (E) 24

Questions 10 and 11 are based on the following chart:

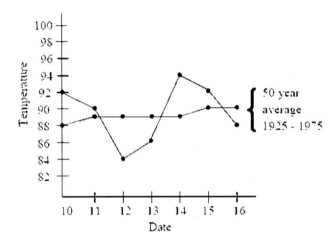

10. What was the percent increase in the maximum temperature from July 12 to July 14, 1979?

    (A) 10

    (B) 10.6

    (C) 11.9

    (D) 84

    (E) 94

11. According to the graph, the average maximum temperature in Los Angeles for the week of July 10 to 16, 1979, was

    (A) much less than the 50-year average for 1925-1975.

    (B) approximately equal to the 50-year average for 1925-1975.

    (C) much greater than the 50-year average for 1925-1975.

    (D) greater than any individual maximum reading for all dates given.

    (E) less than any individual maximum reading for all dates given.

12.

$$a, b, \text{ and } c \text{ are positive integers}$$
$$(b + c)^a = 81$$
$$a \neq b \neq c$$

Quantity A

a

Quantity B

$b + c$

(A) Quantity A is greater.

(B) Quantity B is greater.

(C) The two quantities are equal.

(D) The relationship cannot be determined from the information given.

13.

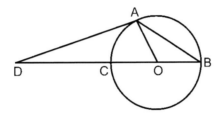

Quantity A

$\angle AOB$

Quantity B

$\angle ADB$

(A) Quantity A is greater.

(B) Quantity B is greater.

(C) The two quantities are equal.

(D) The relationship cannot be determined from the information given.

14.

$$x, y \text{ and } z \text{ are consecutive even integers and } z > y > x.$$

Quantity A

$$\frac{xy + yz}{y}$$

Quantity B

$$\frac{xz + yx}{z - 1}$$

(A) Quantity A is greater.

(B) Quantity B is greater.

(C) The two quantities are equal.

(D) The relationship cannot be determined from the information given.

15. If $a^2b = 12^2$, where b is odd, then a is divisible by all of the following EXCEPT

   (A) 3

   (B) 4

   (C) 6

   (D) 9

   (E) 12

16. 5-liters of water is emptied from tank-A into tank-B. Another 10-liters is emptied from tank-A to tank-C. If tank-A had 10-liters extra water compared to tank-C, how many extra liters does tank-C have now compared to tank-A?

   (A) 0

   (B) 5

   (C) 10

   (D) 15

   (E) 20

17.

A two–pound box of brand A costs $7.88.

A three-pound box of brand B costs $11.79.

Quantity A	**Quantity B**
Cost per pound of Brand A	Cost per pound of Brand B

   (A) Quantity A is greater.

   (B) Quantity B is greater.

   (C) The two quantities are equal.

   (D) The relationship cannot be determined from the information given.

18.

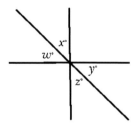

Quantity A	**Quantity B**
$90 - (w + x)$	$90 - (y + z)$

   (A) Quantity A is greater.

   (B) Quantity B is greater.

   (C) The two quantities are equal.

   (D) The relationship cannot be determined from the information given.

19. 0.1% percent of *m* is equal to 10% of *n*, then *m* is what percent of 10*n*?

    (A) $\dfrac{1}{1000}$ %

    (B) 10%

    (C) 100%

    (D) 1,000%

    (E) 10,000%

20. In a certain examination 60% of the students passed in Mathematics, 74% passed in English and 18% failed in both English and Mathematics. If 416 students passed in both these subjects, then what will be the total number of students who took the exam and also number of students who passed in Mathematics and English?

    Select all that apply.

    (A) 770

    (B) 800

    (C) 830

    (D) 400

    (E) 480

    (F) 574

    (G) 592

    (H) 600

Answers and Explanations

1. **Topic: Arithmetic**

   The correct answer is $85.5.

   Let C get x then

   B will get $\dfrac{2x}{3}$

   and A will get $\dfrac{4x}{15}$

   According to the condition

   $\dfrac{4x}{15} + \dfrac{2x}{3} + x = 620$

   $x = 320.7$

   Share of A will be $85.5

2. **Topic: Arithmetic**

   The correct answer is (E).

   Sketch in length AB. Drop a perpendicular from A down to the bottom circumference of the cylinder and call this point C. Then connect C to B and you have right triangle. The height of this triangle is AC, which is the height of the cylinder or 5. The base of this triangle is CB, which is the diameter of the cylinder. Since the radius of the cylinder is 2, its diameter is 4. To solve for AB, use the Pythagorean Theorem:

   $5^2 + 4^2 = AB^2$

   $41 = AB^2$

   $\sqrt{41} = AB$

3. **Topic: Arithmetic**

   The correct answer is (B).

   Average $\times$ Number of terms = Sum of terms

   $16 \times 6 = 15 + 37 + 16 + 9 + 23 + x$

   $96 = 100 + x$

   $-4 = x$

4. **Topic: Algebra**

   The correct answer is (A).

   Since there are 10 cents in each dime, the number of cents in 8n dimes is $10(8n) = 80$. Since there are 25 cents in each quarter, the number of cents in 3n quarters is $25(3n) = 75n$.

   Hence, the number of cents in 8n dimes is greater than the number of cents in 3n quarters. Or you can disregard the n, since it is the same positive number on each side. Thus, you are actually comparing 80¢ in Quantity A and 75¢ in Quantity B.

5. **Topic: Algebra**

   The correct answer is (D).

Substituting $x = 0$ and $y = 1$,

$(x - y)^2 \boxed{?} x^2 - y^2$

$(0 - 1)^2 \boxed{?} (0)^2 - (1)^2$

Then $1 > -1$

Now, Substituting $x = -1$ and $y = 0$

$(-1 - 0)^2 \boxed{?} (-1)^2 - (0)^2$

$(-1)^2 \boxed{?} (-1)^2$

Then $1 = 1$

Since different values give different comparisons, no comparison can be made.

6. **Topic: Geometry**

The correct answer is (B).

The ratio of the sides of $30°-60°-90°$ triangle is $1, 2, \sqrt{3}$, and since the side opposite $30°$ is 2, the side opposite $90°$ is 4. Compare each quantity by squaring the number outside and multiply by the numbers under radical.

$2\sqrt{3} \boxed{?} 3\sqrt{2}$

$\sqrt{3.4} \boxed{?} \sqrt{2.9}$

$\sqrt{12} > \sqrt{18}$

7. **Topic: Arithmetic**

The correct answer is (D).

Average $\times$ Number of terms $=$ Sum of terms

The sum of all five numbers is $8 \times 5 = 40$

The sum of two of these numbers is $(-6) \times 2 = -12$

So, the difference of these two sums, $40 - (-12) = 52$, is the sum of the other numbers.

8. **Topic: Geometry**

The correct answer is (E).

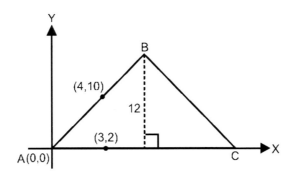

To solve this problem, you need to figure out the ratio between the x and y values in line segment AB. If you look at the figure, AB is the hypotenuse of a right triangle with a side of 12. Without even using the Pythagorean Theorem, you can tell that this triangle is one of the favorite right triangles: a 3: 4: 5. So this has to be a 9: 12: 15 triangle, and the coordinates of point B are (9, 12). All the points on line segment AB are in a ratio of 9 and 12 (which is the same as 3 to 4). The only answer with that ratio is E(6, 8).

9. **Topic: Arithmetic**

The correct answer is (B).

And yet again the slow way to solve a word problem like this is to set up equations.

Letting w and l represent the number of wins and losses respectively, the slow method of setting up equations would yield the following:

$$\frac{w}{l} = \frac{3}{1}$$

$$\frac{w + 6}{l} = \frac{5}{1}$$

Faster way to solve the problem:

	Before		After	
	Wins	**Losses**	**Wins**	**Losses**
1.3				
2.6				
3.9	3(3 : 1)		15	3(5 : 1)
4.15				
5.24				

Bingo! We found the answer on the first try! If C didn't work, we'd move up or down depending on whether the result was too small or too big.

10. **Topic: Data Analysis**

The correct answer is (C).

The increase was $94 - 84 = 10$. The percent increase is found by dividing the increase from the original amount. Thus,

$$\frac{10}{84} = 11.9\%$$

11. **Topic: Data Analysis**

The correct answer is (B).

The maximum temperature for July 10 to 16, 1979, were 92, 90, 84, 86, 94, 92, and 88. These averages to just under 90°. The 50-year average is also just under 90°.

12. **Topic: Arithmetic**

The correct answer is (D).

There are only two ways for a positive integer to a positive power to equal 81 : 9^2 or 3^4. Thus, $(b + c)^a$ could be, say, $(3 + 6)^2$ or it could be $(1 + 2)^4$. In the first case $b + c$ is greater than a. But in the second instance, $b + c$ is less than a. Therefore, the answer is D.

13. **Topic: Arithmetic**

The correct answer is (A).

Since ∠AOB is a central angle, it equals the measure of AB, and since ∠ADC is outside the circle but connects to AB, it is less than half of AB. Therefore, $\angle AOB > \angle ADC$

Alternate method: The external $\angle AOB$ must be larger than either of the remote interior angles.

14. **Topic: Arithmetic**

   Sub topic: Integers

   The correct answer is (A).

   The values of x, y, and z differ by 2 as they are consecutive even integers and x is the smallest.

   Let $x = x, y = x + 2, z = x + 4$.

   Now substitute these variables into the expressions, simplify, and compare.

   Quantity A:

   $$\frac{xy + yz}{y}$$

   $$= \frac{x(x + 2) + (x + 2)(x + 4)}{x + 2}$$

   $$= \frac{x^2 + 2x + x^2 + 4x + 2x + 8}{x + 2}$$

   $$= \frac{2x^2 + 8x + 8}{x + 2}$$

   $$= \frac{2(x^2 + 4x + 4)}{x + 2}$$

   $$= \frac{2(x + 2)^2}{x + 2}$$

   $$= 2(x + 2)$$

   $$= 2x + 4$$

   Quantity B:

   $$\frac{xz + yx}{z - 1}$$

   $$= \frac{x(x + 4) + (x + 2)x}{(x + 4) - 1}$$

   $$= \frac{x^2 + 4x + x^2 + 2x}{x + 3}$$

   $$= \frac{2x^2 + 6x}{x + 3}$$

   $$= \frac{2x(x + 3)}{x + 3}$$

   $$= 2x$$

   Compare:

   $2x + 4 \boxed{?} 2x$

   $4 \boxed{?} 0$

   $4 > 0$

   The Quantity A is greater than Quantity B.

15. **Topic: Arithmetic**

   The correct answer is (D).

Note first this is an EXCEPT question. Now, since $a^2b = 12^2$, and b is an odd integer, let's see what we can come up with. The first value for b that occurs to us is 1, so we get the following:

$a^2b = 12^2$

$(a^2)(1) = 12^2$

$a^2 = 12^2$

$a = 12$

If a equals 12 it is divisible by 1, 2, 3, 4, 6, and 12. So the only choice that remains is D.

16. **Topic: Geometry**

The correct answer is (D).

Tank A originally contained 10 more liters of water than tank C, so represent the initial number of liters in each tank in terms of tank A:

Tank A $= a$

Tank C $= a - 10$

5 liters of water are poured from A to B, and additional 10 liters are poured from A to C. A total of 15 liters are removed from tank A, so it now contains $a - 15$ liters of water. 10 liters are added to tank C, so it now contains $a - 10 + 10 = a$ liters. So, tank C contains 15 more liters of water than tank A.

17. **Topic: Arithmetic**

The correct answer is (A).

$7.88 divided by 2 equals $3.94.

$11.79 divided by 3 equals $3.93.

18. **Topic: Geometry**

Sub topic: Coordinate Geometry

The correct answer is (C).

We should notice first that we are definitely not in a position to say the magnitude of the unlabeled angles is 90°. But we need not make the assumption! We know that $w = y$ and $x = z$ because vertical angles are equal. Therefore, we are subtracting equal quantities from both sides of the comparison, a maneuver which, as we have already seen, will neither upset the balance of the original equality nor interfere with the direction of the in equality. This leaves us with 90 on both sides of the comparison, so we conclude that the original comparison must have been an equality.

19. **Topic: Arithmetic**

The correct answer is (D).

It's time to plug in values for m and n and make use of our translation approach to solving percent problems. We're working with a small percent, so plug in big number for m.

Let's say $m = 2,000$. So, 0.1% of 2000 $= \frac{0.1}{100} \times \frac{2000}{1} = 2$. Therefore, 10% equals 2; rewrite this as $\frac{10}{100} \times n = 2$

Solving for n, you get $n = 20$. Now, translate the rest of the problem: "m is what percent of 10n" can be written as $2000 = \frac{x}{100} \times 200$

Now just solve for x, which equals 1000. The answer is 1000%.

20. **Topic: Algebra**

    Sub topic: Set Theory

    The correct answers are (B), (E) and (G).

    Assume total number of students to be 100.

    Failed in Mathematics $= 100 - 60 = 40$

    Failed in English $= 100 - 74 = 26$

    Failed in both subjects $= 18$

    Failed students in any of the subjects $= 40 + 26 - 18 = 48$

    Students who will pass in both the subjects $= 52$

    If 52 passed, then total number of students $= 100$

    If 416 passed, then total number of students will be $\left(\dfrac{100}{52}\right) \times 416 = 800$

    Number of students who passed in English $= 0.74 \times 800 = 592$

    Number of students who passed in Mathematics $= 0.60 \times 800 = 480$

This page is intentionally left blank

Chapter **16**

Exercise #10

Questions: 20 | Time: 30 minutes

This Exercise includes *20 practice questions*. The questions cover all the question types as explained in Chapter 2 and may fall into any of the following categories - Arithmetic, Algebra, Geometry or Data Analysis. You will find answers and detailed explanations towards the end of this chapter.

1.

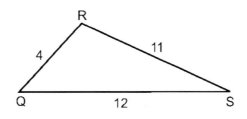

Quantity A	**Quantity B**
The area of ΔQRS	The perimeter of ΔQRS

(A) Quantity A is greater.

(B) Quantity B is greater.

(C) The two quantities are equal.

(D) The relationship cannot be determined from the information given.

2.

$$\text{Set A: } \{2, -1, 7, -4, 11, 3\}$$
$$\text{Set B: } \{10, 5, -3, 4, 7, -8\}$$

Quantity A	**Quantity B**
The median of set A	The average (arithmetic mean) of Set B

(A) Quantity A is greater.

(B) Quantity B is greater.

(C) The two quantities are equal.

(D) The relationship cannot be determined from the information given.

3.

$$
\begin{array}{r}
R \\
+S \\
+T \\
\hline
1W \\
\end{array}
$$

In the addition problem above, R, S, and T are different digits that are multiples of 3, and W is a digit.

Quantity A	**Quantity B**
W	8

(A) Quantity A is greater.

(B) Quantity B is greater.

(C) The two quantities are equal.

(D) The relationship cannot be determined from the information given.

4. $\frac{1}{4}$ boys and $\frac{1}{6}$ girls play soccer at the Union High School, The ratio of boys : girls is 2 : 1. Calculate the fraction of students playing soccer.

(A) $\frac{1}{24}$

(B) $\frac{5}{24}$

(C) $\frac{2}{9}$

(D) $\frac{1}{3}$

(E) $\frac{5}{12}$

5. A fair coin is tossed 100 times. The probability of getting tails an odd number of times is

   (A) $\dfrac{1}{2}$

   (B) $\dfrac{1}{8}$

   (C) $\dfrac{3}{8}$

   (D) $\dfrac{1}{33}$

   (E) $\dfrac{3}{4}$

6. In ΔMNP, $\angle$M is $65°$ and $\angle$P is $40°$. Q is a point on side MP such that NQ $\perp$ MP. Of the following line segments, which one is the shortest?

   (A) MN

   (B) NP

   (C) PQ

   (D) NQ

   (E) MQ

7. Given that $\dfrac{\{(x+y)(x-y)+y^2\}}{8} = 2$, what are the possible values of x?

   Select all that apply.

   (A) -8

   (B) -6

   (C) -4

   (D) -2

   (E) 0

   (F) 2

   (G) 4

   (H) 6

   (I) 8

8.

Quantity A	**Quantity B**
$\dfrac{\sqrt{897(x^2)^3}}{x^{-1}}$	$30(x^6)^{\frac{1}{3}}x^5$

   (A) Quantity A is greater.

   (B) Quantity B is greater.

   (C) The two quantities are equal.

   (D) The relationship cannot be determined from the information given.

9.

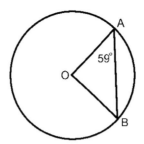

Note: - Figure not drawn to scale.

A and B are points on the circle with center O.

Quantity A	**Quantity B**
OA	AB

(A) Quantity A is greater.

(B) Quantity B is greater.

(C) The two quantities are equal.

(D) The relationship cannot be determined from the information given.

10.

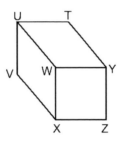

Note: Figure not drawn to scale

Each dimension of the rectangular solid above is an even number. The area of face TUWY is 20, and the area of face WXZY is 8

Quantity A	**Quantity B**
Total surface area of the rectangular solid	Volume of the rectangular solid

(A) Quantity A is greater.

(B) Quantity B is greater.

(C) The two quantities are equal.

(D) The relationship cannot be determined from the information given.

11. Tom is *t* years old, which is 3 times Becky's age. In terms of *t*, after how many years Tom will be just twice as old as Becky?

(A) $\dfrac{t}{3}$

(B) $\dfrac{t}{2}$

(C) $\dfrac{2t}{2}$

(D) t

(E) $\dfrac{3t}{2}$

12.

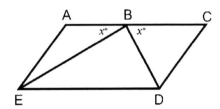

Note: Figure not drawn to scale.

In the figure above, AC ∥ ED. If the length of BD = 3, what is the length of BE?

(A) 3

(B) 4

(C) 5

(D) $3\sqrt{3}$

(E) It cannot be determined from the information given.

13. A magician can double the number of coins given to her in 1 minute. I give her a certain number of coins and after an hour she has a box full of coins. When was the box $\dfrac{1}{4}$ filled?

(A) 15 min

(B) 30 min

(C) 58 min

(D) 45 min

(E) 35 min

14.

Quantity A

Number of inches in one mile

Quantity B

Number of minutes in one year

(A) Quantity A is greater.

(B) Quantity B is greater.

(C) The two quantities are equal.

(D) The relationship cannot be determined from the information given.

15. A coin was flipped 20 times and came up heads 10 times. If the first and last flips were both heads, what is the greatest number of consecutive heads that could have occurred?

    (A) 1
    (B) 2
    (C) 8
    (D) 9
    (E) 10

Questions 16 and 17 are based on the following chart:

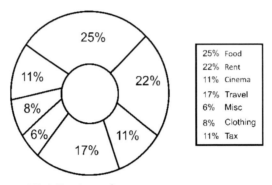

Distribution of expenses

16. Which of the following items amount to the same expenditure as on food?

    (A) Tax, clothing and miscellaneous

    (B) Travel, cinema and miscellaneous

    (C) Cinema and travel

    (D) Rent and miscellaneous

    (E) Rent and cinema

17. A reduction of 2% in taxation enables him to increase his expenditure by one per cent on each of the items, cinema and travel. Then a ratio of 1:2:3 is maintained on the expenditures incurred on which of the following items.

    (A) Travel, miscellaneous and cinema

    (B) Miscellaneous, cinema and travel

    (C) Miscellaneous, tax and clothing

    (D) Miscellaneous, travel and cinema

    (E) None of the above

18.

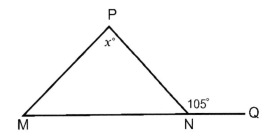

In the figure above, MQ is a straight line. If PM = PN, what is the value of x?

(A) 30

(B) 45

(C) 60

(D) 75

(E) 90

19.

$$15 - x < 2$$

$$2y < 24$$

Quantity A

x

Quantity B

y

(A) Quantity A is greater.

(B) Quantity B is greater.

(C) The two quantities are equal.

(D) The relationship cannot be determined from the information given.

20.

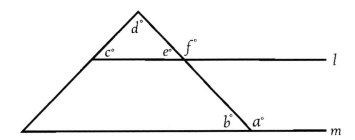

In the figure above, if $l \parallel m$, which of the following must be equal to $a°$?

(A) $b + c$

(B) $b + e$

(C) $c + d$

(D) $d + e$

(E) $d + f$

Answers and Explanations

1. **Topic: Geometry**

   The correct answer is (B).

   First, draw a line segment from point R perpendicular to QS. This is the altitude of ΔQRS, and it must be less than 4. The formula for the area of a triangle is $\frac{1}{2}$ × base × height. The base is 12, and if the height were 4, the area would be 24. Since the height is actually less than 4, the area must be less than 24. You don't have to find the actual value of area, though. Whatever the area is, the perimeter (the sum of all the sides) is 27. Quantity B is bigger regardless of the exact value of Quantity A.

2. **Topic: Data Analysis**

   The correct answer is (C).

   Remember, the median of a group of numbers is the number that is exactly in the middle of the group when the group is arranged from smallest to largest. To find the median of set A, you have to put the numbers in order: $-4, -1, 2, 3, 7$, and 11. Since there are only six numbers, you have to take the average of the two middle numbers, 2 and 3. The average of 2 and 3 is 2.5. To find the average of set B, add up all the numbers and divide by six, because there are six numbers. The sum of the numbers in set B is 15 divided by 6 is 2.5. So, the quantities are equal.

3. **Topic: Data Analysis**

   The correct answer is (D).

   Because you're told that R, S, and T are digits and different multiples of 3, most people will think of 3, 6, and 9, which add up to 18. That makes W equal to 8, and Columns A and B equal.

   There's another possibility.0 is also a multiple of 3. So, the three digits could be 0, 3, and 9, or 0, 6 and 9, which give totals of 12 and 15, respectively. That means W could be 8, 2 or 5.

   Since the columns could be equal, or Column B could be greater, answer choice (D) must be correct.

4. **Topic: Algebra**

   The correct answer is (C).

   The student body is $\frac{2}{3}$ male and $\frac{1}{3}$ female. So $\left(\frac{1}{4} \times \frac{2}{3}\right) + \left(\frac{1}{6} \times \frac{1}{3}\right) = \frac{1}{6} + \frac{1}{18} = \frac{2}{9}$ of the student body plays soccer.

5. **Topic: Arithmetic**

   The total number of cases is 2^{100}. The number of favorable ways is $^{100}C_1 + {}^{100}C_3 + \dots + {}^{100}C_{99} = 2^{100-1} = 2^{99}$. Therefore, the probability of the required event is $\frac{2^{99}}{2^{100}} = \frac{1}{2}$

6. **Topic: Arithmetic**

   The correct answer is (E).

   Draw a quick sketch. Label the important information.

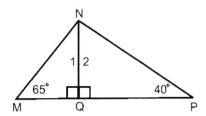

MN and NP are the hypotenuses of ΔQNM and ΔQNP. Therefore, these are greater than MQ, NQ, and QP (the hypotenuse is the longest side of a right triangle). So, eliminate MN and NP. NQ > MQ, since ∠QMN (65°) >∠MNQ (25°) (the longest side is opposite the greatest angle in a triangle).

Eliminate NQ, Similarly, since ∠QNP (50°) >∠NPQ (40°), QP > NQ. Eliminate QP.

Therefore, the answer is MQ, the only remaining line.

The answer is (E).

7. **Topic: Algebra**

   Sub topic: Quadratic Equations

   The correct answer is (C).

   $$\frac{\{(x + y)(x - y) + y^2\}}{8} = 2$$

   $(x + y)(x - y) + y^2 = 16$

   $x^2 - y^2 + y^2 = 16$

   $x^2 = 16$

   $x = \{-4 , 4\}$

   So, the possible values of x are -4 and 4.

8. **Topic: Algebra**

   Sub topic: Exponents

   The correct answer is (B).

   Left side (if we only look at the expression containing x) $= \frac{\left(x^2\right)^3}{x^{-1}} = \frac{x^6}{\left(\frac{1}{x^1}\right)} = x^6 x^1 = x^7$

   Right side (if we only look at the expression containing x) $= (x^6)^{\frac{1}{3}} x^5 = x^2 x^5 = x^7$

   Thus, the expressions containing x are equal in the left and the right columns. This implies any differentiation should come from the remaining numerical part of the expressions.

   If we look at the right column, 30 can also be written as $\sqrt{900}$.

   Thus $\sqrt{900}$ is greater than $\sqrt{897}$ (no calculation is needed). Consequently, the right column is greater than the left column. Hence the correct answer is B.

9. **Topic: Geometry**

   The correct answer is (B).

   Since OA and AB are both radii of circle O, they are equal. In a triangle, angles opposite equal sides are also equal, so ∠OAB = ∠OBA = 59°. The angles of a triangle sum to180°, so ∠AOB = 180 − 2(59°) = 62°. Since the angle opposite AB is greater than the angle opposite OA, AB is greater.

10. **Topic: Geometry**

The correct answer is (A).

Since the area of face TUWY is 20, the dimensions must be 2 × 10.

Remember, each dimension must be an even number. The dimension of face WXZY must therefore be 2 × 4. Since edge WY is common in both faces, the dimensions of face UVXW are 10 × 4.

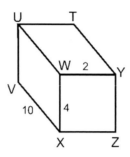

The surface of the rectangular solid is

2 × 10 = 20 (doubled) = 40

+ 2 × 4 = 8 (doubled) = 16

+ 10 × 4 = 40 (doubled) = 80 = 136

Volume equals 2 × 10 × 4 = 80

Therefore, the surface area is greater.

11. **Topic: Arithmetic**

The correct answer is (A).

Set up a chart.

	Now	In x years
Tom	t	t + x
Becky	$\dfrac{t}{3}$	$\dfrac{t}{3} + x$

Let x = the number of years from now.

If Tom is t years old he is 3 times as old as Becky, then Becky must be $\dfrac{t}{3}$ years old.

In x years, Tom will be t + x years old and Becky will be $\dfrac{t}{3}$ + x years old.

Set up an equation based upon your chart.

In how many years will Tom be twice as old as Becky?

$t + x = 2\left(\dfrac{t}{3} + x\right)$ Distribute $t + x = \dfrac{2t}{3} + 2x$

Solve for x

$\dfrac{t}{3} = x$

The answer is (A).

12. **Topic: Geometry**

The correct answer is (A).

Keep in mind that this figure is not drawn to scale. Since AC ∥ ED, we know that the following angles are equal:

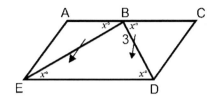

Since ΔEBD has equal angles, the opposing sides are also equal. Therefore, BE = BD = 3.

13. **Topic: Data Analysis**

The correct answer is (C).

In 60 min − box is full.

In 59 min − box is half filled.

In 58 min −box is $\frac{1}{4}$ filled.

Hence C.

14. **Topic: Arithmetic**

The correct answer is (B).

First, set up the numbers for each side:

Quantity A	Quantity B
Number of inches in one mile	Number of minutes in one year
(12" = 1 ft) × (5280 ft in m)	(60 min in 1 hr) × (24 hr in 1 day) × (365 days in 1 yr)
12 × 5280	60 × 24 × 365
Now dividing out 10 and 12 leaves	
1 × 528	6 × 2 × 365
528	12 × 365

Quantity B is obviously greater.

15. **Topic: Arithmetic**

The correct answer is (D).

If the first and last flips were heads, we could have 9 consecutive heads, followed by 10 consecutive tails and the final head.

16. **Topic: Data Analysis**

The correct answer is (A).

Tax, Clothing and miscellaneous = 11 + 8 + 6 = 25% = $\frac{1}{4}$th of his income which is the expenses on food.

17. **Topic: Data Analysis**

The correct answer is (B).

After reduction of 2% in tax: $11\% - 2\% = 9\%$. Increase of 1% each on cinema and travel amount to 12% on cinema and 18% on travel.

18. **Topic: Geometry**

The correct answer is (A).

∠PNM is supplementary to ∠PNQ, so $∠PNM + 105° = 180°$, and $∠PNM = 75°$. Since PM = PN, ΔMPN is isosceles and ∠PMN =∠PNM = 75°. The interior angles of a triangle sum to 180°, so $75 + 75 + x = 180$, and $x = 30$.

19. **Topic: Arithmetic**

The correct answer is (A).

Solving $15 - x < 2$

$15 - x - 15 < 2 - 15$

$-x < -13$

$\dfrac{-x}{-1} > \dfrac{-13}{-1}$

$x > 13$

(Note: Inequality is reversed when dividing by a negative number.)

Solving $2y < 24$

$\dfrac{2y}{2} < \dfrac{24}{2}$

$y < 12$

Therefore, $x > y$.

20. **Topic: Geometry**

The correct answer is (C).

$a = f$, since all the obtuse angles formed when two parallel lines are cut by the transversal are equal.

f is an exterior angle of the small triangle containing angles c, d, and e.

The sum of all angles of a triangle is 180. So, we have $c+d+e= 180$ or $c+d= 180 - e$.

Since f is external to the triangle, we can say $e+f= 180$ or $f= 180 - e$ or $a= 180 - e$ (since $a=f$).

From the above three statements, we can say, $a=c+d$, the answer is (C).

Made in United States
North Haven, CT
27 December 2021